W9-DBE-681

Building-Art: Modern Architecture Under Cultural Construction is a collection of essays by art critic Joseph Masheck. Considering topics in nineteenth- and twentieth-century architecture, its theory and practice, as well as selected achievements by great modernists – Le Corbusier, Ludwig Mies van der Rohe, and Louis I. Kahn – Masheck also analyzes the ideas and artworks of such artists as Giorgio de Chirico and Tony Smith. Contextualizing and culturally speculative, these studies address, among other issues, the distinction between architecture (major and minor) and "mere" building, and between architecture and engineering, drawing the reader into architectural problems that have persisted for at least two centuries. Demonstrating a concern with ongoing modernism, Masheck's essays, which extend to the antimodernist polemics of the 1970s and 1980s, reinvestigate modern architectural tradition in its culture-historical complexity.

BUILDING-ART

CONTEMPORARY ARTISTS AND THEIR CRITICS

General Editor
DONALD KUSPIT
State University of New York, Stony Brook

Advisory Board
MATTHEW BAIGELL, Rutgers University
DIANE KELDER, The College of Staten Island and the
Graduate Center, CUNY
ANN GIBSON, State University of New York, Stony Brook
SUSAN DELAHANTE, Museum of Contemporary Art, Houston
UDO KULTURMAN, Washington University
CHARLES MILLER, *Artforum*

BUILDING-ART

Modern Architecture Under Cultural Construction

JOSEPH MASHECK

CAMBRIDGE
UNIVERSITY PRESS

Published by the Press Syndicate of the University of Cambridge
The Pitt Building, Trumpington Street, Cambridge CB2 1RP
40 West 20th Street, New York, NY 10011-4211, USA
10 Stamford Road, Oakleigh, Victoria 3166, Australia

© Cambridge University Press 1993

First published 1993

Printed in Canada

Library of Congress Cataloging-in-Publication Data
Masheck, Joseph.
Building-art : modern architecture under cultural construction /
Joseph Masheck.
p.   cm.
Anthology of essays.
Includes index.
ISBN 0-521-44013-0
1. Architecture, Modern – 19th century.   2. Architecture,
Modern – 20th century.   3. Architecture – Philosophy.
4. Architectural criticism.   I. Title.
NA642.M25   1993
724'.5 – dc20   92-39223
                                                                CIP

A catalog record for this book is available from the British Library

ISBN 0-521-44013-0 hardback

To the Avery Library
for thirty years

Contents

vii

Illustrations

Preface

THE ART OF ARCHITECTURE led me into general art history, and I like to
recall that the writing of an architectural dissertation finds precedent among
the founders of the modern discipline. Heinrich Wölfflin began architecturally
at that European center of gravity, the problem of normative classicism in the
Renaissance, projecting outward the groundwork of a prestructuralist history
of forms. Also after beginning with architecture, both Aloïs Riegl and Max
Dvořák developed the consciousness of artistic form as embedded in cultural
mentality – an enterprise that has lately proved easier to applaud in principle
than to employ, as they did, in demanding analytical practice. In our ideologically problematic time, their generalists' sense of the art historian's cultural mission is not commonly pursued. The differently global ambitions of
nouveau-academic revisionists who indulge what Nietzsche called a "nihilism
à la Petersburg (meaning the *belief in unbelief*), even to the point of martyr-
dom," only too conveniently enforce the usual American Calvinist-capitalist
intolerance of whatever might actually be aesthetic in art "production."

Assuming that something like a Nietzschean sense of philology crossed
with poetics is still worthwhile with respect to artworks, including primary
architectural "texts," I confess a simpler anxiety, not so much of neglecting
one or another monument or critical touchstone as of pedestrian error. For
the essays collected here, like critical essays in the literary sense, make heavy
use of quotations – bits of source text, sometimes garnered on the run, that
have had to be copied and recopied in multiple revisions. Yes, the scholarly
reader will want to consult the original in case he or she intends to pursue
something further; but doing so becomes even more difficult with many older
and uncanonical or marginal sources, given the now wholesale crumbling of
books printed on pulp paper during the nineteenth century even as a new
librarianship of antihistorical "information science" favors the merely latest
word, crudely oblivious to the historiographic significance of a plenitude of

older texts. Sometimes, one might be the last to consult a given volume. At least I can say that I have never noticed a mistake in transcription that affected sense: linguistic patterns, like crystalline and genetic structures – and not unlike architecture – tolerate more inexactitude than perfectionists of form suspect.

While still a generalist, I have mainly concerned myself for the past twenty years with modern and contemporary painting and sculpture. Perhaps I have consequently become more of an architectural amateur than ever. Some degree of amateurism, however, may at least make certain matters more accessible to readers who, otherwise interested in art as part of the history of culture, are, like many art historians, peculiarly intimidated by architecture. This includes many who need on occasion to remind themselves that the field of culture is considerably larger than the turf of literature or even, today, of grand cultural *theory of theory* (where young scholars now herd up as cultic virgins to one or another high priest).

Two of the present essays are concerned with churches. Two other essays on religious architecture – a subject almost as unwelcome in the New York art world as anything pertaining to the spiritual life in modern and contemporary painting – can be found elsewhere: "The Original High Altar Tabernacle of the Gesù Rediscovered," *Burlington Magazine,* 112 (February 1970), and "Irish Gothic Theory Before Pugin," *Studies* (Dublin), 70 (1981). I will say that one reason I have always been interested in ecclesiastical architecture is that the church is in some sense the palace of the people. To speak from personal experience: when architecture began to interest me in my youth, three churches in Queens (neo-Renaissance, 1930 Shingle Style, and 1937 Mission–Gothic–moderne, in that order) constituted, along with two now defunct department stores (both, I think, by Raymond Loewy), my total experience of *edifices* until about the age of fourteen, when I began to do reconnaissance at the Museum of Modern Art.

As a young student, the first architectural book "laid on" me, as my generation would say, was Geoffrey Scott's insidiously classy classic *The Architecture of Humanism* (1914) with its telltale subtitle, *A Study in the History of Taste.* Fortunately, Everard M. Upjohn – descendant of Hartford Statehouse Upjohn and, beyond, of Trinity Church Upjohn – had the catholicity also to assign Louis H. Sullivan's *Autobiography of an Idea,* from which I take my introductory epigraph, as well as Ruskin's *Seven Lamps of Architecture.* By these means it was possible to build as modern a bridge as one liked between the Scott of classical convention (and social prerogative, in the time of yacht–club "Corinthianism" in America) and the Sullivan of modernist radicality. One sort of did, operationally if not in rigorous theory; and any synthesis so effected had more open possibility than, say, Ruskin, as an "organic" protofunctionalist who, however, hated the modernity of his own age, could have allowed alone.

Thinking back: we must, many of us then and there at Columbia, have been in one way or another obsessed with the problem of classicism. No wonder, at a place where anybody seriously interested was welcome to turn Palladio's, or any other canonical genius's, actual first–edition pages. It happens that at Columbia I rowed lightweight crew, for which it happens that there had just previously been a manager by the name of Robert A. M. Stern. I mention this apologetically, because I sometimes wonder if it doesn't have something to do with my sense that with his "lite" adaptations of classicism Stern, more guiltily than postmoderns who were not Columbians, had seen such an easy, worldly way to sell the family silver.

As a teacher, I am old enough to see some of myself in my own former students of modern art, including certain ex-modernists who are apparently politically unable to acknowledge such traditional nurture. Well, I am in a better position than they to record my own debt to those at Columbia whose *docere/delectare* tutelage in art history – notably Meyer Schapiro's – and more specifically in architectural history deeply influenced me after Upjohn, namely, Howard Hibbard and my mentors, Rudolf Wittkower and Dorothea Nyberg; and also to the staff of the great Avery Architectural and Fine Arts Library there, for a good thirty years of collegial assistance. To Wittkower architecture offered a history of forms, not to be overlooked as to beauty, as vital repositories of cultural signification, in intimate textual affiliation with intellectual history. Nyberg encouraged an alertness to unsuspected resistances and subversions within the classical tradition along with an inspiring, rather Marcusean sense of the unabashed splendor of classicism itself as deserving to be inherited by us all rather than undialectically – and impoverishingly – denied.

The long last essay grew out of a course I taught at Harvard from 1983 to 1986, "Form in the Art-Work." Without the stimulating responsiveness of my few but exceedingly fit students at the Carpenter Center for the Visual Arts (Le Corbusier's only American building), it would not have been begun, let alone have filled out the rambling, unclassical but hardly "picturesque" form it has at last attained.

I am grateful to Donald B. Kuspit for inviting me to produce a book in this series of writings by art critics and especially for his receptiveness to its architectural theme; likewise to Beatrice Rehl, of Cambridge University Press, for her active interest, and to Mary Racine and Cary Groner, also of Cambridge, for editing a complex manuscript. With the proviso that nothing in these very reworked pages is his *fault,* I can thank James S. Ackerman, an almost discouragingly fine writer on the art of architecture, for helpful criticisms early on. Marjorie Welish has my special gratitude as that ideal reader who shows no more patience with whatever is simplistic than impatience with what might rightly be complex.

Sources of Previously Published Essays

Chapter 2 is an expanded version of a chapter in "Irish Church-Building from the Treaty of Limerick to the Great Famine," Ph.D. dissertation, Columbia University, 1973 (Ann Arbor: University Microfilms, 1975).

Chapter 3 was originally published as "The Meaning of Town and Davis's Octagonal Schoolhouse Design," *Journal of the Society of Architectural Historians,* 25 (1966), 302–4.

Chapter 5 is an abbreviated version of "The Pluperfection of de Chirico," in the Galerie Templon exhibition catalog *Bidlo (Not de Chirico)* (Paris, 1990).

Chapter 7 appeared as "Reflections in Onyx," *Art in America,* 74, no. 4 (1986), 138–51, 203.

Chapter 10 is a revised version of a paper presented at "Wilhelm Worringer: Art History or Sublime Hysteria?", a symposium organized by Neil Donahue at Hofstra University, April 1991, and also published in Donahue, ed., *Invisible Cathedrals: The German Expressionist Art History of Wilhelm Worringer* (forthcoming).

Chapter 11 is an expanded version of "Unconscious Formalism: A Response to Andre's Note on the Bechers," *Artforum,* 11, no. 9 (1973), 74–5.

Chapter 12 is an abbreviated version of "Judy Rifka and 'Postmodernism' in Architecture," *Art in America,* 72, no. 11 (1984), 148–63.

Introduction

In his secret heart he did not believe that anything could be *proved,* but believed as firmly that many things might be *shown.*

Sullivan

T HE writings collected here differ, like buildings, in occasion, scale, and material components (old, standarized, or new). More like an architect's oeuvre than a project in "planning," the collection includes occasional structures and full-fledged edifices, classical and otherwise. As to the architect, he might seem to aspire to be a Nietzschean "farmer of the spirit," as if the modern tradition, like the classical one before it, had collapsed, partly under the facile certainties of its own academicism. It is as if, by consulting some of its surviving texts, the architect hoped to retrieve something of spiritual use.

The various essays concern several main themes: the social projection of model buildings (the Panopticon, a nineteenth-century ideal schoolhouse); speculative historical contextualization (Dublin Pro-Cathedral, the schoolhouse, Sullivan's ornament, the Ronchamp Chapel, "soft" postmodernism); the "appreciation" of great artist-architects (Mies van der Rohe; Kahn); architecture in relation to painting (Giorgio de Chirico), sculpture (Tony Smith), and photography (Bernd and Hilla Becher). Recurrent on the theoretical plane are the question of the limits of architecture, whether as against engineering or other essentially nonartistic building (the Panopticon, the "Living-Machine," "Tired Tropes," and, less ostensibly, several other essays), and the working problematics of classicism and functionalism.

The title of the book alludes to the distinction, in German, between *Baukunst* and *Architektur.* "Building-Art," *Baukunst* literally rendered, emphasizes the activity, the very real, artful work of constructing something that might not necessarily have become a matter of art at all. (*Bauwesen,* which implies "knowledge of how to build," is the word for the building enterprise in the ordinary builder's, rather than the civil engineer's, sense.) It retains Germanic evocations of craftsmanly construction that were still welcome at the Bauhaus, often otherwise considered a school of rationalistic design. The term "architecture," by comparison, seems classically idealized, inertly perfect from the start. Invoking "Building-Art" here is meant not to gloss over, but at once to point up and to bridge a discontinuity between building that is tantamount to architecture and architecture itself as an embodiment of theory as well as a fine art. This theme surfaces at several points before submitting to historio-critical consideration toward the end of the book.

The distinction between (nonart) building and architecture is neither arbitrary nor symmetrical, entailing as it inevitably does some sort of architectural transcendental. The noun "edifice" is akin to the verb "to edify" and traces back through connotations of temple building (and altar sacrifice) to the hearth, where, all so metaphorically, something burns away as material and disappears into the upper air.[1] Le Corbusier, who evidently appreciated such things (after two generations of institutionalized modernistic materialist literalism, they would mostly disappear), believed that even in the clinical modern kitchen we still find the space of informal congregation about the stove to be our hearth. This may suggest that even in our world it may still be possible not only to live but *zu wohnen,* that is, meaningfully "to dwell."[2]

"Cultural construction" in the subtitle puns on construction as interpretation as well as building. By and large, the essays, whether reprinted, rewritten, or new, entertain architecture as part of art history and in relation to the wider culture of Europe and America between about 1800 and about 1980. Few pages consist of direct art-critical response to buildings as "texts." Most deal textually with other written texts, sometimes philosophical or literary, sometimes more culturally remote. For the art historian-critic this is, after all, something like responding in kind, while the architect alone can take matters from there, responding in art. Also, "cultural" here does not mean primarily political. It is not a happy fact that so much great architecture is owed to oppression and privilege; but what good does it promise humanity to oblige all to assent to a "radicality" of antiart theory now often as conspicuously determined and enforced by domineering puritans, practically Cromwellians, of upper or upstart-upper class?

Reverence for great buildings or paintings does not necessarily hold the spectator in fetishistic thrall or delusion. Saying so means, of course, that I actually do believe that not all aesthetic "aura" is spurious, in architecture or any other art. By now more often than not, American writers in the sphere of contemporary art criticism hold up Walter Benjamin's challenging 1936 essay, "The Work of Art in the Age of Mechanical Reproducibility," only to maintain, wrongly, I believe, that aura itself, as Benjamin definitively identifies it there, should be over with and was anyway a bad thing for humanity. This is a simplistic and philistine American idea. If the sacred cow really were out of the barn (and without most people ever getting to see it), why shouldn't such critics and art historians seem more relieved than anxious to report the news?

Insofar as this problem is textual, it finds a principal focal point in Benjamin's discussion of film, where the connived, artificial aura of film stars, and so on, is criticized as phony and manipulative – only to be followed immediately, however by a vivid example of *good* aura. True, at the crucial point Benjamin turns from art to nature, and to the innocent visual pleasure taken therein; but all the more obviously in German, in which the art of film is so literally *Lichtspiel,* "light-play," at least one of his two examples sharply evokes films of his own moment, most specifically their technical halation effects. For in defining aura as "the unique phenomenon of a distance, however close it may be" (a Rieglean phrase), Benjamin says, "If while resting on a summer afternoon, you follow with your eyes . . . a branch which casts its shadow over you, you experience the aura of . . . that branch."[3] Furthermore, this important passage may as well echo the art-historical scholarship of Aloïs Riegl, an acknowledged influence on Benjamin, specifically where Riegl says that before classical Greek ornament it would take a stubborn searcher for (pictorial) images to overlook the "beautifully animated, stirring leaf tendrils" (*schönlebendig bewegte Blätterranken*).[4]

Because textual historicity is not a dominant obsession today, even, unfortunately, within the history of art, I might explain that it always strikes me as odd when modern philosophers, aestheticians included, don't seem to care if they recapitulate older, even classic, arguments. In a little book on the subject of philosophy's sense of its own past, Arthur O. Lovejoy's history-of-ideas approach is taken to task, not for being diachronic, nor even for obscuring the context of social life in which only, after all, ideas are lodged, but rather as "atomistic," for suppressing the very interrelatedness of ideas with each other and hence the complexity of their development. Yet we are also told that Bertrand Russell, himself supposed to have benefited early on by not knowing much previous philosophy, came to write that "those who think that philosophy 'really' began in 1921, or at any rate not long before, fail to see that current philosophic problems have not arisen all of a sudden and out of nothing."[5] One could say much the same of the theory and practice of architecture, especially now that 1921, not to mention 1950, is no less historical than 1750, 1450, or 1221, and maybe no less problematic. There is such a thing as architectural literacy, as well as an accumulated literature, in the librarian's sense, of architecture.

Within the general cultural sphere, it is remarkable how a writer as otherwise historically sophisticated as Paul Fussell can be so mistaken in rising to defend the art of architecture:[6]

> In the United States, BAD architecture is rampant because money and profit take clear priority over taste and amenity. [True enough.] But BAD is rampant here too because of the paucity of architectural criticism. [Let's see what this means.] Britain at least has Prince Charles to bitch about architectural ugliness and vandalism and tedium. [Alarm.] We have no such public figure commenting on architecture, and except for [Ada Louise] Huxtable and [*same breath!*] Tom Wolfe, we have hardly any critics who are not the captives of philistine money or university taste.

For one thing, it seems lost on Professor Fussell that the University of Pennsylvania, where he teaches, was the honored academic home of a certain professor of architecture by the name of Louis I. Kahn. In accordance with the populistic "U-" and "non-U" etiquette of Fussell's book *BAD* (1991), "Equality is one of the ideas glorified by the new architecture, and that might be a good thing, but this equality is the equality of ignorance, a celebration of the assumption that no one has sufficient experience or learning to enjoy the allusive exercise required by [*careful!*] traditional architectural details like balustrades, crockets, finials, metopes, or triglyphs." It is no more the function of architecture to rehearse a rebus of formal devices than it is the function of poetry to demonstrate the academic terms for forms and metric feet. At least Fussell does not set out the usual red herrings of the litterateur, "proportion" and "symmetry" as vague absolutes inherited from eighteenth-century Whig aesthetics.

Fussell is a conveniently typical litterateur, by no means an egregious offender. For him to roll on this way would be innocent if he didn't make the mistake of taking a very BAD specific stand, backing (chivalrously, he seems to think) Prince Charles and his architectural expert Leon Krier in the suppression of the posthumous City of London "Mansion House" project of Ludwig Mies van der Rohe. In that campaign – something like averting the execution of an Alberti design in a place already raucous with awful nineteenth-century "Renaissance" pastiches – British antimodernists closed ranks in the Thatcher period. Ironically, by the grace of Elizabeth II Mies had been made a royal gold medalist for architecture in 1959 (see testimonials presented by Sir Basil Spence in the *Journal of the Royal Institute of British Architects* for July of that year), so that Charles's position now publicly contradicts that for which his own sovereign mother was, some time ago, manifestly better advised.

Orthodox modern architecture is, meanwhile, accused of utopianism by our most "pure" theoreticians. But as one only a few years older than the prince of Wales, I can only wonder when the divide opened between his and his contemporaries' pseudoutopian traditionalism, with its strangely Whiggish affection for business, and a more integrally idealistic modernism, whether radical-Tory or Fabian, with (mere) capital honored to "do the honors" for architecture – which I can remember as still causing architectural excitement, including new preservationist excitement for authentic traditional architecture – right about the time Mies received his British medal. Most built architecture owes its realization to one or more of the powers that be, including corporate bodies. Our Fussells would do better to complain about the general cultural effects of money and profit and leave the operations of architectural taste and amenity to people concerned more with their effective exercise in the present than with their mere traditionalizing incantation.

Some would say that for me to revere Mies's work, apart from defending his London project against political conservatism, is tantamount to the quasi-modernist cultural conservatism by which literary writers and readers of the *National Review* and similar journals of the educated right regularly pay their canonical respects to James Joyce. Well, what, one has only to wonder, would their likes have said in 1922; and what do they find worthy in the new "1922" of their own historical moment? The book in hand stops short of the recent

4

past, in which Frank Gehry, for instance, has not been alone in attempting to work through contradictions of modernism and postmodernism (not mere reactionary postmodernism, either). But as its author, I would be dissembling not to ask myself where I have "been," with respect to architecture, since about the time I finished my academic dissertation, in 1973. By the mid–1970s modern architecture seemed – (Richard Meier and a few others excepted – defunct, dissipated in an extended fiesta of undwellable, if buildable, irrelevancies; and there followed those worse reactions, whether of moneyed inhibition fetishized as taste or of the most absurd extravagance, that already typify literal as well as cultural bankruptcy.) Lately, however, there is a sense that architecture has come through something, with the help, I can now see, of a considerable body of negative theory. So it seems worth contemplating our modern classics again, now that we know we cannot afford mere regression.

1

Bentham's Panopticon

An Architectural Perpetration

For B.R.R. in return

WHEN Jeremy Bentham, the father of utilitarianism in social philosophy, met his editor Etienne Dumont in 1788, Dumont, a Swiss former clergyman, already knew the Comte de Mirabeau, whose *Courrier de Provence* soon introduced Bentham's writings on the Continent. Thanks to the popularity of Michel Foucault's *Discipline and Punish* (1975),[1] notoriety has settled upon Bentham's "Panopticon; or, the Inspection-House," a project for a cylindrical prison with radial cells monitored from the optic center (Figure 1). The discussion centers on Bentham's already "improved" version of the basic idea, as published in 1791, of a building 120 feet in diameter, housing 460 inmates who would work for an entrepreneurial contractor (such as himself).[2] A French "résumé" of Bentham's published *Panopticon* scheme was "présenté à l'Assemblée législatif" by the end of the same year in which it was published in the British Isles – notably, at Dublin – in 1791.[3] Almost as expeditiously, Dumont would produce in 1802 a French edition of Bentham's classic of political philosophy, the *Introduction to the Principles of Morals and Legislation* (1789).

At the turn of the eighteenth century, Bentham's project – in a social engineering driven by desperately constrained "self-interest" as a means of effectively overriding free will – synchronically reflects both a new architecture, severe in its deployment of geometric masses and Spartan in its resort to traditional ornamental niceties, and the rise, in rivalry with architecture, of engineering per se – with its demythologized, unrhetorically scientific sense of built structure oblivious to protocols of form. Not that Bentham's Panopticon could be mistaken for a building by Boullée or Ledoux in France. If anything, as presented, it looks today, architecturally, oddly and prematurely Victorian, at once clunky and fidgety, for such a no-nonsense structure. Indeed, it has been taken so unhistorically, like some clever bridge by a forgotten engineer, that in the early twentieth century Bentham was quite overlooked in a pragmatic American re-presentation of his concept.[4] Yet the building, a

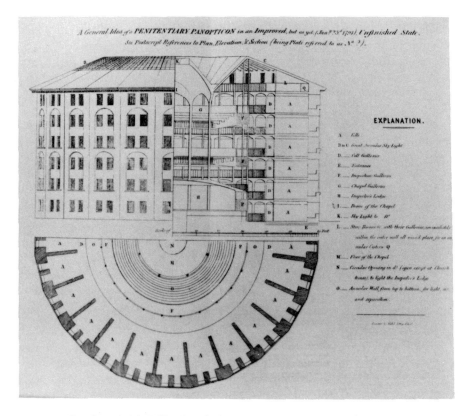

1. Jeremy Bentham (with Willey Reveley), Panopticon penitentiary design. After Bentham, *Works,* ed. John Bowring, vol. 4 (Edinburgh, 1843; repr. New York, 1966).

special case of building as device, but as such also a special *building,* and even Bentham's no-nonsense approach to designing it, have their historical aspects.

Many buildings and projects, before and after him, have come to be related to Bentham's for its main feature of complete radial surveillance. The first quasi-panoptic prison, with radially disposed blocks likes spokes about an axle, though not yet radially visible individual cells, seems to have been built at Ghent in 1772, fifteen years before Bentham began to write. Several prisons in Britain and Switzerland follow upon this, with its eight rectangular blocks surrounding an octagonal "hall of surveillance."

That Bentham's *Panopticon* project was published in Dublin is probably significant in more ways than one. It has already been pointed out that the then "Irish" (exclusively Anglo-Irish) government that subsidized Bentham's 1791 publication had special interest in a prototype "Poor Inspection House" for Irish application.[5] Coincidentally, James Gandon was at that moment setting the major courtrooms of his great Four Courts, Dublin, of 1786–1800, on diagonal axes off a central rotunda. But several Irish prisons of the earlier nineteenth century were in fact designed according to a dynamic of radial surveillance. There were semicircular arrangements of cell blocks with wedge-shaped foreyards at Mullingar (County Westmeath) and Longford, and a similar project for Tullamore (County Offaly); there were longitudinal cell blocks radiating from a centralized lodge not only at the important men's jail in Cork, but also off the corners of a square "castle" at Nenagh (County Tipperary); there were also essentially radially and optically disposed long cell blocks in Down County New Gaol, 1824–30, at Downpatrick.[6] In light of Bentham's work, recent scholars have noticed a tendency for the building at the observing – but also inevitably observed – center of such establishments to declare itself with rhetorical authority a "public" building. Likewise, some Irish workhouses (as many as 150 were built, often to standardized printed designs, between 1834 and the Great Famine) such as Dunshaughlin (County Meath) had rooms radiating from a master's lodge, as was also seen in lunatic asylums like one at Carlow.[7]

Some subsequent Continental works, including projects by a prison specialist, Harou-Romain (1797–1866), echo earlier nineteenth-century American examples, including two prisons on Benthamite lines: the state prison at Richmond, Virginia (1800), by no less an architect than Benjamin Latrobe, and the famously panoptic Western Penitentiary at Pittsburgh (1826), in addition to lesser jails that are variations on Bentham's idea.[8] A. Berthier, a pupil of Labrouste, built a remarkable prison at Autun in the 1850s, the design of which was intended from the 1840s to combine, as had Bentham, cellular with new panoptic features to permit what has been called *surveillance libératrice*.[9]

Despite its being planned ad hoc like some naive contraption, the Panopticon as a structure has various typological sources. Ironically, given Bentham's own drab secularism, at least two earlier eighteenth-century prisons had established religious destinations in calculated lines of sight. Clement XI built probably the first "cellular" prison at Rome in 1703. It was rectangular with "ateliers" at the center, from which a chapel was visible. Later, at Madrid, a cruciform plan with central court had "the cells... ingeniously staggered so that the inmates might see the altar placed in the center."[10] It is also significant, in light of military architecture as protoengineering, that, in the century before, something like a panoptic arrangement of radial chambers occurred in Bernini's arsenal at Civita Vecchia, 1658–63.[11] Further sources include Louis Le Vaux's menagerie at Versailles (destroyed), with royal viewing salon surrounded by seven animal cages, as noted by Foucault;[12] and a century before that, Philibert Delorme's 1559 project for a convent in Montmartre where, without a central observing station, one might assume that the purpose served was by definition one of social *community*.[13]

Foucault's rather Genetesque fascination with specifically penal surveillance has lent intellectual sensationalism to Bentham's idea of a working, ostensibly self-regulating system in which, it should be obvious, the number of jailers is theoretically reduced to one – or to virtually none, since sufficiently pacified inmates would not know if the sole guard was actually on duty.[14] Thus did the project instill its entrepreneurially cheap paranoia. Anyone concerned with humanity of means would prefer to agree with Pugin, whose Hogarthian, moralizing plate of "Contrasted Residences for the Poor" would juxtapose life in a modern, radial poorhouse with its medieval alternative, testifying to a brutalizing neglect of personhood.[15] Pugin's *Contrasts,* it happens, depends on Chateaubriand's *Génie de Christianisme* (1802),[16] which appeared in the same year as the French edition of Bentham's *Introduction.* (More on *génie* shortly.)

The Bentham who, like so many Americans, tried to metaphysicalize utility, or at least to push philosophy aside,[17] promoted his idea as greatly efficacious "par une simple idée d'architecture," and in light of his thought and example some French architecture considered protofunctionalist from about 1800 can reasonably be described as "utilitarian." Lost in his grand sense of a smooth-running and profitable – if incidentally disheartening – social engine, he could not have understood that (his Panopticon included) not all buildings attain architectural significance and not because they might prove too useful. Bentham's notion of "architecture" was "simple" indeed, absurdly reductive, though whether it would have been preposterous to say "par une simple idée du *génie*" becomes an interesting question. Like the Panopticon's all-seeing but invisible guard, himself but a cog in the great exploitation engine that, as social theory, utilitarianism served, Bentham would have had to step outside his frame of reference to create an artwork. Not that it bothered him to speak so glibly of the art of architecture. His utilitarian mentality shared with a new revisionist, engineering alternative to fine-art architecture a sense of the pragmatic suspension of inhibiting conventions. If needs could be satisfied by precedentless, efficient, practically self-generated constructions, aesthetics might wither away.

Twentieth-century functionalist theory in architecture claims roots in the British moralists and also in English romanticism.[18] Bentham's thought, however, was by no means homemade, or even purely British. Admittedly inconceivable apart from the development of early modern political philosophy in England, notably that of Hobbes, Bentham's ideas nevertheless show affiliations of their own with the Continental Enlightenment. "The greatest good for the greatest number," Bentham's famous dictum, has its likely source in the penology of Cesare Beccaria, in whose *Essay on Crimes and Punishments* of 1764 (English translation, 1767), appears the phrase "la massima felicità devisa nel maggior numero," this clearly before Joseph Priestley's employment of "the greatest good of the greatest number" in his *Essay on Government* (1768). Indeed, in France Bentham's appeal must have seemed welcome not as original (and hardly as philosophical) but as corroborative, since the basic notion of utility as an elementary social force looks to the Encyclopedists,[19] specifically, to the idea that "l'utile circonscrit tout," and indeed, it was Claude Helvétius, whom Bentham studied and acknowledged,[20] who had worked out a theory of utility as basis for ethics.[21] Bentham was sufficiently conversant with his work to imagine Helvétius taking interest in the Panopticon.[22]

Bentham was of course concerned with political economy in the modern sense of "economy" that he, Adam Smith, David Ricardo, and others advocated.[23] Contemporaneously with the Panopticon project, at his brother Samuel's work town for Prince Potemkin at Crichoff in the Ukraine, which he visited in 1786, Bentham began his *Defence of Usury* (critical of Smith's *Wealth of Nations, 1776*), likewise in epistolary form.[24]

Originally, the concept of an "economy" by no means centered on the economy of money: any functionally sufficient system was an economy, such as the economy of nature. In any system, efficiency has its benefits, although the notion of "aesthetic economy,"[25] especially concerning a beauty of simplicity of means, is less immediately to the point here than an idea of the systemically operational that should be considered in connection with the rise of engineering in Bentham's time. And yet, utilitarianism facilitated the sense of the economic as implying an efficaciousness uncomplicated by values, so that by high Victorian times the English word "economy" could connote outright opportunism.[26]

It is significant that Bentham projected a building at all: for an empirical application of social philosophy he turned to, or rather, toward, architecture. This is explicit in the opening words of his preface to his proposal for the building (which was begun but never finished): "*Morals reformed – health preserved – industry invigorated – instruction diffused – public burthens lightened – Economy seated, as it were, upon a rock – the gordian knot of the Poor-Laws not cut but untied – all by a simple idea in architecture!*"[27] Even before turn-of-the-century French "Revolutionary" architecture took on its grander project of housing a new social man, European architecture was undergoing a radical neoclassical purge of previous, baroque ornamentalism.

Had this tropism been followed through historically, however, Bentham could only have encountered complication at the start, for Alberti's approach to prison design in the early Renaissance would probably have been inconveniently humane. The building type of the prison arises in *De re aedificatoria* not in book 4 devoted to public works, but in a chapter (13) of book 5, "On the Works of Individuals," meaning works of special purpose not required by the whole people collectively, along with such other special-purpose architectural needs of magistracies as granaries, treasuries, arsenals, emporia, dockyards, and stables.[28] Humanist that he is, Alberti himself first invokes the ancients, who had three distinct classes of prison: night-detention centers for the moral instruction of crude vagrants, prisons for debtors and those who merely "require the tedium of prison life to set right their wayward lives," and what we would call penitentiaries for "those who have committed abominable crimes, those who are unworthy of the light of day or of contact with society, and who are soon to suffer capital punishment or be given over to darkness and shame."[29] Although ready to follow the ancients "in all other respects," Alberti finds the Roman penitentiary idea rather heartlessly pagan:

Anyone who determined that this last category be an underground chamber, like some fearful tomb, would be proposing a penalty for the criminal more severe than what the law itself or human reason should demand. Even if such men (who are beyond redemption) deserve the ultimate of all penalties for their crimes, it would be expected of republic and prince alike that they should not be wanting in compassion.

No, he says, you will just have to "use large blocks of hard stone, held together with iron and brass," to try to make the prison strong enough. He further suggests "a lining of boards, lofty barred openings, and so on, although not even these will prove large enough or strong enough to prevent anyone intent on freedom and safety from escaping, should you give him the opportunity here to demonstrate the extent of his natural strength and ingenuity." For, Alberti says, in an aside whose worldly application of an eye-of-God idea anticipates the less troubled Bentham, "to my mind they are quite right when they say that the only impregnable prison is the eye of a vigilant guard."[30]

In Italian architecture of the Enlightenment period, two important theoreticians of stripped-down architectural protofunctionalism, Lodoli and Milizia, both had ascetic reason to affirm ornamental simplicity. Carlo Lodoli (d. 1761) was a Franciscan monk whose personal humility was highly respected in the Venetian society to whose sons he taught new ideas that threatened established classicism. Bentham would have been less interested in that than in the fact that, according to the reports of Francesco Algarotti (*Saggio sopra l'architettura*, 1756), Lodoli's first principle was necessity, allowing in architecture only what is "veramente in funzione," with concern for the "natura della materia."[31]

The more complex Francesco Milizia, whose *Roma delle belle arti del disegno* (1792) notoriously compared the then-new sacristy of Saint Peter's (as the worst structure in Rome) with the Cloaca Maxima, the ancient sewer, as the best,[32] is associated with Jansenism, that Catholic sort of puritanism.[33] Piranesi's *Parere su l'architettura* (1765) had already "explicitly attack[ed] . . . principles of absolute linguistic coherence . . . founded on naturalism"[34] – and attacked Algarotti too – when Milizia published his *Dizionario delle arti del disegno* (1797). In the latter, architecture is a "language for ingenious (*ingegnose*) and significant (*significative*) dispositions of edifices."[35]

Before publishing the *Parere*, Giovanni Battista Piranesi had already produced (beginning c. 1745) and reworked (1761) the etchings of his great *Carceri*, or *Imaginary Prisons*, series. In her stimulating essay on it, Marguerite Yourcenar notes, by the way, that the Cloaca Maxima was the only outlet of the ancient Mamertine Prison. Yourcenar's comment that "here stone, iron and wood have ceased being elemental substances – they now become no more than a constituent part of the edifice with no relation to the life of things" evokes Bentham's all but economically indifferent sense of building materials. Of Piranesi's penal spaces she writes, "Nowhere sheltered from sound, one is nowhere sheltered from sight either . . . and this sense of total exposure, total insecurity, perhaps contributes more than all else to making these fantastic palaces into prisons." Here the ominous machinery deployed in these famous etchings is found to consist, all the more ominously, of commonplace building-construction equipment, while Piranesi himself is seen to stand, not with the inmate as sufferer but on the side of "public punishment, with Roman law and order."[36]

It is all the more urgent in view of utilitarianism, and especially in the case of a prison, to consider what radical plainness or deornamentalization of the late eighteenth century, already opposed by Piranesi, entailed. Even if the claim of an architecture governed by "necessity" in Milizia's *Principi di architettura civile,* published between 1781 and 1800,[37] plagiarizes Algarotti's account of Lodoli's position,[38] Milizia's chapter "On Edifices of Public Security" has a section, "Prigioni" (Prisons), in which negative ornamentation is very much to the linguistic point.

"Architecture must know how to brutify (*imbruttire*) itself," this Italian contemporary of Beccaria and Bentham says in his *Principi,* introducing the subject of prison design, where some negative-ornamental necessity can be supposed "more or less evident." For it is in its standing apart from but also beside *società* that the prison's appropriate (or classically, decorous) ornamental incivility makes its civil point. Subtly enough, Milizian penal "brutalism" admits of ornamental distinction between civil and criminal imprisonment, with "sadness" (*malinconia*) as keynote of the civil prison versus "horror" (*orrore*) in the criminal. It is of course the extremity of the latter that calls for more categorical definition. If it is no surprise that here Milizia thinks first of the most earthbound and primeval of the classical orders, the Tuscan – actually, of the abstract *proportions* of the Tuscan, minus even the grave beauty of its actual columns – his effort is to push back still further than that, before or below the dignity of the orders at all, into a kind of ultraviolet, preornamental zone. His thoughts about heavy, haphazard, and shadowy stonework on "double-thick" walls with narrow and deformed openings and "cavernous" recessed entrances comprise a penal aesthetic – "cruel members that may cast the most severe shadows" – that does not exclude "decorations of frightening sculptures and inscriptions," while "all, in sum, must breathe darkness, terrible menacing ruins, as a deterrent to crime."[39]

A contemporary example of such deliberately "frightening" sculptural ornament as Milizia imagines serves to show its apotropaic power as anything but to the good, should governing authority be itself unjust. I refer to the stinging Milizian *orrore* of the tympanum relief over the entrance to John Traill's Kilmainham Gaol, Dublin (constructed 1796), which shows five chained serpents intertwined and impacted in a semicircular field framed, along with the doorway, by a massive band of almost literally wormy vermiculated rustication. Beginning with the rebellion of 1798, and well into the twentieth century, countless Irish patriots passed under this threatening relief, some great ones only once.

Milizia's consideration extends to materials as well as to brutal form and takes an obvious extremist pleasure in vividly imagining a prison's exterior walls as tiled smooth for security while planted amid boulders clamped and bolted together, and having a deep, steep-sided moat beyond. It would be rash, however, to take this aesthetic delight, which is by no means divorced from the essence of ornament, as Sadean. Unlike Bentham's day and night of enforced paranoia, Milizia's linguistically and socially utilitarian deterrent-sublime is itself to be complemented, he says, by an interior less penal than correctional. (Bentham affects to attempt much the same distinction but can no more conceive an architectural expression of it than he can permit himself to imagine its human reality.) Indeed, the "completely *orrendo* [exterior] aspect, far from ruling out a commodious and healthy interior," might best be designed like a cloister with cell and guards' doors interspersed, the former placed according to seriousness of crime and opening onto an airy courtyard (how far can this be from the Panopticon?). There would be "ample corridors allowing for work spaces" (as in actual contemporary American workhouses, Milizia says). Latrines need to be cleverly designed to avoid stench, even if this means using (more expensive) iron rather than wood – hygiene, ventilation, and general healthfulness being important "everywhere, even in these sad places." This intimidating-looking prison is ideally located not in the country but in town, near the courts and less exposed to seditious attack, but also in marked ornamental and "instructive" contrast with beautiful nearby buildings. It is not beautifully plain but ornamentally significantly grave, all the more so in juxtaposition with its civil neighbors. If a materialist functionalist would tend to enroll the Panopticon as pure architecture, possibly purer than anything rhetorical, in light of Milizia's meditation on prison architecture it is relatively artless.

While the rise of engineering in later eighteenth-century France began to pose a challenge not so much of one aesthetic against another[40] as of pragmatics against aesthetics, French architecture in the "Revolutionary" period was already preoccupied with the question of ornament and utility. The simple cylindrical form of Bentham's model prison evokes the elemental geometry of the French, even if by default – Bentham being too concerned with the mechanics of the program to think about it that way, whereas French architects were consciously essentializing form. Thus the basic disposition of the Panopticon is in its radial organization not unlike the famous spherical Newton cenotaph (1784) of Etienne Boullée, or a cemetery or columbarium by Claude Nicolas Ledoux, even if they go further, geometrically as well as symbolically, that is, from cylinder to sphere.

The very title of Ledoux's book, *L'architecture consideree sous le rapport de l'art, des moeurs et de la législation* (1804), recalls – or even alludes to – that of Bentham's major utilitarian treatise published in French two years before. Mundane parallels might include Ledoux's concern with underground vaults for food storage, where Bentham experimented with a "frigidarium" and planned one for the Panopticon. More importantly, Ledoux as much as resorts to a notion of self-regulating energy in his theory of architectural ornament: for him "decoration," defined in *L'architecture* (1804) as "the expressive character, more or less simple, more or less complex, which is given to each edifice," has animate and even self-justifying qualities:

> It distinguishes the altars that dispute eternity with the Supreme Being from the fragile palace sustained by temporary power. It brings surfaces

13

to life, immortalizes them, stamps them with all feeling and all passions. It modifies the irregularities of fate, humbling the ostentatious and uplifting the diffident; it stigmatizes ignorance and elevates knowledge, and justly apportioned, it gives to nations the luster which makes them shine, and plunges into savagery those peoples ungrateful or heedless . . . who neglect its favors.[41]

As far beyond Bentham's understanding, as beyond Boullée's insistence that architecture is a realm of intellectual form (not mere fancy building), indeed, was Ledoux's comprehensive attitude toward ornament, which by no means simply ("reductively") eliminated ornament, but took it as linguistically functional.

"Appropriateness will offer us the analogy of proportions and ornaments . . . it will show at first glance the reasons for the constructions and for what they are destined," says Ledoux in his *L'architecture*.[42] But he says so in a way that hangs everything on classical thinking in extension of the moral aspect of classical *decorum*. In itself, self-regulating economy has no expressive potential except parsimony – a reason, perhaps, why Bentham's penal pile doesn't even look significantly "simple." It is one thing to let things be where shared values prevail, such as a sense of the moral significance of ornament perhaps more deeply inscribed in Western architectural theory than the classical doctrine that had conveyed it (as would soon be seen by its rich proliferation in the anticlassical writings of Ruskin).

Bentham, out to humiliate the inmate of his Panopticon (he could have denied this, but negating an unfortunate's humanity is enough to humiliate), cannot be credited with an expressive humiliation. Not that no one ever claimed one, however: in 1868, a socially prominent British architect would wonder why he lost a competition for a Poor Law "asylum," or workhouse, since he had only followed the rules. "You consider my elevation ugly," wrote George Gilbert Scott, Jr. "You have a right to your own opinion. It is, however, fair to mention that the first of the instructions to competitors directed that the building should have 'no architectural pretensions whatever.' I have endeavoured to carry out this instruction."[43] There is no need to get into the details of the case, but one may well wonder what a demand or a claim for an effectively architectureless building, even by some naive understanding of ornamentation, might mean, given mere blankness of ornamentation as by no means beneath architectural civility around 1800.

How can ornamental blankness signify where the quasi-industrial utilitarianism of the Panopticon (not so crisp, at that) does not? How should one approach a distinction between accidental or even awkward nakedness, as it were, and significant, even noble, nudity in architectural art? All this begins to suggest how the Panopticon both relates to and differs from the stoically noble ornamental starkness of categorically fine-art architecture by Boullée, Ledoux, and others – much later mobilized on behalf of an "autonomous" modern functionalist architecture by Emil Kaufmann in his classic *Von Ledoux bis Le Corbusier* (1933).[44]

A telling moralism shows in Milizia's claim that simplicity cannot consist in mere *privazione* of ornament, lest a bare wall be the most beautiful:[45] to the extent that the operative term is privation, this inevitably evokes the scholastic notion of evil as the privation of good. For Milizia's ideal prison to be linguistically significant in its very withholding of ornamentation indicates an essentially architectural position, whereas the lack of ornament in the Panopticon, thanks to Bentham's efficiency and economy, exercises no such significance. The Panopticon should basically count instead as a work of engineering – of actual civil engineering, as well as of metaphoric social engineering – playing a different and strictly utilitarian game. That in realization the Panopticon turns out to have been surreptitiously finessed into (mediocre) architecture, however, will nevertheless have to affect Foucault's discussion of the building, as even the rudimentary published Panopticon design is more demonstrably architectural than anyone relying on Bentham's verbal program alone would suppose.

Ledoux held that "in a factory (*usine*), round and square piers, or shafts combining both, seem more appropriate (*convenables*)" than conventional (classical) orders.[46] By virtue of the fact that it was severely "utilitarian," in more than a pun, the Panopticon raises questions, important to modern architecture, of nil or zero-degree ornamentation, of engineering in rivalry with architecture, and of anatomical structure. And Milizia's conception of significantly negative ornament, readily affiliated with the concept of the nude at the absolute center of the classical aesthetic in painting, sculpture, and architecture alike, leads in turn to the matter of anatomy and of the articulated vertebrate skeleton to a sense of scientifically determined and rationally unembellished "engineering" structure.

At its root, the concept of ornament never implied anything superfluous: from its ultimate Indo-European source the term connotes a fulfilling expressive follow-through of integral form.[47] About 1800 in France, and to some extent elsewhere, this root sense was newly exposed as a downplaying or virtual elimination of conventional ornamentalism as so much rhetorical superfluity – assuming for now that plain talk is not just another rhetorical mode – and to have rendered prominent the possible ornamental expressiveness of a building as a whole. There is philosophical support for this largely antibaroque development in Helvétius's *On Man* (1773) as well as in writings of Diderot and d'Alembert, where an integrity of simplicity of "character" is opposed to "the superfluous."[48] One almost begins to pick up on a moral sense of "Ornament as Crime," to use the famous 1908 title of Adolf Loos's early modernist polemic.

Curiously, what with modernist architecture today so often rejected as "utopian," literary utopias have not necessarily assumed that unornamented architecture meant pure, ideal architecture – certainly not *News from Nowhere* (1891), by William Morris, who in at least one narrative is a principal progenitor of modernism in design.[49]

In the modern orbit of Le Corbusier the physiological and anatomical understanding of tectonic structure leads to a distaste for external decoration as almost an indignity to the human body, in what might as a matter of fact constitute a reference to Benthamism: "In that definition all fine *utilitarian* architecture lies; in the breathing unity of masses entirely adequate to their function. Decoration can be revolting, but a naked body moves us by the harmony of its form. Thanks to certain of our architects, we have houses that are splendidly naked."[50] These are the words of Ozenfant, who later in the same punchy "Purist" book *Art* (1928), known in English as *Foundations of Modern Art* (1931), includes a full-page aerial photograph of a five-armed radial prison at Copenhagen under the provocative caption "Order at the service of Liberty," this in a section entitled "The Technic of Happiness."[51]

Already in 1750 Rousseau had expressed his conception of a moral ideal in terms of nudity and in a disapproval of ornamental trappings as wasteful or vain: "L'homme de bien est un athlète, qui se plaît à combattre nu; il méprise tous ces vils ornements qui gêneraient l'usage de ses forces, et dont la plupart n'ont été inventés que pour cacher quelque difformité."[52] Diderot respected the nude body so much that he warned the artist to stop at its skin and refrain from anatomical inquiry: "The deep (*profonde*) study of anatomy has spoiled more artists than it has perfected. In painting as in morals it is dangerous to see under the skin."[53]

Boullée, in his *L'architecture: Essai sur l'art*, likens "the skeleton of architecture" to "an absolutely nude, skinned," presumably load-bearing, wall.[54] Ledoux, anticipating an important modernist preoccupation, not only of Le Corbusier but of modernist architects in Germany and Russia, began to see the orderless condition as appropriate to industrial building.[55] It was quite in the spirit of Boullée and Ledoux that the Marxist aesthetician Plekhanov would recall in his *Art and Social Life* (1912), which devotes two chapters to "Art and Utility," an architect's remarks in a debate of the revolutionary convention, in 1793, on a proposed National Assembly hall: "When architecture came up for judgment, a certain [Léon] Dufourny asserted that all buildings 'should be as plain as a citizen's virtues.' 'What end is served by superfluous decoration?' he added. 'Architecture must be regenerated by geometry.' "[56]

According to Emil Kaufmann, J.-N.-L. Durand indulged a veritably iconoclastic rejection of traditional architectural ornament (almost as if it were a trapping of the enemy). "Laughable and fruitless" he called the classical orders, and accused them of adorning "by vain and costly means" whereas "nature and common sense display such sure and simple means even in bare construction." Kaufmann is happy to report that Durand thought that for all buildings the "Mechanismus" of composition might be the same.[57] One does find in functionalist theory of the time a sense of the engineering aspect of anatomy[58] – including a kind of skeletal structurality that persists with the (originally naval) engineer Buckminster Fuller's geodesic dome. That, while an obvious manifestation of engineering more than of architecture, is also the product of a consciousness of man as a creature at home in the biosphere.[59]

Architectural orderlessness may not be synonymous with architecturelessness, but it only highlights the question of a building's being significantly architectural. Neither may it be as easy to depart entirely from the realm of the poetic (including the architectural) as Jeremy Bentham supposed. Despite the "programmatic dislike and distrust of metaphor" that drives Bentham's attempt to find a neutral or scientific vocabulary for moral theory, the literary theoretician Kenneth Burke has observed that Bentham himself "calls such idealizing words," "metophorically enough, 'eulogistic coverings' or 'fig leaves.' "[60]

There is also, however, a positive sense that the body astutely adorned can display depth of character in external expression – an office both practical and lofty, much as Ledoux understood the manifest expressiveness of ornament to be. Consider Tolstoy's describing of his central character in *Anna Karenina* (1875–7), whose restrained deployment of clothing (which Carlyle would have liked) indicates more astute than inhibiting taste: "Her black dress with its rich lace was not conspicuous on her, either; it merely served as a frame, and what one saw was Anna alone, simple, natural, elegant and at the same time gay and animated"(1.22).[61] Ledoux's saying that decoration humbles the ostentatious and uplifts the diffident, he implies that within the self-regulating system of decorum semiotic falsehood is automatically ruled out: ostentation punishes itself, while by something like a less-is-more principle diffidence rewards itself with taste. Socially, evil itself displays its guilt against a natural decorum, since "governors will inhabit huge, luxurious abodes as empty of contentment as they are full of bitterness," and "the walls of the financier will carry the spoils of a hundred families."[62]

"Variety will give each building its proper physiognomy,"[63] the architect Ledoux writes, implying an interplay of the generic and the individual, of regulation and self-regulation, that recalls seventeenth-century theory of emotional expression (Le Brun, anticipating Darwin) and connotes vital mechanism within an encompassing system of nature. Bentham, too, thinks of the body: in his utilitarian treatise he says his basic idea "is to the art of legislation what the science of anatomy is to the art of medicine . . . nor is the body politic less in danger from a want of acquaintance with the one science than the body natural from ignorance in the other."[64] Yet his sense of the metaphorical body as anatomical object is tantamount to one of mechanical structure, not to a physiological complex.[65] Whereas the inert "bodies" of physics and anatomy stay put unless something sets them moving or move until something stops them, the living bodies of physiology have independence and self-sufficiency as systemic entities (traditionally, the "soul," *animus,* of an organism is manifest in independent *animation*). Bentham's attempt to institute a social kind of physiology by anatomical means could only prove robotic, but it bears interesting similarities to certain contemporary notions of self-regulation on a social scale, and also with a new sense of engineering construction as unimpeded, rationally self-evident structure.

Despite the fact that engineers to this day converse in a Newtonian dialect of "forces," Malebranche already disputed the concept of (Newtonian) force in favor of a very different principle of "least action" by which God works in nature,[66] letting things more or less take shape on their own, neither determining everything nor abandoning the system (as with Descartes's and

Leibniz's sense of the world's clockwork, the latter famously spoofed by Voltaire in *Candide,* 1759). Contemporaneously with the Panopticon, Kant claimed in the *Critique of Judgment* (1790) that natural bodies differ from works of human art in being "self-organizing."[67] In a broad view, any number of instances of self-regulation become evident, even as regards social behavior. Thus in Malthus's *Essay on the Principle of Population* (1798), society is subsumed in a kind of human natural history whose "checks to population" include "all those customs, and all those diseases, which seem to be generated by a scarcity of the means of subsistence," these as "constantly operating with more or less force in every society."[68] Less acknowledged but important in popular life was spontaneous submission to a simple "Method" of grace, followed by equally automatic social formation, among the Methodists. Wesley writes as if the development of his own movement seemed self-regulating owing to its adherents' trust in God: "As they had not the least expectation at first, of anything like what has since followed, so they had no previous design or plan at all, but every thing arose just as the occasion offered." Here, indeed, is a spiritually preoccupied inverse utilitarianism unlike the monstrosity of Bentham the atheist's will-crushing superego for somebody else: "They saw or felt some impending or pressing evil, or some good end necessary to be pursued. And many times they fell unawares on the very thing, which served the good, or removed the evil."[69]

But when the French Revolutionary military engineer Lazare Carnot, in his "Essay on Machines in General," less subtly dismissed the Newtonian notion of forces as "metaphysical and obscure,"[70] he was not necessarily prepared to embrace Malebranchean "least action." Carnot's was the voice of a new pragmatic, that of engineering. What seems most telling in the engineer's frame of mind is a kind passive immersion in structural problems versus an active imposition of (classical) artistic forms, so that architects' and engineers' very notion of what their task was grew different. To the new mentality the "Latin" of conventional classical architectural form came to seem almost an arbitrary vernacular imposed upon a supposedly more fundamental reality of mathematical and physical science. Because function was now asked to speak more directly, in deference to nature's ways, the classical ornamental tradition was challenged at its metaphysical basis (the linguistic as natural).

What might seem definitively architectureless is the "engineering" alternative that about the turn of the eighteenth century was institutionally defining itself away from a fine-art architecture itself standing in the clear rational light of neoclassical orthodoxy, the pure geometries of the one resembling the pure geometries of the other. Nobody would expect Bentham's Panopticon, such a severely utilitarian thing, to be an architecturally glorious affair; but there would be good reason to consider it as related to the emergent civil-engineering tradition just then defining itself as distinct from the poor-relation subcategory of "military," in relation to "civil," fine-art architecture.

Much more has been written about the concept of "genius" in respect to poetic – especially the romantic poet's – superrational inspiration than has been about ultrarational creativity in *le génie,* the new eighteenth-century field of engineering. In 1759 Edward Young asked, "What, for the most part, mean we by genius, but the power of accomplishing great things without the means generally reputed necessary to that end? A genius differs from a good understanding as a magician from a good architect: that raises his structure by means invisible; this by skilful use of common tools. Hence genius has ever been supposed to partake of something divine."[71] Diderot wrote in an unpublished fragment, "On Genius," where small-minded attention to detail is "utilité . . . domestique," of that "rare machine *(machine rare)*" that can grasp phenomena in their workings. Here the same concept presents itself in distinctly quantitative terms: "The man of genius knows what he leaves to chance, and he knows it without having calculated the chances for or against, this calculus being entirely in his head."[72]

Nor did the poet's genius simply give way to the engineer's. All along there was an unapologetically metaphorical *génie,* or "genius," of artistic and architectural inspiration. Thus among several varieties of "Génie" classed in the *Encyclopédie,* Diderot and D'Alembert include *Génies en architecture,* these, however, being not invisible inspirers of architects but symbolic-ornamental "genius" figures, something like agents or angels of inspiration that might appear in classical architectural circumstances (like the Roman "victories" from which angel representations derive).[73] Similarly, in 1787 Viel de Saint-Maux published his *Letters* on ancient and modern architecture "in Which Is Found Developed the Symbolic Genius Presiding Over the Monuments of Antiquity."[74] The empathetic aspect of noble building did not wither when such metaphor disappeared: it was in his *Génie de l'architecture* (1780), concerned with "Analogy of This Art with Our Sensations," that, for one thing, the engineering-conscious Le Camus de Mézièrs had maintained that a prison ought to look and seem like a prison.[75]

Nevertheless, the very term and concept of "engineering" – *le génie,* as in *le génie civil* – holds interest, evoking as it also does both genius in the abstract (as in Chateaubriand's title) and the individual genius, as in Boullée's fanfare "A Newton" at the opening of his manuscript *Architecture: Essai sur l'art.* He writes, "Esprit Sublime! Génie vaste et profond! Etre Divin! Newton!"[76] And in Boullée's apostrophe there may echo a passage in the 1750 discourse by Rousseau already mentioned: "Les Verulam, les Descartes et *les Newton,* ces précepteurs du genre humain, n'en ont point eu eux-mêmes; et quels guides les eussent conduits jusqu'où *leur vaste génie* les a portés?"[77] The term *génie,* in the sense of civil engineer, was stable by about 1759.[78] Earlier, within official classical architectural theory, Félibien, secretary of the Royal Academy of Architecture under Louis XIV, had explained in his *Principes de l'architecture* (1699) that military architecture is different from civil architecture by being hardly concerned with ornament, and that architects who specialize in fortifications are distinguished from others by being called *ingenieurs,* "perhaps because of the ingenious inventions that they are obliged to put to use in the tasks that present themselves" (1.13).[79]

The Ecole des ponts et chaussées, Paris, was founded in 1741, the Ecole du génie at Mézières in 1748, and the Parisian Ecole des mines in 1783. Once the Ecole polytechnique was established in 1794, mainly for the training of army officers (emphasizing construction and mining and rather scornful of mechanical engineering as civil and workaday), Ponts et chaussées, Mines and another special Ecole du génie militaire became postgraduate "schools of application" following Polytechnique studies. Also, from 1815 on, the title *ingénieur civil* identified an engineer not in state employment; once the Paris Ecole centrale des arts et manufactures, a private institution, was started in 1829, emphasizing mechanical engineering as of serious industrial importance, many of its graduates joined a "Société des ingénieurs civils."[80]

The culturally uninhibited, even iconoclastic, can-do attitude of the engineer became a point of professional pride in France in the nineteenth century, its attitude of productive competence challenging a cachet of classical education in moral values and cultural sophistication that still attached to a traditionalist social ideal of the *honnête homme* in the eighteenth century.[81] In his account of his own project for a country house for a *"mecanicien"* – which it is fair to translate as "mechanical engineer" – Ledoux praises engineering, in 1804, as "this precious art which the futility of this century seems to disdain."[82]

All this is in association with what today we call engineering, of which the practitioner is *l'ingénieur,* and in which creative cleverness in problem solving is obviously more to the point than an appeal to cultural precedent. The engineer is in the simplest sense a figurer-out, whose cleverness is *nearly* a virtue, good if not noble. Obviously this engineering has its prehistory, especially as regards hydraulics, ballistics, and so forth, but this history is not a *historia* in the same sense as the history of architecture, however told.[83] In accruing sophistication, engineering, busy, as it were, forgetting architecture, was like a new language still derived in some ways from the old. By an interesting contradiction, the early development of civil engineering in the eighteenth century[84] at first extended, before it disconnected from, the Renaissance tradition of the antique orders, although it deserves to be remembered that certain matters of what we would consider civil engineering were not alien to Vitruvius in his uniquely surviving classical treatise on architecture. Thus the *Science des ingénieurs* of Bernard de Bélidor, a Catalonian-born artillerist, published and republished in the century from 1729 to 1830, "included a concise manual of architecture, with a textual and pictorial description of the five classical orders of columns."[85] The *Génie de l'architecture* (1780) of Le Camus de Mézières, who designed the cylindrical Halle aux Blés[86] in Paris, represents a moment of sophisticated transition: while informed by mechanics, it considers general massing to be the same kind of proportional problem that the artistic system of the orders served to control. Otherwise, in a proposal of 1800 for a new London Bridge consisting of stone piers and iron spans, the ironwork was to consist principally of tangent circles, but with twinned Greek columns on the piers set atop the cutwaters (at least they would be baseless Doric!). Similarly, on a suspension bridge over the Rhône near Tournon in 1824, built to the designs of a M. Seguin, pairs of square pylons supporting the cables do their best to behave as classical columns, with a thin molding applied down to about the height of a capital from their tops.[87] Could it have been, however paradoxically, a sense that the glory of architecture might be mislaid that led such nineteenth-century protomodernist partisans to cling to its ideal classical elements?

Developments in specifically naval "architecture," a field already recognized by Milizia as a subcategory of military architecture (whence sprang civil engineering), tell something of sophisticated "utilitarian" construction around 1800. Seventeenth-century naval vessels had received such grand quasi-architectural ornamentation, like the ornamental systems of the great contemporary châteaux,[88] that an entire school of carvers led by Pierre Puget "tried to insist that the basic structure of warships should be devised to suit the arrangements of the sculptured groups"; to impress being one of the working functions of a warship.[89] But what we now mean by naval architecture really began in the early eighteenth century, when the calculus made comprehensively engineered ship design possible. Ironically, Isaac Newton stood on the wrong side of an early controversy, believing that one ideal hull shape of least resistance could be mathematically derived.[90] In a *Traité du navire* (1746) Pierre Bouguer inaugurates a new version of a theory-and-practice justification familiar from French civil architecture: "Experience would be the best means of perfecting naval architecture, if it were possible; but it is plain enough that practice is insufficient in many cases. It is certain that if this alone is capable of perfecting some parts, it has need, in an infinity of others, to be aided in the light of theory."[91] A new excitement in ship design around the turn of the century is reflected in a remark of Ledoux, one of that architect's more vivid anticipations of Le Corbusier: "What builder would not attain utter transport if one told him of an edifice three hundred feet tall, raised in the middle of a stormy sea?"[92] Notably for the theory of ornament, the important British naval architect J. Scott Russell, designer of the renowned *Great Eastern* (1808), had studied sea waves and "evolved a system of design, known as the *line* principle, by which certain lines in the shape of a ship were related to the shape of ocean waves."[93] We tend now to associate such thought with the postwar heyday of functionalism, when texts by the mid-nineteenth-century American sculptor Horatio Greenough, collected under the title *Form and Function* (1947),[94] were found to celebrate the ship hull as a pragmatic revelation of formal beauty. In a book published at the Bauhaus in 1926, however, Kandinsky juxtaposed on facing pages, à la Corbusier, a schematic line drawing of a three-masted, square-rigged "sailing vessel" and a photo of a model of the exposed hull framework of "a motor freightship," these both rationally comparable as "line-point constructions."[95]

The general emergence of civil engineering, including modern naval architecture, would deserve a place in art-historical consideration of the architecture of 1800 for its conditioning of form and structure even if Boullée and Durand had not been institutionally involved in its emergence. The first determinations of architectural dimensions by the principles of physics (Newton's "natural philosophy") were made in the early 1800s by Louis Navier at the Ecole des ponts et chaussées – that is, the School of Bridges and Causeways (or "Roadways"), as against architecture in the sense of the *beaux-arts* – which, founded in the eighteenth century, was the wellspring of French civil engineering. Boullée himself taught at the Pont et chaussées. Jean Nicolas Durand, his pupil, became an army engineer and taught architecture at the Ecole polytechnique when it opened in 1795. Durand published both *Receuil et parallèle des édifices en tout genre, anciens et modernes* (1801) and a *Précis des leçons d'architecture données à l'Ecole polytechnique* (1802–05). In the latter, certain Benthamite reflections appear: "If we observe the progress and development of intelligence and feeling, we shall find that in all periods and in all places, all the thoughts and actions of men have originated in two principles: love of comfort and dislike of any kind of pain"; or, "Public and private utility, the happiness and preservation of the individual and of society, this is the...good of architecture."[96]

Now of these theorists, it is Durand of the Polytechnique who seems uniquely concerned that, while the prison exists for the maintenance of public tranquillity, "one can be detained while not being guilty"; hence "one must only be punished after being judged." Here too is a rather anti-Piranesian aesthetic by which the art of architecture is to play less a penal than a penological role. With health and security established as priorities, "the architect could concern himself with making such a place bearable by all possible means, far from seeking to make it horrible by the ridiculous spectacle of chained, piled up columns in one way or another imprisoned in the walls, etc."[97] If anything, Durand himself could be said to have *avoided* the panopticon in prison design: despite thinking of a radial disposition for a library (not unlike Sydney Smirke's later ironwork reading room, begun in 1854, for the British Museum), in his typological plates a prison is conceived in rows of parallel blocks, hardly different from a barracks.

Durand's thought evokes the utilitarian outlook. Defining architecture as "the art of composing (*de composer*) and executing all buildings, both public and private,"[98] Durand states its "so interesting and noble goal" as "public and private utility (*l'utilité publique et particulière*)"; yet even he does not dissolve architecture into construction. Rather than retreat into Vitruvian *utilitas,* he elaborates the subtler principle of *convenence,* which implies appropriateness, suitability, into a more pragmatic triad of its own: "For a building to be *convenable* it must be *solide, salubre* (healthy) and *commode.*"[99]

Where Durand pursues an economic argument against the classical orders it is indeed in virtually utilitarian terms of pleasure measured against pain: "According to most architects, architecture is less the art of making useful buildings (*de faire des édifices utiles*) than that of decorating them"; yet if only because conventionally classical *décoration architectonique* is expensive, it remains to be determined whether such decorative "pleasure (*plaisir*) compensates for the cost that occasions it."[100] In the eighteenth century, Marc-Antoine Laugier was criticized for rationalizing the priority of the orders, only to consider secondarily the "addition" of doors, windows, and such as "need" dictated. Laugier's idealized primitive hut, the foundation of his (otherwise protofunctional) architectural theory, was dismissed as a "fabrication" that could only be "natural" because it was so coarsely instinctive as to amount to a natural production by default! The larger point is that the traditional orders simply do not form "the essence of architecture."[101] Laugier himself, Durand says, faced the fact that "necessity alone" was the origin of the art of architecture, whose fundamental goal was none other than "public and private *utilité*."[102]

When a building is planned to be suited to its "*usage* or purpose," it will have a "character of its own," and if it is planned "in the most economical, that is to say the simplest, manner, will seem as large and magnificent as possible" – then why worry about "beauty" anyway?[103] If Durand goes rather far in making beauty, or something supposedly just as good, a simple consequence of "the most suitable and economical disposition," there is nevertheless merit in his claim that "in architecture, far from being an obstacle to beauty, as is commonly believed, economy is, on the contrary, its most fecund source."[104] Economy is the mother of Durand's beauty, and he criticizes the Paris Panthéon for not having been built on a (note for Bentham) circular plan, which would have been the most economical way to produce a single chamber of even greater area.[105]

It was precisely to the gross mechanical serviceability of the Bentham Panopticon, which struck him as typically British, that Louis-Pierre Baltard, a student of Ledoux who himself had corps-of-engineers experience during the revolutionary wars, took objection. In an *Architectonography of Prisons; or, Parallel of the Different Systems of Planning of Which Prisons Are Susceptible* (1829) Baltard writes, by no means sentimentally, "The English bring into all their works the genius for mechanics which they have perfected, and they thus want their buildings to function like a machine worked by a single motor."[106] Foucault quotes this sentence,[107] only to maintain that Bentham's Panopticon "must not be understood as a dream building: it is the diagram of a mechanism of power reduced to its ideal form; its functioning, abstracted from any obstacle, resistance or friction, must be represented as a pure architectural and optical system: it is in fact a figure of political technology that may and must be detached from any specific use."[108] One does get Foucault's endlessly restated main point about the growth of surveillance from Napoleonic times to the present, for example his apt quotation from a text of 1808 that "no part of the Empire is without surveillance . . . and . . . the eye of the genius who can enlighten all embraces the whole of this vast machine . . ."[109]

Not altogether unlike Bentham himself, however, who (as it were) stamped out metaphor only to have his stamping out be covertly metaphoric,[110] Foucault loved to work his terms over until the terms themselves were the substance of the discussion as much as anything else. Cryptoaesthetic as that may be, he notes the novelty in Bentham's day of cylindrically constructed "panoramas."[111] Actually, the term "panopticon" was still being applied a hundred years after Bentham, and in French, to artwork set up in diorama fashion for projective gazing: there had indeed been, for example, the "panopticon art gallery" of Joseph, Graf von Deym (for the mechanical organ of which Beethoven composed music);[112] but at the end of the nineteenth century Strindberg could still write of "figures . . . immobiles comme dans un panopticon."[113] The speculative gaze of Foucault surveys and projects in every direction, like Bentham's efficient jailer, whose own anxiety must be that he can only be sure of one cell at a time. Yet quick as Foucault is to occupy the privileged lookout Bentham has prepared for him, that station, in typical literary fashion, is inadequately *observed*.[114]

Dream building, no; but building – even, like it or not, architecture – yes.[115]

In considering Bentham's critical reputation here, however briefly, it should be noted that there is an early Benthamite instance of the machine metaphor for a working functional(ist) building, which we always associate with Le Corbusier in architectural modernism. In the January 1835 issue of the *Westminster Review*, which Jeremy Bentham founded, there appeared an anonymous article (probably by Colonel Perronet Thompson) on the current Houses of Parliament projects, maintaining that the new building should be "a powerful machine of nicest force, calculated at once for the most vigorous and gentle operation, as the different occasions shall demand – of wondrous power but composed of a multitude of parts adjusted to a thousand special functions, yet combining for the production of one grand general effect."[116] Le Corbusier's own "machine for" metaphor was considerably more organically informed than this, but the remark deserves to be pursued because here, perhaps, are the very terms of the twentieth-century functionalist formulation, but subject to a different governing principle because the larger *function* that all subfunctions come together in fulfilling is the production of a "grand effect." Latter-day American functionalists tended to drop from theory this comprehensive semiotic function of the building as an artwork (only to see a simpleminded "semiotic" reinstalled more recently), which is obviously more difficult to defend than gross practicality. Nevertheless, in the architecture of Boullée and Ledoux such "functionalism" in the service of concepts – here the national dignity of the seated parliament – was strong.

Interest in Bentham considerably outlasted interest in his better-mousetrap Panopticon scheme. Carlyle critiques Benthamism in *Heroes and Hero-Worship* (1841) while managing to forgive Bentham himself on grounds that he dared to seize hold of the modern world's (ignoble) ways. First comes the utilitarian attitude as wrecker of myth and poetry, in a remark that happens to anticipate Marx:

> The living TREE Igdrasil . . . has died-out into the clanking of a World-MACHINE. "Tree" and "Machine": contrast these two things. I, for my share, declare the world to be no machine! I say that it does *not* go by wheel-and-pinion "motives," self-interests, checks, balances; that there is something far other in it than the clank of spinning-jennies, and parliamentary majorities; and, on the whole, that it is not a machine at all! – The old Norse Heathen had a truer notion of God's-world than these poor Machine-Skeptics.[117]

This leads Carlyle into his attack on Bentham's influence – punning on the name of John Stuart Mill:

"Well then, this world is a dead iron machine, the God of it Gravitation and selfish Hunger; let us see what, by checking and balancing, and a good adjustment of tooth and pinion, can be made of it!" Benthamism . . . is the culminating point, and fearless ultimatum, of what lay in the half-and-half state, pervading man's whole existence in the Eighteenth Century. It seems to me, all deniers of Godhood, and all lip-believers of it, are bound to be Benthamites, if they have courage and honesty. Benthamism is an *eyeless* Heroism: the Human Species, like a hapless blinded Samson grinding in the Philistine Mill, clasps convulsively the pillars of its Mill; brings huge ruins down, but ultimately deliverance withal. Of Bentham I meant to say no harm. But this I do say, . . . that he who discerns nothing but Mechanism in the Universe has in the fatalest way missed the secret of the Universe altogether.[118]

That Bentham is excused (and not sarcastically) for manfully mastering the game may have some importance, later, for the French cult of Gauguin (himself aware of Carlyle) as a charmingly crude "hardy." In the painter Maruice Denis's Whitmanesque sense, Gauguin "fully justified Carlyle's etymological play on words with *genius* and *ingenuity*"; "Something of the essential, of the profoundly true," Denis says, "emanated from his savage art, from his rough common sense, and from his vigorous naïveté."[119] Denis must be referring to Carlyle's *Past and Present* (1843), where the word holds importance in what strikes the modern reader as, if anything, a mechanical-engineering context. It is after speaking of how, with the progress of the labor movement and "the Inventive Genius of England, with the whirr of its bobbins and billyrollers shoved somewhat into the backgrounds of the brain," a fairer distribution of goods might prevail, that Carlyle pits true "genius" – in Milton's sense of divine inspiration – against the supposed mere outward formalities of high-church religion.[120] In American culture at least, there is the related problem of a tendency to take the detachedly beautiful (including art) as, for better or worse, feminine, while upholding whatever is efficaciously engaged (applied) as masculine. In a thickheaded Emersonian strain of thought, utility itself is practically world sanctifying, at least as far as it remains possible for anything to be.[121] But consider, from *Anna Karenina,* again, where the dissemination of Bentham's ideas is specified – "He also read another article on finance, in which Bentham and Mill were mentioned" (1.3)[122] – the utilitarianism exposed in the statement that in America "they put up buildings in a rational manner" (6.22).[123] Could this word "rational" have been written with more disdain?

To Aldous Huxley, who takes up Bentham and his Panopticon in an essay written shortly after World War II on, appropriately, Piranesi's *Carceri,* the societal problem of the Panopticon is that if a (rather British) sense of "tidiness" gets (rather Germanically) out of hand, "mechanical efficiency" is as much an enemy of liberty as anarchy at the opposite extreme. Just so in Bentham's time, and thanks partly to him, "From being sub-humanly anarchical, prisons became sub-humanly mechanical."[124] Huxley, who too rather likes the figure of Bentham himself, refers, without observing Tolstoy's own awareness of

Bentham, to the chapter in *War and Peace* (4.1.10) recounting the spirit-breaking imprisonment of the character Pierre by a more heartlessly systematic than innately corrupt French military ("It was the system, the concatenation of circumstances").[125] "Today," according to the British novelist fascinated by the sheer structural "pointlessness" of Piranesi's fantasy prisons as emblematic of a very modern spiritual *acacia*,[126] "every efficient office, every up-to-date factory is a panoptical prison, in which the worker suffers... from the consciousness of being inside a machine."[127]

What seems, after all, so inhumane about the Panopticon is its treatment of persons not only as mere bodies but hardly even as that, except in the most detached geometric sense of a social geometry within a social engineering. Perhaps, once effectively despiritualized, the "humanistic" Enlightenment had no defense against newly tyrannical monstrosities of "natural law." With man's soul disacknowledged in favor of an abstract well-being conveniently adaptable to efficient utilitarian-industrialist production, "panopticons" were to provide labor in the form of useful – meaning productive – citizens. (Note the barely disguised social geometry of slavery itself [not even a reciprocal serfdom], with the state's hands washed clean.) With no place for its moral case to be heard, the socially guilty soul would just have to march off in enlightened chains along with the disorderly body. In the seventeenth century, Spinoza, with his profounder moral geometry, and then in Bentham's day, Hegel, aware of Spinoza on the subject, could have argued this better than I can here.[128]

Social control, understandably the first consideration in designing a prison, is in this context no longer a mere theme but, in the interest of brutally decentered "genius" or guiding spirit of sheer and absolute Efficiency, effectively the entirety of the penal program. Social control itself is posed as an essentially mathematical or geometric rather than moral problem, whereas in their geometries the French architects of eighteen hundred were investigating the nature and qualities of architecture. Is it any wonder that something of the enforced utilitarianism of the Panopticon can be found in the disposition of a British commercial office block of the 1970s?[129]

The Panopticon would be easier to reserve to "social engineering" if it were essentially (or purely) a mechanism, even an essentially optical mechanism, through and through as Foucault has it. Insofar as function tends to be manifest but reflexive rather than latent but mediated in engineering structure, Bentham's Panopticon was a civil-engineering contribution to industrial engineering, even to "management." But that is not the whole story, for, at the same time, it took more definite architectural form.

It was after shipbuilding experience that Samuel Bentham got the idea ("in consequence of the limited number of officers at his disposal": *DNB*) for his panoptic or "Central-Inspection Principle" workhouse while visiting Jacques-Ange Gabriel's then new and ultraclassical Ecole militaire, on the Champ-de-Mars.[130] Samuel Bentham's project does anticipate his brother's penitentiary idea, but its architectural interest more simply concerns eighteenth-century civil engineering as leading into functionalist modernism. Each of the twelve sides of his five-storied, flat-roofed polygonal workhouse consists simply of broad strips of large mill or factory windows separated by low horizontal wall bands on each floor (with a thinner but similar band at the top).[131] In the elevation shown in the published plate, two angled walls project flat on either side of the entrance face of the polygonal structure as if narrowing toward the left and right "ends." As such, Samuel Bentham's "Industry House," a workhouse in the sense of a combination of factory and dormitory, anticipates the American "daylight" factory, which, as Banham has shown, vitally influenced European modernist architects in the early twentieth century.[132] Now between Samuel Bentham's late-eighteenth-century, utterly "utopian" industrial workhouse and the twentieth-century protomodernist factories, a historical way station of sorts may be supplied by a building designed in 1858, quite literally by a military "civil" engineer working for the British navy. Colonel G. T. Greene's Boat Store, at the Sheerness (Kent) Naval Dockyard, built in 1859–61, was "discovered" for functionalist architecture by the architectural photographer Eric de Maré and first published in 1957.[133]

As for Jeremy Bentham's Panopticon, designed with "frugality and necessity more attended to than appearance,"[134] whatever part of the original conception influenced by his brother Samuel's workhouse increases with alterations in the second version, such as the provision in each cell of two big five-by-four-foot glass windows. Bentham says, "My instructions to the [note:] architect were, *Give me as much window as possible*..."[135] That the "chapel" function of the central space is much more emphatic in the second version (and the appropriate text more obliging) is no doubt an appeasement of establishment interests on the part of the secularist Bentham, who would work to found University College, London, as pointedly nonsectarian (and have himself embalmed, seated in a glass case, to oversee its board forever). So it is also related typologically to such later eighteenth-century polygonal "chapels" of the Methodists[136] as William Thomas's Surrey Chapel, Southwark (1782–3), or else even the interior of Soane, the modernist's proposed Tyringham (Buckinghamshire) Chapel, of 1800.[137] But Bentham's actual building was also in general more a work of architecture, not just a giant mechanism perhaps belonging by default to the new category of engineering, than has been supposed.

The published plate, which shows the 1791 revision described in Bentham's "Postscript" that was haltingly under construction until governmental abandonment in 1813,[138] is understood to have been drawn up by "Mr. Revely" (*sic*), whom Bentham describes as his "professional adviser."[139] This must mean Willey Reveley (1760–99), a feisty student of Sir William Chambers who in 1794 edited the third volume of James Stuart's *Antiquities of Athens* and who lost a commission (not the only time) for a county infirmary at Canterbury after "exasperating" his clients by daring to insist that his plans "be executed under the supervision of a 'common Carpenter ... in order to save the expense of an [on-site] architect.'"[140] Now Reveley, even if here expecting to work without prototype, would, as a student of Chambers, have had to agree that his Panopticon design, with its split six-story elevation and section over a half-circular plan, resembles in upside-down reversal Palladio's then well-known reconstruction of an ancient theater (of which any panopticon is of course an inside-out inversion), as illustrated in Daniele Barbaro's 1556 edition of Vitruvius (an illustration that had already inspired Inigo Jones to conclude that Stonehenge was a Roman temple!).[141] As a fine-art architect, Reveley actually belonged to the maverick and progressivist Hellenic "left" that by the turn of the century was undercutting the academic authority of the essentially Roman academic classicism in which Chambers himself had loomed large.[142]

More than merely rendering what Bentham had verbally proposed, Reveley must have been responsible for sophistications that become more glaring when one consults this perhaps not so eccentric structure *qua* architecture. Consider, for instance, the shallow round-headed insets on each of the twenty-four faces (of what was originally to be a round structure), framing and linking pairs of windows on the second and third, and then the fourth and fifth, stories of the brick exterior. These appear descended from the Roman relieving-arched exterior wall treatment of, notably, the fourth-century Basilica at Trier.[143] In this "round" context, one even finds echoes of the arcuated exteriors (not to mention the cellular infrastructure) of the Colosseum and other amphitheaters, of which the Panopticon is obviously a functional inversion. Furthermore, with its addition of a "quadrangular front" to house officers, this taking up five cells' width of "dead-part," and "projecting, say for instance 20 feet" beyond the circumference of the building (i.e., by one-sixth of its diameter),[144] suddenly the overall plan becomes, oddly enough, almost pantheonic. If there was any metaphysical absurdity in that, it did not trouble Jeremy Bentham. Reveley did discuss the Pantheon with Bentham, and also at least one modern "engineering" structure, "Hughes's Riding Amphitheatre, near London, [where] the supports, I am told, are of iron silvered."[145]

Without delving further, as into the Panopticon's vaulted quasi-dome (a sort of gabled doughnut) with its oculus over the Panopticon's central space, or deep into the general question of ancient Roman "industrial" architecture, suffice it to say that by an almost postmodern historical displacement Roman architecture would seem to have become this new maverick Greek revivalist's default or "junk" mode – especially with "frugality and necessity more attended to than appearance" by Jeremy Bentham himself.[146] However he would have conceived his own role in the matter, Reveley probably deserves to be considered at least coarchitect of the Panopticon. The building is not exactly a precedentless piece of engineering after all, but a proposition interpolated, crudely enough, into the field of architecture. Perhaps even in that it is rather Roman, and open to estimation as such by a "utilitarianism" located within rather than without, architectural history, all the more so for its evocation of so literalized (and exclusive) a Vitruvian *utilitas*.[147]

2

Politics of Style
Dublin Pro-Cathedral in the Greek Revival

For Anne Crookshank

HIS NATIVE DORIC
> Newspaper headline in Joyce's *Ulysses*

"Our native Doric."
> Remark later in *Ulysses*

THE essentially modern notion of a "romantic classicism" in European art and architecture about 1800 concerns an effective resort to antique, classical, but most definitively Greek types and forms.[1] Antiquarians still speak of a "battle of the styles" in the nineteenth century, and there is an obvious sense in which the Gothic Revival challenged Enlightenment classicism only to be rivaled by a new Hellenism, especially in secular public buildings. However, modernists see a more complex, as it were philological, situation in which, from the mid-eighteenth century, the study of Greek architecture undercut a Roman orthodoxy firmly established since the Renaissance, with the new Greek defensible as *only more truly orthodox* than the old Roman precedents.

In this, also, one "rationalism," the Greek, would vie with another, the Gothic, for already in the eighteenth century the Gothic appealed to a new engineering mentality despite its religious connotations. Even from the standpoint of twentieth-century secularist rationalism the Greek has its counterpart claim, with the romantic-classical Greek revivalism of the German architect Karl Friedrich Schinkel (1781–1841), notably, underlying, it is often said, the "classic" architectural modernity of Ludwig Mies van der Rohe (1886–1969). An important white paper of the International Style claims, in 1932, "In design, the leading modern architects aim at Greek serenity rather than Gothic aspiration."[2] It was, of course, the more ostensibly rational and totalizing geometric simplicity of Greek, versus the ("picturesque") complexity, especially of Gothic architecture, that recommended it to modern sensibility, often

29

enough in a markedly secularist spirit. All the more remarkable, then, should be the building in Greek Revival style of the most prominent Roman Catholic church in nineteenth-century Ireland.

The Greek Revival in architecture entailed critique of all prevailing, that is to say, Roman, classicism, including the British and Anglo-Irish "neo-Palladianism" derived from the writings and buildings of the Venetian Andrea Palladio in the Renaissance, but also resting on an ancient Roman basis. Once Greek architecture was directly confronted as a still accessible utterance, with nothing like a "Septuagint" for it on paper, even Palladio's own *Quattro Libri dell'architettura* (1570), the object of such deference in the eighteenth century, would be left in the critical position of a vernacular vis-à-vis the long distinguished, but no longer primary, "Vulgate" of Vitruvius's *De Architectura* (first century B.C.).

At the intellectual center of the original British neo-Palladian movement – which itself came to influence French neoclassical architecture in the later eighteenth century – stood Richard Boyle, the third earl of Burlington, earl of Cork and lord high treasurer of Ireland. Although Ireland indeed saw so much significant neo-Palladian building that the style is now as vital to the country's cultural self-definition as the medieval Romanesque, it is interesting to ask what is Irish in works in which textbook correctness of disposition and detail ruled over anonymous "classical" if not slavish workmanship. An extreme example: why wonder who "designed" the beautiful facade of the Provost's House at Trinity College, Dublin, of 1759, given that Burlington's prior employment of a Palladio drawing in his possession for the identical facade of the London house of General Wade, 1723–4, can itself hardly be considered to have comprised an act of *disegno?* To this day the Palladian style remains sufficiently normative to supply classicizing cosmetics – and usually a visibly defective air of "proportion" – to a multitude of bumbling speculative buildings. One might turn to the modern philosopher Heidegger for a sense that once the Greek truth shines through to modern insight, its discarded Latinate husks are more fetishized than ever in a bourgeois cult of demythologized rational progress and empty, denobilized wealth.

In the British Isles, three historiographic phases of early modern interest in Greek sites and antiquities are discernable: first, preliminary seventeenth-century accounts and an eighteenth-century "archaeography" of the monuments; then a specifically romantic Hellenism at the turn of the century; and finally, a political Hellenism aware of the struggle of contemporary Greece for independence from the Ottoman Empire.[3] If the English cultural impact of the Greek War of Independence (1821–33) was, excepting Byron, less than signal, Ireland was in a rather different situation before Catholic Emancipation, which was only attained during the Greek War. As early as Lord Mountjoy's brutal subjugation of 1600, Pope Clement VIII had "placed the Irish war on the same footing as the war against the Turks";[4] and Irishmen were to share in the successive phases of modern Hellenism, antiquarian, romantic, and surely – what with Greece rising up against the Ottomans – political. Not that the Catholic Irish majority were in a position to do much major building;

yet if the British might still prefer not to have the question of the Greek War of Independence arise,[5] any Greek Revival oblivious to it is unthinkable. Especially before Catholic Emancipation was attained in 1829, the Irish parallel should hardly have needed to be spelled out.

Architecturally speaking, the Greek Revival would imply a critique of all prevailing, essentially Roman classicism, "neo-Palladian" classicism not excepted. But the inner circle of the founding generation included one who looked at architecture and thought about politics rather independently, Burlington's Irish friend George Berkeley, Bishop of Cloyne.[6]

Actually, there was some Ascendancy, or Anglo-Irish, participation in the early, exploratory stages of Hellenism, and this included Bishop Berkeley. In 1717 Berkeley was in Monopoli (Puglia), within the ancient pale of Magna Graecia.[7] Little more than a year later he wrote, in Rome, "This gusto of mine is formed on the remains of antiquity that I have met with in my travels, particularly in Sicily, which convince me that *the old Romans were inferior to the Greeks,* and the moderns fall infinitely short of both."[8] Berkeley's own sense of classicism must have gained not only from his friendship with Burlington, but also, we can now suppose, from direct experience of Palladio's architecture in 1719,[9] on a second visit to the Veneto. His 1718 remark gives a sharp glimmer of what would emerge about 1750 as a distinctly modern, revisionist, Greek-informed, and pointedly alternative classicism, threatening to established convention.

Even before James Stuart and Nicholas Revett's 1749 proposal for the expedition that would issue in their influential *Antiquities of Athens Measured and Delineated* (1762–1816), other Irishmen were exploring the more visibly Hellenistic East. The antiquarian Richard Pococke, later bishop of Ossory and then of Meath, who was in the area between 1736 and 1740,[10] published *A Description of the East* (1743–5) and other accounts.[11] In 1749, the first expedition to set out for the eastern Mediterranean after Stuart and Revett's proposal was a markedly Irish enterprise, including as it did Francis Pierpont Burton (later Lord Conyngham),[12] James Caulfield (later first earl of Charlemont), and the artist Richard Dalton, whom Robert Adam identified as both "infamously stupid" and Irish.[13] Another sign of Hellenic interest at the midcentury: in 1753 a Huguenot by the name of John Gast earned a theology doctorate from the University of Dublin with a thesis on Greek history.[14]

From the other side of the Irish Sea arrived in Dublin, in 1769, Thomas Cooley, the mentor of the important establishment architect Francis Johnston. Significantly, Cooley was then already familiar with the plates to Thomas Major's *The Ruins of Paestum* (1768), a vital early publication of the most influential Greek precedents for the baseless Doric order. The plates were edited by Robert Mylne, a Scots architect and engineer in whose office Cooley had served (and who as a Protestant had the distinction of belonging to the Accademia di San Luca).[15] A decade later, none other than James ("Athenean") Stuart himself designed a 1780 freestanding octagonal banqueting house, modeled on and named for the Temple of the Winds in Athens, built at the Marquess of Londonderry's Mountstewart House, County Down.[16]

The door to architectural Hellenism opened wider after the Grand Tour began to extend below Naples, taking in the major site of Magna Graecia at Paestum. Study of the travel literature has now shown that of turn-of-the-century British accounts taking cognizance of Paestum and its great Greek temples (to be described as awesome by Shelley), the earliest, Henry Swinburne's *Travels in the Two Sicilies,* in two volumes (London, 1783, 1785) was republished in Dublin in 1786.[17] In 1790, Lord Charlemont lectured on his experiences in the 1749 expedition at the Royal Irish Academy;[18] and from about then dates another garden structure, a Doric temple at Belline House, County Kilkenny, with primitive tree-trunk Doric columns[19] – a feature also hinting at influence of earlier eighteenth-century French theory.

There are also popular and folkloric indications that Greece and the ruins of the more Hellenic East were on the Irish mind from the turn of the century. The roving Chevalier de Lactocnaye, who thought that by its size and ancient political structure of local kingdoms, Ireland evoked ancient Greece, heard of a gentleman "who assumed the title of *Lord Peloponnesus, Earl of Greece.*"[20] It was claimed that Ireland had been *colonized* by ancient Greeks, if with doubt attached that the colonists may instead have set out from Scythia[21] – and even Bishop Berkeley made a Scythian reference.[22] (Would the Abbé Barthélémy's story *Les Voyages du jeune Anarcharsis* [1789] have been known, with its timely praise of Greek liberty?) Furthermore, a certain romantic trope bespoke Ireland as a country of ruins, mostly medieval but nevertheless likened to those of the ancient Levant. The town of Kilmallock, County Limerick, sacked in 1570 and then left devastated in the wake of Cromwell, was called Ireland's "Baalbec or Palmyra" in 1812.[23] This notion must have been widespread, for by 1821 it was reported that "foreigners, relying upon bardic accounts, would naturally expect to meet in Ireland with ruins similar to those in Palmyra";[24] and even a foreigner could affirm in 1839 that "l'Irlande peut, en tout vérité, être la Palmyre de l'Europe; elle est le pays des ruines."[25]

Politically, it was dangerous enough for British rule that Irish sympathy for the French Revolution had crossed religious lines. Now here was Henry Grattan, the great Irish parliamentary voice for an independent nation, referring to ancient Greece in arguing in 1793 for the extension of suffrage to Irish Catholics: "I have heard of Athens, that cruel republic, excluding so many of her children from the rights of citizenship; but she had only the wisdom of Socrates and the light of Plato: she had not, like you, revelation to instruct her."[26] Byron, that definitive English philhellene, wrote in a letter of May 3, 1810, "I see not much difference between ourselves and the Turks."[27] Finally in 1829, with the Russians advancing against the Turks while the Irish were demanding religious freedom, the Duke of Wellington decided at once for "Greek liberation abroad and Roman Catholic emancipation at home."[28]

By the time Alexis de Tocqueville visited Ireland in 1835, modern Greece was independent and the Catholics of Ireland had emancipation. Yet the Roman Catholic bishop of Kilkenny, questioned on the Catholic population's being "half-savage," as claimed in England, reminded Tocqueville of the Irish struggle in these terms: "I must admit that it is in part true. But whose fault is it, if not theirs who have reduced them to this state of bad government? *What became of the Greeks under the Turks?* Before 1792 we could have no schools, we could not be called to the bar, the magistry was closed to us, we could not possess land."[29] Two years later a French writer who, inspired by the Greek War of Independence, had already penned *Vendéennes et chants hellènes* (1826), visited Ireland on a mission announced by a slogan at the front of his *L'Irlande* (1839): "Justice pour l'Irlande!"[30]

It was against such background, in 1815, that a new Greek Revival Roman Catholic Pro-Cathedral of Saint Mary began to rise on Marlborough Street, in still officially Anglican Dublin, with its heroic *baseless Doric* hexastyle portico reiterating the classical Athenian Theseum (or Temple of Hephaestus) (Figure 2).

Why this great and excellent church should have been overlooked for generations as a work of art is a question of social as well as art history. By social history I refer to a historical deletion of a national patrimony of which both sides should all along have been prouder. If in saying so I cross a certain line, let me take advantage of my outsider status to add that I believe this could not have occurred without an element of cultural chagrin on the oppressor's part. For the pro-cathedral is not outranked by any other church in the country; yet its significance entails Continental (Catholic) relations and parallels distasteful to those who would have thought only themselves sufficiently capable or properly entitled to admire a pretty "Georgian" ankle.

The pro-cathedral, banished like all substantial Catholic buildings before Emancipation from too prominent a site, was for too long marginalized. Aside from faith and class, the insularity of an abiding antiquarian approach discouraged the comparative study of Continental architecture, let alone theory – of which, however, Catholic churchmen in Ireland about 1800 were much more likely to have been aware. To the antiquarian mentality the Greek and Gothic Revivals were mere excursions from the reassuring Roman-and-Renaissance academic orthodoxy based on Vitruvius's *De Architectura* and guarded in London by Sir William Chambers and in Dublin by his disciple James Gandon, from whom the torch would be passed to Henry Aaron Baker as master of the Dublin Society architectural school. Thus the alarmed reaction to the new understanding of Greece is evidenced by the bitterness of Chambers' general sense of "Attic deformity"; he and his followers held their Latinate fort.

Only in the last generation of art history, thanks to studies in eighteenth-century French architectural theory, has it been possible to comprehend how the Dublin Pro-Cathedral is in fact a monument of distinguished rank in the history of early modern architecture. Crucial here is the understanding of a deep-set identification in early eighteenth-century French theory between the Greek and Gothic architectures,[31] long thought by a superficial stylistic to be like oil and water. Beginning with the Abbé Cordemoy's *Nouveau Traité de toute l'architecture* (1706) – from which, by the way, the radical British architect of 1800, Sir John Soane, "painstakingly wrote out . . . and commented upon

2. Dublin, Pro-Cathedral of Saint
Mary, 1815–25. Exterior. Early photograph by William Lawrence. Courtesy
of the National Library of Ireland
(Lawrence Collection).

... a translation"[32] – the Greek and Gothic modes were likened in abstract
structural terms. Out of a complex debate between Cordemoy and the engineer
Amédée-François Frézier, from 1709 to 1712, came a sense of the early Christian basilica as linking classical and medieval architecture in an age of Constantine that was conceived of as "la sainte Antiquité."[33] The best visual model
of this ideal was Claude Perrault's reconstruction of Vitruvius's basilica at
Fano, published in his great 1673 edition of Vitruvius and reprinted in a handier
Abrégé... de Vitruve (1674).[34] Here was what Cordemoy specifically advocated
in analogy with the structural clarity of Gothic arcading; namely, a continuous

interior peristyle (unbroken, enclosing a wall-like range of columns), a feature still grandly conspicuous in the Dublin Pro-Cathedral.

Most exemplary of the new critical understanding in later eighteenth-century architecture, especially church building, was the church of Saint Philippe-du-Roule, Paris, designed by J. T. F. Chalgrin (future author of the Arc de Triomphe) in 1764 and begun a decade later (Figure 3). Even commentators otherwise unused to considering Irish architecture in relation to its general European counterparts have for some years noticed how much the Dublin church, long loosely attributed to a John Sweetman, of Raheny, County

3. Jean-François Chalgrin, Saint-Philippe-du-Roule (conceived c. 1766), begun 1772. Engraving, eighteenth century. After W. Hermann, *Laugier and Later Eighteenth-Century Theory* (London, 1962).

Dublin, resembles Saint Philippe-du-Roule, especially for the nave peristyle with continuous entablature curving around behind the altar (Figure 4). This handsome Doric feature – the Doric order being specifically recommended as appropriate to "édifices sacrés" by another influential, later eighteenth-century French theoretician, J.-F. Blondel, under whom Chambers is said to have studied[35] – would have evoked the highest praise from Cordemoy and from a better known protomodernist, the Abbé Marc-Antoine Laugier, as well. As for the severity of the Doric itself, it happens that etymologically "Dorian" terms are "tropes of violence," words that "contain more than the flavor of racial conquest."[36]

An important alteration of the Pro-Cathedral interior that diverges from Saint Philippe-du-Roule, from the original designs for the Dublin building, and also from the large and excellent working model of it that still exists, is a pair of large semicircular, quasi-thermal windows springing over the peristyle from the front of the apse into the nave.[37] Although the church as it stands, with dome on rather elegant pendentives and the modern quasi-thermal windows, is still sometimes found less satisfactory than the original project, what is telling in light of French theory is that with these features the building is at least as much like Perrault's ideal basilica as is Saint Philippe-du-Roule itself. Arguably, whoever altered the design only brought Saint Mary's closer to what the wisest French critics of the eighteenth century held up as the very

4. Dublin, Pro-Cathedral of Saint Mary, 1815–25. Interior with apse. Early photograph by William Lawrence. Courtesy of the National Library of Ireland (Lawrence Collection).

model of "holy antiquity." The actual designs were sent to Dublin from Paris, and any relation to an early Christian basilica or the modern Paris church was all-too-much protested while the Pro-Cathedral was still under construction: "The design is not taken from St. Maria Maggiore at Rome, St. Philip du Roule at Paris, or any other building in existence: those churches are in the Roman, whereas the Metropolitan Chapel is in the Grecian style."[38]

In 1803 the land was purchased for the Dublin church, in Penal Law terminology still but a humble, if soon metropolitan, "chapel." In a sense the architectural history of the project begins in 1808, when the baseless Doric Nelson Pillar (destroyed by nationalists, 1966) designed by William Wilkins – author of *Antiquities of Magna Graecia* (1807), with influential plates of the baseless Doric from Paestum – was erected by Francis Johnston in the middle of what is now O'Connell Street,[39] which is to say, right in front of the first site considered for the Pro-Cathedral – apparently still too prominent a place for a major Catholic church. Instead, construction began there in 1814 on Johnston's Ionic temple-fronted General Post Office, with a competition opened for designs for the cathedral building somewhere else. However appealing it may be to imagine the great new Doric column with a massive Doric pro-cathedral standing immediately behind it, it does seem unrealistic to have the church comprise an ensemble with a monument to Lord Admiral Nelson only a decade after 1798, when French troops had landed unsuccessfully in County Mayo in support of the United Irish (and many better-off Catholics sided with the British authorities).

Significant in the Penal circumstances is the fact that, as for the Orthodox Christian churches of Ottoman Greece, which were not permitted to vie with local minarets,[40] the Catholic Relief Act of 1782 expressly prohibited a Catholic church from having a "steeple."[41] Not only would that have been unconscionable on the site first considered, but it could well have predisposed those involved in the project to think of a Greek-temple disposition instead of something Georgian-classical (not to mention Gothic).[42]

The fundamental basilican concept was under discussion in Catholic circles in Dublin even in this earliest stage of projecting a pro-cathedral. John Milner, the ranking Catholic "Vicar-Apostolic for the Western District of England," was in Ireland in 1807–8 expressly to oppose any compromise emancipation conceding a British government veto in hierarchical appointments; this was against a conciliatory effort by assimilated Catholic gentry. Milner was a significant early enthusiast of the Gothic Revival in church architecture.[43] However, the new antiquarian enthusiasm for Gothic architecture in which he shared might possibly have carried a specifically English nationalistic tinge, as was the case with a friend of his, John Carter.[44]

By his own report on Ireland, published in 1808, Milner was already musing on the general appropriateness of the basilican form for a cathedral: "It is . . . to be observed that a large cathedral . . . was meant to be a basilic [*sic*], or corps of building for various religious purposes. This idea has never once found place in the brain of any of our modern cathedral reformers: no wonder, then, they have made so many blunders and so much havoc in them."[45] Moreover, his Gothic interest notwithstanding, should a Greek style have been proposed for a church it was to Milner's mind "infinitely preferable to have a perfect work of the latter kind, than a caricatura of the former."[46] Indeed, while the Pro-Cathedral was being built in Dublin, he himself commissioned a Greek Revival seminary chapel (1817–19) at Oscott, near Birmingham.[47]

It is worth wondering whether Milner or anyone else in Catholic circles might have known an illustrated seventeenth-century account of the early Christian basilica and its continuation in Greek Orthodox architecture. The brief epistolary text of Leone Allacci (or Leo Allaticos, or Allatius), *De Templis Graecorum recentioribus* (Cologne, 1645), treats the Orthodox church as having managed to preserve an ancient Greek Christian architecture despite oppression by an unbelieving imperial power.[48] If this work became newly timely, there were several copies of it in the library of Trinity College, Dublin, before 1835.[49] And Allacci's early account of Christian "temples" in Ottoman Greece includes a church plan with an exterior peristyle continuing around a semi-circular apse, inversely like the Dublin church as built.

As to the actual authorship of Saint Mary's Pro-Cathedral: the name of an amateur, John Sweetman, was indeed long entertained. The building was begun in 1815,[50] roofed, including the fine dome (an afterthought), in 1820, opened in 1825, and finally consecrated, after Emancipation, in 1834 (still without its temple-front porch, executed only in the next decade by J. B. Keane).[51] Ending a history of denials, Edward McParland has affirmed that the domeless and thermal-window-less wooden model of the Pro-Cathedral, which the building committee put on public view in July of 1816, indeed "confirms the evidence of the only two known early (and useful) drawings for the church, that the inspiration behind the design is French," in fact, in line with French churches "designed under the influence of Laugier," and, of course, "related to St. Philippe-du-Roule."[52]

Some time during the construction of the Pro-Cathedral, Sir Richard Morrison (1767–1849), whose work is taken as Palladian-into-eclectic, is believed to have had a supervisory role. Is it possible that during his long career as a supposed jack-of-all-styles, Morrison, around the turn of the century, may perhaps have more categorically eschewed Roman for Greek classicism than has been understood? What if his supposedly chill Palladianism at some point began to count as Greek? He did name his (architect) son William *Vitruvius*, but that was in 1794. According to Craig, in remodeling two country houses in County Kildare, first at Lyons in the 1790s, then at Carton, after 1815 – "he straightened the curved Palladian colonnades . . . using baseless but un-fluted Doric columns."[53] Morrison made the Hellenist's pilgrimage beyond Rome to Paestum in 1821, that is, soon after the Pro-Cathedral was roofed.

In any case, the winning project in the design competition was a submission known as "the Grecian design marked P." According to Michael McCarthy, this "P" stood for *pontifex*, the true architect having been a priest. Apparently he was the later archbishop John Thomas Troy, an Irish Dominican and former prior of San Clemente in Rome, who was interested in archaeology and in the baseless Greek Doric order at Paestum in particular. He knew the secretary of both Stuart pretenders in Rome, and he also knew firsthand the modern churches of Paris, including Saint Philippe-du-Roule. McCarthy sees the dome and pedimented portico as "suggested by Soufflot's Panthéon" (originally, Ste. Geneviève), but his point is that "it is not surprising, in the light of the *entente cordiale* between Catholic Ireland and Napoleonic France, that Archbishop Troy should obtain the plan and model of his new cathedral from the United Irishman in exile in Paris, John Sweetman, who had been intimately associated with Wolfe Tone." Moreover, "since Sweetman was in Paris and lived close to Chalgrin's church, it is understandable that Troy should have entrusted the draughting of the plans and the making of the model to his care."[54] Whether or not the case for Troy–Sweetman will stand, this is all the more interesting today because it has scarcely been a decade since a distinguished authority continued to minimize the Greek Revival while begrudging the Pro-Cathedral's similarity to Saint Philippe-du-Roule as "more obvious in the model than in the church as built."[55]

The Greek Revival, of which the Dublin Pro-Cathedral is a major monument, struck at the root of established, and establishment, (Roman) classicism by rendering it dated, hence by no means absolute. Earlier eighteenth-century Greek reconnaissance, however meager it seems, was already drawn by a current of deep-set importance for Western architectural and cultural history. In a sense, just what Martin Heidegger tells us as moderns about the displacement of the Greek language by Latin, and about how the installation of Latinate thought has shaped Western thinking (this now seen as if through the widening cracks of a doomed structure), may be taken as visibly intimated in the mid-eighteenth- to early-nineteenth-century displacement of Roman (and Latinate renaissance) by "revived" Greek architecure.[56] As ever in doctrinal dispute, the problem can if necessary be made to turn on a single fine point, here the necessarily critical, direct beholding, rather than by resort to canonical *Latinate* text, of the baselessness of the prior, and as Vitruvius himself would now have had to accept, definitively *Greek,* Doric order.

That visible evidence of Irish consciousness of the Greek War of Independence may be uncommon, as a certain Whiggishness still insists,[57] does not mean that the Greek Revival wasn't also a liberationist expression on the part of Irish Catholics – and dissenters, too – whose struggle was undeniably parallel with that of the modern Orthodox Christians in the newly romanticized motherland of democracy. If not very many major Irish churches were built by Catholics in the Greek or any other mode, Saint Mary's does not stand alone. My favorite cousin of the Pro-Cathedral is James Cusack's 1849 Franciscan "Abbey Church," in Galway town, which is not world-class but is at least true-blue. Given the Irish Catholics' social position, however, Dublin's Hellenizing Pro-Cathedral was a building of tremendous symbolic importance at a critical moment. That in early nineteenth-century Ireland the Greek Revival offered a politically alternative classicism, vis-à-vis the Roman classicism of the establishment, is implicit in its embrace by members of the pre-emancipated Catholic hierarchy, including not only Milner but Peter Augustine Baines. And in this too there may have been parallels elsewhere, notably in Germany.

The Pro-Cathedral was nearing completion when Baines, a former Benedictine monk of Ampleforth, was consecrated titular Bishop of Siga (Mauretania) in Dublin in 1823. In a text of the next year he toasts the Roman Catholic Church for its conservation of classical artworks ("*offer[ing] them as models to the world*") and speaks of Greek Orthodoxy as akin to Catholicism,[58] as Anglicans interested in the Byzantine Church since the seventeenth century have claimed. Later, anticipating by more than a decade the argument in Ruskin's *Stones of Venice* (1851–3) that Gothic art is not barbarous, Baines continued to pay his respects to antiquity: "The Christian Church . . . includes within its pale nations of every clime, language and custom; from the polished Greek and Roman to the rude and uncivilized barbarian."[59] Significantly, he would come to oppose what he saw as the excesses, Gothic-archaeologizing, of A. W. N. Pugin.[60]

The newly opened Dublin Pro-Cathedral did not seem strange to that peripatetic German, the Prince Pückler-Muskau – whose negative impression of the Anglican clergy Schopenhauer applauds.[61] "It is a handsome building," Pückler-Muskau wrote, stating as enthusiastically as inaccurately that "the interior is a large oval, with a colonnade of Ionic [sic] pillars running round it, surmounted by a beautiful dome . . . "[62] I mention Arthur Schopenhauer also because it is apparent that between writing the first (1818) and second (1844) volumes of *The World as Will and Representation* he too had evidently given fresh thought to the beauty of the Greek Doric order. He was aware, in fact, of "recent measurements . . . at Paestum."[63] And if Catholic cosmopolitanism had made modern French architecture less alien to Irish Catholic churchmen than it would have been to the Anglo-Irish, Germany itself offers certain parallels to the Irish situation. Something of an analogy may be drawn, for instance, in the years of the Greek War, with the struggle of Bavarian Catholics against Prussian Protestant domination of a consolidated Germany, because "the enemies of the Catholic Church were also the enemies of Bavarian nationality, and the friends of the supremacy of Prussia."[64]

On Protestant dynastic grounds there was closeness between Britain and Prussia, and once liberated, Greece was to be ruled by a Bavarian prince, Otto von Wittelsbach. Crowned Otto I in 1832, he moved into the Greek Revival "Old Palace" at Athens (1837–41), designed by a Prussian-born Münchener, Friedrich von Gärtner.[65] If it would be simplistic to equate the Berlin of Karl Friedrich Schinkel, and England, on one side, with the Munich of Gärtner and especially Leo von Klenze, and Ireland, on the other, the Catholic Bavarian situation does show similarities to contemporary Catholic Ireland, against the background of Anglo-Prussian closeness. Gärtner was in England in 1819–20;[66] and Schinkel, who had recently finished his Berlin Cathedral of 1817–22 (now demolished), visited Liverpool in 1826. There he analyzed the new (1823–4) Greek Revival Saint Andrew of Scotland (Presbyterian) Church by John Foster, Jr.[67] Conversely, Harvey Elmes visited Berlin to study Schinkel's Hellenizing architecture firsthand before winning an 1836 competition for Saint George's Hall, Liverpool, with his own Greek Revival design.[68] By 1841

Anglo-Prussian interests were close enough to allow agreement on alternating Anglican and Prussian Lutheran bishops of Jerusalem.[69]

In Bavaria the opening years of the nineteenth century had witnessed an extreme, late-Enlightenment hostility toward the Catholic Church. In 1816 – which is to say while the Pro-Cathedral was rising in Dublin – the bishops appealed for relief to Maximilian I, king of Bavaria, and a concordat between church and state was realized the following year. Everything changed with the accession of Ludwig I (1825–48). Himself a philhellene,[70] Ludwig oversaw a major revival of Catholic culture in Bavaria. Under him religious orders regained establishments of which they had been stripped, and the splendid churches of Bavaria were rescued from ruination while "several new ones, models of architectural beauty," were built.[71] Even the transfer of the University of Ingolstadt to Munich, in 1826, belongs to a nineteenth-century recovery from seventeenth-century "troubles" – in that case, occupation by Gustavus II of Sweden – as when Cardinal Newman would set out to found his Catholic university in Ireland.

Pleased to design Greek churches for Lutheran as well as Catholic use, Leo von Klenze himself advocated the classical Greek style as most suitable for Christian churches. He may have been at pains to argue why, in a handsome portfolio of Greek ideas for churches, published as early as 1822; but it is notable that there he does not hesitate to cite a precedent in, yes, Chalgrin's Saint Philippe-du-Roule.[72] The exterior flank of the Dublin Pro-Cathedral, as executed, even has something of the crisp heft of von Klenze's Propyläen on the Königsplatz, in Munich, of 1846–50.[73] In Scotland, where national discontent with the post-Union English state (Presbyterian) church broke out in the 1830s and 1840s,[74] Klenze is known to have influenced the Greek Revival church architecture of Alexander Thomson after 1850.[75] Neither can the generic sources, Greek (Lysicrates Monument) as well as Roman (Julii Monument) overrule the possible derivation of a certain cylindrical cupola with saints as atalantes, this surmounted by a shallow dome and topped by a stone cross, atop a significant Greek Revival church in Cork, George Richard Pain's Saint Patrick's (1836), from one of Leo von Klenze's published plates.[76]

A remote but telling parallel to Saint Mary's Pro-Cathedral in Dublin can be found in the Christianized Doric Hellenism of an important – and almost exactly contemporary – Scandinavian church, the Church of Our Lady, which is the state (Lutheran) cathedral of Copenhagen. Built between 1807 and 1829 by Christian Frederik Hansen, it has a baseless Doric portico at the end of a huge rectangular block and a stocky square tower over the entrance wall.[77] Artistically, Copenhagen Cathedral looks more aware, in its Hellenism, of avant-garde French architecture of the new generation of 1800. Politically, it has an anti-British association of its own: Hansen's church was built because the old cathedral was destroyed when Nelson bombarded Copenhagen on September 5, 1807. Similarly, at Saint Mary's, Dublin, and the Church of Our Lady, Copenhagen – which the sculptor Thorvaldsen fitted with colossal Christian statues in antique Greek style in the 1820s and 1830s[78] – we confront a Christianization of the Greek antique at a time when the Greek War of

Independence was an urgent manifestation of opposition to alien political and religious domination. As an art–historical phenomenon, this should be seen as contrasting sharply with the Revolutionary secularization of Christian themes and forms in late eighteenth-century France.[79] The rise in German literary culture of a dual enthusiasm for Greek antiquity and Christian belief by the Schlegels and others must have been important internationally.[80]

The Dublin Pro-Cathedral is not the only Irish Catholic church of the period built in the Greek Revival style. And if the Greek Revival was not widely adopted by the Church of Ireland – the obvious exception is Saint Stephen's, Upper Mount Street, Dublin, of 1824, by John Bowden – it is all the more significant that it throve among the Presbyterians and other dissenters of Ulster.[81] These people, who had taken part in the beginnings of the national struggle when the United Irish movement was founded at Belfast in 1791, took readily to the classical Greek style for churches built (with government aid) during and in the decade after the Greek War of Independence.[82] Two remarkable Ulster examples of about 1840 by John Millar in County Down are the Presbyterian Church at Portaferry, an amphiprostyle Doric temple, and Holy Trinity, Kircubbin, the latter based on a Doric temple illustrated in *The Unedited Antiquities of Attica* (1817).[83] All the Irish – Protestant or Catholic – who chose to identify themselves by architectural style with an idealized Greece of antiquity must have been aware of the struggle in contemporary Greece for national self-determination and religious freedom, the Presbyterians no doubt with their own grassroots, Greek-democratic understanding of a "sainte antiquité."

Appendix

The specialist reader will not have had difficulty in gaining a sense of how I apply the term "Greek Revival," with Saint Mary's Pro-Cathedral as a winning, cosmopolitan instance of the style. But because others may wonder how I distinguish Greek Revival from previous, general-purpose Roman classicism, especially in much humbler churches where the evidence is subtler, allow me to attempt a generalized distinction based on years of obsessive looking at Greek Revival buildings of the early nineteenth century in America as well as in Ireland and England.

The temple front with low-slung roof, obviously in either case ultimately Greek, is a main feature of both systems, but to characteristically different effect. The front of a Greek temple is the short, gabled end of a structure that is itself essentially columnar but prismatic, whereas in the Roman tradition – which until about 1750 represented all of accessible "antiquity" in Western Europe – the concept of the temple front is already that of a "porch," attachable as so much decorum applied rhetorically to an otherwise self-sufficient main block, and to its long side at that. Of course, buildings without temple fronts occur in both the Roman-Renaissance and Greek Revival systems; but the gabled quality of Greek architecture seems so strong that, unlike Roman classic revivals of 1400–1750, the gable-pedimental concept dominates Greek Revival buildings as something more comprehensive than an ornamental feature, to the point where the building as a whole presents itself as templelike – and, at that, rather more "institutional" than "domestic" – with or without a literal temple-pediment, or orders of columns at all. For Greek architecture glories in the gable, as well as in the pure rectangular prism (or the balanced cluster of prisms); and even if the main facade of a Greek Revival building should happen to be a "long" side, the spread of an encompassing gable will often nevertheless dominate it. Devotees of Anglo-Irish neo-Palladianism know the temple front as central ornamental feature, overseeing, as it were, a long wall; but emphatic gabling tends to make the whole building more of a "temple" again.

Suppose we consider overall effect rather than details, standing back even from general period characteristics including scale, and ask, for instance, why Edward Lovett Pearce's south front of the old Parliament House, Dublin (1729) – now part of the Bank of Ireland building – should not be thought Greek, whereas Smirke's forecourt of the British Museum (1823), in London, definitively is. If neither facade carried a pediment, the Parliament entrance would still connote more the "open arms" (in Palladio's own figure) of a Palladian country house, while that of the London museum is more like a temple precinct. There in fact are temple fronts in both cases, but Pearce's merely presides as if at table; Smirke's is a consummation into which the entire peristyle is drawn. Gandon's House of Lords front of the same Dublin building, from the 1780s, might be taken as interestingly transitional: think of it as a "House" front with a porch and see its Palladianism; think of it as the hefty, sublimely blind flank of a "Bank," hugely pedimented, and begin to see the opposite – as can only be confirmed by Gandon's notion of Greek temple-front *windows* in a drawing for the counterpart Foster Place facade.

Let me go a little too far from an admittedly modernist viewpoint and claim that in a sense every neo-Palladian building is essentially a house, noble or Whiggishly genteel and bespeaking ease in personal or collective worldly authority. By contrast, every Greek Revival building, even an ordinary 1840 Presbyterians' farmhouse in upstate New York, is in some sense a contribution to the civic order. As such it is likely to imply a different kind of restraint, beyond taste, perhaps even – perish the thought that the term should be borrowed from Ruskin's Gothic – ennobling the commonplace by "sacrifice."

At least this approaches an explanation of why, when I began to look into the subject in the late 1960s under Anne Crookshank, I tended to subsume under the category of the Greek Revival some Irish Catholic churches of the early nineteenth century which Georgianists who had not run out of material simply consigned to a vague "classicism" beyond the pale of *classy* taste. McDermott and Brioscú's photographic survey[84] now makes it visually convenient to see that in Dublin alone a number of buildings exhibit the Hellenizing domination of the temple-front concept as a major gable end. Among these are John Bowden's Saint Stephen's, Upper Mount Street, c. 1827; the little porch of Saint Catherine's Convent, Lower Baggot Street, after 1827; the almost orderless Methodist Church, now Saint George and Saint Thomas's,

Great Charles Street, 1828; John Keane's Saint Francis Xavier's, Gardiner Street, 1829–32; John Leeson's Saint Nicholas of Myrna, Francis Street, 1829–34; John Boulger's Saint Andrew's, Westland Row, 1837; Patrick Byrne's Saint Paul's, Arran Quay, 1837 (portico 1842); the Presbyterian Church in Adelaide Road, 1840; Isaac Farrell's former Wesleyan Centenary Church, Saint Stephen's Green, 1843; even the massive Hellenization of an otherwise basically Palladian facade at John Bourke's Mater Misericordiae Hospital, Eccles Street, 1861; and even Patrick Byrne and Stephen Ashlin's portico to Saint Audoen's, High Street, added only in 1898; plus the belated former Dublin Hebrew Congregation Synagogue, South Circular Road, c. 1925; (not to mention the vaguely dated but still impressive mini-Greek-temple belfry of Adam and Eve's, Merchants Quay). In fact, I would rest my case with Bourke's Chapel of the Holy Cross at Conliffe College, 1876, where a Hellenizing temple front levitates absurdly, assisted by Baroque volutes, in trying to play out the old Palladian "class act."

Years ago, I tried in a thesis for Trinity College to defend as Greek Revival such churches and, especially, others by James and George Richard Pain at Dunmanway, Ovens, and the Ursuline Convent at Blackrock, all in County Cork, with (now we know, George Richard Pain's alone) the temple front of Saint Patrick's, Lower Road, in Cork city, of 1836, and James Cusack's Abbey Church, Saint Francis Street, in Galway town, of 1849. Today, all of these buildings, including the Pro-Cathedral, are at last noticed. Yet Craig, who kindly helped me when I was a student years ago, still hedges with the terms "classical" and "neo-grec" (the latter more properly reserved for a form of late Victorian ornament), putting all these long overlooked works, including the Pro-Cathedral itself, under a heading "Roman Churches for the Roman Church."[85]

I mention every pertinent Dublin example shown by McDermott and Brioscú in order to point out that all these are religious buildings. Where the temple fronts of the Catholic churches are punctuated by sculptures at eaves and gables in the manner of Greek *akroteria,* the effect is only more pronounced. Still we are told that, except for some courthouses and the Pains' jail at Cork, there was almost no Greek Revival in Ireland, or that Saint Mary's Pro-Cathedral was as much as unique. Yet not only churches but other Irish buildings to this day taken as insignificantly late or bad Palladian, or as Adamesque or, especially, as "Regency," owing to ornamental details, are virtual Greek Revival buildings, some of them significant as such.

That the Greek Revival was certainly not widely adopted by the Church of Ireland of the establishment, but instead manifested itself in Catholic circumstances and among the Presbyterians and other dissenters of Ulster, in their province of a province, during and soon after the Greek War of Independence, cannot be insignificant. John Millar's County Down examples, again, are outright Doric temples.

Needless to say, these are literally provincial buildings, whereas Saint Mary's Pro-Cathedral is metropolitan, indeed, cosmopolitan. But one also cannot see the Pro-Cathedral in its sophistication without transcending the assumption that Irish architecture, per se, is provincial vis-à-vis anything in Britain. This great building begins to suggest the cosmopolitanism previously connoted by Edmund Burke with the adjective "European," built as it was around the time the romantic nationalism of Beethoven, for instance, became so international as to inspire *Irish Songs* as well as *The Ruins of Athens*.

3

An American Utopian
Schoolhouse Design

For C.E.

SOME time ago, Barbara Wriston called attention to two schoolhouses designed by Ithiel Town (1784–1844) and Alexander Jackson Davis (1803–
92), as they appeared in *The School and the Schoolmaster* (1842), by Alonzo
Potter and George B. Emerson.[1] One of the projects is simply rectangular in
plan, the other uniquely octagonal. Both were published in Potter and Emerson's book as models for school districts looking for schoolhouse designs, and
as such they continued to circulate in a number of later publications – the
octagonal school,[2] notably, in Henry Barnard's *School Architecture* (1848).[3]

The model school on octagonal plan, which deserves attention, was apparently an original design by Town and Davis (Figures 5 and 6). In an
appendix to Potter and Emerson's book the building is accompanied by a
statement of the two architects that reads, in part: "The design for a schoolhouse intends to exhibit a model of fitness and close economy. It differs from
a design published by the Common School Society of New-York, in being
more simple, without the belfry, and complete in the octagonal form."[4] There
is, however, a manuscript among A. J. Davis's papers that appears to be a
draft of this statement but in which the words "by Mr. Town" are inserted
between "design" and "published."[5] On the other hand, three untrimmed
copies of an engraving of what is probably the other Common School design,
attribute that work to "Alex. J. Davis."[6] Nevertheless, it cannot be wrong to
assign the octagonal schoolhouse project to the partnership of Town and Davis.

The cross-aisled octagonal plan, which deviates from absolute bilateral symmetry only in giving up a walled-off lobby used also for recitations, has four
square porches (the rear one a woodshed connecting with two privies), attached
on the main axes and locking the resultant Greek-cross form inside a circular
path (the path would disappear in later reproductions). That the design is so
absolutely centralized, at least from without – and triply so: octagon, Greek
cross, circle – and that it is set forth in something of an ideal program, suggest

5. Ithiel Town and Alexander Jackson Davis, Octagonal schoolhouse. Elevation.
After Alonzo Potter and George B. Emerson, *The School and the Schoolmaster*
(New York, 1842).

that it embodied ideological meaning. I suspect that the project implies a
knowledge of Continental pedagogical theory, as well as reflecting familiarity
with garden design, possibly including early ideal pedagogical architecture in
a garden context.

In *The Schoolmaster,* the second title in the book already mentioned, George
Emerson shows sophistication in garden history in a passage suggesting suitable plants for flowerpots: "I can only recommend our wild American plants,
and . . . remind the reader that there is hardly a country town in New-York
or New-England from whose woods and meadows a hundred kinds of flowers
might not be transplanted, of beauty enough to form the chief ornament of a
German or English garden, which are now neglected only because they are
common and wild. Garden flowers need not be excluded."[7] Tellingly, this
takes German gardens as open to a *jardin anglais* irregularity: these pointedly
wild wildflowers might be at home in such a garden, in a way that they would
not be in a geometrical Italian or French classical one.

To show what he has in mind, in the same section of the book G. B.
Emerson quotes from a source identified as "Cousin, *The School at Bruhl*":
"The outside of the building is as agreeable as it is convenient; it is situated
on the prettiest side of town, and has no communication with any other
building. It has a magnificent view over a delightful country, a large kitchen-

6. Ithiel Town and Alexander Jackson Davis, Octagonal schoolhouse. Plan. After Alonzo Potter and George B. Emerson, *The School and the Schoolmaster* (New York, 1842).

garden, and two flower-gardens."[8] This is curious. Town and Davis's free-standing octagonal school, with a central lantern above, is recommended for its flexibility – "The octagonal shape will admit of any number of seats and desks (according to the size of the room), arranged parallel with the sides . . . or on such principles as may be preferred" – however, "The master's seat may be in the center of the room and the seats be so constructed that the scholars may sit with their backs to the center, by which their attention will not be diverted by facing other scholars on the opposite side." In fact, it lacks side windows, specifically so that "the attention of the scholars will not be distracted by occurrences or objects out of doors."[9]

The authority in question has to have been Victor Cousin (1792–1867), a philosopher of pedagogy and aesthetics and Minister of Education under Louis Philippe. Cousin himself was concerned not only with education in the abstract, including the comparative study of European educational systems, but also with the publication of model schoolhouse designs. Appended to a volume of his works dealing with public instruction in Germany, Prussia, and Holland (1841) are plates showing specific plans, elevations, and sections for seven different schoolhouses meeting varying local requirements of accommodation.[10] In light of the consideration that the school have "no communication with any other building" one notices that none of these exhibits is centrally planned (some have symmetrical facades, some do not). Indeed, a tendency to avoid modeling his officially recommended buildings on centralized plans would seem to accord with Cousin's own attitude toward geometric form. Along with his own voluminous *Fragments philosophiques* there appears a "Dissertation on the Metaphysics of Geometry" by Vincent-Augustin Fribault, who shows a strong prejudice against regular geometric figures as capricious and unempirical.[11]

If George Emerson's text raises the issue of garden associations, and if his knowledge of Cousin points to a Continental educator interested in ideal schoolhouse architecture, these facts in themselves seem to lead no further. The problematic character of the Town and Davis octagonal project derives from its centralized plan, with connotations of the garden that are more explicit.

But if the Americans were cognizant of modern French pedagogy, they surely knew that in contemporary Germany Friedrich Froebel (1782–1852) was already enacting an ideal conception of schooling itself as a process of gardening. Froebel's *Education of Man* (*Die Menschenerziehung*) came out in 1826. Although it may not have been entirely translated into English until 1877, Froebel had set up the first *Kindergarten* in 1837, and by mid-century the idea was being transmitted. A school for kindergarten teachers (*Kindergärterin*) was founded in 1849, and by at least 1855 a sort of Froebel-in-a-nutshell by a disciple had appeared in English, Bertha-Maria Marenholtz-Bülow's *Woman's Educational Mission; Being an Explanation of Friedrich Froebel's System of Infant Gardens*. It would be difficult to press the *Kindergarten* metaphor further than Marenholtz-Bülow does: "As the name implies, the children are to be viewed as plants under the eye of the intelligent gardener, whose care and duty it is to nurse them with love and gentleness, to train them so that body and soul may put forth their shoots, and the flower of childish innocence expand without the bud being crushed or blighted."[12]

Froebel's positive liking for regular geometric forms is conspicuous in his invention of the famous "gifts," the Froebelian wooden, geometric toy blocks that would make such a deep impression on Frank Lloyd Wright as a boy in the 1870s. Wright would never forget these "smooth and shapely maple blocks with which to build, the sense of which never afterwards leaves the fingers: so *form* became *feeling*. . . . What shapes they made naturally if only you would let them!"[13] Marenholtz-Bülow herself had thought explicitly of architecture when she described the "Third Gift: The Cube Divided into Eight Smaller Cubes": "The different *buildings* and figures which can be executed with these eight cubes are in part represented in the accompanying engravings, from which it will be seen that there are three ways of arranging the cubes, namely, either surface to surface, or surface to edge, or edge to edge."[14]

In Froebel's own writing the garden metaphor is actively sustained; but what is crucial is that, in his view, while the liberating context of the garden allows the child to develop freely, it does so according to a symmetrical inner geometry. His imagery even suggests the wildflowers of George Emerson: "Look at the plants which you call weeds, and which, grown up here compressed and constrained, scarcely permit one to guess at their inner symmetry; but look at them in free space, in field and flower-bed, and see what a symmetry, what a pure inner life they show, harmonizing in all parts and expressions: a regular sun, a radiating star of the earth springs up" (*Education of Man*, 1.8).[15]

It is a recurrent theme in *The Education of Man* that the natural flowering of the child is a formal and regular thing. But if Froebel's metaphor for schoolchildren is a field of flowers, even wildflowers, each regularly organizing itself alone, one might ask why a centrally planned school should not inhibit the very unfolding of the freedom Froebel intended to cultivate.[16] In a tender passage he regrets that all education is necessarily an imposition, and for this very reason it is all the more important that the child's environment – the specially contrived setting for his or her free growth – be carefully and consciously, since necessarily, controlled: "For let us confess, that, when we speak of the development and cultivation of our children, we actually should speak of the swathing and binding of them; indeed, we should not at all speak of a training which coheres with the development of the spiritual, of the desire and will of man, but of a stamping and moulding, however proudly we all believe ourselves long since freed from this spirit-deadening view" (*Education of Man*, 4.B.f.94).[17]

The fascination with regular polygons that Froebel reveals in his invention of the "gifts" and in the section on geometry in his *Education of Man* (4.B.n.100) titled "Knowledge of Forms" accords, then, with his sense of the ultimately liberating character of carefully imposed regularity.

To some extent, the octagonal plan of Town and Davis's schoolhouse can also be associated with earlier garden architecture. At least one architect and garden planner of the Baroque, Joseph Furttenbach (1591–1667), who knew Galileo and was probably stimulated by his geometry,[18] designed ideal garden schools. In her *History of Garden Art*, Gothein reproduces "A Little Garden of Paradise – Design for a School Garden," identified as coming from Furttenbach's *Architectura civilis*.[19] Two comparable designs appear in Furttenbach's *Architectura universalis* (1635).[20] In each case the square pattern of the garden as a whole breaks down into four separate, subordinate square gardens. Dividing arbors intersect at a basically square, but eight-sided structure (the corners are chamfered). In the first case, this building is called a "Capella"; in the second, a "Bibliotecha." The Furttenbach plans, remote as they stand, adumbrate Town and Davis's in form, in meaning (by their garden associations), and even in mode, sharing the ideal and programmatic qualities of speculative paper architecture.

Postscript

In the twenty-five years since I wrote this, my first article, my sense of the octagonality of the Town and Davis schoolhouse as occurring along a certain international revisionist axis has deepened even as the project seems more telling in relation to contemporary American culture.

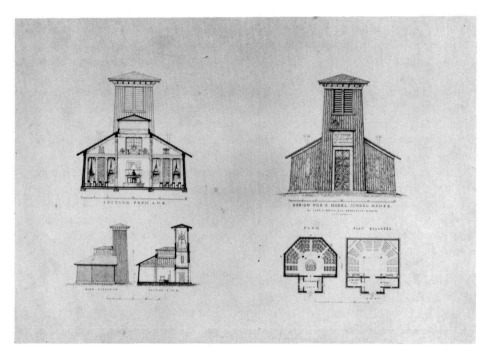

7. Ithiel Town and/or Alexander Jackson Davis, Design for a model schoolhouse, c. 1837. Engraving. Avery Architectural and Fine Arts Library, Columbia University, New York. Photograph courtesy of the Avery Library.

First, I trust it will dispel more confusion than it will create to explain that both the octagonal schoolhouse project presented in Potter and Emerson's book and the previously undiscussed "rectangular" project (not an insignificant carpenter's Gothic example there accompanying the octagon) are of specifically "rustic" board-and-batten construction, with battered exterior walls. They are different but related.

The significant design mentioned here as rectangular can also be considered semioctagonal, except that when "enlarged" by filling out the two dead corners of its auditorial plan with small rooms, the result is a rectangular block on the exterior. In its two alternatives, this schoolhouse with square entrance tower no doubt represents the New York Common School Society project (1834?), for which elevations, plans and sections were published as "Village School-House" in Davis's *Rural Residences* (1837).[21] I illustrate the uncut plate (Figure 7) where it is purportedly by Davis – although it was given singly to Town in the Davis manuscript, as noted. Possibly Davis meant to credit Town with the germ of the unconventional polygon idea? Because the square entrance tower makes it look so much like a secularized (or for that matter, ordinary Calvinistic) country church, it is worth recalling that it was in 1838 that Ralph Waldo Emerson delivered his famous Divinity School address at Harvard, in which was proposed, in effect, a redeemerless Christianity of his own ego –

likewise, of course, yours and mine. One might think as well of the little one-horse, wooden and similarly rustic "School of Philosophy" that this messiah of "self-reliance" built on the grounds of the house he bought in Concord, Massachusetts, in 1834.

The other, purely octagonal project, which does seem to be by Town and Davis together, has no ostensible equivalent to a church tower. Instead it has a quasi-functionalist glazed central lantern. All the more relevant, however, in view of the churchlike aspect of the tower-fronted "Town *or* Davis" school-house, is that centrally planned – and also often enough octagonal – chapels carry something of a European history in respect to nonestablished or dissenting religious denominations. Salomon de Brosse's Huguenot "Temple" at Charenton in the seventeenth century[22] may thus anticipate a proliferation of nonconformist examples in Britain, including a Unitarian (formerly English Presbyterian) Chapel at Colegate, Norwich, of 1756. There is, too, an entire category of Methodist chapels whose design, sometimes claimed for John Wesley himself, was engendered by the protocols of original Methodist camp-meeting worship rather than designed as such by Wesley.[23] Taken together, all such churches imply potential in the centralizing idea as a possible cultural clean sweep of precedent in one or another fresh and idealistic, institutional start. Yet insofar as an analogously inaugural impulse drives the Town and Davis schoolhouse project, one might further consider the markedly Reformational character of the European religious prototypes in light of the exclusionary, essentially Protestant, nonsectarianism of the early nineteenth-century public school movement in the United States, including, notoriously (against the press of Continental immigrants in the nineteenth century), the Common School Society of New York.

In American culture of the immediately postfederal period of self-definition, the architectural partnership of Town and Davis had a significant place. Town, an ex-carpenter, was probably more like the engineer of the outfit; Davis was more fine-arts-attuned. When they designed the model schoolhouse, Ithiel Town already held an 1820 patent for the "Town Truss" that made it possible to build covered bridges with a continuous diagonal web of ordinary lumber, with no arch required[24] (it must then have been a pleasure to design the new national Patent Office of 1832, housing a patent of one's own). As early as 1835 Town designed a New York shop front of iron. Alexander Jackson Davis, also known as a painter of landscape and architectural subjects, was responsible for the collection of art and architectural books and prints in the firm's "architectural rooms." This collection was the main reference for a new artistic sophistication in the New York mercantile culture of the time, in the social circle of Dr. David Hosack.[25]

Davis's middle name (like the given names of the landscape designer Andrew Jackson Downing) can only remind one of the initial struggles of lower- and middle-class Jacksonian democracy in American politics of the time. The April 1835 issue of the *American Monthly Magazine* attacked Town and Davis for the supposedly bastardly Greco-Roman temple-plus-dome design of their New York Customs House (later the United States Sub-Treasury; now Federal Hall)

of 1832, speaking of the "vandalism" of their Indiana State Capitol at Indianapolis, 1832–35.[26] May we infer from this some old-guard cultural reaction
assuming a posture of Euro-academic orthodoxy? Today it seems all the more
amazing that sophisticated minds steeped in the terms of classical eclecticism
– not merely in historic forms but in an established syntax of classical recom-
bination (e.g., the steeple and temple front in Gibbs's St. Martin-in-the-Fields,
London, and the temple and dome in Soufflot's Ste. Geneviève, Paris) – could
also set themselves freshly to the task of designing such a homegrown school.

Perhaps the partnership of Town and Davis exemplifies a creative dialectic
of the pragmatic and the historical. That it would probably be easier to liken
Ithiel Town to Ralph Waldo Emerson under a category of protofunctionalism,
is part of a problem that pursues Americans even today. Isn't it possible that
what has so often been rationalized as a quasi-spiritual as well as protofunctional
aesthetic of Emersonian simplicity and integrity – with the Shakers doubly
applauded as fetishists of simplicity who nevertheless liked machines – was
really the perfect aesthetic for the conversion of the hand-tool worker of the
family farm and village into the obedient industrial worker of the new local
mill? As early as the winter of 1837–8 one finds, in a review of an exhibition
of machine-made products in Massachusetts, utter delight in a new perfectionism of operational skill that renders hand craftsmanship futile if not crude.[27]
With Emerson's countermetaphysical importance to latter-day American
"functionalism" a large subject, it is enough to note that his citation of "the
masonry of Eddystone lighthouse or the Erie canal," tying neatly in with a
happy capitalist sense of the status quo in his "Thoughts on Art" of 1841,
adumbrates later materialist-functionalist praise of the same (Cornish) lighthouse, built in 1756–9 with concrete.[28]

As for the more idealistic European philosophical background: already in
the generation previous to Froebel the pedagogical reformer Johann Heinrich
Pestalozzi, a Swiss former student of theology, had likened the *educator* to a
gardener tending fledgling organisms unfolding according to innate natural
law.[29] And actually, it was in turning from the study of architecture, at Jena,[30]
to pedagogy, that Friedrich Froebel had met Pestalozzi and been influenced
by him. It was in an American reformist context, in educational journals of
Connecticut and Rhode Island, that between 1838 and 1848 the young Henry
Barnard had published parts and versions of what became his *School Architecture; or, Contributions to the Improvement of School-Houses in the United States*
(1848). And Barnard himself wrote on Pestalozzi, while his other writings
include a pamphlet on the Deweyesque theme of *Manual Labor and the Use of
Tools* (Hartford, 1871), as well as *Papers on Froebel's Kindergarten with Suggestions
in Principles and Methods of Child Culture in Different Countries* (Hartford, 1884;
revised from *Barnard's American Journal of Education*). One begins almost to see
the metaphysical underpinnings of Town and Davis's otherwise essentially
architectural idea.

In their modern edition of Barnard's book, Jean and Robert McClintock
treat the definitively octagonal design as an example of a then-new type of
pattern book for "whole buildings," in which were "created building types

and forms that have no historical counterparts." They rightly consider my essay, now revised here, an attempt "to show the possible origin in Froebelian pedagogy of an original schoolhouse design."[31] While grateful for the acknowledgment (rare enough in the art world), I tend to think that nothing is without historical precedent, and worry that the American wish to *be* so, which may be know-nothingism even in the political sense, is a serious cultural problem. Not that the McClintocks would necessarily disagree; but their attention to the spirit of precedentlessness in which the Town and Davis design was disseminated as a how-to-do-it type, helps me in turn to see its Americanism all the more clearly. So, for that matter, does Sibyl Moholy-Nagy's admiration in terms of "form and function" of an octagonal log blockhouse of 1808 in Maine, or of the (similarly problematic?) precedentlessness of circular Shaker barns, from 1823 on, as the insight of a sophisticated European modernist.[32]

Speaking of the more preposterously American: originally I avoided mention of octagonal houses, which appear at midcentury, especially in upstate New York. I did so because the subject seemed potentially distracting from the seriousness of the Town and Davis schoolhouse as an idealizing and innately ideological project, one by no means altogether ad hoc, in the seriously speculative invention of an important building type. I have been aware of octagonal houses, especially of a fine example outside Hamden, New York, that is quite near, it happens, one of my favorite fishing spots. I have also admired the Moore House, on Castle Street, in Geneva. For them, however, one can no doubt thank Orson Squire (!) Fowler, a phrenologist from Fishkill, New York, whose *The Octagon House: A Home for All; or, The Gravel Wall and Octagon Mode of Building* (1849) – and note the awkward disjunction, in the subtitle, between the pragmatic and the formal – marketed the octagonal house idea, "wholly original with the author," as giving more space per linear foot of wood and promising less heat loss through the walls.[33] Fowler's own Fishkill house (1849–58) was destroyed in 1897; if there is anything to regret, however, it is that in America the phrenological house should so typically have outproduced, and outlived, the Froebelian school. As for the Hamden example, the house of John Hawley, an Englishman, and locally supposed to have been provoked by buildings Hawley knew in England, it was built contemporaneously with Fowler's in 1856.[34]

Projects like these are all the more interesting as they encompass at once utilitarian and design aspects, yet to the neglect of "good" (assumedly classical) proportion in the abstract. That Town and Davis themselves still thought in proportional terms seems evident in their falling back on such basic ratios as 1:1 and 1:3 in specifications that Henry Barnard relays informally, and with implicit flexibility: "In the design given, the side-walls are ten feet high, and the lantern fifteen feet above the floor; eight feet in diameter, four feet high."[35] But in take-it-or-leave-it form, and all the more so when depending on ultrapragmatic American craft tradition, the very question of proportion was bound to be left behind as a residuum of fine-art, and upper-class, "architecture." In eighteenth-century England, James Gibbs, basing his method on

Perrault, had already reduced the question of proportions in the orders to arithmetic ratios; and once William Halfpenny's influential *Practical Architecture* (1724) reduced it handily to mere tables of inert dimensions, an entire genre of mechanically formalizing how-to-do-it books was spawned.[36]

If Town and Davis's schoolhouse was a kind of fine-art "gift" – to allude to one of Ralph Waldo Emerson's essays as well as to Froebel – to the common life, an answer to common needs and no more hopelessly utopian than the bestowal of literacy on children, then as a cleverly original invention it might have undermined the architectural authority that made it possible. Before applauding, however, consider a larger problem: no matter how radicalized in theory, the holy remnant of pure architecture would become more reserved than ever to the upper class. Make way, everybody (else) for (mere) "building," by *builders,* at first, like the local raisers of barns and houses who would contract to build such schools as these – with or without the classical pilasters still furnished on the interior of the other, semioctagonal, published design.

Prepare, too, for the notion that paying a little extra for ornament, to go ahead with those interior pilasters, should definitively make for a matter of architectural art. And yet, by the turn of the century the Froebelian *Kindergarten* metaphor itself found architectural fulfillment in the modernist ornamental theory and practice of Louis Henri Sullivan. In his *Kindergarten Chats* (1901–2) we find the claim that in schools of architecture "we need men . . . who can grasp the significance of youth, the social value of democracy and of creative art. . . . The *kindergarten* has brought [N.B.] bloom to the mind of many a child. . . . But there is, alas! no *architectural kindergarten* – a garden of the heart wherein the simple, obvious truths . . . are brought fresh to the faculties and are held to be good because they are true and real."[37]

4

Note on Sullivan and the Rarefaction of Bodily Beauty

For S.E.R.

I T is said of Jean-Nicole Durand, the pupil of Boullée who taught architecture in the new non-fine-art engineering context at the Napoleonic Ecole po-lytechnique, that his "insistence on a utilitarian, functional, logical architecture contributed, through the American students in Paris, to the functional struc-tures of the Chicago School."[1] Certainly an applied-scientific, if not exactly "polytechnique" sense of building was vital in the genius of Chicago archi-tecture, Louis Henri Sullivan, whose Paris study, undertaken in 1874 after he left MIT, was at the traditionalist Ecole des beaux-arts.

Sullivan was fascinated by the problem-solving mentality of engineers with-out expecting or wanting to reduce architecture to engineering.[2] Not only was he too concerned with beauty, but perhaps also with *scientia,* for that. In the notes and drawings that would eventually comprise his *System of Architectural Ornament According with a Philosophy of Man's Powers* (1924), his thought seems deeply affected by New England transcendentalism, though even the distinctly Emersonian self-construction informing his own pragmatic would never have sufficed in itself. For him, Whitmanesque generosity of poetic spirit was vital too.[3] However, there also seems to reverberate in Sullivan's writings some-thing of Schopenhauer[4] – by way of the contemporary aestheticism of Whistler[5] – or even of Oscar Wilde. In Chicago in 1882 Sullivan could have heard no less "aesthetical" a critic than Wilde, in person, describe the outside of W. W. Boyington's recent (1869) and prominent Water Tower on North Michigan Avenue as "a castellated monstrosity with pepper boxes stuck all over it," only to praise the pumping machinery within as "simple, grand and natural."[6] He would surely have shared Wilde's admiration of the keenly functional heavy industrial machinery as natural, organic, anatomical – even as bodily kinetic.

Sullivan's larger project cannot be reduced to a way station on the road to some mechanical functionalist notion of design, thanks to which fine art (presumably evidenced in architecture by the ennobling rhetoric of ornament), should at last happily wither away. His modernism, in its own right fully accomplished in a much more than utilitarian fashion, corroborated tendencies already shaping the future of architecture in nineteenth-century Europe and America respecting biological as well as engineering form.

Not that Sullivan's newly "organic" architecture of "form following function" would have been exactly welcomed into the influential, moralized nature aesthetic of John Ruskin.[7] In the second volume (1846) of *Modern Painters* Ruskin angrily (or anxiously?) denies any identification of beauty with utility as a "degrading and dangerous supposition" that confounds "admiration with hunger, love with lust, and life with sensation." To make any such identification is "to assert that the human creature has no ideas and no feelings, except those ultimately referable to its brutal appetites. It has not a single fact nor appearance of fact to support it, and needs no combating, at least until its advocates have obtained the consent of the majority of mankind, that the most beautiful objects of nature are seeds and roots; and of art, spades and millstones" (3.1.4.2).[8] And the midcentury American rural stylist Andrew Jackson Downing chimes in, "A head of grain, one of the most beautiful of vegetable forms, is not so beautiful as a rose; an ass, one of the most useful of animals, is not so beautiful as a gazelle; a cotton-mill, one of the most useful of modern structures, is not so beautiful as the temple of Venus."[9]

In his mature essay "On Poetry," in the *Kindergarten Chats*, Sullivan will specifically reject the "fancy... that a man may create a great work by reproducing a Greek temple, or any past vital work," since no such work is possible without one's "in his own way having held communion with the flow of life." No; "a great work, for us, must be an organism – that is, possessed of a life of its own; an individual life that functions in all its parts; and which finds its variations in expression in the variations of its main function, and in the consequent, continuous, systematic variations in form, as the organic complexity of expression unfolds..."[10]

So strong is Sullivan's "*organic* organic," however, all the more as perpetuated by his disciple Frank Lloyd Wright, that we Americans must remind ourselves that this familiarly given sense was not that of even the French scientific tradition – to us, the supposedly all too "mechanical" French sense of the *organique* inherited by Le Corbusier.[11] Ironically, it becomes a complicated matter to understand Sullivan himself when, in the same place, he condemns academic, beaux-arts architectural composition as "a mechanical, not an organic process.... indeed, the very antithesis of an organic process." This is especially so insofar as Continental naturalists themselves, in extension of Enlightenment *Naturphilosophie,* tended to project onto the natural realm a geometric regularity not unlike the assumed symmetrical beaux-arts ground plans.[12]

On the other hand, within the more fundamental seventeenth-century French "geometric" view, even anti-Cartesians conceived of nature as sufficiently structural and reversible that, with an "organic" implication we begin to recognize, *composition* was already mechanically complementary to *decom-*

position, as where Pierre Gassendi says that the things of nature are experi-
mentally "reduced, as though decomposing them, to understand of what
elements and according to what criteria they are composed."[13] Insofar as this
begins to connote composition and life versus decomposition and death, Sullivan's unabashed sense of an animating soul as projected in architecture could
have found a scientific analogy in Pasteur's sense of molecular dissymmetry
as characteristic of the organic realm, with the carbon atom as almost a sign
of life, or at least its departed matériel. (The renowned Pasteur was teaching
at the Sorbonne during Sullivan's Paris visit.)

At home in Boston, consider the popular influence, after 1846 – when Louis
Agassiz arrived to teach at the technical institute now known as the University
of Lowell, in Massachusetts – of the great Swiss naturalist whose own early
study in comparative anatomy had been personally encouraged by Alexander
von Humboldt and Baron Cuvier. In an article published posthumously in
the *Atlantic Monthly* in 1874, which discusses Cuvier (and hardly mentions
Lamarck, more commonly appealed to by functionalists for his notion of
types), Agassiz comments on the aesthetic aspect of natural selection in a way
that would have appealed to Sullivan for its implication of a certain creative
force over and above strength (structure?) and beauty (ornament?) alike:

> It would not be difficult to bring together an array of facts as striking
> as those produced by the evolutionists in favor of their theory, to show
> that sexual selection is by no means always favorable to the elimination
> of the chaff and the preservation of the wheat. A natural attraction,
> independent of strength or beauty, is an unquestionable element in this
> problem, and its action is seen among animals as well as among men.
> The fact that fine progeny are not infrequently the offspring of weak
> parents and vice versa points perhaps to some innate power of redress
> by which the caprices of choice are counterbalanced.[14]

Most Sullivanian in this is the challenging freedom of operating under an
evolutionary influence that cannot be known or projected in advance.

Sullivan, who could turn familiarly to – among other naturalist texts – (Asa)
Gray's School and Field Botany "for a simple exposition of plant function and
structure,"[15] did not so much decorate his buildings with plant motifs as allow
the buildings themselves to flower metaphorically, as if out of their own
sensitively practical articulation, especially, and as if embryologically, in an
ultimate refinement of the (also Wildean) "skin" precisely as surface. It is by
virtue of this that his artistic practice deserves to evoke the most venerable
sense of ornament as being a fulfilling, expressive follow-through, which is
anything but a superaddition, excrescence, or superfluity.[16]

His art unfolds against the background of a newly organized nature and
new notions of its stylization in art. The older *Naturphilosophie* was a poetic
cult of, above all, regular natural – especially plant – structure, from the
eighteenth century on, as in the work of Lorenz Oken, which Darwin considered "mystical." Sullivan's art also manifests a more culturally affirmative
sense of specialization and refinement that can be attributed to his notions of

an unfolding "organic" democratic society and of natural phenomena as manifestations of an "unknowable" as in the biology studies of Herbert Spencer.[17]
In some notes he even seems to take a late, artist's place in that rather literary
tradition of culturalizing natural science. "The seed-germ," he writes, "may
...thus be considered... as a container of energy, forming of its own will
sub-centers of energy in the course of its [N.B.] functioning development
toward the finality of its characteristic form – the expression of its identity."[18]

Ruskin could not have denied Sullivan's intimate grounding of his ornament
in organic nature. If necessary, he might have rationalized (and minimized)
Sullivan by referring his ornamental gift to his Boston mentor, Henry Hobson
Richardson, the grandson of the chemist (and Protestant theologian) Joseph
Priestley. Even so, he would have found it difficult to accept that an Irish-
American, of all people, should have succeeded so magnificently in creating
a post-Ruskinian form of modern ornament beyond his sphere of influence.
Surprisingly, Peter Collins attempts to contain Sullivan, in his ornament, as
(simply) "the culminator of Ruskinianism," relegating him to a plurality who
"invented a type of terra-cotta panel which, in its appropriateness as well as
its beautiful and original detailing, showed the real applicability of Ruskin's
theories."[19] Yes and no: it is going too far to say that "Sullivan (especially
after Wright began to work for him) shows his genius especially as an orna-
mentalist, or as what would today be called a 'stylist' – that is to say, a man
who can put an attractive sheath around someone else's structural frame,"[20]
namely, his (Danish-American) partner Dankmar Adler's. (Unfortunately,
Philip Steadman has seconded Collins's censoriousness toward Sullivan, one
root of which may be Ruskin's shameless bias against the Irish.)[21] As for
Ruskin's own theory; while it is modernist of him to argue everywhere against
classical idealization and on behalf of stylization fresh and free, it then becomes
almost duplicitous of him to negate sarcastically an "ideal" Greek-style lion-
head ornament in favor, on the same page, of a thoroughly naturalistic, un-
stylized drawing of a tiger's head by John Everett Millais – as happens in his
second "Lecture on Architecture and Painting" (1853).[22]

Sullivan's ornamental stylizations of nature, often obviously generated with
draftsman's or engineer's compass in hand, are sometimes taken as the charming if almost regrettable residue of the premodern tradition of furnishing
ornament at all, something like respectable and forgiveable returns to nature
applauded for at least eschewing the obsolete classical-ornamental vocabulary.
Yet nothing more clearly marks the historical recurrence of classicism itself
than the cleansing call to return to the prototypical forms of "nature." The
stylization in Sullivan's ornament is at least as lively as the nature motifs with
which it engages. And despite a great struggle of the nineteenth-century academic mind to acknowledge the fact, not only is stylization never a crudity;
it almost by definition entails abstracting idealization.

Recently, James O'Gorman has sought to squeeze Sullivan out, or divide
him up, between H. H. Richardson as forebear and Frank Lloyd Wright as
legatee. To Gorman's eye, Sullivan himself began to bloom only when Richardson's rising Marshall Field Wholesale Store (1885–8) stimulated his Audi-

torium Building (1886–9), also in Chicago. "By this time, Sullivan's ornament had developed from the stiffly constructed, angular patterns of [Frank] Furness toward the continuously curvilinear forms, perhaps derived in part from Viollet-le-Duc, in which the underlying geometric structure is overlaid by more animated and more luxurious foliage. Wright was to call this Sullivan's 'efflorescence.' "[23] Once Wright's ornamentalism takes over, Sullivan can be practically dismissed. O'Gorman's revisionism is understandable in reaction to a long-standing cult of Sullivan as a kind of bodhisattva stopping short of the gate of true modernity, alongside certain European figures who likewise participated in the decorative-art style of the art nouveau. After modernist loss, there has understandably come loss of interest in extending any rationalization of the kind.

A principal exhibit in O'Gorman's case, however, an 1875 Sullivan lotus design, needs to be reconsidered more historically. Sullivan's imaginative development of vegetal ornament occurred within a context of design reform and ornamental art theory in America (notably in Boston), as well as in England, in the latter part of the nineteenth century. By the testimony of *The Autobiography of an Idea* (1924), Sullivan hated his lower-grade schooling in Boston in the early 1860s. In about 1867–8, his father, a teacher of dancing, "thought he would teach his son drawing. His son thought otherwise. His son detested drawing. The prospect of copying a lithographic plate setting forth a mangle, a step-ladder, a table, a mop and a pail, was not alluring."[24] This sort of how-to-do-it lesson, by the way, had its contemporary architectural counterpart not simply in the traditional handbooks of classical ornament but also in such pattern books of predesigned, otherwise Ruskinian, hypothetical Gothic ornamental details as Joseph Barlow Robinson's *Gothic Ornament Adapted from Nature* (London, 1857) and *Architectural Foliage Adapted from Nature*, the latter an album of lithographic details published at New York by J. O'Kane (perhaps in 1868).[25] It was at about the age of twelve, in 1868, that Sullivan first became aware of architecture, coincidentally (?) with his transfer to a cheerful new school building.

Now from precisely 1870, as Sullivan proceeded to English High School, Boston, dates the important Drawing Act of the Commonwealth of Massachusetts, which, influenced by contemporary British design reform, made art instruction mandatory.[26] Sullivan just missed benefiting from it in grammar school, though it is unlikely that his beloved high school teacher of general subjects, Moses Woolson, would have been unaware of the new legislation. What he leaves unsaid in the *Autobiography* is, with Woolson encouraging "nature study with open book," namely Gray's *School and Field Book of Botany* ("Louis's playground"), and Gray himself visiting the class from Harvard for an occasional lecture,[27] whether this involved actual drawing on Louis's part, which hardly seems unlikely.

O'Gorman insists that "Sullivan may have been a student of nature from early childhood . . . and at least one drawing from 1875 records him dissecting a lotus in pursuit of its structure; but he first learned how to transform nature into ornament in Furness's drafting room," in Philadelphia, in the summer of

1873.[28] However, it seems worth considering what was already going on in the Boston schools under the influence of the Drawing Act. Charles A. Barry, who was teaching drawing in 1870 when the act was passed,[29] was supervisor of drawing for the Boston public schools. In 1878, he published a *Primer of Design,* which offers a stylized lotus as its prime figured example of "historical ornament" worthy of study, copy, and individual variation.[30] This seems at least as relevant to Sullivan's personal stylization of the lotus as does the work of Furness, who perhaps did not so much advance a "transformation of nature into ornament" as withhold anything like the incised linearity of Victorian "neo-Grec" ornamentation from his aggressively sliced and cut-away (proto-"brutalist") piles of brick and stone. In Boston the influence of the Drawing Act was manifest, whether the teenaged Sullivan would have known he was in the swim of art-educational reform or not.

According to Connely's biography, Sullivan went to Philadelphia, dissatisfied with M.I.T., to gain some office experience in preparation for the Ecole des beaux-arts: recommended by his teacher William Ware, he was referred by Richard Morris Hunt to Hunt's pupil Frank Furness, of Furness & Hewitt, who held that "a building should proclaim its use" (Sullivan would also soon be exposed to the thinking of Viollet-le-Duc, in Paris).[31] He admired Furness's facility at freehand drawing, exercised in the summers at Cape May, New Jersey, where "he spent his leisure copying seaweeds and flowers, out of which drawings he fashioned his designs in terra cotta."[32] When Hewitt, the partner, found him copying his own Moorish ornament and objected, young Sullivan left to rejoin his family in Chicago, after barely more than this one summer (of 1873) in the Furness office.

Then, working in Chicago that autumn, he got to know John Edelmann, office foreman for the firm of William Le Barry Jenney, who had already worked for Denkmar Adler. His close friendship with Edelmann, which he carried with him to Paris and back, would prove vital to Sullivan's subsequent development. In the spring of 1874 Edelmann introduced the eighteen-year-old Sullivan to his sports club, whose president had worked as architect and civil engineer in New York. Called "Lotos Place," this was located south of the city on the Calumet River. Its members, who soon included Sullivan and his older brother Albert, competed in rowing as well as track and field and Greco-Roman wrestling, and slept in the Lotos club boathouse on weekends. As a student in Paris in the autumn of 1874, Sullivan designed a room interior with pistil and stamen ornament, and dedicated one of the project drawings to his Chicago friend. Another ornamental drawing, also dedicated to Edelmann, on April 17, 1875, soon before Sullivan left Paris, offers as "centerpiece" of an ornamental fresco an eight-petaled flower with the petals turning into thistles, in turn punctuated with antennae.[33] Returning to live with his family, Sullivan was also back at Lotos Place with Edelmann, who now occasionally drew in Sullivan's old M.I.T. notebook. Following one of these Lotus Place sketches Sullivan himself, on August 5, 1875, made not one but two analytical drawings of a lotus bud, one "before fructification," showing "position and structure of ovaries," the other giving "cellular structure."[34] Beyond the symbolic erotics, in doing so Sullivan – busy working out mind and body with an Edelmann whose homemade and sophomoric but earnest idealist aesthetic concerned "noble thought nobly expressed,"[35] and who also had an architectural notion of releasing "suppressed functions" – was also measuring his direct (and unclassical American) experience of botanical nature against the codified European ornamental tradition.

In 1875–6 Edelmann's firm was the source of Sullivan's first two commissions, decorative "frescoes" for a synagogue and an evangelistic "tabernacle" in Chicago. In the Sullivanian wording of the Chicago *Times* of May 21, 1876, "the underlying idea" of the latter project was "botanical": "the anatomy of plants if geometrically treated – the structural growth is carried throughout the forms, and the leaves and flowers are seen geometrically – that is, without perspective – as one sees their lines when pressed in the herbarium."[36] Back at the boathouse, Sullivan and Edelmann (who was then drawing Lotus Place members exercising and skinny-dipping) both made negative comments on marriage in the notebook. Sullivan's Lotus Place sports activity apparently faded after the 1877 season, with his friend gone away to try farming; but before long Edelmann returned and fixed up Sullivan, then developing an interest in engineering as if in compensation for his so far successful but only decorative architectural practice, with a job at the firm of Burling & Adler, where Sullivan would find in Denkmar Adler his intellect-engineer partner. Then, in a sense, the lotus began to attain to fully sublimated statement.

But the lotus motif itself was not only accruing symbolic significance in "lotus-eater," aesthetic movement terms; it was also of serious art-historical interest. It will suffice to mention a later but crowning example, by William H. Goodyear, of the Brooklyn Museum: *The Grammar of the Lotus,* to appear in 1891. Goodyear tried to establish the lotus in its various botanical parts and growth stages as *the* originating motif for even categorically Greek-classical architectural ornament. He devotes an entire chapter to "Lotus Form Mistaken for Papyrus,"[37] and twice illustrates, as if demonstrating the absolute source for every possible radially lobed or sunburst design, the "Dried Ovary Stigma of the Lotus After Seeding; from Nature."[38]

What the lotus drawings of 1875 really suggest, then, is not some special debt to Richardson (as O'Gorman would have it), but rather the growth of Sullivan's own ornamentalism out of the commonplaces of a generation, the last of the nineteenth century, whose fundamental reconsideration of the ornamental stylization of nature constitutes an important chapter in the prehistory of abstract art as well as of architectural modernity. More like Whistler, in painting, than one might suppose, only more urgently and profoundly than Whistler, Sullivan developed a gift for ornamental articulation (away) *from* nature into a virtually *symboliste* sense of the independent "life" of artistic forms and structures. Tellingly, Lauren S. Weingarten, discussing a previously unknown, more symbolist second version (1893), handwritten in French, of the architect's essay "Inspiration" (originally 1886), points to French critics' praise of Sullivan's Transportation Building at the 1893 World's Columbian Exposition, in Chicago, as exercising sympathetic contemporary symbolist understanding of ornament as a fine-art spiritualization of otherwise material(ist) building requirements.[39]

In view of the fresh symmetries of his own stylized organic ornament, it is significant that Sullivan was disillusioned at the Ecole des beaux-arts by an academic cult of the typically symmetrical plan in architectural design that resulted in what for him was a too-detached cleverness[40] – which, in a sense, mutates into an opposite (asymmetrical) extreme under a later academization of modernism, thanks to the doctrine that " 'the plan should generate the facade,' as Le Corbusier was fond of saying."[41] The freshly regularized patterns – based on and so evocative of organic growth – that enliven in epidermal layers the surfaces of his buildings relate more subtly than one would think (though precisely in dialectical opposition) to the beaux-arts tradition of academic plan-composing against which Sullivan, as cultivated as he was, inevitably had to rebel.

To turn, say, from the finely lined terra-cotta facade and bronze entryway panels of Sullivan's Guaranty Building of 1894–5 in Buffalo, to a beaux-arts design such as the fantastic and rather questionable plan of 1897 for a gambling casino on a pier by Louis-Hippolyte Boileau (this projected in a drawing today said to show "the fine, nervous lines and radiating masses typical of student projects of the late 1890s")[42] is to see the hollow grandiloquence of beaux-arts linearity and symmetry dissolve into scaleless, meaninglessly inflected, almost escutcheon-like patterns. The fanatical form-generating system of the academy is seen dying even as the young American's ornaments, themselves often enough oddly symmetrical and escutcheon-like, germinate with new life (Figure 8). It is as if Sullivan had faced up to the empty formality of the graphic plan and converted *it* to useful, properly decorative purpose (classical forms having become "floating signifiers" anyway within the academic tradition).

Contemporaneously, in *The Sense of Beauty* (1896) the American aesthetician George Santayana negates "a sordid utilitarianism that subtracts the imagination from human nature,"[43] yet nevertheless affirms the claim of utility, at least in determining architectural types. Under the theme "Form" he says, "The non-imitative arts supply organisms different in kind from those which nature affords. If we seek the principle by which these objects are organized, we shall generally find that it is likewise utility. Architecture... has all its forms suggested by practical demands," so that "we have the same intrinsic materials to consider as in natural forms."[44] Santayana's remarks themselves exceed Yankee pragmatism, going all the more against the grain – rather like Sullivan's, though more aristocratic – of his own broadly idealist character.[45] Perhaps any materialism here reflects influence from the theoretical writings of Gottfried Semper, who taught in (and designed) the Zurich Polytechnicum, notably *Der Stil in den technischen und tektonischen Künsten; oder, praktische Aesthetik* (Style in the technical and techtonic arts; or, practical aesthetics, 1860–1),[46] a work that Santayana may have known from his student days in Germany in 1886, if not earlier. Aloïs Riegl had not yet articulated his dialectical response to Semper, especially with his sense of artistic materials as offering only re-

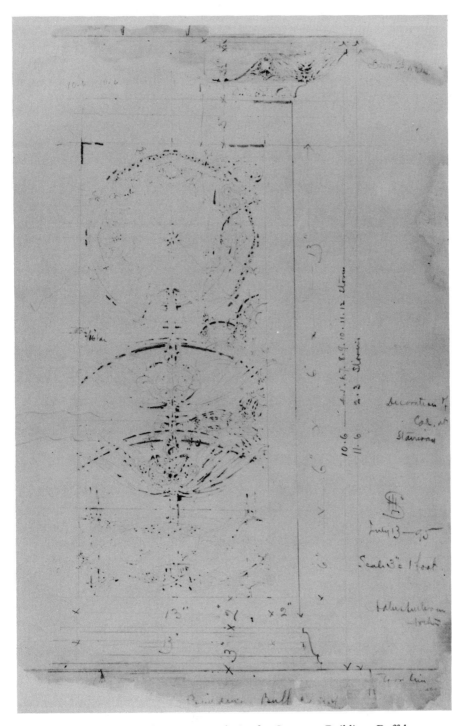

8. Louis Sullivan, Design for ornamented pier for Guaranty Building, Buffalo, New York. Pencil drawing, dated July 13, 1895. Avery Architectural and Fine Arts Library, Columbia University, New York. Photograph courtesy of the Avery Library.

sistance, negatively, as "coefficients of friction" (*Reibungskoeffizienten*), in the generation of artistic form.[47]

As in nature, where mutation may make for adaptation or grotesquerie, the economy of formal convention has a problematic edge – a matter that becomes clearer in Santayana's section, "Expression." Here the philosopher speaks specifically of "the expression of economy and fitness." With "waste ... a sort of pungent extract and quintessence of folly," fitness gives beauty a leg up. In an essentially conservative way, this happens only as "the fit form becomes fixed in a type" (as in Lamarckian zoology), which in turn makes for a highly problematic "aesthetic propriety"; hence "the much-praised expression of function and truth in architectural works."[48]

Ironically, this is why the patrician Santayana can seem better prepared than, say, the more radical and more obviously modernist William Morris to entertain the possible beauty of "an iron bridge," just because he is so well prepared to assign it a certain inferior status: "though it certainly possesses and daily acquires aesthetic interest, [it] will probably never, on the average, equal a bridge of stone."[49] Like a social upstart, the new type of structure made of industrial materials can be admirable under the limitation of its inability to accumulate sufficient aesthetic capital to challenge unqualified, highclass beauty. This anticipates Le Corbusier's opposite, Perraultean advocacy of moderns against ancients, not to mention much vulgar antimodernist polemic.

Likewise negatively Corbusian is the fact that Santayana puts a limit on flat roofs. He holds that "no fitness of design will make a building of ten equal stories as beautiful as a pavilion or a finely proportioned tower; no utility will make a steamship as beautiful as a sailing vessel," despite the fact that "added charm" can accrue once such "forms" are "established."[50] Had he been familiar with such a challenging contemporary work as Sullivan's thirteen-story Guaranty Building, Santayana might have been abler to realize that there was no reason a fine new building could not have a "tower's" edge, if not that of a precious "pavilion." In the last analysis, there is no reason even a prison, or any other building given over so extremely to utility, should not necessarily also stand as a work of art. Concerned that beauty be, as it were, stretched and sustained over the bulk of a building ten stories tall, Santayana might have considered the essay "Ornament in Architecture," published in *Engineering Magazine* in August 1892. In it, Sullivan argues for, in effect, an allover expressivity: "An ornamented structure should be characterized by this quality, namely, that the same emotional impulse shall flow throughout harmoniously into its varied forms of expression – of which, while the mass-composition is the more profound, the decorative ornamentation is the more intense," both, however, springing "from the same source of feeling."[51]

It is sobering to think that that major aesthetic exposition of Sullivan's, "The Tall Office Building Artistically Considered," appeared handily in *Lippincott's* magazine only in March of 1896, which is to say, one month after Santayana sent the manuscript of *The Sense of Beauty* (already rejected by Macmillan and other Boston publishers) to Scribner's in New York.[52] Here the architect faced head-on the modern building type that was basically "materialistic, an exhibition of force, of resolution, of brains in the keen sense of the word. . . . the joint product of the speculator, the engineer, the builder." "Problem: How shall we impart to this sterile pile, this crude, harsh, brutal agglomeration, this stark, staring exclamation of eternal strife, the graciousness of those higher forms of sensibility and culture that rest on the lower and fiercer passions? How shall we proclaim from the dizzy height of this strange, weird, modern housetop the peaceful evangel of sentiment, of beauty, the cult of a higher life?"[53] Certainly not merely by decorating it. For in rising to the challenge in a sequence of steps from "social basis" to "literal material satisfaction" to "the elevation of the question . . . to the plane of elementary architecture as a direct outgrowth of sound, sensible building," and finally "to the beginnings of true architectural expression, through . . . sentiment," Sullivan sees himself as ultimately confronting "the imperative voice of emotion," which asks, "What is the chief characteristic of the tall office building?" Santayana might well have appreciated Sullivan's empathetic and expressive response, which transcends mundane utility: "And at once we answer, it is lofty. This loftiness is to the artist-nature its thrilling aspect. . . . the eloquent peroration of most bald, most sinister, most forbidding conditions."[54]

"What Is an Architect?" asks Louis Henri Sullivan in one of his *Kindergarten Chats* (1901–2, revised 1918). That Sullivan cheerfully welcomes the engineer to the building task along with the blacksmith, stonecutter, shoveling navvy, the president as well as the trainman of the railroad, the steel mill superintendent, the banker, merchant, policeman et al., also *dis*qualifies him as a fine artist, "a real architect – an architect *solus*."[55] For what defines "the true function of the architect" as such is a more creative (even in a sense mimetic) as well as comprehensive task, "To initiate such buildings as shall correspond to the real needs of the people." Saying so, Sullivan can only wonder, "How shall I infuse such unmistakable integrity of meaning and purpose into the word, *initiate,* the word, *correspond,* and the phrase, *real needs of the people,* that mutton-heads and knaves can't use them for their own shameful purposes, by effecting a change of significance in the formula?"[56] For "the real architect is . . . not a merchant, broker, manufacturer, business man, or anything of that sort, but *a poet who uses not words but building materials as a medium of expression*"; hence, "to be truly great, really useful, he must impart to the passive materials a subjective or spiritual human quality which shall make them live for other humans . . . "[57] A certain sublimation is necessary that thought may "flower and exhale the perfume I call architecture," "UTILITY" being something the architect must "organize, integrate and [N.B.] glorify."[58]

According to Adorno, the real function of art lies precisely in its lack of ostensible function: "If any social function can be ascribed to art at all, it is the function . . . [of having] no function." It is not fair to make this sound like mere formalism, as Hans Belting is today far from alone in doing.[59] The point is not art's purposelessness (which, anyway, is by no means the same as pointlessness), but its transcendental capabilities. There is the simple idealist value of a useful art engaged uncompromisingly; but there is also art's own spiritual utility, for which worldly purposelessness itself might only, in the end, serve as occasion or means. With their ever-admired yet ever-problematic ornamental elements and, what is more, their entire ornamental-expressive aspects, Sullivan's buildings advance in the useful art of architecture a rarefaction (almost by definition beautiful) of utility, in analogy with the sublimation of bodily beauty. "He knew his anatomy," the great architect would remember of another of the Lotos Place oarsmen, "and had devised special exercises to develop each separate muscle in his body. So when in the sunlight he walked the pier for a plunge, he was a sight for the Greeks, and Louis was enraptured at the play of light and shade."[60]

5

De Chirico's Pathos of Lost Antiquity

For M.B.

THE painter de Chirico writes in his novel *Hebdomeros* (1929), "On the plain are... the river which goes through the middle of the town and the bridges which are true works of art."[1] I notice this because at a certain point in a course I regularly teach, I like to discuss Cézanne's *Mont Sainte-Victoire,* the painting with a central tree and a long viaduct bisecting the right-hand side, which is in the Metropolitan Museum in New York. For some time I have been struck by an ambiguity in Cézanne's motif that is in one sense submerged, and in another exposed, in representation. The formidable stone arcuated construction traversing the valley of the river Arc was, before anything else, a nineteenth-century railroad viaduct insinuating itself, let's say "Ponts-et-chaussées"-style, into the abiding landscape. Yet prior to its being represented by Cézanne, the structure alluded in a more "Ecole-des-beaux-arts" manner, to the categorically antique but also anciently engineered form, altogether appropriate to a valley in Provence, of a Roman aqueduct.

I am reminded, too, of a famous photograph, itself rather Chiricesque, by André Kertesz, *Meudon,* 1928, in which a steam engine and tender are seen to cross a viaduct above a construction site at the end of an old city street. This image suggests the industrial cityscape of Stockton as observed by a writer whose name the classy de Chirico might never have willingly pronounced, namely, Engels, in a book he would surely have preferred to ignore: *The Condition of the Working Class in England in 1844* (1845). Engels says, "The railway from Manchester to Birmingham passes over the town and the whole ravine in which it lies by means of a lofty viaduct" (chap. 3).[2] Kertesz's photograph is much more beautiful than, say, Edouard Baldus's *Pont du Gard,* c. 1855 – to pit a great twentieth-century photo of a railway viaduct against a commonplace nineteenth-century photo of a Roman aqueduct – and largely due to its motif, which is evocative of Engels. But then de Chirico would probably have preferred not to hear even of photography at all!

Today, if not a hundred years ago when barely a generation old, Cézanne's (nasty modern?) railroad viaduct shows itself as abstractly mimetic, partly by ex post facto virtue of the (charmingly ancient?) classical antetype of the aqueduct. In a sense, the viaduct had only naive historicity – not unlike, I think, the way de Chirico's novel depends ploddingly on the simple past tense[3] – until Cézanne painted it into modernity, after which its form could be said to vibrate between the poles of modern engineering and ancient art. And de Chirico's spiritual suspension between ancient and modern identifications, or evasions, has something of the character of Cézanne's preconstructed motif as rendered, perhaps not without symbolic struggle, in *Mont Sainte-Victoire*.[4]

In 1888, when Cézanne might have been painting this undated *Mont Sainte-Victoire,* Giorgio de Chirico was born – in Greece, a fact of birth that surely pleased him more than that he was born at the end of the already dingy nineteenth century. But how oedipal would have been such a contrived self-definition, given that the reason he was born in the classical homeland rather than in his father's country was that his father was actually a civil engineer working there on the construction of the Thessalian railroad, as Whistler's father had done on the Saint Petersburg–Moscow railway a generation before. Both fathers died overseas at this railroad work, leaving their teenaged, aesthetically inclined sons in circumstances of privileged Schopenhauerean detachment.

De Chirico himself seems to have sought an easy agreement between the classical and a temperamental modernity of his own, with tailored arcades and draftsman's space-geometries reiterating the first modern classicism of the aristocratic fifteenth-century Renaissance. It was all too easy for him to condemn the Vittorio Emmanuele II Monument (1885–1911) – as he did in a well-known 1919 text, "On Metaphysical Art" – while standing as aloof from architectural modernism as did certain patrician Anglo-American philo-Florentines of the years before and during World War I. Whenever the essentially Germanic and romantic Renaissance revivalism of his *Rundbogenstil* arcades puts us in mind of modernistic Italian Fascist architecture[5] – and then of utterly penal latter-day "postmodernist" designs by, for example, Aldo Rossi[6] – it is not without reason that we suppose we see through de Chirico's hairsplitting self-prescribed post-1920 "classicism."

Tafuri, in likening Rossi's work to the "emptied sign" of de Chirico, permits him a harmlessly ineffectual "linguistic" hermeticism. His claim that "the accusations of 'fascism' hurled at Rossi mean nothing, given that his attempts to recover an aristocratic ahistorical status for forms preclude naive verbalizations of content and all compromise with the real" sounds as much like an apology for de Chirico as it is for Rossi. But in both cases the resultant "emptied sacrality," in Tafuri's apt phrase, is just what strikes some of us as quasi-fascist.[7] All true classicism, however, of whatever period, requires the essentially subjunctive conviction that, confronted by new conditions and constructively alive to their possibilities, one is doing what the worthy immortals would have done in the circumstances. Needless to say, that requires living in the present more than de Chirico (or for that matter Rossi, in Tafuri's estimation) was prepared to do.

It's not just the image-contents of his art that seem suspended in inert gas under a bell jar, but de Chirico's spirit too. His was a socially privileged fantasy, hardly even escapist insofar as it constituted the lifetime indulgence and display of an only slightly wayward *bon goût* of patrician restraint. It was by no means a spiritually privileged mystic vision. De Chirico's paintings are no more "mystical" than bedtime stories for a toga party – despite the fact that in his own day even secularized modern art did not lack the possibility of spiritual transport for the truly mystically inclined.[8]

De Chirico's vacancy, supposed to be portentious, the artist himself presumed accounted for by a problematic desire to descend in a symbolist line from Arnold Böcklin, in fin de siècle Munich – it not being as easy to choose our own artistic fathers as one might think. But Böcklin and Max Klinger – that men's-club semimodernist – on both of whom de Chirico wrote enthusiastic essays, have always held special appeal for those antipathetic to any radical modernity after the secession moment of 1900. Not without reason was Heinrich Wölfflin's 1897 advocacy of Böcklin followed by Julius Meier-Graefe's 1911 denunciation. Robert Goldwater's argument that none of this German art deserves anyway to count as symbolist could rightly extend to de Chirico.[9]

Besides Böcklin, the standard accounts of de Chirico's cultural formation in Munich mention his readings in Schopenhauer and Nietzsche – usually without even distinguishing between the two philosophers. De Chirico may indeed have hero-worshipped Nietzsche, but he didn't seem to absorb Nietzsche's critique of Schopenhauer. What could be less Nietzschean, after all, than to will an inert "enigma." Apollonian composure must be won by struggle, not assumed in pacifistic retreat. As to aesthetic ideology in the Munich of de Chirico's youth: what does seem worth considering in light of the painter's Sicilian family background, and his aristocratic airs, both, is his possibly surprising receptiveness to a certain Munich "Stimmung," what with the schematic *Rundbogenstil* arcades that appear in so many of his architectural compositions. As a handy instance of the freestanding arcade there was Friedrich Gärtner's Feldherrnhalle (Hall of the Generals), built in 1840–4 off the Max-Joseph-Platz, a close variation on the famous Loggia dei Lanzi on the Piazza Signoria, in Florence, of five centuries earlier (1376). The sheer abundance of the Italianate *Rundbogenstil* (round-arch style) in Munich must be relevant. Notwithstanding the usual discussions of Turin's squares by de Chirico scholars, nineteenth-century Italianate (and Hellenic) Munich must have been a perfect, even inevitable, site for de Chirico's architectural incubation.

Less conspicuous but at least as significant in contemporary Munich architectural history would have been Baron Geymüller's studies of Italian Renaissance architecture. Geymüller expounded a thesis tracing the origins of Italian Renaissance architecture to the court of the thirteenth-century German king of Sicily, Frederick II.[10] This was a contemporary theory with its own German romantic precedent[11] that would have appealed to the de Chirico who hated Gothic form and urgently required the security of a timelessly ideal classical grounding for himself.[12] What a perfect ideal for young Giorgio, too: this Frederick II, as the German royal son of a Norman Italian mother.

One need not know the novel *Hebdomeros,* with its various epiphanies of strongmen, to sense the passivity of de Chirico's lonely-heart idealizations in so-called metaphysical or classical space. It seems almost discourteous to refer to the private personality of this artist who lived with his mother while on army duty in wartime, and whose images of biscuits and candies were of pleasures he couldn't indulge owing to a sensitive stomach.[13] In *Spurs* (1978) Derrida considers idealist detachment in a way that seems to me in this con-nection rather Chiricesque: wondering whether the detachment of (his) truth exiles the philosopher, specifically Nietzsche, Derrida speculates: "Distance – woman – averts truth – the philosopher. She bestows the idea. And the idea withdraws, becomes transcendent, inaccessible, seductive. It beckons from afar (*in die Ferne*). Its veils float in the distance. The dream of death begins. It is woman."[14] Together, idea and woman "form a history.... history itself [perhaps], a history which philosophy alone, inasmuch as it is included therein, is unable to decode."[15] It seems fair to bring this in because often what de Chirico meant by "Metaphysical" painting seems to be merely a *look* of *philosophy.*

Magritte, who was stimulated by de Chirico's work, shows a livelier sense of incongruity. If I can never quite comprehend de Chirico's sense of himself as "Metaphysical" it is because the question always returns me to the defin-itively "Metaphysical" poetry of the seventeenth century and its revival by T. S. Eliot and the other Imagist poets, which I have already explored in respect to Magritte.[16] In the essentially juxtapositional imagist frame of mind, true "Metaphysical" poetry resembled an early structuralist tendency in an-thropology to formulate disjunct but vividly concrete-specific clusters of par-ticulars.[17] For the imagists and for Magritte, what Dr. Johnson had called the original metaphysicals' "heterogenous ideas yoked by violence together"[18] always detonated fresh poetic meaning.[19] De Chirico, however, simply smoothed the strangeness between things, and times, into a make-believe imagic consistency – quite like what Eisenstein contemporaneously dismissed as mere "brick-by-brick" editing in film, in contrast to his dialectical montage – and especially as packaged in a classy, reactionary, antimodernist, Renaissance revival picture space.[20] And it might be argued, by the way, that in architecture from Perrault on, no true classicist was ever altogether antimodern.

It is perhaps easier than ever to see de Chirico's Magrittean art-within-art interiors, especially in the works depicting paintings on easels, as personally expressive despite the artist's frigid – or, as he would have preferred to main-tain, Nietzschean-aristocratic – detachment from any affect but melancholic detachment itself. Noticing that in these indoor, introverted "views" the ceil-ing bears down as inside upper limit of a small, all too securely closed space of consciousness, may mean finding the only trait of German Expressionist painting – and also film – typical of de Chirico. This becomes self-conscious where the protagonist of *Hebdomeros,* produced in 1929, muses, "He would have liked to tell him that he hated views and only liked bedrooms, . . . especially the corners of bedrooms and low ceilings."[21] But de Chirico, who in 1920 had likened Max Klinger's images to cinematography,[22] was surely aware of just such a device in contemporary German film.[23] *Hebdomeros,* however, de Chirico's mid-life (crisis?) novel, is worthy of an excursus as contributing to the larger problem of sources, originality, influence, and even appropriation. Reading it hasn't exactly converted me to de Chirico's cause, but it has illuminated his sad but never quite tiring search for historical depth in lieu of any passionate involvement with modernity.

Plodding in structure, as if written a page a day, and as nostalgic for the German postromantic afterglow of the Sezession in the author's youth – the automatically evocative word *Stimmung* is affected several times – as for a groundless classical ideal, *Hebdomeros* nevertheless shows some nice surrealist strokes and flashes of visual metaphor. As aesthetic self-justification it can be embarrassing: "This is why Hebdomeros preferred to stay and pretended to take an interest in all the pictures and works of art, extremely mediocre in fact, which he knew by heart because he had seen them ever since his childhood."[24] Yet when sufficiently bitter in its antimodernity it shows some contemporary wit: "A magic word shone in space like Constantine's cross and was repeated right down to the far horizon, like an advertisement for toothpaste: *Delphi! Delphi!*"[25]

Whenever, as novelist, the artist camps, blaspheming his own classical ideal (and perhaps even the venerable Winckelmann who made such identification possible?), the reader is on his own. Early on, Hebdomeros, the protagonist, projects the utter passivity of his awe of athletes onto these "accomplished gentlemen" themselves, "men with good proportions, perfectly happy in body and mind, . . . absorbed in their favourite occupation: *the construction of trophies.*"[26] Later, "the Prefect's wife . . . insisted that her husband should spare the athletes the fatigue of . . . early rehearsals, and that he should allow them to restrict themselves to *tableaux vivants* representing the death of Patroclus, combats between the Greeks and the Trojans and other facts taken from Homeric poems. But these gentle and insistent entreaties were always in vain." Such wit the aesthete author attempts with only partial success to contain by fiat a bunch of athletes "looked at Hebdomeros with an air of scornful irony, and then, at the way out from the stadium, dug each other in the ribs and laughed among themselves when they met him."[27]

Hebdomeros had not yet appeared when Walter Benjamin was stimulated to embark upon his endless *Passagen-Arbeit* (Arcades project) by reading Louis Aragon's then-new surrealist novel *Le paysan de Paris* in 1926.[28] Benjamin, who called surrealism "the death of the last century through farce,"[29] was in archeological search of just that lingering, all too temporal nineteenth century from which de Chirico tried so hard to escape into a distant classical eternity.

Others have already likened *Hebdomeros* to *Gradiva,* a novel by Wilhelm Jensen that had charmed Freud, of which I have more to say.[30] However, the antecedents of both trace back further to the "first" Renaissance nostalgia for antiquity, in its architectural setting, at the very origins of the novel as a literary form. For *Hebdomeros,* like *Gradiva,* also resembles that ultimate example, the mysterious *Hypnerotomachia Poliphili* (1499), which is of great interest in relation to Renaissance architecture. And this locates his own novel, like so much that tends to make de Chirico precious, in the fifteenth-century romance with antiquity itself.[31] Structurally speaking, all three works are romances in which the hero traverses the world in a search for a love strongly identified with classical antiquity, except that in de Chirico's case there is no human love object in what is essentially an aimless search for meaning. Even aesthetic delight comes and goes like the wind. It is the world that moves, that drifts by Hebdomeros, who is as passive and inert as the spectator of a melodrama.

Jensen's novel, which appeared in 1903, is fully titled *Gradiva: A Pompeiian Fancy,* and *Hebdomeros* too recalls destroyed Pompeii, in a passage likening body poses to ancient sculptural types.[32] This, however, also entails a certain literary appropriation by Freud himself, with *Gradiva* thereby made available to the surrealists subsequently and indirectly. Freud, who not only thought (male) creative artists pursued intuitively paths similar to those of scientific psychoanalysts, but envied the immediate appeal of their work to women,[33] liked to think of himself as a litterateur. His involved (re)telling of *Gradiva,* in "Delusion and Dream in Jensen's *Gradiva*" (1907), has been described as "written with such delicacy and beauty of language as to rank high and to compel admiration for its literary qualities alone." Indeed, a Munich reviewer wrote on its appearance in 1907, with de Chirco living in Munich, that "many professional writers must envy" Freud's prose.[34] Understandably (if also no doubt competitively), Freud's own account, or recounting, of the novel in analytical paraphrase, is somewhat longer than Jensen's original text.

Beyond *Gradiva,* if not Freud's essay on it, as possible source, Jensen himself had never seen the original ancient sculpture that led his own love-seeking (but love-overlooking) protagonist on, having been inspired, he later told Freud, by a copy of the – not Roman, but Greek (that is, otherwise even more "original") – relief seen probably in the Antikensammlung in Munich, where, of course, the young de Chirico could easily have seen it for himself.[35] Freud didn't see the ultimate source sculpture in the Vatican museum until some months after he had published his study of the modern novella stimulated by it. In any event, in his analysis of the story Freud concurs with Carl Jung, who had called his attention to *Gradiva* to begin with, that the psychological germ of Jensen's creation was a relationship between a brother and a sister. (By the time he finished *Hebdomeros,* might de Chirico have known of Oscar Levy's recent discovery of the dubious manuscript of *My Sister and I,* in which his idolized Nietzsche confesses his own incestuous relationship with his sister?)

De Chirico's first wife, Raissa Calza, was an archaeologist who directed excavations at Ostia Antica, the port of ancient Rome. For the somewhat obvious reason that it calls up Freud's own deep-set archaeological metaphor,[36] indulged in "Delusion and Dream," the painting *The Archaeologists*, dating from 1929 – in which two featureless, monumentally seated figures, a pair of friends, hold in their laps like prizewinners on a game show all they can carry of Greco-Roman architecture in model form – would surely have charmed the founder of psychoanalysis as he combed over Jensen's *Gradiva* (not to speak of a sculptural version, in bronze, *The Archaeologists [Orestes and Pylades]*, of 1940).

In de Chirico's work of the 1960s, still frowned on by some, what is taken for weakness may be a lowering of his guard. Particularly in stereotypically "noble," equestrian paintings like *Divine Horses of Achilles: Baliose and Xanthos*, 1963, and *Ancient Horses*, 1965, toylike animal forms, not to mention model-railroad-scaled Greek architectural accouterments, have a certain shyly honest fictiveness. In *The Mysterious Baths*, 1966, even the ideal of the, preferably ruling-class, ephebe, that recurrent motif in *Hebdomeros*, attains a curious stasis, as if in maturity one came to live with certain ambiguities as stably familiar states. Here, and maybe even more in *Ulysses' Return*, is an invasion of interior by exterior realms suggestive of the Magritte who was sparked by de Chirico early on. And in such later works de Chirico permits himself a romantically ingratiating, pasty paint quality, a more defenselessly "personal" touch.

Especially significant, to be sure, is *The Departure of Hebdomeros*, 1969, which sports lurid volutes typical of *luxe*-French, halfway "modernistic" decor of the 1930s.[37] As if in some out-of-body experience, an interior punctuated by "exterior" incident has an expressive-oppressive ceiling seen impossibly from above and without; in two different places one of a pair of huge Hollywood-baroque white volutes touches the ceiling, or outside, while its mate stays put, inside and below. This is perhaps as gaga a testamental image as an old man may well have sought to produce, and not uninteresting as such. Here, despite a business-suited, post-Roman pedagogic figure and his ephebic disciple (as in the novel), another, competing persona of the metaphysical artist departs this pacific salon in a rowboat that seems to come equipped with its own convenient little canal. This image of so futile, unanchored and yet traditionally architectural an imaginary past at last carries enough of its own surreal conviction to reflect favorably back upon earlier work.

Where Ernest Jones, in turn, sums up Freud's account of Jensen's imaginary lovers who never found each other in their home town, but only in the ruins of ancient Pompeii, he stresses *Gradiva*'s essential conflation of a remote historical past with a needy present in which remedial justification is sought: "The ancient time of two thousand years ago when the pair were supposed to have known each other is equated with the forgotten period of their actual childhood."[38] For this modern artist who thought he wanted Greece but might have settled for Rome (had not the upstart Mussolini laid claim to that), a vision of the aristocratic Italian Renaissance seems to have provided resort from a horrible world of modernity, railroads, engineering and, in general, the rude real world of other men. If de Chirico could never overcome his antimodern sense of exile from an idealized Renaissance, or Roman, or Greek architectural past conjured up for reassurance, perhaps he did attain an essentially romantic *idea* of architecture, acquired in his youth in eclectically classical Munich, thereby acquitting himself, his parents, and at least the nineteenth, if not the twentieth, century.

6

Textual Life of the Living-Machine

For Meyer Schapiro

Voici la machine à émouvoir.
Le Corbusier on the Parthenon

FIRST in a review of an exhibition of paintings by Le Corbusier, in 1972, and later in my *Historical Present* (1984), I have speculated that this great architect's modernist dictum, probably equally beloved and despised, "A house is a machine for living [in]," which is a refrain in his classic treatise *Vers une architecture* (1923), might have come out of thoughts on Rousseau prompted by an entry in the *Journal* of the nineteenth-century painter Delacroix. Man is the subject, and in the entry for May 1, 1850, Delacroix describes him as "that brute...that machine made for living, for digesting and for sleeping."[1] A modern edition of Delacroix's text appeared in the same year as *Vers une architecture,* and although Le Corbusier composed *Vers une architecture* from articles that had "all appeared by January 1922" in the journal *L'Esprit Nouveau,*[2] he would have known of the preparation of Delacroix's *Oeuvres littéraires* (1923), including the *Journal,* by Elie Faure, the art historian among his purist colleagues. Whether or not the notorious figure was at least detonated in the mind of Le Corbusier by Delacroix, it deserves further attention as to background but also as to later repute.

Of fundamental importance to the meaning of the "machine for living" trope is the precedent, in classical architectural theory, of Vitruvius's distinction between the "machine," which is complex, and the simple "organ" or instrument (or "engine," in the sense of agent). As Le Corbusier certainly knew, Vitruvius devotes the first chapter of Book Ten – as Jean Martin titles it in his classic French Renaissance translation of 1547, with beautiful plates (and annotations) by the sculptor Jean Goujon – to "What Sort of Thing a Machine Is; and of the Difference Between an Organ and It Which Is Invented from Its Start by Necessity." By return to this classic French source, we who are used to a modern English sense of the "organic," especially in contra-distinction to the mechanical, are obliged to perform a serious revision. For what Vitruvius and Martin, following him, understand to be implied by the notion of the machine or the mechanical is virtually the opposite; namely, it is a complexity of interrelated movements (inevitably social), in operational resemblance to the workings of nature – whereas the organ (or instrument, or engine)[3] is literally simple and used by one workman (like an extension of the individual body). Among engines, says Vitruvius, "there are those which move mechanically, others like tools" (10.1.3), which Martin renders as "with the ingenuity of art (avec ingeniosité d'Art)" versus "like an organ or instrument (organiquement)."[4]

Despite philological subtleties in the prime text, Vitruvius's fundamental distinction, carried by Martin, is clear: machine connotes animate, spirited, functioning nature – just what we would have been led to expect from the organique. In the phraseology of Martin, "Our forefathers, seeing how Nature thus performs her works, took her as example and in seeking to imitate her ways of going about things, stimulated (as it is believed) by some divine spirit, invented many useful things (utilités) for our life, finding means to render many a thing easier by machines, and others still by organes..." (1.4).[5] Ob-viously, this sense of "machine" as natural, or of nature as animately me-chanical, is pre-Cartesian, and in the sixteenth century would inescapably have recalled the dictum of Thomas Aquinas that "art imitates nature in its mode of operation." It is also, however, orthodox Vitruvian, this very Corbusian con-ception of the supposedly "organic" machine (that sense, ironically, only fur-ther confirmed by Le Corbusier's freewheeling recourse to the more contemporary, biological notion of organism) as inscribed already by Martin on the Vitruvian cornerstone of French classical theory.

From the Greek come organon, for instrument, organ, or methodology, and the Latinized organum, also conveying simplicity, as in Francis Bacon's (in-ductive) Novum Organum (1620).[6] Actually, Bacon's essay "Of Building," in The Essays or Counsels Civil and Moral (1625; published in French, 1734), approximates the "machine for living" idea, but inappropriately for Corbusier. Bacon opens this essay on the country house with the statement, "Houses are built to live in, and not look on; therefore let use be preferred before uniformity, except where both may be had."[7] While this might be relevant as a defense of utility or "function," the subservience of Bacon's sense of art, including his dismissal of classical "uniformity" or symmetry (to be seconded by Ruskin in the nineteenth century), would have seemed to Le Corbusier like part of the problem rather than part of the solution.

In rationalizing organic vitality, even as it seeks to vitalize rationality, Le Corbusier's dictum has strong Cartesian overtones. With Vitruvius-Martin in mind (a Vitruvius annotated by Guillaume Philandrier had appeared in 1545, but Martin's stood definitive until Claude Perrault's, of 1673), Descartes's sense of mechanism does not seem "antiorganic." In the Discourse on Method (1637), often employing an architectural metaphor of building on foundations for his systematic thinking, Descartes recounts that old German streets built up helter-skelter struck him as "ill-proportioned" compared with (new French) towns planned by military engineers (sect. 2). Turning organically to the anatomy of the heart, however, he is far from arguing from abstract function to concrete form. Bodily "organs" are givens: the valve opening into the main artery is "oval because of its structure"; movement "follows . . . necessarily from the mere disposition of the organs" (sect. 5). Likewise, "natural movements which bear witness to the feelings . . . can be imitated by machines as well as by animals," and even a clock "composed only of wheels and springs" shows "nature working . . . according to the disposition of . . . [the] organs." The problem for us moderns is that (to risk an oversimplification) by *nature* Descartes meant physics, not biology, yet it included what we mean by biology, and entailed the same wonder of life and soul. Hence we actually come closer to Corbusier in his *Meditations on the First Philosophy* (1641), than anywhere in the *Discourse;* here the philosopher bespeaks "that whole machine (*machine*) made up of bones and flesh such as may be discerned even in a corpse, which I have called my body." Less orthopedically: "And so . . . what am I? A thinking thing (*une chose qui pense* [a thing that thinks]), that is to say, which doubts, understands, affirms, denies, wills, and does not will, and which also affirms and feels" (*Medit.* 2) – adding, in a word highly significant to Corbusier, that being a thinking thing means that he is "un esprit," in the sense of mind or soul.[8]

Certainly there is a whole Cartesian aspect to what could be called Corbusier's poetry of reason. Yet along with the recurrent *machine à habiter* motif of *Vers une architecture* (translated as *Towards a New Architecture*) there is also the rather more Pascalesque application, specifically to the Parthenon, of "machine à émouvir," or *machine for moving* – "moving," that is, in the sense of provoking emotion.[9] In another observation, published posthumously, the great modernist responded to the spiritual rigor of the temple's structure as manifesting superhuman sublimity: "The Parthenon, awesome machine (*terrible machine*), pounds and dominates. . . . "[10]

In theory of the high classical period, specifically a 1699 glossary by André Félibien knowingly following Vitruvius, the distinction is still observed between a *machine* of many parts and a simple *organe ou instrument*.[11] Surely not until the impact of industrialism, for which Le Corbusier had a contemporary enthusiasm, would the twin notions of the "mechanical" and the "organic" become polarized in their familiar way. As late as Coleridge the organic still connoted the instrumentality of a tool in use, like the "engine" of Vitruvius.[12] Traditionally, the body as what we would call an organism was considered more like a "machine," anyway, than like any particular *organe*.[13]

In the eighteenth century, there is some obvious Corbusian precedent in La Mettrie's conception of *L'homme machine* (1748), itself revisionistically relying on a Cartesianism of animals as "organically" complex, functioning machines. (*Man a Machine* followed upon La Mettrie's atheist *Histoire naturelle de l'âme* [Natural History of the Soul], 1745, which might have made Descartes wince.) In one passage the materialist La Mettrie maintains that "since all the faculties of the soul depend to such a degree on the proper organization (*organisation*) of the brain and of the whole body that apparently they are but this organization itself, the soul is clearly an enlightened machine (*machine bien éclairée*)."[14] Further, "This innate force in our bodies... resides in the organization of the whole body (*organisation de tout le corps*)"[15] – a comment whose sense of significant overall distribution and simultaneous interrelation of parts leads back to seventeenth-century French aesthetics.[16] In addition, it has been noticed that in the *Encyclopédie*, it is in the article on "Méchanicien," interestingly enough, that the claim is made that, thanks to Harvey's discovery of the circulation of the blood as well as Descartes's geometrical philosophy, modern medicine has "assumed a wholly new aspect," what with "the animal body, and in consequence the human body... considered as a real machine."[17]

The modern sense of an essentially biological organic depended not only on the development of biology as a science but also on the established analogy between a building and the human body as a staple not only of Renaissance humanist architectural theory, beginning with the mathematician Luca Pacioli's *Divina Proportione* in the fifteenth century,[18] but also, on the other hand, of Renaissance anatomy itself. Andreas Vesalius's classic *De humani corporis fabrica libri septem* (Of the [N.B.] Fabric of the Human Body in Seven Books, 1543), of wide importance for the fine arts, was joined by other treatises of quasi-architectural interest.[19] Even Galileo, in whose world of mechanics "machines" also included animal bodies, discovered in anatomy a certain intrinsic proportional fittingness.[20] While the subject of human proportion in architectural theory, from the Renaissance to Le Corbusier's "Modulor," is vast, here is a significant instance from Etienne Boullée in the generation of 1800, to whose work Le Corbusier's has often been related: "It is therefore proved that proportion and harmony in bodies are established by nature, and that, through the analogy which they have with the human organism (*notre organisation*), properties deriving from the essence of bodies have power over our senses."[21]

At least two great classical architects of the seventeenth century studied anatomy firsthand, and in so doing found meaningful structural differentiation in the functional parts of bodies. Le Corbusier would have liked the fact that in *Méchanique des animaux*, Claude Perrault's third volume of *Essais de la physique* (1680), Perrault, a physician, turns readily to an engineering analogy in which he "compares... muscles which act counter to one another in an arm with the shrouds on a boat-mast which counterbalance one another."[22] Christopher Wren, though apparently not so strong on the civil-engineering side as he would have liked,[23] assisted in brain dissections and took a discriminatingly quasi-architectural interest in animal structure: "Among [his] diverse new experiments in anatomy... were schemes of several fishes dissected, in which the fabrick of the parts appear'd very often irregular, and differing much both from brutes, and one another."[24]

In terms of modern comparative anatomy from plants upward, the principal development about 1800 was of a functionally comparative sense of structure. First among the scientists was Comte de Buffon, who published his literary classic, the "Discours sur le style" (1753), while at work on his vast *Histoire naturelle* (1749–1804).[25] With his natural-law approach Buffon "endeavored to incorporate biological phenomena in their entirety as a link in the great law-bound world process."[26] Even the architectural professional could admire Buffon: Charles-François Viel de Saint-Maux, government "Architect of the Paris Hospitals," who wrote *De l'impuissance des mathématiques pour assurer la solidité des bâtimens* (1806), may have "censured the 'gigantic and fantastic' projects of the modernists,"[27] but he had also published a project for a large-scale monument dedicated to Buffon and his great scientific project: *Projet d'un monument consacré à l'histoire naturelle dedié à monsieur le Comte de Buffon* (1779).

J. B. Lamarck, who has relevance in the matter of protofunctionalism for his theory of "types,"[28] tried to insist, in his *Recherches sur l'organisation des corps vivants* (1802), against Baron Cuvier, that animal classes evolve in a continuous sequence. In his view, and by his distinctly architectural metaphor, all vertebrates "appear to be constructed upon a common plan."[29] In *Philosophie zoologique* (1809) Lamarck maintains that in organisms it is "the needs and uses of parts" that "have developed these same parts."[30] Cuvier, for his part, wrote that the functions constituting animal "économie" tally up in "*trois ordres* [three orders]," each of which, including "organs" of movement, can be considered – and note the return to the nature mechanism – "like a partial machine coordinated with all the other machines that in ensemble form this world."[31]

Discussions of Lamarck in respect to Le Corbusier often fix on his notion of "types" in evolution vis-à-vis the standardized *objet-type* of purist industrial design. To follow Madeleine Barthélemy-Madaule, however, in maintaining that Lamarck was not really concerned with the doctrine of "types" but with "transformism," that is, the notion of one form turning into another (with types as consequential), is to find new pertinence in a corrected Lamarck.[32] Noting the subtitle of section 6 in Lamarck's *Histoire naturelle des animaux sans vertèbres* (1815–22), "On Nature, or the Power, in Some Sense Mechanical, that has Given Being to the Animals and Made Them Necessarily What They Are," Barthélemy-Madaule elucidates this as "a transfer of God's power to nature," as a "purely executive power" that "does not include decision making, and therefore does not include setting goals. The execution is 'mechanical.' "[33] But this mechanism is rather more abstract than the machinery one is accustomed to imaging; for Lamarck transformed the eighteenth-century sense of visible anatomical structure into the nineteenth-century dynamic of an abstract "organization."[34]

Important for architectural theory is Lamarck's conception of functions as having primacy over actual organs, with the latter following suit. "I could prove that it is neither the shape of the body nor of its parts that gave rise to the habits and to the way of life of animals. On the contrary, it was the habits, the way of living, and all the influencing circumstances, that, with time, shaped the body and parts of animals," Lamarck claims in his *Discours de l'an VIII* (1800).[35] In the *Philosophie zoologique* (1809), which begins by distinguishing artificial systems ("art") from nature, organic from inorganic nature, the "*series*" is "the design of organized being," "*circumstances*" are (negative) "obstacles" to its "production," and "stimulating *needs*... give rise to *actions* that

81

modify the organs" (thus causing the diversity of species).[36] In Lamarckian usage, then, "utility ... designates the exercise of a function and through it of an organ."[37] Hence, "Function creates form," according to Geoffroy Saint-Hilaire's *Principes de philosophie zoologique* (1830).[38] But it was thanks to Lamarck that the sense of the primacy of function over organ regained credit after the second half of the nineteenth century.[39]

Apropos of the currency of Bergsonism as well as of Corbusier's involvement with the group "L'Effort moderne": according to Barthélemy-Madaule, "In the *Philosophie zoologique,* the concept of *effort* intervenes between needs and organic modifications."[40] Despite misunderstanding at two extremes by Darwin and Bergson,[41] Lamarck's emphasis, it seems, was on neither catastrophic elimination nor on vitalistic will, but rather on fortuitous rise to occasion – as, oppositely, with the Lamarckian disappearance of unused organs (so suggestive of the superfluousness of ornament in modern architectural theory).

For obvious reasons, nineteenth-century biological imagery in architectural writing has been more observed than has architectural imagery in biology, such as Lamarck's – not to mention the more commonplace George Ogilvie's *The Master Builder's Plan; or, The Principles of Organic Architecture as Indicated in the Typical Forms of Animals* (1858). Remarkably, at several points a classic paper of 1860 on the asymmetry of organic molecules employs the architectural metaphor of a stairway: all material things, Louis Pasteur says, divide according to agreement of forms and repetition of identical parts into two categories, those that look the same in mirror reflection and those that do not: "a straight (*droit*) stairway, a stem with paired leaves, a cube, the human body," versus "a winding (*tournant*) staircase, a stem with spiralling leaves, a screw, a hand, an irregular tetrahedron."[42]

The greatest French art critic of the time would seem to have had some importance for the origins of Le Corbusier's house-as-machine idea. In the section on Delacroix of his "Salon of 1846," Baudelaire writes, "There is no pure chance in art any more than in mechanics. A happy invention is the simple consequence of a sound train of reasoning whose intermediate deductions one may perhaps have skipped, just as a fault is a consequence of a faulty principle. A picture is a machine, all of whose systems of construction are intelligible (*dont tous les systèmes sont intelligibles*) to the practiced eye."[43] This is not irrelevant, even though the term machine as applied to a painting more technically connoted the overblown compositions relentlessly cranked out within the academic system. By the way, one also finds a strong case for artistic contrivance in an essay of the same year by Baudelaire's admired Edgar Allan Poe, "The Philosophy of Composition," which is an exposition of how the poem "The Raven" was composed to produce an "originality of combination"of certain verse forms into stanzas, since "originality ... is by no means a matter, as some suppose, of impulse or intuition. In general, to be found, it must be elaborately sought ... "[44] Otherwise, in his more famous "The Painter of Modern Life," probably written in late 1859 and early 1860 and published in installments in 1863, Baudelaire, with his urbane polemical antipathy toward any romantically virginal sense of nature, writes, "Everything beautiful and noble is the result of reason and calculation (*le résultat de la raison et du calcul*)."[45] And in speaking of modern harness and coachwork as drawn by the fashion-plate artist Constantin Guys he says, "In whatever attitude it may be caught, at whatever speed it may be running, a carriage, like a ship, derives from its movement a mysterious and complex grace which is very difficult to note down in shorthand. The pleasure which it affords the artist's eye would seem to spring from the series of geometrical shapes which this object, already so intricate, whether it be ship or carriage, cuts swiftly and successively in space."[46]

This latter remark is all the more interesting if there is any chance of its depending on an American source. In "American Architecture" (1843; collected 1853), an essay admired by Emerson in *English Traits* (1853) but then long forgotten until it attained new fame a generation ago as protofunctionalist, the American sculptor Horatio Greenough writes, "Observe a ship at sea! ... observe the gentle transition from round to flat, the grasp of her keel, the leap of her bows, the symmetry and rich tracery of her spars and rigging.... Behold an organization second only to that of an animal.... Could we carry into our civil architecture the responsibilities that weigh upon our shipbuilding, we should ere long have edifices as superior to the Parthenon, for the purposes that we require, as the *Constitution* or the *Pennsylvania* is to the galley of the Argonauts."[47] Baudelaire refers to Stendhal at the start of "The Painter of Modern Life" for the thought that "Beauty is nothing else but a promise of happiness." Since he is known to have plagiarized much of his essay "Edgar Allan Poe: His Life and Works" (1852; 1856) from articles in the American *Southern Literary Messenger* (1849–50),[48] and if he had also been exposed to the writings of Greenough, who reveled in his own definition of beauty as the "promise of function," Le Corbusier's later tropism toward pragmatic America might find a more American source (with Stendhal behind it) than even he would have suspected.

More remotely, Tolstoy employs in *War and Peace* (1869) the lingering Cartesian image of a rationalist timepiece in conjunction with the Corbusian *machine à habiter*, this with a specifically medical twist that anticipates, in turn, an otherwise simple derivation *from* Le Corbusier soon after *Vers une architecture* was published. Late in the novel, Napoleon, annoyed by a persistent cold (!), exclaims, "What do the doctors know? They can't cure anything. Our body is a machine for living. That is what it is made for, and that is its nature.... Our body is like a perfect watch meant to go for a certain time; the watchmaker cannot open it – he can only adjust it by fumbling his way blindfold. Yes, our body is a machine for living, that is all" (3.2.29).[49] Then, in *Anna Karenina* (1875–7), against the grain of the utilitarian, Benthamite thinking of the character Levin with his "theory of dairy farming according to which the cow was only a machine for converting fodder into milk, etc.," Tolstoy puts this perhaps transutilitarian thought into the mind of Dolly: "The argument that a cow was a milk-producing machine was suspect to her. She could not help feeling that such arguments could not be of any real use to farming" (3.9).[50]

This itself, however, reads very like an approving allusion to an often-quoted remark of Baudelaire in his "Salon of 1859": "The whole visible universe is just . . . a sort of fodder that the imagination must digest and transform."[51] Le Corbusier, to whom the later "American methods" of Frederick Taylor, the famous "efficiency expert" (*Principles of Scientific Management, 1911*), were by no means unattractive[52] (not to mention Henry Ford's consultations with Lenin on the Soviet Union's New Economic Policy), would have noticed Tolstoy's agrarian skepticism toward the industrial bias of this supposed American virtue in the following bureaucratic exchange, later in the same novel: " 'American methods,' said Sviazhsky with a smile. 'Yes, sir. There they put up buildings in a rational manner . . . [*sic*].' The conversation passed to the abuse of power by the United States authorities . . ." (6.22).[53]

With the huge growth of engineering in the nineteenth century, the possibility of a "machine for living" approached. The boast of a speaker on the fiftieth anniversary of the Ecole centrale des arts et manufactures, Paris, 1879, showed the terms of a new industrial ideal anticipating Le Corbusier's own fascination with modern engineering and the twentieth-century cult of functionalism it served to inspire. Nevertheless, Le Corbusier himself would have seen a gauntlet thrown down in front of the art of architecture in those early claims of what the perfect graduate of the engineering school was supposed to be able to *bâtir* on demand: "To build a house, a machine or a work of art: it is all the same to him. To adapt the available means in the most rational manner to the assigned goal, with neither unintelligent prodigality nor damaging parsimony; to calculate everything; to prepare everything in advance; to forget nothing; to achieve the most useful, convenient and least expensive solution with the aid of ingenious combinations: such is the Centrale civil engineer, the brain that sets in motion all efforts destined to create the projected ensemble."[54] Already, however, Viollet-le-Duc was disappointed with what the demigods of applied mathematics actually produced, accusing those very engineers who extended the scientific study of materials of being "perhaps less disposed than others to establish a concord between the forms that they gave to the material and its own properties."[55]

Of course it was an optimistic policy of possible rapprochement with modern, 1920s engineering and industrial production that Le Corbusier pursued with his colleagues of the journal *L'Esprit Nouveau* (The new spirit). Today's skeptical critique would take that as happily materialistically as Le Mettrie would have, two centuries before, except, that is, to condemn as "utopian" any quasi-Enlightenment expectation of general human progress. Fortunately, Alan Colquhoun has advanced a subtler analysis of the problem, denying a simplistic "Bentham-like relation between form and function" in the larger program of Corbusier, who even in *Vers une architecture* wrote that "architectural abstraction has the particular and magnificent property that, rooted in the brute fact it spiritualizes it, because the brute fact is nothing but the materialization, the symbol, of the possible idea."[56] According to Colquhoun, Le Corbusier took the real difference between engineer and architect, who otherwise "start from the same foundation," as concerning the architect's deliberated "manipulation of . . . [the] feeling of harmony," which exceeds the (relatively inadvertent) admirable efficiency of the engineer's problem solving.[57] It is possible to take this remark formalistically: "If he said, 'The house is a machine for living in,' it was not so much to annex architecture to a branch of empirical science as to use the machine as a model for a work of art whose form and structure were determined by laws internal to itself."[58] To be sure, the idea has its political aspect: "In a tendency related to the *rappel à l'ordre* in postwar Paris, the architecture of the machine age was seen as overcoming history to achieve a kind of transhistorical classicism."[59] Yet Colquhoun's analysis helpfully reopens the aesthetic question of Corbusier's machine ideal.

Under the title *The Human Machine* (1908) the English novelist Arnold Bennett uses the "machine," specifically the automobile, as an extended figure for the human body, "the machine which was designed to do this work of living," as dominable by will, in reflections.[60] "Your 'character,' " says Bennett, "as it is to-day, is a structure that has been built almost without the aid of an architect; higgledy-piggledy, anyhow" – though "occasionally the architect did step in and design something."[61] Analogy between building and body has, of course, a rich textual history (e.g., 1 Corinthians). Bennett's otherwise unremarkable text intimates a triangulation between body as building and body as auto "machine," engendering building as machine – which Le Corbusier himself would also relate to the modern auto. An iconoclastic progressivism itself evokes Corbusian rhetoric: "The human machine is an apparatus of brain and muscle for enabling the Ego to develop freely in the universe by which it is surrounded without friction";[62] also, "The heart hates progress, because the dear old thing always wants to do as has always been done. . . . The brain alone is the enemy of prejudice and precedent, which alone are the enemies of progress."[63] And if Bennett can sound Lamarckian-evolutionary mentioning "the modifications which the constant use of the brain will bring about in the general values of existence,"[64] he can also evoke the briar pipe of the last illustration of *Vers une architecture*[65] as well as the very glassware (of popular Duralex brand) of the Purist "L'Esprit nouveau," saying that the ordinary man is frustrated because "what he wants is a pipe that won't put itself into his mouth, a glass that won't leap of its own accord to his lips . . ."[66]

Well before World War I, an element of proto-Dada mockery of scientific literalism was already emergent in the French avant-garde. Erik Satie's hilarious "Memoirs of an Amnesiac" (1912) purport to give details of certain crackpot, pseudoscientific techniques for dealing with musical sound – this by a composer who ten years later would make light of Le Corbusier and Amédée Ozenfant's "Purist" earnestness: "Something terrible has happened. . . . My subscription to *L'Esprit Nouveau* has just expired . . . yesterday. . . . Yes . . . I'm 'all of a dither' about it."[67] Satie's humor, however, points up the fact that the efficiency aesthetic of *Vers une architecture* also emerged, if not so simply as many of its enthusiasts or detractors would say, into a contemporary debate between vitalism and mechanism in science, this also reflected in "dystopian" fiction.[68]

In Germany, the art historian Paul Westheim noticed the metaphor early on, writing in a 1922 survey of contemporary French architecture that Le Corbusier "regards a house as a machine for living (he cites a modern ship's cabin as the most perfect example of this), a chair as a machine for sitting. 'Washstands are machines for washing. Twyford created them.'[69] It is the engineer who understands today how to heat, to ventilate, to illuminate." Thanks to the work of Henry Van de Velde, Adolf Loos, and others, Westheim can add, "Such ideas are not new to us in Germany." Aware of Le Corbusier's knowledge of early German modernist design,[70] and the Swiss architect's sense that German theoretical progress had in practice been left unfulfilled, he also quotes the expressionist architect Hans Poelzig to the effect that "purely technological form" is thrown aside once it becomes outmoded, whereas "the art form is eternal and is not destroyed without detriment."[71] Westheim understands with unusual subtlety that Le Corbusier was not simply trying to "propagate the machine form anew," or to "substitute the engineer for the architect." No:

> Beyond the simple demand for functionalism he is governed also by an aesthetic attitude.... He rises above the level of pure functionalism.... The engineer has reached the standard of excellence in his construction when he has found the most concise, useful, and economical solution for a particular purpose. He thinks of the purpose, and the form results by itself. He then immediately and unhesitatingly abandons this form again, for the sake of a new purpose. Le Corbusier, on the other hand, wants architecture, wants the shaped form, wants the same thing as the cubist painter, who relies on *esprit,* logic, and adherence to the laws of mathematics.... He admires the way the engineer poses the problem correctly, figures it out practically and logically.... He holds him up as a model to encourage the architect to cast off false ballasts and rid his construction of obsolete and alien elements.[72]

In England, Bergsonian vitalism was challenged by a new mechanistic extremism, about which a new antimechanist critique developed, including, on the philosophical plane, E. A. Burtt's *The Metaphysical Foundations of Modern Science* (1924) and Alfred North Whitehead's *Science and the Modern World* (1925), the latter with its emphasis on "organism." Like Le Corbusier's *Vers une architecture,* H. G. Wells's novel *Men Like Gods* – which Aldous Huxley would satirize in *Brave New World* (1932) – is dated 1923 (though it apparently was already circulating in 1922). In that year, the Soviet writer Yevgeny Zamyatin (Eugene Zamiatin) wrote (in words that Le Corbusier, the wildly enthusiastic author not only of the chapter "Eyes Which Do Not See, 2: Aircraft," in *Vers une architecture,* but also of *Aircraft* [1935], would have liked), "The word *airplane* contains all of our time. It also contains all of Wells."[73] One wonders if the Swiss architect could at least have known of Zamyatin's novel *We,* written in 1920–1 (to appear in English in New York only in 1924), in which a mechanist "ethos" is "first represented in the planes and angles of architecture."[74]

Within Russia, Moisei Ginzburg's *Style and Epoch* (1924), certainly influenced by the *L'Esprit Nouveau* articles from which Le Corbusier composed his

Vers une architecture of the year before, is a formidable document on the side of technical optimism, wherein, as Frampton also points out, the naval warship takes the place of Corbusier's passenger liners and the locomotive that of his bourgeois automobile. *Style and Epoch* is all in all more simply mechanist in its enthusiasm – as industrial as possible, in fact – than the dialectic of "Engineer's Aesthetic and Architecture" in Corbusier's book.[75] Indeed, Ginzburg's love of the machine is happily materialist, as against the threat of "abstractness" in modern art.[76] He comes closer to Corbusier where the machine itself can only be conceived in organic, anatomical terms: "We can sense in every architectural monument, in its most austere design, the presence of some kind of internal dynamic system."[77] Particularly interesting, here and now, in a chapter on "Industrial and Engineering Organisms," is Ginzburg's discussion of the machine and such "engineering structures" as the crane "that have grown out of the same modern needs."[78] "While the organism of the machine is massive and solid, indended for movement along the ground, the structure of the crane is light, as though devised to fill the urban skyline with its well-proportioned silhouette."[79] It is almost as if the crane, as a second-order – not to say more sublimated – machine, deserves loftier, more confidently architectural, standing.

In the same year in which Le Corbusier's text was published in English, there appeared at Paris Elie Faure's puristically entitled *L'esprit des formes* (1927), the fifth and conclusive volume of his *Histoire de l'art*. Faure's volume displays considerable photographic evidence of the purist machine aesthetic with regard to architecture especially, but even, à la the Cartesianism still manifest in Tolstoy (and soon in Paul Valéry), with respect to medicine. Like the famous juxtapositions of archaic and classical Greek temples equated with old and up-to-date automobiles in *Vers une architecture,* Faure juxtaposes on facing pages a flying buttress of Chartres Cathedral (Henri Le Secq had initiated such structurally abstracting photography of the French cathedrals in the mid-nineteenth century) with a similarly composed detail of one springing leg of, yes, the Eiffel Tower. One suite of four illustrations, however, entails a "clinical" efficiency quite literally. The images, which have in common a recumbent figure either dead, dying, or under treatment or revival, are, in sequence: a Giotto painting described as a "composition organique"; a documentary photograph of a patient under surgery in a modern operating room tagged "composition organique naturelle"; another "composition organique" painted by Rembrandt; and a tiresome "composition naturaliste" in paint that seems to show medical instruction over a patient, this last by one Henri Gervex (1852–1929). It is noteworthy not only that the significant paintings count as the "compositions organiques," but that the specifically clinical, body-shop aspect of the new hospital photo is actively opposed to the hopelessly naturalistic painting (in which a rail holds the viewer off from too close a sight of the patient while attendant figures garbed in white might almost as well be just as busily changing a tire in an auto race).

As regards the very influential 1927 English edition of Corbusier's book, how telling is it that a distinction between two different verbs for "to live" in the French seems lost in Frederick Etchells's – *Vorticist artist!* – translation? Where "a house is a machine for living in" is followed up with "baths, sun, hot-water, cold-water, warmth at will, conservation of food, hygiene, beauty in the sense of good proportion. . . . "[80] Le Corbusier uses the verb *demeurer* first, "to stay," only later in the text, as if challenged by his own excitement with engineering, employing *habiter,* with its more spiritual connotation of thriving inherent in "to dwell"; yet by 1927 even he was worrying about misconstrual of his metaphor;[81] thus one might say that while hot running water is all well and good for a place to park yourself for a while, living a life in a home, at home in the world (perhaps all the more in the modern world), ought to entail something more, something at least equivalent to a beautiful machine that can fly. Perhaps to some extent the simplistic ironing out of Le Corbusier's organic-mechanistic thinking in later Anglo-American functionalism begins right here in the Etchells translation of 1927.

In 1928, on the heels of the Englished *Towards a New Architecture,* came two hostile allusions to Corbusier's text (this would become an antimodernist cliché, especially in England), one haughty and the other frumpy. I. A. Richards, the literary critic, opens the preface, dated May 1928, to his *Principles of Literary Criticism,* with this sentence: "A book is a machine to think with, but it need not, therefore, usurp the functions either of the bellows or the locomotive" (since a bellows is actually more an *organe,* it should probably not, anyway, be likened to the literal or metaphorical French-architectural *machine*).[82] More diffusely, the *machine à habiter* figure, as excessively Cartesian-mechanistic, is grist for considerable middlebrow satire in *Decline and Fall,* Evelyn Waugh's novel of the same year.

As a poet in touch with purism, Paul Valéry, on the other hand, can be seen employing much the same figure as Richards, only more sympathetically:

A fine book is first of all a perfect *reading device,* the properties of which may be defined with some exactitude by means of the language and methods of optics; at the same time, it is a work of art, a *thing,* though one having its own personality, showing the features of a particular way of thinking, suggesting the noble intentions of an arrangement both successful and determined.[83]

Shortly after the appearance of *Vers une architecture* Valéry had published a pair of dialogues, "L'ame et la danse" and "Eupalinos; ou, l'architecte" (1924), of which the shorter, first piece, "The Soul and the Dance," has an extra character who, at one point, speaks of the human body as "la machine des mortels" and remarks, "Et notre système vivant n'est-il pas un incohérence qui fonctionne, et un désordre qui agit?"[84] In other words, the living body is pretty much like a contraption that somehow manages to work (one may think, in the extreme, of Jean Tinguely's abstract yet hilariously anthropomorphic motorized sculptures). But in Valéry's *Idée fixe,* a 1932 dialogue between a doctor and his friend that contains exchanges of semiclichéd scientific-mechanical and humanistic-spiritual ideas, one speaker calls attention to "one of our most vital actions, that of eating and digesting. Generally speaking, we're a one-way tube!"[85] (Again, shades of Delacroix.)

Even in the present informal reconnaissance, the idea of the house as a "machine for living [in]" entails a rich historicity despite Le Corbusier's own hurry-up, clear-the-decks purist attitude in 1923. The phrase is still catchily antisentimental, and sure to upset conservatives. The Nazis made easy disparaging use of the Corbusian term *Wohnmaschinen* (living-machines) as dehumanizing in implication, in propaganda against modernist public housing projects.[86] One does wonder if Le Corbusier realized that the bourgeois humanism he took for granted might disappear, or if he had so much implicit confidence in it, at least in the decade after World War I, that the shiny new engineered world that charmed him was a bracing spectacle from which he, maybe even *we* his later readers, could always expect to return.

His fascinating English book *Aircraft* (1935) records a remark from a lecture of 1931 "before an audience of 3,000 which booed and hissed"(!): "Birth of the new *biology* of contemporary building – steel and concrete."[87] Now, with a sense that a whole new mode of manual craftsmanship was called for by the aircraft industry,[88] the world of metal and machines seemed charged with potential for a perhaps higher-order organicism (more like what the classics meant anyway), since "All things in life are 'organisms.' "[89] "The time has come," he continues, "to create the *organisms* of modern society: dwellings, cities, buildings of determined function."[90] In *L'Esprit Nouveau*, in 1924, the architect had already written of such forms as "shells, birds, large prehistoric skeletons," which he called "the first introduction to the mechanics of things."[91] Now he penetrates deeper into the biomechanical mystery, reflecting on a scientific report on certain large birds of the Himalayas:

> The great gliding birds traverse the sky by means of the supporting plane of their wings; but these wings are neither flat nor rigid: they are tilted, and it is by imperceptible modifications of the supporting plane that these great gliders keep in the air for hours without moving their wings. What a beautiful lesson for those who cling a little stupidly to the extreme materialist theory of to-day which lays down that every solution derives strictly from 'deductive' (as they say) analysis.[92]

Then again, in his happy record of a visit to America, the America of modern Europe's great fresh start, *When the Cathedrals Were White* (1938–9), Le Corbusier, echoing Valéry and Delacroix, says of New York, "A city has a biological life," much as "it is justly said of man that he is 'a digestive tract with an entrance and an exit.' "[93] How tantalizing, those casual quotation marks! Might one even find buried here words of Descartes himself? For there is also a discussion of digestive mechanics at the beginning of Descartes's *Treatise on Man* (1622), if, by now, anyone cared to know.

Remarks of the semiotician Jan Mukařovský, in the Prague Linguistic Circle, on the question of a supposedly self-evident architectural functionalism when it was newly problematic in the 1930s, acquired new relevance fifty years later in the time of superficially "semiotic" architectural theory. To

Mukařovský, whose speculations deserve some close attention, "There are potentially present in every act and its results functions other than those which the act obviously fulfills. Indeed, because man is the agent of the act, all the primary functions rooted in his anthropological organization are potentially present" (except when some are "incompatible with the thing or act").[94] No fewer than four different "functional horizons" obtain in architecture, only one of which is immediate purpose. Of the others, historical purpose entails typological precedent; social purpose includes symbolic functions as well as available resources; and an "individual functional horizon" allows the creative revision of established norms, with consequent possibilities for future development – "Every use of a human creation, whether of a material or an immaterial thing . . . " being "to a certain extent its 'misuse,' an alteration of its function."[95]

Still, an identifiable aesthetic function has the special business of a "dialectic negation of functionality" in that it "contradicts each [other] function and every set of functions." Of this special function, which "does not emerge suddenly . . . as something added and supplementary but is always potentially present," and which "prefers to occupy a space vacated by all the other functions" (such as by atrophy), no object cannot be the vehicle, nor is there anything "which necessarily has to be its vehicle." As "the dialectic negation of semioticity itself (cf. the transformation of the communicative function in a literary work or in a painting)," the specifically aesthetic function effects both conservation and change – witnessing Henri Van de Velde's commending the purposefulness of the machine precisely as a matter of beauty.[96]

Elaborating on the aesthetic function in architecture, Mukařovský maintains that it can manifest itself even in the most "practical" buildings, and that, while it "does not come from the outside but is absolutely immanent in architecture," it tends to appear added, especially to the exterior, as exceeding "a required function."[97] He argues against the tendency to isolate architecture from arts thought to be more hermetic, "arts [that] function only in the sphere of spiritual culture, whereas architecture functions simultaneously in spiritual and material culture."[98] Architecture, which is not unaffiliated with the other arts, also affiliates, of course, with the extra-aesthetic world. So there is something *to* the functionalist view that "the aesthetic function is a consequence of the undisturbed operation and perfect coordination of the other functions" (as in the usual "machine" terms), even if one usually confronts, not "the possibility of attaining a total harmony" but rather "a choice among several ways of violating it."[99]

Mukařovský is concerned that the operational urgency of Corbusier's figure not be exempted from history: "The comparison of an architectural creation with a machine (Corbusier) is an extreme expression of the tendency of a period toward the least ambiguous functionality in architecture, but in no way is it a supratemporal characteristic."[100] As for fascism as the outside frontier of the purist aesthetic of sheer efficiency: Adorno and Horkheimer, refugees from the Nazis during World War II, warn in their *Dialectic of Enlightenment* (1944), "The subjective spirit which cancels the animation of nature can master a despiritualized nature only by imitating its rigidity and despiritualizing itself in return" (Excursus 1).[101] That, however, is not what Le Corbusier, nor for that matter, Descartes, was doing.

Between 1933 and 1936 Denis de Rougemont had composed reflections on the modern world, including fascism, called *Penser avec les mains* (Thinking with one's hands, 1936). Under the heading *Machines à penser* (Thinking machines), in a chapter entitled "La pensée prolétarisée" (Proletarianized thought), Rougemont maintains, "It is a dull romanticism, an archaeologism happily out of fashion (see Ruskin), that refuses itself the mechanical aids by which the spiritual act of creation might insert itself into what is given, sure of the swiftness of a shock."[102]

Cautioning that his comments on the matter are not final, by the mid-1940s Roman Ingarden felt discontent with then-common recourse to organic metaphor for architecture. For Ingarden, sophisticated biological organisms are too thoroughly hierarchical, while the "functions" performed by whole buildings or parts thereof are not as systemic as biological ones: witness the sovereignty of the central nervous system.[103] Also, most architecture seems to tend too strongly toward an inorganic, if not antiorganic, regularity: "The spatial forms of the masses that occur in the architectural work of art differ necessarily in their fundamental type from the forms found in the organism. They are always – to put it paradoxically – concretizations of certain idealizations of abstract geometric formations,"[104] while the regular forms of nature are really all too irregular.[105] Following Aloïs Riegl, Ingarden also notes, "It is precisely the fact that organic forms undergo alteration or even transformation within the framework of the architectural work which allows us to conclude that there is no fundamental affinity between architecture and the organic world, but instead a profound opposition between these two realms."[106]

The English critic Sir Herbert Read, speaking in America soon after World War II, called attention to the different matter of how "Le Corbusier's intransigent definition of a house as 'a machine to live in' " might inherit or subsume classical aesthetic decorum as one of the functions that architecture socially serves. Read points to the eighteenth-century architect Sir John Vanbrugh's term "State" (as in "stateliness") for one of his aims in designing princely houses, along with "Beauty and Convenience." Read is aware that here "we are up against a sociological factor, for 'State' in Vanbrugh's time was the quality of a certain manner of living: the manner of the typical oligarchs of the seventeenth and eighteenth centuries." Hence "Vanbrugh would have been neglecting the strict functional requirements of his task if he had been any less extravagant and, in our eyes, irresponsible. Indeed, Vanbrugh himself claimed that his houses were the most convenient ever yet planned."[107] Read could assess "oligarchical" decorum so calmly because as a democratic socialist in the line of William Morris he knew quite confidently the kind of society, as well as the kind of architecture, required by modern life, and in that, in postwar Britain, he was hardly alone.

One significant Catholic artist of the Left would eventually mobilize Le

Corbusier's *machine à* figure against heartless secularization: in 1947 Jean Char-lot commented on the decrepitude of church architecture in officially atheist modern Mexico and adapted the Corbusian "machine à" figure perhaps sur-prisingly readily, as "machines for praying," to the ruinous old colonial churches of the people. (Certain textual details confirm that Le Corbusier was on his mind.) "The Catholic architecture that fell upon Mexico as a spread *arras* of liturgical embroidery is now in tatters; it fits only loosely over a land churned deep by successive revolutions," writes Charlot. "The planners who had the faith and muscle to build these *machines à prier* are present as a mound of skulls piled in a niche of the splendid habitat which their brains once con-ceived and wrought."[108] What could be less "clinical" than that?

Internationally, Le Corbusier and his *machine à habiter* were practically household words as features of the modern movement by the opening of the 1950s, even in Russia. Le Corbusier had already designed the Centrosoyus (later, Ministry of Light Industry), 1928–36, in Moscow (without going to supervise its construction), while a famous project for the Palace of the Soviets was rejected by Stalin in 1931. In Solzhenitsyn's novel *The First Circle* (1968), set in 1949 in a Stalinist prison outside Moscow disguised as a technical in-stitute, among the topics of intellectual conversation is "how someone called Carbusier [*sic*] (or something) was building houses for other people some-where" (chap. 25).[109] This might as well allude to a 1948 report in the Soviet *New Times* that Le Corbusier's new apartment houses in Geneva " 'looked like an absurd, alien growth,' had 'nothing in common with the people,' and were therefore 'doomed to wither away.' "[110] In the West, of course, the catchy "machine for living," taken equally simplistically as connoting a dehumanizing mechanization of life, circulated most widely in populistic antipathy to mod-ernism in general.

Thanks to the onset of a popularized, and simplistic, essentially utilitarian (and antimetaphysical) notion of functionalism in architecture and design – in the dissemination of which the Museum of Modern Art, despite its connois-seurly acuity, was influential[111] – by the early 1960s the once-optimistic mod-ernist aesthetic extrapolated from efficient industrial production was in critical crisis. Peter Collins, concerned with the notion of architectural typology by which buildings might come somewhat automatically "off the rack" to meet stereotyped needs, wrote of Louis-Pierre Baltard's 1829 criticism of Jeremy Bentham's Panopticon – that it was a mere "machine worked by a single motor" – saying that Baltard "had the insight to perceive the basic analogical fallacy upon which it, like so many other misleading aspects of the new theory of Functionalism, was based. . . . Thus we see the beginning of the functional theory of the machine age, for this phrase could hardly have expressed more clearly the idea of a prison as a 'machine for living in.' "[112]

Even Kenneth Clark could write in 1963, "To find a form with the same vitality as a window moulding in the Palazzo Farnese I must wait till I get back into an aeroplane, and look at the relation of the engine to the wing. That form is alive, not (as used to be said) because it is functional – many functional shapes are entirely uninteresting – but because it is animated by the breath of modern science."[113] Putting it this way, Clark was of course extending on behalf of science and its otherwise inanimate works the concept of the soul rather than taking the well-trodden but drearier route of conceding quasi-aesthetic value to whatever "works."

Well before postmodernism, contextuality arose as an issue in architecture. Early modernist buildings might enjoy a healthy obliviousness to surrounding structures, like new truths establishing themselves in and against prevailing error, while with Le Corbusier and others the new field of "planning" widened the scope of design to a macroarchitectural scale. By 1960 the notion of a building's "blending into" its surroundings was already a cliché in the popular critique of architecture, though if new was good and old was now so bad, most people were quite unvexed by the question of whether virtue ought to "blend into" vice. No machine, of course, blends into its surroundings, except for the absurdity of "streamlined" encasings added to machinery in the 1930s in order to render it functional *looking* by domesticating it in a drapery of sheet metal skirts. Of itself, machinery doesn't really blend into anything except – if one proceeds carefully – other machinery.

In 1967 the British architects Alison and Peter Smithson said, "A building today is interesting only if it is more than itself; if it charges the space around it with connective possibilities – especially if it does this by a quietness that up to now our sensibilities have not recognized as such at all, let alone seen clearly enough to isolate its characteristics – to see that it presents us with the new, softly smiling face of our discipline."[114] These remarks might be taken to anticipate the affirmative but inevitably neutralizing contextualization sought, notably by James Stirling, under the postmodernism of the 1980s.[115] Worth recovering here is, instead, an orthodox modernist sense, more profoundly cubist (and comprehensively structural) than simply postimpressionist (and unifyingly designed), of a building's relation to its immediately surrounding *space,* on behalf of which the Smithsons offer their flexible, rather John Deweyesque sense of "connective possibilities" without needing to specify termini for such connections – not to mention their rather Nietzschean intimation that worthy struggle on behalf of such purely architectural conception might produce perceptibly gratifying results.

On Le Corbusier's death in 1965, André Malraux already testified, "His famous phrase 'A house is a machine for living' doesn't by any means give the whole picture. The picture it really paints is, 'The house must be the jewel-box (écrin) of life.' The machine for happiness (la machine à bonheur). He always dreamed of cities, and his projects for 'radial cities' are towers rising from immense gardens. This agnostic built the most gripping church and convent of the century."[116] If Malraux was right, possibly the *machine à habiter* idea, in its fuller sense, was not altogether alien, after all, to what Martin Heidegger, otherwise hating the technomodernity that Le Corbusier and the purists loved and insisting instead on a Greek-metaphysical sense of *techne,* would himself have more poetically, but rigorously, termed a *dwelling place.*[117] This subject would rightly require a different essay; but it is enough to acknowledge that the terms of Le Corbusier, cold-blooded though they may have sounded to some, then and still, were the words of a passionately engaged working artist.

We can now only wonder how Le Corbusier might have extrapolated his machine-age metaphor in our pervasively electronic culture. Lucen Kroll, who designed and built the remarkable Maison Medicale, Mémé, for the medical faculty of the Catholic University of Louvain in the early 1970s,[118] attacks not the computer but rather a computer domination of design, ever more rigid, that might instead have rendered manufactured building components newly variable. Of order, Kroll says, "there are (at least) two kinds: the *mechanical* and the *organic;* both are mathematical insofar as they involve the imposition of measure, but behind them lie quite different approaches, for the mechanical dominates while the organic composes."[119] Whereas modernism tended to be "autistically" detached by its imposition of dominating and overdetermining will,[120] by becoming more "permeable," open to social consultation and aware of physical context, architecture "takes root, needed . . . becoming a natural process, almost biology."[121] With allowance for individual alterations (in multiple dwellings, especially), "A process of accretion starts, which grows like a biological organism."[122] Unfortunately, the computer itself has so far only tended to extend disadvantageous mechanistic architectural thinking into the electronic sphere: "Engineers and contractors, powerful and methodical by nature, have tended to adapt the computer tool to their own image, so much so that they are unable to imagine it otherwise,"[123] accustomed as they are to grinding out "over-precise" but "provisional hypotheses" with a deceptively definitive look. Now, Kroll argues, "One must . . . dismantle some of the automation."[124] For "we need to construct a habitat through industrial means, but architects instead use the habitat to pursue an industrial image."[125]

Even in recent postmodernist discourse, however, one can discover, as Matei Calinescu has in Gilles Deleuze and Félix Guattari's *L'Anti-Oedipe: Capitalisme et schizophrénie* (1971), a distinct echo of Le Corbusier's signature literary figure of the "machine for living [in]." In this case, Deleuze and Guattari consider man's unconscious mind as *une machine désirante;* and according to their anti-Freudian "nonanthropomorphic 'productive theory,' " "the unconscious works like an industrial unit . . . a factory of desire" (Calinescu).[126] Such a conception of the psyche itself is now indebted, all over again, to some, at least, of Le Corbusier's own complex network of operational sources and working influences.

7

Reflections in Onyx on Mies van der Rohe

For M.M.B. on his retirement

The feeling for the splendid is not original by nature . . . , for this is properly a mixed feeling combining the beautiful and the sublime, in which each taken by itself is colder. . . . Accordingly, the German will have less feeling in respect to the beautiful than the Frenchman, and less of what pertains to the sublime than the Englishman; but instances in which both appear in combination will be more suitable to his feeling. . . . In love, just as in all forms of taste, he is reasonably methodical, and because he combines the reasonable with the noble he is cool enough in each feeling to occupy his mind with reflections upon demeanor, splendor and appearances.

> Kant, *Observations on the Feeling of the Beautiful and the Sublime*

CAN it have been his hundredth anniversary? This means that Ludwig Mies van der Rohe was only five years younger than Picasso and already pushing 50 when Elvis was born, even though my generation, at least, associates him with the 1950s. As with Picasso the abiding eminence inspires historical retrospection. Amid present-day historical anxieties that have become utterly manneristic, the Museum of Modern Art – once the Vatican of the "modern movement," now looking more like a Neiman Marcus – celebrated Mies's centennial with an exhibition of some 450 drawings, some of projects unseen until now, as well as models, photographs of buildings, furniture, a full-scale exemplar of one of the snazzy chromed steel columns that Mies first designed for the famous Barcelona Pavilion, and even a mock-up detail of his New National Gallery at Berlin – the building which represents the great architect's final apotheosis alongside Schinkel, author of the Berlin Altes Museum (1823–30).

The master's two manifest masterpieces, the Barcelona Pavilion and the Tugendhat House, were still under construction while Henry-Russell Hitchcock was writing *Modern Architecture: Romanticism and Reintegration* (1929). Those of us who tuned in a whole generation later would have an easier time with the structural "expressivity" of Mies's later gridded boxes, but Hitchcock announced the architect's rationalism as a hopeful eschewal of Expressionism – in his words, Mies's "earlier weirdness."' It would be unfair to make too much of the slap, but something here already suggests a problem of stylistics that pursues us today, not only in architecture but also in painting – where a superficial sense of "expressionism" has been challenged by willfully super-ficial, often cynically parodic forms of abstraction. Indeed, few today bother about what always concerned Mies as spiritual value in art: no wonder there hardly seems time to wonder about the place of Kandinsky and Klee, for instance, in the Bauhaus context. Next slide, please!

Let's go back to the great moment of the Barcelona Pavilion (1928–9; Figure 9) and the contemporary Tugendhat House, at Brno, Czechoslovakia (1928–30); and let's think, first, about that elegantly *schlank* chrome-plated column. For this element, cruciform in section, has almost heraldic (not simply signature or trademark) status in respect to Mies's supposedly "reductive," but actually essentializing, architecture. Is it needless to say that this column – which really ought to be called a pier or post because it isn't round – far from being given, in the sense of the orthodox classical orders, was most actively willed?

The form involves simplification, but there is more to it. The Modern's centennial exhibition made it possible to see in the flesh how the Barcelona and Tugendhat piers also differ. The former is sheathed in chromed sheet metal fixed with screws along the edges of the four fins; the latter looks more unitary – and Brancusian – with its chrome sheathing elegantly rounded on the fin ends without ostensible seam. As the Modern's 1:5 mock-up detail of Berlin's New National Gallery (1962–7) shows, the cruciform pier takes another, open form at the end of Mies's career, as composed (somewhat Tony-Smith-wise) of four dark T beams, flat end out.

The condensation of a support into something so slender, spaced so far from the next one, must have entailed a virtually Gothic sense of progressive structural shrinking and tightening, from lighter roof and lighter pier to prac-tically no roof on practically no pier. Or if Mies's classicism were as simple a matter as it once might have seemed, how is it that the beautiful Barcelona-Tugendhat post, that technically distilled toothpick of a pier, is like nothing in architectural antiquity so much as the impossibly hyperattenuated columnar elements of fantasy architecture despised by Vitruvius in Roman mural paint-ings? Vitruvius, who anciently notes that, "instead of columns," mere "reeds" are there employed, condemns these as "things which are not at all, and which cannot be because they have never been" (!). As Dorothea Nyberg has pointed out, Claude Perrault made an interesting comment on this passage in his 1684 edition of Vitruvius, in the context of the ancients-and-moderns dispute, ob-serving that Vitruvius "has not been believed": "My opinion is that what he says . . . here has served only to provide the model," that is, the no-no sounded like a neat idea.² All this relates to a complex of ideas in which "Gothic" breaches of classical law became validated in a new and protomodern "engi-neering" aesthetic capable of its own "classic" logic and no longer requiring formal precedent. Better to ponder this deeper stylistic, perhaps, than to keep

9. Ludwig Mies van der Rohe, German Pavilion, Barcelona, 1929. Interior. Photo-graph courtesy of the Museum of Modern Art, New York.

on filing Mies's buildings as either Schinkelesque and neo-neoclassical or asym-metrically oddball-modern.

With Mies's gleaming post in mind, I am beginning to rethink his primi-tivizing elementalism as not unlike the rich ambiguity of (a different) primi-tivity and (a similar) urbanity in the sculpture of Brancusi. Mies's shining needle of a post has a better than vaguely Brancusian aspect, all the more for its similarity, in section, to a cruciform stone base type developed by Brancusi and employed, notably, under the sleek, polished bronze *Bird in Space* (ca. 1941) in the Museum of Modern Art. Consider the perhaps small gaps in this sequence of motifs: *Bird in Space*/propeller form/Barcelona chair/Barcelona-Tugendhat "column"/Corbusian biplane structure. Of course, to speak of Mies's lintelless post (in analogy with Brancusian baselessness) in this way is to approach it as a freestanding sculptural object.[3] In architectural space the thing is also an active punctuation that tends, practically, to be out of the way and, formally, to relate across space to the plane of a nearby wall – which brings us to the other singularly stunning element of classic Barcelona-Tugendhat conception.

Subject today to extremes of possible negative apprehension – Veblenesque

97

"conspicuous consumption," uptight bourgeois *luxus,* revolutionary puritanism, or a 1980s-style, might-as-well-eat-cake inflationary splurge – is the
splendid, pristine onyx, yes, *onyx,* freestanding major wall of this, the
German state pavilion for the international exposition at Barcelona. Kant
says that the splendid combines the beautiful with the sublime, and, for me
as a youth, at least, Mies's sheer splendor here occasioned unalloyed admiration. I did not know about the onyx until years later, even if, at the
stage of adolescent Miesophilia, that would have been all right with me.
Pure splendor didn't seem to need so much apology back then anyway,
except that youth has a way of sidestepping the unpleasant struggles of the
parental generation in favor of whatever big guy gets big things done (witness
Mies's own early monument to Bismarck).

At any rate, I went right for the sheer magnificence of that Barcelona wall,
in its apt proportions, its obviously astute placement in the plan and space
and, undeniably, its heady extremism – all in all, a perfectionist ideality in
which anything like a literally semiprecious materiality would have meant only
a bonus of delight. Not that I was wrong either, and it might be simplistically
pseudoradical to imagine as much. For one thing, the lithe visual massiveness
of that onyx wall lets it participate with the thin plane of the roof and the slab
of the floor in a set of three kindred sculpturesque planes. Thanks to Wolf
Tegethoff, we now know that the Barcelona wall was not monolithic, but
was built hollow, like a box, of slices from one block of the rarest *onyx doré*
from the Atlas Mountains, which Mies (who had apprenticed in his father's
stonemason business) was thrilled to find at a German stone contractor's place.[4]
Hence, it can be seen at once as something of an extension and something of
an inversion of the use of marble veneer as interior "cladding" – much as the
Barcelona Pavilion itself, as a De Stijl/suprematist totality, is like a spatial,
"inside" counterpart to Mies's massy, "outside" brick monument to Karl
Liebknecht and Rosa Luxemburg, of three years earlier (destroyed by the Nazis).

After all, the pavilion was a real showpiece. Functionalistically, it had to
satisfy fewer utilitarian requirements than a fair-sized gas station (and does
not Ed Ruscha's pop, and popular, 1963 *Standard Station, Amarillo, Texas,*
followed by the silkscreen *Standard Station,* of 1966, with its perspectively
plunging flat roof and spindly posts, involve at least some covert Miesian
spoof?). Artistically, the pavilion was so pure as to amount to an open-form
sculpture in which, it just so happened, one could walk around – an "installation," in a way, exemplifying Weimar German with-itness simply in
exhibiting itself.

As Mies's textbook example of ultramodernity, the Barcelona Pavilion was
significant not only for the critical cause of the as yet unbaptized International
Style but also in the popular diffusion of functionalist ideas after World War
II. Just how such classic work of Mies might be seen as refined, not merely
reductive, as architecturally imaginative and affirmative rather than nihilisti-
cally protominimal, by now necessarily concerns two important aphorisms
long associated with Mies, but which have histories, or at least prehistories,
of their own, the more famous being "Less is more." Some years ago, a notes-

and-queries column in the *New York Times* sought to trace this one back to Hesiod ("The half is more than the total," *Works and Days,* 40), with the more telling "Not so honest would be more honest," from Lessing's 1772 play *Emilia Galotti,* followed up by an allusion, two years later but much closer to home, by the poet Wieland: "And less is often more, as Lessing's Prince has taught us." Additionally noted was a monologue in Browning's "Andrea del Sarto" in which a painter tells his wife and model that he knows at least twenty other painters who do "much less" than a fortuitous smear caused by an accidental swipe of her gown against a wet canvas: "Well, less is more, Lucrezia."

The other, more problematic, Miesian dictum, that "God is in the detail[s]," has been clouded by misunderstanding. A few years ago a distinguished art critic quoted it as if it concerned *proliferate* detail, which is the opposite of its true sense. With this saying Mies unambiguously meant to identify a moral, caring perfectionism in seemingly insignificant craftsmanly matters, such as the clear-cut sharpness of an unadorned corner or the perfect join of two smooth blocks or panels. Recently, opinions were aired in "Chapter and Verse" columns in *Harvard Magazine* as to the source, which a consensus associates with Aby Warburg, while some insist on a further connection with Flaubert. Some twenty years ago, however, when I asked Rudolf Wittkower, who was active in the Warburg Institute from 1934 to 1956, about it, he testified categorically that Warburg himself took the eventually Miesian dictum from the historian Jules Michelet.

The real meaning of "God is in the detail" (or, more riskily, "the details"), is worth getting at. Once, a cousin of mine in the building trades, whom I was helping to build a utilitarian hunter's shack, used this craftsmanly commonplace: "You're not building a church." Well, by the same token, in whatever he designed, Mies was *always* "building a church." This true sense of Mies's dictum, and why it is weakened in the plural form, may be clearer in light of a passage in Kant's *Observations on the Feeling of the Beautiful and the Sublime:*

> There is a certain spirit of minutiae (*esprit de bagatelles*) which exhibits a kind of fine feeling but aims at quite the opposite of the sublime. A taste for something because it is very *artful* and laborious – verses that can be read both forward and backward, riddles, clocks in finger rings, flea chains, and so on. A taste for everything that is overparticular and in a painful fashion *orderly,* although without use – for example, books that stand neatly arrayed in long rows in bookcases, and an empty head that looks at them and takes delight, rooms that like optical cabinets are prim and washed and extremely clear, together with an inhospitable and morose host who inhabits them. A taste for all that is *rare,* little though its inherent worth otherwise might be. . . . Such persons stand under great suspicion that in knowledge they will be grubs and cranks, but in morals they will be without feeling for all that is beautiful or noble in a free way.[5]

The factor of sublimity that makes Mies's "splendor" possible rules out the "spirit of minutiae" and affirms simplicity as a function of care in respect to elements of larger wholes. (What could be less merely "reductive"?)

Of course, the splendid overlaps with the monumental, and on that, in Mies's work, the history books refer to his winning 1933 project for a new Reichsbank in Berlin. Early in that year the Nazis came to power, and one does wonder how far Mies would have obliged their sweet tooth for the monumental. Matters are not helped by an article published by the young Philip Johnson at the end of 1933: from culturally "reactionary" and "conservative" Nazis, Johnson distinguished others, "revolutionaries who are ready to fight for modern art," and offered that "a good modern Reichsbank would satisfy the new craving for monumentality . . . " (with friends like this . . .).[6] Even if one allows that a phraseology of "art for the times" obtained in the secessions of the turn of the century, and that an established Hegelian rhetoric enabled Mies himself, as innocently early as 1924, to speak of architecture as "the will of an epoch translated into space,"[7] the problem of the emergence of a Miesian monumentality, just when the Nazis were shopping around, remains.

An article appeared in the United States a year after Johnson's wherein one Walter Curt Behrendt, the very "Baurat or Architectural Advisor to the Finance Ministry" of the "former" German government (no party mentioned), speculates on modern or "experimental" architecture as appropriate to the times, illustrating works of Mies; it isn't easy to tell where this bird, ultra-corporate in attitude, was coming from, but *The Magazine of Art* (sponsored by the American Federation of Arts) liked one passage enough to print it in big letters on its back cover: "Comprehending reality means for the architect no less than the recognition of the new ideas of order rising up out of the creative and formative forces of the times and integrating his own work with these ideas."[8] *Whose* ideas of order; *whose* monumentality?

This whole problem gets frustratingly tangled: "monumentality" can be esthetically good or bad; if totalitarians of the right have craved it, so have totalitarians of the left, not to mention nontotalitarians; and it can be avoided out of ungenerous cravenness too. Even with plenty of new evidence around us some people still honestly do not understand how readily big-time capitalism translates under strain into protofascist forms. Others cannot conceive of any apolitical neutrality, not even, or especially, for one genuinely absorbed in art – as if all not with one were necessarily against. Also, by a line of thought in which the Reformation still echoes, some would deny that even a downright evil artist might be capable of good work – this, oddly but often enough, despite resort to the Baudelairean-Satanic as somehow cute (what do they think evil *is?*). Anyway, it was with the Reichsbank project that Miesian "monumentality," not intimated even in the "city-planning" aspect of earlier public housing work, bloomed.

While Mies's architecture is citified and citifying, his sense of the city included professional-class "garden districts" before such turfs split off into suburban realms of their own after World War II. This is part of a larger contradiction in Mies's generation, with its fantasy "garden cities" projected from drawing boards in Paris and Berlin, while for Mies personally there was experience of a bush-league city, Aachen (Charlemagne's church notwithstanding), before the big time in Berlin. I mean that after 1937, when Mies came to America, a "super-block" like his campus for the Illinois Institute of Technology, or even the Seagram Building on its agoraphiliac terrace, should probably be "thought back" as Euro-urbanistic, instead of mistaken simply as Westchester-corporate – even if as time passes the distinction eventually lose its edge and becomes antiquarian. Yet there is indeed something amusingly, dudishly assimilationist in thinking of Mies actually designing a "ranch house," which the Resor House, on Resor Ranch, near Wilson, Wyoming, was to be – even though the magnificent Tugendhat House was already "urban-fringe" and the ranch-house stereotype, with its own Wrightean roots (Mies was carrying some coals to Newcastle, too), got popularized only later.

Two well-known drawings from the Resor House project (1939–40) make use of photocollage. In this they anticipate the reproduction of Picasso's *Guernica* mobilized to define the plane of a major wall in Mies's 1942 project for a "Museum for a Small City," which has, in addition, two planes (walls) defined by horizontal strips of rather late-Monetesque, water-lilian landscape photographs sliced through by the thin verticals that support the roof – plus a couple of sculptures (yet *more* Kolbes?) punctuating the space near and far.

The Resor House studies also rely on the concreteness of photocollage elements to convey the fictive concreteness-to-be of built planes in imagined architectural space. The graphic space-constructions of El Lissitzky would be pertinent, except his isomorphic, diagonal perspective is a "real" system for evoking a poetic space, whereas Mies, more pragmatically seeking a metaphorical equivalent, keeps literalness rhyming with literalness. This, I think, is why his pasted-on pictures are all parallel and head-on as well as flat on the sheet. The Resor drawings, as a result, have a synthetic cubist aspect, with the "architectonic" of cubism literalizingly manifest in the architectural design.

One Resor drawing has three photocollage elements representing architectural planes with the three elements of significantly different sorts: all are technically photographic, but one "is" so much woodgraining, à la Braque; the next, in the middle ground, is an art reproduction; and the third, which is the only one not in color and which by a nice irony represents a transparent window-wall (or rather the view therethrough), is the only "photographic photo" per se. Because, as Tegethoff reports, the reproduction is actually a *detail* of a painting by Klee, there is a sequence, too, from the woodgrain as mere arbitrary "sample," to the Klee as a significant portion, and on to the big, spliced, CinemaScope *unendliche Landschaft* of the West, cowboys and all.

To read back, from (for the European at least) a "natural" landscape that is only culturally conventionalized to a still charming degree, past the Klee as art (and Expressionist-Bauhaus art at that), is to come up against the dumb inertness of the woodgrain, which might as well be Formica. Such a progression involves the whole large question of a modern architecture so totalized that it can only use sculpture for visual "load-bearing" relational-compositional purposes, and that, needless to say, has little unaccounted-for wall surface to spare for painting. Here a quotation, by way of Tegethoff's book, is interesting as much for its conviction as for its tinge of defensiveness: Herr Tugendhat, it seems, once said of the living and dining areas of his famous Brno house, "The incomparable patterning of the marble and the natural graining of the wood do not take the place of art, but they do participate in the art, in the space, which is here art."[9] Tegethoff, incidentally, while identifying the Klee image as a detail from a 1928 painting called *Colorful Repast,* does not remark the possible expressive/Expressionistic appropriateness of that work for a dining area.

The (nineteenth-century?) landscape panorama in the "rear" of the same photocollage is transfixed by one of Mies's slim piers and by an even slimmer window mullion, an idea on which the other Resor House study, which is barely a "drawing" at all, concentrates. Here only a panoramic, Tetonesque (Wilson, Wyoming, is near Grand Tetons National Park) landscape photograph appears, cut through vertically by a post and a mullion at left and a mullion, then post, at right, with a few faint lines defining and extending the posts and understatedly framing the expanse of glass wall as almost completely "soaked up" with the view. There is a certain precedent for this, and for Mies's other sliced-through landscape photographs, in the vertically sliced "phototriptychs" by the photographer F. Holland Day, at the turn of the century; but, given the intrinsic sublimity of the Western landscapes used by Mies, what really come to mind, from a decade later than Mies's Resor project, are the "zips" of Barnett Newman's "American-sublime" paintings, especially those with a panoramically horizontal format.

In a spirited attack on latter-day attempts to set photography over and against painting, the abstract painter Richard Hennessy once illustrated this very Resor House drawing in dual juxtaposition with, on the left, a Muybridge Western mountain landscape photo of about 1871, and, on the right, a 1961 Newman: for Hennessy, these works by the two other artists represent extremes of "the romantic sublime in its geological and human manifestations," with Mies's implied synthesis as "a touchstone of twentieth-century humanism, proposing a particular relationship between ourselves and our landscape."[10] Today one might also detect hints of self-consciousness here, with the urbane European slicker doing "The Big Sky" as a number, or even the Resors themselves as sophisticates self-producing their own, Marie-Antoinette-like mise en scène of "ranch life"; yet Mies's poetic projection retains an independent ingenuity.

The "expressivity" of Mies's later architecture is so highly sublimated that it has little to do with whatever Hitchcock once meant by his early "weirdness." However surprisingly, it can indeed bear some analytic comparison with abstract expressionism. Even mentioning Pollock in the same long breath as Mies van der Rohe is not necessarily as farfetched as might have been supposed. Peter Blake, the architectural historian, knew both men (of Mies he said, "like Jackson, he wasn't verbal but intuitive"); Pollock, it happens, was fascinated by Mies's "Museum for a Small City" idea, and he and Blake toyed with building such a structure to house his own paintings, behind his Long Island studio.[11] By at least the late 1940s, work by Mies can indeed be looked at with Pollock in mind – that other master of the abstract-sublime, who hailed from the next county from the Resors (the cowboy posturing of Pollock tends to be discounted nowadays, but does he not bear the name of Jackson, Wyoming?).

Those who see merely "mechanical" grids in the facades of (especially) Mies's later high-rise buildings ought to drop the middlebrow complacence (encouraged by Saul Steinberg cartoons) and look more receptively. Even in two dimensions, on the facades and flanks of tall buildings – and the skyscraper, too, has its esthetic of sublimity – Mies's sense of an articulated "all-overness" not unlike Pollock's makes itself felt. For example, the rectilinear structural expressiveness of the exteriors of Mies's pair of beautifully mutually offset apartment blocks in Chicago at 860 and 880 Lake Shore Drive, 1948–51 (Figure 10), shares in a polyphony of overlapping linear systems that not only stops short at the corners, and is hence discretely composed on each face, but consists as well of superimposed major and minor networks. The boldest grille consists of the floor bands and the principal vertical supports that occur every four windows (behind which the apartments were intended to be "open-plan"); and it has been noted that in each set the two inner windows are actually larger – wider – than the outer ones, which varies the overall rhythm.[12] As with Pollock's classic "drip" paintings, this heavier, wider-gauged system overlays that of the unequally but regularly spaced window mullions, which is itself undercut by light horizontals at the window openings, less than halfway up from each floor. At the same time, the major grid, almost like a solo part against a *basso continuo,* takes control of the overall scale, making more visually manageable each building face as five or three *bays* wide, rather than comprising twenty or twelve confusable units. (It seems relevant that Mies used to listen to Bach while he worked at the drafting table.)

Mies himself must been at home in Chicago, what with its important earlier modern architecture, its Bauhaus School (later Chicago Institute) of Design, directed by his Bauhaus colleague Moholy-Nagy, and his own new home base, the Illinois Institute of Technology (originally Armour Institute), which he got to shape from 1939 on – its individual buildings and its increasingly subtle and complex plan.

If the art of the time of one's birth becomes crucial in the development of one's historical consciousness – well, then, here is where I came in: with Mies van der Rohe's beautifully squared-away, ultratech Minerals and Metals Research Building for I.I.T., dating (as I do) from 1942, which I first encountered in a magazine when I was a teenager. I went for it straightaway, along with Mondrian, whose classic compositions its *fachwerk-* (or half-timber-) like bricked-in end treatment and fine-tuned rectilinear siting in relation to sister structures it immediately recalled. Hero worship made me not only want to become an architect, but to study specifically at Illinois Tech, what with the

10. Ludwig Mies van der Rohe, Apartment houses at 860 and 880 Lake Shore Drive, Chicago, 1948–51. Photograph courtesy of Hedrich-Blessing.

presence there of Mies's spare, ascetic little interdenominational chapel as well as his Crown Hall (1952–6) – the school of architecture and in a sense the master's temple of *Baukunst,* or "building-art."

For Chicago, too (I also remember as news), Mies projected a magnificent convention hall in 1953, known on the outside by its giant cross-bracing and, for the interior, by another remarkable photocollage, in which a vast plain rectangular chamber is defined by the crystalline trusswork of a nobly high roof of amazingly broad unsupported span, marble-paper walls and a pasted-on crowd scene below. The enthusiastic crowd photograph deserves attention. It both repeats (like wallpaper) and is truncated, *en collage,* like so much tele-vision footage. Placards indicate that it comes from the Republican convention of the previous year, 1952, when Eisenhower defeated Senator Robert A. Taft, who had condemned the New Deal as socialistic. At the time the Korean War was in full swing, with Americans fighting as U.N. troops. President Truman had already fired General Douglas MacArthur, Allied commander in the Pacific during World War II and U.N. commander in Korea, for wanting to attack Communist China. In the ensuing election I rooted for Adlai Stevenson, the Democratic governor of Illinois; but Mies, whom I see as a temperamentally conservative refugee who had become an American citizen during the war, in 1944, must, forgivably if not ideally, have shared the manifest Eisenhower enthusiasm of the Chicago convention crowd.[13] Otherwise, being able to remember back before Mayor Daley's "townie" Nazism of 1968, also in Chi-cago, means that I can actually still feel uplifted by Mies's big American flag (actually a real toy one) hanging down, calm as a grazing horse, into an *aula maxima* (no suburban "center," this) for his adopted hometown.

Strange, now, to think back to a time, 1958, when the Seagram Building was new. Allow me to sketch in some more personal background: it was around this time, even arguably with this building, that Mies attained his widest renown. When I was a youth, Jack Kerouac was working within walk-ing distance on his famous novel of the age *On the Road* (1957); not that this would have meant anything to me: I was watching television. But as a teenager I would occasionally visit the Museum of Modern Art, and I remember mul-tiple trips to admire Junzo Yoshimura's traditional-style Japanese house (with "beat" Zen garden), erected in the museum garden in 1953. Later came a full-scale mock-up, inside the Modern, of a corner of the coming Seagram Build-ing, this with real bronze detail and supplied with mirrors, above and below, for vertical extrapolation – which made you feel unnervingly suspended half-way up the plunging facade.

My adolescent hero worship of Mies was as unbounded as that mock-up with its infinitely repeating, not to say regressing, mirror images. I can even understand how the elegantly limber rigor of Mies's "classicism," so like a handsome and practically Tolstoian military rectitude, must have felt as libi-dinal as some other kid's seeing a recruiting poster and dropping out of school to join the Marines. No wonder a passing shock of aesthetic recognition came, in maturity, on first sight of the former Nazi buildings by the Königsplatz in Munich, though it then became easy (easier, apparently, than for some who now toy aesthetically with cheap thrills of fascistic extremism) to distinguish Paul Ludwig Troost's fetishistic frigidity – using stone like Styrofoam, fixing a kind of sparely pleated detail as if with loads of starch – from the humanely cool self-possession of the real Miesian thing. All this must have its oedipal aspect, as Mies himself – who, tearing away from traditional architecture, had the brainstorm of the onyx wall in a stoneyard (like his father's) – might have understood. My father was an engineer, and I clung to Mies for sublimating the mundane-technical into something higher, namely, art. More and more, in maturity, I find in the engineering aspect of Mies's work a mysterious source of splendor.

My access to at least the threshold of the technical mystery might be by roundabout return, through art history and theory, to the would-be philo-sophical banter of high school in the time of the Seagram, when a few of us would hang out and talk, often enough about Wright and Le Corbusier and Mies. Thanks to the brothers who taught us, anything philosophical was somehow Thomistic, whether for or against. And Thomism, the scholastic philosophy, is certainly relevant to Mies, who as a boy attended the cathedral school at Aachen. It seems that later, having asked Peter Behrens, their master, what the task of architecture is, and gotten no adequate answer, the young Mies and his budding architect pals, who already knew that what they were after concerned the nature of truth, were "delighted to find a definition of truth by Thomas Aquinas: 'Adequatio intellectus et rei,' or as a modern phi-losopher expresses it in the language of today: 'Truth is the significance of fact.' "[14]

My Miesianism would carry along even to later study of the protomodern "rationalist" view of the Gothic, with Gothic structure as almost an antetype for civil engineering by the eighteenth century in France. So imagine the earlier impact, practically simultaneous with the Seagram Building, of the paperback of Panofsky's lectures, delivered at a Benedictine monastery in 1951, on *Gothic Architecture and Scholasticism* (1957). Understandably, specialists have criticized the book, but the totalizing logic of its vision, in sympathetic application of the Thomistic system, is just what lent it utterly Miesian appeal – as, for instance, with its, well, Panofsko-Thomistic "postulate of clarification for clarification's sake,"[15] or the parallel Panofsky draws between gestalt psy-chology and Saint Thomas's remark, "The senses delight in things duly pro-portioned as in something akin to them; for the sense, too, is a kind of reason as is every cognitive power."[16] Even now I am tempted to relate to Mies's "Gothically" attenuated cruciform pier of the Barcelona Pavilion and Tug-endhat House Panofsky's exposition of the "*Pilier cantonné*, the columnar pier with four applied colonnettes," which "permitted the 'expression' of the trans-verse ribs of the nave and side aisles" in Gothic churches.[17]

It wasn't just a question of getting New York blasé, once everybody had talked about the Seagram Building and it was there to be taken for granted, nor even the lump-it acceptance of "modern" as a look, ostensibly on grounds of efficiency, that becalmed my Miesomania – and not only mine. The shocking demolition of old Pennsylvania Station in 1964 took a lot of fun out of the modern movement in New York, whether in the sense that the death of a father begins to make the oedipal affair seem moot, or at least by affecting even great modern buildings with a touch of survivor guilt. (I do remember, when the great station was threatened, wishing its splendid steel-and-glass train shed could be saved and used for a museum of abstract expressionism, with big canvases hanging on wires in the vast free space, and I may or may not have been influenced in this by Mies's projected "Museum for a Small City.") When Charles Luckman Associates – a name that deserves to live in infamy – replaced one of the great buildings of this hemisphere with a glitzy office slab and a giant redneck-suburban trash can in 1968, students of architecture were afloat, if not adrift, in theory and, reasonably enough, in politics, over and against the aesthetic matters of building.

Mies was a hero of art, and today we are offered "stars" instead of heroes. Perhaps only the deep-seated philistinism of the query "What's hot?" can explain how a prodigal son of Mies, Philip Johnson, has kept busy with his stylistic boutique, or account for an I. M. Pei, also in Corbu eyeglasses, as passing, in effect, for a Louis Kahn. The equivalent in writing on art is all the hurried, newsy verbiage, especially a form of "theory" as promotional as anything else, that mounts up in unmanageable volume yet never really *builds*. Even Fredric Jameson, justifiably attacking the philistinism of Tom Wolfe, jogs right along without a lost breath into an irresponsible claim that post-modernism, too, "was . . . the recognition of a basic failure on the architects' own terms . . . the Mallarméan 'zero degree' of Mies's towers quite unexpectedly began to generate a whole over-population of the shoddiest glass boxes in all the major urban centers of the world."[18] Yet to make of Mies's work a "Mallarméan 'zero degree' " of architecture is ill observed, if not, for that critic, oddly simplistic in its sense of reductivism. And since when do we blame bad follower work on a good master? No; we need more careful and sensitive critique than the hubbub of the market permits (and there is indeed a market for theory too) – not just more picking of teams. Exemplary in this regard is still Meyer Schapiro's critique of Lewis Mumford's *The Culture of Cities* (1938) as pseudo-radical.[19]

Meanwhile, at this writing, abstract painting and sculpture have already been "hot" again for months, and even minimalism, believe it or not, is getting warmer. Sorry, but Mies, as ever, is still positively cool.

Postscript

Adolf Loos's remark that "the architect is a bricklayer who has studied Latin" might apply with special profundity to Mies. The architect Aldo Rossi quotes it only to caution that Loos himself was defending a simple sense of the building task, akin to those of less cultivated craftsmen, against all " 'modernist' architects" whose work has facilitated a "utopia that is a slave to power."[20] But thanks partly to the influence of Rossi, among others, the different critical problem at the moment (1992) is that otherwise useful antiutopian critique has tended to delete whatever innate, bricklayer-like value there is in the work of individual artists such as Mies.

Despite the ornamental plainness of his surfaces, Loos, for his part, had tolerated more artifice in the handling of materials than later functionalists ready to invoke his name or Mies's would admit. Two newspaper articles published by him in Vienna in 1898 are significant. In the first, "Building Materials," Loos as much as adumbrates the gleaming onyx wall of the Barcelona Pavilion in condemning, à la Ruskin and also Morris (whose still recent revisionist wallpapers may be alluded to), the unacknowledged slavish labor that a finish of luxurious simplicity implies: "People say 'material' but they mean 'work.' . . . Our hearts will beat with reverential awe at the sight of the polished granite wall."[21] As interested in new possibilities for poured concrete as he is ready to abhor its use to simulate stone, Loos regrets that his sense of material integrity is misconstrued: "It is characteristic of our Viennese situation that I who am against the violation of materials, who have combated imitation energetically, am dismissed as being a 'materialist.' Just look at the sophistry: these people who attribute such a value to materials that they have no fear of their becoming characterless and who freely resort to surrogates."[22] Clever argument! – as if, say, using vinyl to imitate marble indicated not so much a phoniness of plastic as a kind of idolatry of marble. For his special pavilion, it might be argued, Mies had the exceptional opportunity to take a luxury material in stride.

In the second article, explaining his "Principle of Cladding," Loos, stimulated by the materialist theory of Gottfried Semper, frames his principle as a kind of double negative: "The law goes like this: we must work in such a way that a confusion of the material clad with its cladding is impossible." By this standard, no metaphorical substitution of one material for another is ruled out, only any one material standing in, with absurd literalness, for itself. "That means, for example, that wood may be painted any color except one – the color of wood."[23] All the more interesting in light of Jean Baudrillard's oddly puritanical sense of stucco work as tantamount to vulgar "plastic" culture[24] is Loos's example that "stucco can take any ornament with just one exception – rough brickwork,"[25] meaning that since stucco is customarily used to clad just such walls, it may look like anything but that sort of work (otherwise, why bother?); likewise for him, a by no means offhand analogy with underwear: "Woven underclothing" or tights "may be dyed any color at all, just not skin color."

Three quarters of a century later, under the two epigrams " 'Less is more' (Mies)" and " 'Less is a bore' (Venturi)," Charles Jencks devoted a chapter of his since-influential critical history of modernist architecture to "The Problem of Mies."[26] As if shaken by the liberal skepticism of Lewis Mumford, Jencks performs a public disenchantment in which both Mies's "Platonic" idealism (just as crudely, Aristotelianism too) and his "elitism" are scandalized as "farce." Jencks sets out from "The Case Against 'Modern Architecture,' " in Mumford's *The Highway and the City* (1964): "Mies van der Rohe used the facilities offered by steel and glass to create eloquent monuments of nothingness"; having "the dry style of machine forms without the contents," these issued in an "apotheosis of the compulsive, bureaucratic spirit."[27] Bashing Mies with Karl Popper's postwar anti–Platonic classic *The Open Society and Its Enemies,* he invokes "social context" only to proclaim by a barefaced, Spencerian evolutionism that "as civilization becomes more open, it makes more semantic distinctions between building types, a discrimination which Mies's 'neutralizing skin' does everything to ignore."[28] "As civilization becomes more *open* . . . "?! Today it would be better to say that as culture becomes ever less escapably multinational-corporate, it makes more *merely* "semantic" distinctions, between human lives or tasks as well as between buildings or commodities.

Jencks plays to the grandstand by brushing aside discriminations that "only a connoisseur" could make: if Y is content to see less than X does, one had better defer to X's report.[29] He is right that "in the best of Mies's work we are brought up to the question of belief."[30] But where he claims that at Mies's Lafayette Park development, in Detroit, of 1955–63, "Bathroom vents, television aerials, etc. shatter the pretensions of 'perfect form,' "[31] he not only exaggerates, he perhaps betrays an idealism frustrated or repressed: if anything, the Lafayette Park townhouses look quite tolerant of such minor disarray of everyday life. I myself have recently observed that at the largely ignored Colonnade Towers, near New York but in unfashionable Newark, a spin-off of Mies's Chicago apartment house projects standing beside an abandoned public housing project of low blocks, even the current tenants' bedraggled "draping" of the window walls with bedspreads and sheets has not spoiled the crisp, drip-dry appearance of the elegant towers facing each other across a (still tidy) lawn.

Far too impatiently does Jencks dismiss Mies's 1952 Chapel at Illinois Tech, in Chicago, for supposedly not looking like a chapel, without even entertaining the thought that it might be a finely wrought understatement specifically conceived as the chapel for a technical institute. To allude to the famous chapter of *The Education of Henry Adams:* if Mumford meant that the cult of the dynamo, somehow minus the idolized dynamo, might suggest the holy architectural cultus that Henry Adams otherwise celebrated in *Mont-Saint-Michel and Chartres,* one might prepare to agree. Together with the I.I.T. Boiler Plant, finished before the Chapel in 1950 and itself a towering bricked-up box with "clerestory" windows and even a "flying buttress" of angle-iron – features that might all too easily have suited the cliché of a college chapel – the Chapel may in fact form an interesting pair in opposition, as a small pure horizontal block with three-bay-windowed front giving, without distraction to worshipers, an inviting and hardly semiotically ambiguous view of the altar and altar cross to passersby without distracting worshipers within.[32]

In any case, that, in practice, buildings are not so much antiornamental as perfectionistically ornamental totalities is the real basis for inquiring how their starkness does and does not carry over from Loos. In steel and bronze, in glass and even marble, Mies, this great classicist of the technological age who was in fact the son of a stonecutter, was not so unlike a stonemason who had studied Latin after all.

8

Post Tenebras Lux
Speculations on Ronchamp

For M.G.C.

L E Corbusier's pilgrimage chapel of Notre-Dame-du-Haut, Ronchamp, stands on a hill named Bourlémont in the Vosges Mountains, above the river Saône, not far from the Swiss border. This, the famous "Ronchamp Chapel," replaces a nineteenth-century church heavily damaged in World War II, though there is said to have been a church on or near the site since the fourth century and a pagan temple before that. Le Corbusier began his designs in 1950, and the church was built between 1953 and 1955. Although Ronchamp was taken as an abrupt or even unforgiveable departure by some orthodox modernists, certain aspects, at least, of the genesis of the church may be traced back to the immediately postwar years and perhaps even much earlier.

The freewheeling formal jouissance, the decorously billowing voluptuousness of this functioning Catholic church dedicated to "Our Lady," obviously rankled certain "functionalists" as much for their own puritanism as for its ostensible religiosity. An architectural "crisis of rationalism" was declared.[1] Certain critics, including Lewis Mumford and Nikolaus Pevsner, would try to rationalize the odd building as a modern-eclectic recollection of German expressionist projects of the 1920s – as out of character as that would have had to seem to Walter Gropius and Sigfried Giedion.[2]

Immediately, the communist art historian (and future mayor of Rome) Giulio Carlo Argan was furious. Questioning Ronchamp's "downright druidic" primitivism as idolatrous, Argan saw Le Corbusier's departure from rationality as "gratuitously" counting for religiosity: "So," he asked sarcastically, "after the *machine à habiter,* Le Corbusier now wants to patent a *machine à prier?*"[3] Actually, as a Catholic artist, Jean Charlot, for one, was quite at ease with the idea of a *machine à prier.*[4] Really, why not a *machine à habiter* for God? Argan thought the church rather baroque (an idea Le Corbusier did not like)[5] yet contradictorily neoplastic in its spare whiteness. As to neoplasticism, however, he managed to ignore the beautiful irregular rectilinear fenestration of the south wall as comparable to the spirit of, say, Mondrian's *Composition No. 3 with Color Planes* of 1917 (Gemeentemuseum, The Hague), in which varying rectangular pastel rectangles are suspended with a beautiful asymmetric tension in a continuous field of white. Argan was enraged that Le Corbusier, a nonbeliever, should duplicitously advance religion as social control, claiming that Ronchamp's "ostentatious primitivism isn't religious at all, it's political."[6] He simply didn't think a modernist religious architecture possible, since modernism is essentially secular[7] (a not uncommon circular argument).

Peter Blake, unconstrained by a simplistic, and basically materialist, sense of function, was not the only critic to excuse the Ronchamp Chapel as sculpturesque: "The great curved masses ... might be the result of some acoustic determination, as Corbu declared; but they formed, together with the deep, irregularly spaced slot windows, a mysterious aura that was as reminiscent of the catacombs or the massive stone monasteries of the Middle Ages as it was of some dimly understood spatial concepts of today and tomorrow."[8] Later, Charles Jencks could concede it highly metaphorical but not religious standing, at least not on its designer's part.[9]

What becomes more interesting to consider, a generation or two after Ronchamp, is how such a definitively spiritual commission could have been approached by an artist-architect whose own occasional remarks on spirit (including a "Poem to the Right Angle" written in the time of Ronchamp) tended, at least in America, to be dismissed as mere poeticizing promotion for an essentially materialist program.

For two reasons I cannot follow Argan in thinking that here Le Corbusier may have been like an eighteenth-century cleric reading Voltaire in private but dispensing public pieties.[10] What difference does it make, in the first place, what the architect's possibly confused religious intent, if any, was compared with the possible religiosity of the result? Nor is this simply a theoretical problem of intentionality in art: since early in the Protestant Reformation, one of the sharp distinctions between Catholic and Reformed understanding concerns the Catholic insistence that even an unworthy priest effects worthy sacraments, sacraments being sufficiently a matter of (objective and social) form not to depend for their efficacy on the (subjective and individual) spiritual worthiness of their agents.[11] How, then, to take a working Catholic church by a religiously inactive Protestant architect?

Second, on the personal side, it is not really so easy to be sure where Le Corbusier (Jeanneret) himself was "coming from," beyond the too-simple fact that he was not religious in adulthood. Apparently the claim that with his mother and pious live-in aunt the architect was brought up a Lutheran[12] takes literally a wisecrack about being Luther's subject rather than the pope's that probably indicated only a very general affiliation with reformed Christianity. General-purpose Swiss Calvinism is no doubt more to the point, including Zwingli, with his vision of a primitively pure Christianity restored.[13] It also seems significant that Le Corbusier referred to his ancestors as Albigensians –

heretics of the twelfth and thirteenth centuries who ate no meat and held the body in such contempt that they believed Christ a phantom incapable of suffering, death, and resurrection.

More on Protestantism later; but something basic that deserves to be established is characteristically Protestant insofar as it displays the biblical literacy of a layman. For at least one of Corbusier's famous dicta should be documented as scripturally conversant: "Eyes which see not," a slogan of the architect's *Esprit Nouveau* period that resounds in *Vers une architecture* (1923), deserves to be considered a fairly obvious biblical allusion (Isaiah 6:9; Jeremiah 5:21; Ezekiel 12:2; Mark 8:18). However ironically, the residual religious culturality of a modernist like Le Corbusier would have run deeper than that of those today brought up on loss of faith in modernity itself, let alone in God.

Whether or not one considers the cult of inspiration through nature in which the young Jeanneret indulged as culturally Protestant, it is known that an initial inspiration for the Ronchamp Chapel – most specifically for its hollow "bivalve" roof – came when the architect picked up a crab shell on a Long Island beach in 1947, and marveled at its structural strength. In this, it would seem, is a topos of some significance. Lamarck had been fascinated by shells;[14] but the primevally religious connotations of sea shells were a topic of discussion in France from the early 1920s, when in burials from as early as the Paleolithic in the Dordogne, shells from the remote Mediterranean were found, and likewise on the Côte d'Azur, from the Atlantic.[15] In the 1920s Le Corbusier was already interested in prehistoric, "non-Hellenic" shrines as "aspects of the Mediterranean tradition,[16] and that the shell in question was that of a crab has some such interest in relation to this chapel of the Virgin, since the growth of the crab and other crustaceans, is mythically associated with the lunar vicissitudes of the female principle.[17]

More art historically, while one might think of the nascent inspiration of the crab's shell as rather Northern, even "Gothic," in light of a remarkable drawing of a crab by Dürer, a similarly fascinated exotic naturalism can also be found in Italy perhaps even before mannerism, and with antique precedent at that.[18] And if loose comparison is sometimes made between Ronchamp and projects of the German expressionist architects, it may also be to the Northern point to note a remark critical of Michelangelo's dome of Saint Peter's – soon to be admired, for art and engineering alike, in Le Corbusier's *Vers une architecture* – by a member of the expressionist "Gläserne Kette" (Crystal Chain), Hermann Finsterlin, in the spring of 1920: "Does not the dome of St. Peter's peer out Lilliputlike from the depths of Messina like a giant sea urchin whose spines have been removed?" In the same letter Finsterlin puts an odd, unclassical twist on classical architectural anthropomorphism when he muses on the human body as "a building composed of the tiniest, most emancipated single-cell structures," wondering, "What if we are only living architectural cells, Lilliputian elements that build themselves into the giant proliferation of their organic machinery?"[19] There is, too, Gide's admiring description of the shell-like, clay mud huts of the Massas people of the Congo, as recounted in his *Travels in the Congo* (1927).

Moreover, it happens that the irregular ground plan, at least, of the Ronchamp Chapel uncannily resembles the plan of the contemplative thatched *cabane* of rock, so nature-attuned, this called the "Maison de Philosophe," built for (though never occupied by) Jean-Jacques Rousseau by the Marquis de Girardin on the grounds of his estate at Eremenonville, near Paris, c. 1778. As published in plan, elevation, and section in an engraving, the plan of this little nature-contemplative hermetic cell for the famous quasi-Calvinist Swiss philosopher was itself quite like the form of a clamshell, and with bulging walls of irregular thickness and a door and two windows in one curved side.[20]

It is worth considering that, provided Le Corbusier's picking up of the crab shell on Long Island is accurately dated to 1947,[21] he probably did this on the East End of the island, where at the time he could conceivably have been conversing with Marie-Alain Couturier, the French Dominican priest who did so much for modern art and artists, including Le Corbusier, and who had spent the war years on the East End and was in fact revisiting New York in 1947.[22] In any case, the architect's own early thoughts, with Ronchamp approaching, are interesting: "The crab shell . . . will be placed on the stupidly but usefully thick walls; to the south, the light will be made to enter. There won't be any windows – the light will enter everywhere, like a stream."[23]

But Le Corbusier was then also already in the midst of an unsuccessful religious project in the south of France that included a pilgrimage church, his 1946–8 "City of Contemplation" in the Sainte-Baume mountains, near Marseilles. This was built to develop the shrine near the cave where, according to the medieval *Golden Legend* (popular until the Reformation), Mary Magdalene, after having convinced the citizens of Marseilles to destroy all their "temples des idoles" and replace them with "églises chrétiennes," spent the last thirty years of her life without earthly sustenance. She lived, it was said, without even water – the absence of water on Bourlémont was part of the program of Ronchamp, and the reason for its rain-scooping waterspout – in a mountain grotto prepared for her by angels.[24] By the early thirteenth century this grotto was taken to have been at La Saint-Baume[25] (more on which, later). The commission, opposed by the hierarchy but defended by Father Couturier, entailed housing for pilgrims and at least one chapel. More or less relatable to Ronchamp in this project are some wildly snaking garden walls[26] and a rather wartime, Quonset-hut-like chapel.[27] But there was also a projected idea for an underground church,[28] a notion that deserves a short side trip.

While ambassador to Japan in 1926, Paul Claudel, the Catholic mystic who died in the year the Ronchamp chapel was dedicated, wrote an extensive description of "an underground church." Given his fascination with the hand as a symbolic motif, Le Corbusier would have noticed Claudel's siting of his imaginary cathedral near Chicago, in commemoration of a Eucharistic congress there and also due to the way, on the map, the Great Lakes suggested to him a giant paw print in the middle of the American continent.[29] Made of reinforced concrete, "a kind of homogeneous . . . material . . . obedient to our hands," the vast, Boullée-sublime "tabernacle" of a church "would be an organism, the most sacred of all, the Heart."[30] Now that "mankind is billowed like a flood, and the Church is swallowed up" as Trinity Church, in New York, is swamped by the towers of Wall Street, Claudel muses, the visionary church might gravitationally retreat underground; and this giant catacomb would be entered via an immense trapdoor so that people might naturally "run down in bulk like grain to the bottom of the silo."[31]

Inside, Claudel's fantasy building would be like a "double Colosseum," an earthly dome surmounted by a heavenly one, and "it should be exactly like the two valves of a shell."[32] Important too is water symbolism obviously evocative of Ezekiel's vision of the Temple, with an immense basin of water covered by an "upper shell," while "the dome . . . could be deeply creased like those great scallop shells which are aptly called holy water stoups," made of concrete.[33] "Understood as a tabernacle and a Holy of Holies,"[34] the envisioned church entailed a Christian, as well as Jewish, sacral darkness: "The Catacombs come in the train of the hidden home of Nazareth, the cave of Bethlehem, the Arimathean's tomb."[35] Claudel's rather literary proposition was not so eccentric as to go unread: Jean Charlot was pleased to discuss it with the writer in New York while Claudel was French ambassador to the United States (1927–33).[36] Still, the project would not be so interesting but that two decades later, soon before taking up the Ronchamp Chapel, Le Corbusier himself actually projected an underground church, dug right into the stone of a mountaintop, at a pilgrimage site.

What, however, could be more different from an underground church than the Ronchamp Chapel crowning its hilltop site and attuned to the "four horizons," as noted in sketching the site? For one thing, it is no mere literalization of an architectural simile to acknowledge that views of the chapel lend it a certain tentlike aspect, and to recall that in *Vers une architecture* Le Corbusier reproduces something that later readers have tended to overlook: a line drawing identified in the English edition of *Towards a New Architecture* (1927) only as a "Primitive Temple" but actually a well-known scholarly reconstruction of Moses' movable Tabernacle in the desert.[37] It had been with deliberate antipathy toward the Canaanite containment of God in a particular temple-dwelling that originally "the prophets set up the tabernacle, that is to say, the mobile tent where God in the desert freely dwelt with His people, but as a traveler, always retaining His freedom to leave, and never belonging to the land through which He was passing"; furthermore, the Jerusalem temple retained some tent features, though traditional reconstructions of the tent-tabernacle are themselves influenced by the sense of the Temple.[38] It remains to be considered that Ronchamp is not only a pilgrimage church, but one designed by a Swiss whose family history included religious exile from France. Meanwhile, the Jewish architectural matter has major Christian analogical interest, for the incarnation statement of the prologue to John's Gospel that reads, "The Word was made flesh and dwelt amongst us," literally means "... and pitched his tent amongst us."[39]

It is possible that Le Corbusier's early ideas for the Ronchamp Chapel were substantially more evocative of the Temple of the Old Law than the visible results. Supposedly, Romchamp simply overthrows the classic modernist flat roof that Le Corbusier himself had done much to establish; at least one interior study, however, shows a flat ceiling, and it seems relevant that the actual Temple of Solomon was flat-roofed.[40] Too, Le Corbusier thought of having the Ronchamp Chapel windowless; the cubical chamber of the Holy of Holies, housing the Ark, was windowless, in accordance with Yahweh's intention to "dwell in darkness" (1 Kings 8:12).[41] Le Corbusier could easily have learned such lore of Jewish temple history from Ernest Renan, whose writings he is known to have enjoyed in his youth; and in respect to Corbusier as begetter of the modernist *maison,* it is worth noting that Renan was the first to consider Solomon's Temple specifically "domestic."[42]

Apropos of "Our Lady of Ronchamp": when the dark enclosure of the Holy of Holies carried over as an "altar-room" enclosed by curtains in the early Christian church, this was symbolically likened the Virgin's womb[43] – that is, to the anatomical basis of her title as "Seat of Wisdom" (in respect to the Son as Logos). If such matters seem like arcana in regard to a presumably agnostic twentieth-century architect, it would hardly have been arcane for him to know another of these honorific titles from the Litany of the Blessed Virgin Mary, "Ark of the Covenant." Father Couturier had arranged with Léger in 1946 to decorate the facade of Notre-Dame-de-Tout-Grâce, at Assy (consecrated 1950), with a mosaic mural of selected titles from this litany also featuring the Virgin's other principal womb-metaphoric title, "Arch d'Alliance" (Ark of the Covenant).[44] Le Corbusier's modern church is also seen as shiplike; and one might even think of that other ark, beached on Mount Ararat, in passing from the (independently) projected subterranean pilgrimage chapel to the built one in full sail atop a hill. Why not, indeed, an ark upon a sacred hill in restatement of Ararat and Horeb-Sinai on the humbly venerable Bourlémont, especially by reference to this well-known and, for Notre-Dame-du-Haut, altogether appropriate Mariological metaphor borrowed from Judaism.

As built, Ronchamp is by no means windowless, but its highly articulated lighting is part of the wonder of the interior, especially the slit of light that floats the otherwise massive roof as it drapes down from three of the four walls on slender points, and the great southern *mur-lumière,* or "Wall of Light," perhaps the most beautiful wall in twentieth-century architecture. This south wall of the church is indeed a special feature (Figure 11).

Unlike the other walls, which make use of brick and stone from the former church on the site, the Wall of Light consists of two curved thin planes, widely and separately diverging (the architect is known to have been musing over dam construction). According to Danièle Pauly, the "skeleton" (*ossature*) of this wall is composed of piers, of beams that join and breach, and of prefab-

11. Le Corbusier (Charles-Edouard Jeanneret), Notre-Dame du Haut, Ronchamp (Haute-Saône), 1950–4. Interior of south wall. Photograph by Ezra Stoller © Esto.

ricated spars (*poutrelles,* i.e., as of an aeronautical wing) bracing the interior and exterior envelopes, which in turn consists of metal lattice sprayed with concrete. The whole long stretch of wall, inside and out, then, consists of two nonparallel concrete "membranes," each four centimetres thick; and "one can imagine this construction as a skeleton (*squelette*) over which is stretched, on the interior and the exterior, a skin (*peau*)."[45] On the inside, the wall plane bends back off the vertical from east to west, whereas on the outside it is most battered back at the west end and straightens toward the east; in other words, the church tapers like an upside-down ship hull to a "prow," with all the old symbolic significance of the *navis* (ship) of a church "nave."

From inside to out, the wall is cut plastically through by window openings. "Ave Maria" texts are inscribed on glass set back in deep "reveals" or recesses on the interior. In Le Corbusier's 1950 presentation model of the church, since destroyed, the south wall had a "more cautious" pattern of window piercings.[46] Now, its twenty-seven rectangular openings, of various dimensions and irregularly distributed, cubically carve the wall.[47] It is the astutely asymmetrical fenestration pattern as well as the highly plastic recessions that make the south wall so extraordinary. With the window openings much wider inside than out, and to such dramatic effect, one may recall, from the late eighteenth century, the "star"-like openings in the domical "sky" of Boullée's huge spherical project for a Newton monument, these "figured and formed by small openings pierced, funnel-like, into the exterior of the vault from its exterior until, reaching the interior, they take the figure proper to them."[48]

The singular effect of this curtain-like yet massive-looking wall relieved by deep wells of light leads one naturally to wonder about possible historical antecedents. Pauly has adduced several possible sources, none farfetched, including the Villa Adriana, known in Corbusier sketches dating from a 1911 visit; oriental Jewish cemetery steles, of which Le Corbusier kept a 1930 photo clipping; the Sidi Brahim mosque at El Atteuf, in the valley of M'zab, in southern Algeria, visited in 1931; the kitchen wall of an Indian house; and a Sardinian funerary stele known as "Torre dei Giganti."[49]

Ackerman affirms the imperial Roman idea in suggesting the general type of "Roman cryptoporticos where rectangular apertures serve to light vaulted passages," such as that at Hadrian's Villa: "These were probably the source of Renaissance applications as in the court of the Palazzo Massimi in Rome."[50] The generally Hadrianic possibility is also promising thanks to the type of the grotto or *serapeum,* cut out of the living rock to a kind of periscopic light chimney, this also as imaged by Piranesi.[51] I might add to the roster of possibilities the massive brick wall with large, deep-set windows and niches for statues – of which there is one such in the Ronchamp wall, for a statue from the old church – in the flat outside wall of the D-shaped western exedra (which may have served ritual purpose in this otherwise commercial building) of the Mercatus Traiani in Rome, built just before the Villa Adriana earlier in the second century. Indeed, when Pauly speaks of a "desolidification" of mass at Ronchamp whereby, from a hefty tower at the principal door, the wall unfurls to the right,[52] she might almost be echoing, to different purpose, Giedion's description of the wall of the Mercatus Traiani: "In principle this room presented a dematerialization of the surface of the wall, in the manner that was raised to perfection in the later Basilica of Constantine."[53]

Whatever its origins, the Wall of Light is perhaps the most notorious feature of the chapel to those who reject Ronchamp for untruthfulness to materials by applying a too narrowly materialistic formalism. In reality a subtler unity of gestalt prevails. True, the seemingly bulky curl of the south wall as underpinning the similarly bulky curl of the roof may be pedantically "false" insofar as both are actually light, framed structures (the thin faces of the "balloon" wall actually being far enough apart to constitute a long inverted hallway, if not a room, and the roof in a number of studies conceived as an airplane wing). Nevertheless there rings true a surprisingly "classical" concinnity of wall taper and roof taper, which is also to say, of the most prominent feature in plan with the most prominent feature in elevation. The self-professed modernists objected to the church as an unforgivable departure from a correct, that is perceptually self-evident, rationalism; but here, if anything, a higher and more poetic sense of form, itself by no means irrational, is in effect. No need to appeal that the heart has its reasons.

So wonderful a church, however, could never have constituted a mere formal problem. Perhaps turning again to the South, where Le Corbusier had worked on the unexecuted City of Contemplation at La Sainte-Baume, will suggest what personal investment of spirit may have informed Ronchamp. For the country around Marseilles, in Provence as well as Languedoc, was dear to the Protestant ancestors of Le Corbusier who, under persecution, had fled to Switzerland. I am thinking in particular of the local history, but also the fascinatingly ruinous landscape and architecture of Les Beaux de Provence, where the Magdalene legend held local association as tenaciously as in Le Sainte-Baume, on the other, easterly, side of Marseilles.

For some twenty years now – ever since, as a student driving through Provence with my old friend Bjørn Rye, I first saw the hoary hills of Les Baux – I have meant one day to tell why they made me think so strongly of Ronchamp. Popular descriptions of Les Baux, its ghost town and strange geomorphology, comment on the mysteriousness of the place. The mystery is deeply architectural, with vacant or fragmentary classical structures close by abandoned primitive chambers dug out of the soft natural stone (bauxite), and now exposed to the elements like overscaled cells in some gigantic fossil body.

Around the hill and former medieval castle of Les Baux, situated some six miles from Saint-Rémy, the hillsides are pocked with cavelike chambers. Parts of the castle and some dwellings are literally hewn out of the native rock, so that the ruinous blurring of nature and culture that charms Chateaubriand in the *Génie du Christianisme* (1802), for instance, seems to take effect before one's eyes. No wonder the nineteenth-century neo-Provençal poet Frédéric Mistral, who lived in this town where freestanding Renaissance window frames are silhouetted against the sky as in some surrealist film, renewed the idea of Mary

12. Les Baux de Provence, cave architecture in the hills. Photograph by the author, c. 1967–8.

Magdalene's hermitage. In one particular exposed rock chamber (Figure 12), where blocky niches were cut into the inner wall in an irregular orthogonal pattern, I first thought about Le Corbusier's Wall of Light at Notre-Dame-du-Haut.

Les Baux is old enough to have a Carolingian cemetery, and some of the cave ruins are said to be medieval, though its baronial status was undermined in the fourteenth century and its seat dismantled by Louis XI. Then in the sixteenth century it became the refuge of Protestants during the Wars of Religion, and in the town the old "Temple Protestant," of 1571, still displays the motto *Post Tenebras Lux* (after darkness, light). But Les Baux was fairly destroyed by Richelieu in 1632, and its Huguenots fled, yes, to Switzerland – Le Corbusier's people's "Albigensians"?[54]

If so, this cosmopolitan modernist architect's own complex attitude toward the classical tradition finds a sort of local kinship. Though a linguistic separatist writing in the old local Provençal, in his long poem *Calendau* (1867) Mistral celebrates, out of local pride, not only the Pont du Gard but the Roman triumphal arches of Carpentras, Cavaillon, Saint-Rémy and Saint-Chamas – ignoring those no longer extant, including one at Arles that had been recently destroyed.[55] In this, the popular poet of the local tongue has behind him a sophisticated counterpart in the nationalistic Renaissance French of the six-teenth-century (Catholic) poet Joachim du Bellay, whose cycle of twenty-five sonnets "Les antiquités de Rome" (1558), written in Rome, ironically exercises a Pateresque nostalgia for France and for the French language versus, or rather, *contre,* Latin.[56]

The local tradition of a poetry of the simple life was still observed in 1919, when Roger Fry visited Les Baux by bicycle on the recommendation of Ottoline Morrell. After the visit the (Protestant) aesthete wrote to Marie Mauron of her literary "apostolate" at Les Baux, "There I saw life as it should be, a life where poverty and wealth are accidents of little importance, where one can enjoy the things of the spirit without ceasing to be a peasant."[57]

Wandering in such a French place, where the sixteenth century looks so recent, one can also think of the great architect of the French Reformation period, Philibert Delorme. If Le Corbusier himself has a describably Delormean aspect, it probably shows in connection with the engineering of Ronchamp, that highly irregular building, and especially in its aeronautical-modern "vaulting."[58] Not irrelevant, at Les Baux itself, however, if one is thinking of the Ronchamp turrets and "prow," is an early seventeenth-century campanile with empty windows at the top and its own diagonally projecting wall buttress, this attached to the church of Saint-Vincent and known as the "Lantern of the Dead."

I am thinking, now, that it may not have been so wrongheaded of some critics to react against Notre-Dame-du-Haut as a church proposing to be not only modernist but *catholique,* but not for the reasons supposed. To adopt a post-Reformation and pre-ecumenical – but also pre-Résistance and prewar – distinction: if there was anything not altogether *catholique* about the Ronchamp chapel, that may be because there is about it something rather elusively personal that just might be distinguished as *chrétienne,* in the sense of Protestant. It may not be going too far to add that if that old distinction means next to nothing today, that may be thanks, not to the indifference but to the spiritually generous ecumenism of such "Christians" as Le Corbusier – who built this church of *Our Lady* against extraordinary artistic as well as institutional odds.

9

Kahn: The Anxious Classicist

In memoriam Robin Walker

Louis I. Kahn (1901–74), the Estonian-born Philadelphian and most celebrated American architect of the 1960s, has seemed a last major "form-giver" in an unchallenged modernist sense. Saying so is hardly a slight against Frank Lloyd Wright, who died in 1959, nor against Le Corbusier, who died in 1965, nor even against Walter Gropius or Ludwig Mies van der Rohe, who both died in 1969. All of these men belonged to the founding generation of World War I, long since canonically installed. Kahn, self-made in the good sense, had practiced architecture in obscurity for years, working mainly on public housing and on what the 1950s called "developments." He was engaged in architectural design for a good two decades when, with the Yale Art Gallery (1951–3), he emerged into the limelight of that first (and last?) generation fully confident in modernism as a new tradition succeeding to the architectural mantle of the Renaissance itself, where the Renaissance tradition had so long maintained institutional authority.

With Kahn's works now surveyed,[1] I want to respond to some of them singly; but I also wonder about that general classical inheritance that partisans of the International Style tended to take negatively for granted as "traditional." For some of the geometric formalism, especially of plan (not necessarily symmetrical), of the Roman antique that lay at the heart of the European academic tradition, seems embedded, however elusively, in the new tradition of modernism that wrote over it. In Kahn's case, where a high modernism passes perhaps into a late one, any neo-Renaissance classical recall may be more acute than a simple matter of conservatism: knowing, self-conscious classicism may itself be more or less inevitably mannered, as otherwise "High Renaissance," mid-sixteenth-century architecture outside central Italy, not only Venetian but French, can testify. In and above the specifics of Kahn's designs, one sees signs of Romanism, yes, but refracted, as it were, through a Renaissance sophistication and with mannerist potential. Nothing is the same on its second time around, and if Kahn's work is neither precedentlessly modern nor naively revivalistic, it might mark not some arty neomannerism of the postmoderns to come, but rather a more integrally or inevitably (mortally) mannered phase of "classical" modernism itself.

Kahn's was a plain style, yet artful. By the American folk distinction of the plain and the fancy it would have to count, for its sheer refinement, as fancy, however unembellished – its very plainness being rather Roman at that. Typical Kahnian Romanisms include not only circular and other centralized plans, but segmental arches, coffering, enthusiastic employment of brick and concrete, a tendency to orthogonal wall division evoking ranges of classical orders, and the markedly regular disposition of pavilions and buildings in ensemble, even when asymmetric. While none of these is unique with Kahn, all like traits do seem germane to his aesthetic.

Perhaps more profoundly than with any other major architect since the founders, Kahn's Romanism was passed through the lens of the Roman Renaissance, just as in his theoretical statements there echoes an essentially Renaissance humanist rhetoric stimulated, though not developed, by Vitruvius in antiquity. That for five hundred years the Greek essence had been treated like a Roman scent bottled and packaged in the Renaissance and marketed in the premodern academies is significant for the kind of mystic-sounding noble office that a generation ago Kahn was by no means alone in ascribing to the nearly gnostical magic of form and light in architecture and, bolstered by grandiloquent rhetoric, to the almost priestly role of the architect. How pompous, after all, Vitruvius himself can sound.

It now seems sure that Kahn was more than superficially familiar with Rudolf Wittkower's classic treatise in Renaissance architectural theory, *Architectural Principles in the Age of Humanism* (1949; 2d ed., 1952; 3d ed., 1962), which another student of Wittkower's (other than myself), since turned architect, Colin Rowe, sent him early in 1956.[2] Wittkower's book shattered an old Burckhardtean sense of the Italian Renaissance as secularist that was all too expediently welcome, with practically Freemasonic enthusiasm, in America. (It was no coincidence that Jacob Burckhardt himself was the teacher of Wölfflin, the lawgiver of formalist art history.) But just what, with the *Architectural Principles* in hand, could one at last expect to fathom? How, in setting Platonic and Neoplatonic ideas of the mathematical harmony of the cosmos to explicitly Christian purpose, the Renaissance architects of centralized churches had in fact set up a decidedly spiritual "sympathy between the microcosm of man and the macrocosm of God."[3] Significantly, Kahn himself took happily to the task of designing proper sanctuaries, Jewish or Christian.

To some, any such metaphysics suits Louis Kahn's supposedly "mystical" sense of architecture, much as his centralized plans supposedly indicate a return, if not a retreat, to Palladianism. For one thing, Wittkower's was not the only available metaphysic of centralized building, and in context it was by no means mystical. All the more in view of Kahn's transcedental musings, which seem so unusual in our cynical time, it deserves to be noted that Wittkower's treatise stood quite hard-nosed beside at least one other known and still interesting

British text whose ostensible spiritualism might now be more problematic in terms of protomodernist utopianism. I refer to a book first published by the architect William Richard Lethaby under the title *Architecture, Mysticism and Myth* in 1892, and revised in a series of articles in *The Builder* in 1928, these in turn eventually republished posthumously, when *Architectural Principles* was in its second edition, as *Architecture, Nature and Magic* (1956). What with its more scholarly work in intellectual history to do, the *Architectural Principles* understandably steers clear of Lethaby. After all, the mystique Wittkower had carefully to isolate was itself a humanist one, and as such demanding of historical criticality.

Yet here already, in the form of a practitioner's reflections, was a direct attempt at a cosmological sense of architecture with special attention to the sacred or royal building on a central plan, and from well beyond the pale of classical or even European architecture at that. Considering the sense of the "heavenly" and kingly in centrally planned buildings, Lethaby (1857–1931), this surveyor of the fabric of Westminster Abbey whose "main thesis" was "that the development of building practices and ideas of the world structure acted and reacted upon one another,"[4] notes foursquare palace halls, for instance, as "especially appropriate for monarchs claiming to be kings of kings and sending out their commands east, west, north and south."[5] Oddly akin to Louis Kahn's otherwise basically Bramantesque High Renaissance Romanism is Lethaby's plan for a Byzantine-type royal palace at a site called Mashita, east of the river Jordan, with vaulted square hall, four transept spaces and openings cut diagonally in through hefty corners.[6]

Since about 1970, the spread even in traditional religious circles of a populistically mystical, syncretic "mandala" literature has only obscured the clarity with which such subjects as the cosmological implications of foursquare architectural plans could appear before the turn of the 1960s.[7] Lethaby himself held the respect of modern critics. Lewis Mumford wrote in a 1957 foreword to a reprint of his collected papers (first edition, 1922) that Lethaby's critique of the old academicism deserves to extend to "the modern academicians, who bow and genuflect piously, with the same verbal formulae, the same deadly imitativeness, before the Palladios and Vignolas of the modern movement, Le Corbusier and Mies van der Rohe."[8] To the humanist cult of imposed regularity and ideal proportions, Meyer Schapiro, with whom I remember discussing Lethaby about 1970, still opposes Lethaby's thinking as growing empirically out of artistic experience,[9] this in a tradition in which academic classicism was opposed by William Morris, Philip Webb and other early moderns. The point, for the time being, is that Wittkower's *Architectural Principles*, while surely Kahn's cup of tea, does not in itself account for Kahn's so-called Palladianism, which, even if Palladio himself had been more simply classical and Roman (say in the manner of Bramante) would still be unorthodox, not to say mannerist, and in its own way irreducibly new. At the least, Kahn would have to carry forward something of the visible historicism of specifically eighteenth-century neo-Palladianism, as some contemporary architecture has done all too self-consciously, with (manneristic) complications of its own.

It also says something about Kahn's situation that the 1960s produced in art a style of sculpture offering itself as styleless, minimalism, where the very insistence on regular geometric forms as blank, neutral, cool, and antiformal finds precedent in the more extreme formal elementalism of Enlightenment neoclassicism,[10] that categorical neoclassicism in whose genesis earlier eighteenth-century British architectural neo-Palladianism had a formative role. The modern founders had inherited from the nineteenth century an anxiety to come up with a truly modern style, but (just?) before postmodernism, modernist architects often liked to think of their work as otherwise styleless or transcending style. While no art is styleless – in rhetoric, the "plain style" makes its own rhetorical point – it is tempting to see a kind of zero-degree rhetoric not only in minimalism but in functionalist architecture before it, with precedents in Roman engineering and other sorts of unornamented utilitarian construction. Like the American minimalists in sculpture, Kahn must have known something of the dilemma of the clean modernist slate that may propose itself as a rather Latinate and rhetorical *tabula rasa*.

It does now seem amazing that – thanks largely to Sigfried Giedion, who broadcast a basically functionalist appreciation of imperial Roman engineering construction – an extended argument about "monumentality" in architecture could develop in Kahn's time innocently, it seems, of authoritarian taint. More difficult to understand is how talk by and about Kahn on the mystique of "light" not only goes unchallenged today but is enthusiastically affirmed despite pressing critique of a lingering pseudocultic Enlightenment resort to imagery of divine illumination.[11] Perhaps architects merely thrill to rhetoric, as to big aqueducts? "All I can say is that architecture, per se, does not exist": in a way, what a typically imperious, American thing for our hero to say (in a videotaped interview). Or perhaps it is simply that the empty rhetoric of our American culture vies with that of Rome itself.[12]

If by now the modern tradition of ideal form and geometric order that derives from Renaissance humanism, and which includes Louis Kahn, is open to criticism as a bourgeois aesthetic of enforced hierarchy and control, authoritarianism as such is not necessarily part and parcel of all deference to classical precedent. Besides, a fashionable bourgeois antihumanism appears today in cynical denial of access to classical and other high culture, a cultural scorched-earth policy that under revisionist colors bitterly preserves social prerogative over and against any possibility of a humanism for all. But if Kahn's art itself is better than reactionary – not simply more than Renaissance-revivalistic, updated, and certainly not a mere closing down of modernism and a handing back to bankrupt bourgeois tradition of hard-earned modernist cultural capital – perhaps this will be apparent in its own subtler tensions.

Louis Kahn's Romanism is a recovery, especially of an antiquity itself long before recovered for humanism and stabilized not only as officially true but also as contingently modern, with new classics of its own already accumulating by about 1500. If some of his own most important works were to appear in ruination (as, under his theoretic influence, younger architects have liked to muse), their archaeological ground plans would suggest Roman imperial architecture of the second to fourth century. Still, much in Kahn's production is specifically Bramantesque, harking back to Bramante at that moment of 1500, and in equivalence with the ideal moment of Raphael in High Renaissance painting,[13] and it is not without reason that an excavated octagonal basement from 1500 might well look like an excavated octagonal basement from A.D. 300.

Yet I wonder further, in terms of style, if, in some sense reconstituting, not reiterating, the once-definitive truth of (Roman) classicism, and thus in some sense recapitulating the once-canonical High Renaissance formulation, Kahn – quite unlike a younger generation that would ransack the classics of the Avery Architectural Library for formalist fashion plates – wasn't himself rather like a sixteenth-century "outsider believer" (French and also Protestant) such as Philibert Delorme. Away from Rome, the very Romanism of the High Renaissance might have its own maneristic potential under pressure of having antiquity and modernity alike, to attain. That Delorme – not unlike the distinctly Venetian Palladio – looks middle-of-the-road compared with full-fledged French mannerism, but not compared with Roman architecture of a generation before him, may be as much a question of sophistication as of provincialism.[14]

In self-consciously catching up with the Italian Renaissance in France, "saying it his way," Delorme tended to effect an all the more unwittingly contemporary quasi-mannerism, a style open to Gothicisms of ungrammatical, directly engineered (even protomodern) form not covered by the Latinate grammar books.[15] Delorme's urgency, not to say anxiety, about the cool regularity that marks the High Renaissance in Italy is obvious in his published scheme for correcting a too-medievally irregular chateau by inserting extra blocks between ones already standing irregularly about a court, so as to render the whole ensemble symmetrical.[16] A Gothically rooted fascination with vaulting and "creatively" engineered roof timbering; a rather sculpturesque approach to the wall, including the attachment of a cylinder to its vertical plane;[17] occasional odd "orioles"; even a picturesqueness of roof silhouette that led Delorme to dilate on exotic chimneys in his treatise, *Architecture* (1567): such can be found in productions of Kahn the "last modernist" as well as in the thinking of Delorme as a rather anxiously French "Renaissance" architect.[18]

To do something of the kind in our time, to (re)approach the heart of Italian Renaissance architecture from a distance, one would somehow have to override the earliest foundational struggle of modernism – emergent by about 1700 in (French) architectural theory, and after 1750 inescapable in practice – as challenging institutionalized Roman authority in critical confrontation with Greek architecture. Much more than a matter of surface style, that neoclassical development was an unseating of establishment models by recourse to prior standards, and was critical and radical as such. It was also metaphysical; for while evidence of Roman engineering was still to be seen in brick and mortar, the prospect of a certain *abstract* classicism opened up, in which the ostensibly precedentless structural understanding of modern engineering (versus architecture as institutionalized fine art) might actually find deeper roots in the pure tectonics of Greek architecture than in the Roman pragmatics advocated in Kahn's time on behalf of a particular functionalism by the likes of Sigfried Giedion.[19] Call this metaphysical primitivism if necessary, but it may be the deepest wellspring of the modern tradition. And if, in entertaining such a markedly Roman classicism as he did, Kahn also went in a sense against it (as with Delorme, whose [inadvertent] mannerism could not but deviate from a then-modern Roman absolute, the Bramantesque), his results now attain a new classicality of their own.

Turning self-effacingly to the side, with its flank on Chapel Street, the Yale Art Gallery in New Haven, of 1951–3, amounts to Louis Kahn's historical debut. Along the long blind flank four continuous stone string courses protrude from a facing of Roman brick. At the time, this was a rather wild ornamental indulgence, pardonable insofar as the bands "express," as one used to say, the floors behind the wall.

Owing to a tendency to take glass curtain walls for granted in high modernist architecture (a tendency that in the 1950s was already pointed up in popular caricature), it is worth remarking, not only regarding the smaller entrance wall but even more in reference to the split garden facade, on the long back "campus" side of the gallery, where one squarish plane is set considerably forward of the other, a deference to the classic "International Style" of, say, Le Corbusier's Salvation Army (City of Refuge), Paris, of 1929–33, which was perhaps the most beautiful allover glass facade of its type. This finely honed facade of Kahn's really consists of two distinct squarish walls, like a foreground and middle ground in painting, each framed by stone left and right. A similar treatment of the entrance wall relieves a structure that might otherwise have sat like a boxcar on the city corner. Even the building's admired cylindrical interior staircase, not indicated on the exterior (nor again in more forceful return within Kahn's later British Art Center across the street), recalls in an introverted manner an often-overlooked cylindrical pavilion in front of Le Corbusier's Paris building.[20]

Today, perhaps the most remarked feature of the Yale Art Gallery is its cast concrete coffered ceilings – or better, étages (floors), such heft have they, with their exposed triangular-prismatic honeycombed undersides (Figure 13). Early on, Kahn had thought of using a continuous tetrahedral steel space frame – not unlike certain early experimental structures by Alexander Graham Bell, and quite like the contemporary engineered structures of Buckminster Fuller. The chunkier cast concrete result, a continuous slab pricked with triangular-prismatic coffers, related to an idea already being used by Kahn's associate Anne Tyng, who was a kind of link with Fuller.[21] But one may also want to note the hexagonal cellular structures of about 1950, and the tetrahedral ones of about 1960, of Tony Smith, the minimalist sculptor who had once worked for Frank Lloyd Wright. A decade later, Ludwig Mies van der Rohe would employ a significantly different coffering system, arguably more Greek than Roman, for the ceiling of the New National Gallery, Berlin (1962–3): there, large inset squares frame further inset grids of subsquares, in a typical

13. Louis I. Kahn, Yale University Art Gallery, New Haven, Connecticut, 1951–3. Photograph by Grant Mudford, courtesy of the Philadelphia Museum of Art.

simultaneity of major and minor scale systems that also marks large glass-walled building facades by him, in which there is more "composition" than many observers suppose.

Vincent Scully says that Kahn was "a Romantic-Classic architect" who "was beginning modern architecture again . . . with heavy, solid forms derived from structure rather than from pictorial composition through which modern architects of the twentieth century had . . . attempted to rival the freedom of abstract painting. . . . So Kahn's work . . . is . . . never pictorial."[22] That seems too sweeping, but it could well apply to the once denoted "Primary Structures" of the minimal art that paralleled the florescence of Louis Kahn's decidedly inorganic architecture. Mies was no minimalist, despite the generalizations of antimodernists; but the uniform and continuous poured concrete triangular clustering-into-hexagonal coffers of Kahn's Yale Gallery ceilings, dark and chunkily faceted, practically adumbrate the extreme formal single-mindedness of American minimalist sculpture of the 1960s. Indeed, as a photograph

(c. 1952) shows, the matrix used to mold them, with ranks of equidistant pyramids, uncannily resembles Tony Smith's black steel *Hubris* (1969), with its ranks of identical pyramids occupying half the surface of a plinth. Nevertheless, the hexagonal, "chair caning" coffer pattern of the Yale Art Gallery ceilings is as unforgettable, qua coffering, as Kahn's later Kimbell Museum's suppressed (neo-Roman but also Corbusian) barrel vaults.

Of two dubious but interesting unexecuted skyscraper projects on which Kahn worked between 1952 and 1957, one, the "City Tower," for Philadelphia, also evokes Buckminster Fuller — if not also the aging Wright's fantasy of an icily faceted "mile-high" erection. While irregularly shaped floors in this design recall the evenly stacked free-form floors of Mies's well-known expressionistic 1919–21 "glass skyscraper" projects, their skewing from floor to floor, supported by cockeyed beams, makes for a dizzy, irrational effect. To walk around the model is to discover, not some steadily winding helix but swaying profiles lurching from one position to another. It is as if, with experimental extremism, Kahn were rehearsing an escape from Architecture as We Know It.

The other projected office tower, for Kansas City, Missouri, is rectilinear yet also odd, especially in the wooden model that looks like an ultracraftsmanly night table of vaguely Chinese style, what with a big space left open between the upper floors and the base. Actually, "raising" a tall building in a like manner, from top down, by means of a tower crane (a technique perfected in postwar France but resisted in America by organized labor) is neither without historical precedent (as in early Soviet modernism) nor without issue: there is the Corbusian elevation of bulk in Gerhard Kallman, Michael McKinnell and Edward Knowles's then-recent Boston City Hall (1962–7); and the uptight ultraglitz of the firm Kevin Roche John Dinkeloo's overrated Ford Foundation Building (1967)[23] only distracts from the fact that it is much the same thing, only with "unbuilt" belly glazed in and planted like an immense terrarium.[24] Both projects display an engineerly gamesmanship out of control, whereas Kahn's gift was classically architectural.

Picture a sheet of graph paper with one square blackened in, this as the kernel of an incipient plan; and treat the blackened square as a corner with two walls of unit thickness at right angles.[25] The basic corner comprised of walls of unit thickness is enough to engender a closed, rectangular, and more or less independent space enclosure, whether a room or, as often with Kahn, a freestanding pavilion, or even an urban space. Next, one will want to project another room or pavilion whose walls, I suggest, Kahn would tend to conceive as generated in counterpoise, corner-to-corner but alongside the kernel unit in an adjacent row of squares. Once one thus breaks loose from thinking of the second space as simply an attached room sharing the same first corner — either as just the next box in a row or else as diagonally elicited, like a cubist "switchover" or checker (and, either way, the unit corner may already seem overloaded) — it will come naturally to think of another, complementary pavilion, or at least the first corner of one. The result may not be without human connotation of proximity, interdependence, even the immediacy of a couple

14. Louis I. Kahn, Bathhouse, Jewish Community Center, Ewing Township, New Jersey, 1954–9. Photograph by Grant Mudford courtesy of the Philadelphia Museum of Art.

sculpturally sharing one "shoulder," though the immediate point is an innately formal structural affiliation of space units that do not simply materially abut.

This logic of volumes affiliated by corner relations, visible or implied, is given with understated intelligence in a recreational bathhouse built by Kahn for the Jewish Community Center in Ewing Township, near Trenton, New Jersey, in 1954–9 (Figure 14). Twenty years ago, Colin Roe interpreted the larger project for the Jewish center proper, together with American work by Mies van der Rohe, as a retreat from the International Style "free," or open, plan with flat roof, which to him connoted a rejection of the modern *zeitgeist* and a "classical" retreat.[26] This I tend to take as a defense of a deeper, "abstract" classicism, as against this structure's ranks of pyramidal miniroofs as manneristic (and soon all too fashionable). In any case, the larger project exemplifies a certain Kahnian clustering of cells into unequally sized but affiliated nodal points in a continuous nexus, as in Row and Robert Slutzky's analysis of Mondrian's painting *Broadway Boogie-Woogie,* of 1943–4, in terms of an architecture of "phenomenal transparency" that itself offered something of a "Mannerist malaise."[27]

It is, however, the humbler bathhouse that concerns me now. And since the "housey," hip-roofed pavilion in series would become a Kahnian cliché of neoacademic modernists, one admittedly remote early modernist instance of a foursquare pyramidal roof should not be forgotten: a 1910 project by Le

Corbusier for an art school. Notably for Kahn's way of thinking about composition, the poolside bathhouse seems tellingly fundamental, and as such deeply analogous to the interdependency of plane, volume and space in cubist and subsequent modernist painting of any "linguistic" complexity. Kahn's Ewing bathhouse stands firmly against any lingering nineteenth-century academic sense that tasks too modest are insufficient for *Baukunst,* promising only mere building. Here is the simple building dignifying of human-activity that one might permit oneself to imagine Heidegger (in some better version of his own corrupted humanity) projecting, as the then-recent author of "Building Dwelling Thinking" (1952).[28]

As the 1960s opened, the Richards Medical Research Building at the University of Pennsylvania in Philadelphia, of 1957–65, located Kahn securely on the still unruffled modernist map. The Richards towers, highlighted by the Museum of Modern Art with an exhibition and official monograph while still under construction,[29] rise from a fascinating "knight's-move" ground plan that is at once regular and varied: a row of four (and one different) square units in a row, plus one perpendicular and a last off axis, at one end.

Perhaps because such Richards details as the inverted, or negative, corners became a "brutalist" cliché in the last decade of presuming modernist hegemony, one may now want to pick at this once master-piece design. The concrete piers show Kahn's fineness of thought in the splitting in half, and half again, of a corner pier into (a) solid half-pier, (b) quarter-width break, then (c) quarter-width solid; however, just where such a pier is engaged in a brick wall, the equation breaks down with the heft of the half-pier excused, so to speak, to disappear into the unaccounted mass of the wall. Nevertheless, something of a modernist equivalent to the classical relation of freestanding to engaged column, and on to *pilaster,* occurs where the vertical concrete piers are set flush with the wall. If so, this is a case of nicely extreme ambiguity between the rhetorical and the ad hoc.

Trademarks of the Richards Building are its brick "chimneys," slit wide across their tops like boxy wooden organ pipes. With other forms in Kahn's work such as bifurcations of the wall mass by a slit, the "chimneys' " crisp profiles against the sky may embody something of Kahn's direct experience of Egyptian architecture (which already held modernist appeal to Corbusier and others a generation earlier), to judge by the starkly formal shadow in a 1951 pastel travel sketch by Kahn of the Egyptian Temple of Horus at Edfu. The high–low lintels of the windows of the Richards towers are a rather Corbusian feature (e.g., Unité d'habitation, Marseilles, 1947–52), while, speaking of the "chimneys," what about some allusion in them to the unconventional chimneys, minus their nutty "prairie" slabs, of Wright's 1913–18 Midway Gardens, in Chicago?

At La Jolla, California, stands the Salk Institute for Biological Studies, of 1959–65, after the Richards Building, probably Kahn's best-known design. This photogenic structure is an interesting case of mirroring, whereby reflected irregularities, including Corbusian anglings of facade planes, comprise a linear symmetry.[30] With the channel of space between the two main masses poised, as if for aeronautical takeoff, toward a fantastic view of the Pacific, an effect somewhat self-consciously sublime is held like a permanent pose.[31] Yet to imagine the view thus framed to be of a river instead of an ocean, may call to mind the pair of long, closely spaced blocks, also mirroring one another, and nothing if not self-conscious, of Vasari's mannerist Uffizi, perpendicular to the Arno, in Florence. Elements of the project, notably, the large cylinders of a separate "meeting house" in a model of c. 1961, seem struggling to emerge into such succeeding works as the great capital complex of Dhaka, in Bangladesh, on which Kahn had already started by 1962.

But first, the big question of the Renaissance centralized church arises with Kahn's early thoughts for the First Unitarian Church and School, Rochester, built over the decade 1959–69, with a twelve-sided sanctuary set into a square plan. This gave way in the developing project to influences from Frank Lloyd Wright's Unity Temple, also Unitarian, at Oak Park, Illinois (1906–8). Unintimidatingly monumental, crisp, shadowy inset shafts in the brick walls of the Rochester church, especially where they occur in an up-and-down, A–B–B–A sequence of large and capped versus small and open-topped, are also reminiscent of the front of Wright's prior – and secular – masterpiece, the Larkin Company's " 'A' Administration" Building in Buffalo, built in 1904–6 and demolished (after dereliction) only in 1950. They even recall an alternation of low bollards with full piers on the ground front of Wright's 1909–10 Robie House, Chicago (a passage subtle enough to confuse the workmen who first mistakenly built five identical piers).[32] Wright himself was then soon to be struck by centralized plans as working "basic schemata" of architectural design (something like empty gestalts), thanks to diagrams in Paul Frankl's Wöfflinian *Die Entwicklungsphasen der neueren Baukunst* (1914).[33]

Kahn's known respect for the noncredal religiosity of the Rochester congregation should not lead to making too much of its Unitarianism, at risk of losing sight of the challenge of sophistication-within-orthodoxy in Renaissance form that Wittkower had worked to restore. In this project and other contemporary work Kahn's strong element of Renaissance Romanism does come into view. Having already related to Donato Bramante's device of a circle lodged in larger horizontal semicircle the supposedly "minimalist" work of Robert Mangold in painting,[34] I observe something similar in Kahn's designs: the distinctive motif of a segmental crescent, or classicizing "thermal," window centered directly over a vertical slit – as in contemporary projects for a Tribune Review Building, Greensburg, 1958–62, and a Fleisher House, Elkins Park, 1959, both in Pennsylvania.

If it seems too un-Unitarian to think of the Bramante who planned Saint Peter's in the Vatican as a centralized church, Wright's Unity Temple itself, as I have written before, uncannily resembles the massive structure usually said to represent one of the rising crossing piers of Bramante's Saint Peter's, as under construction, in Raphael's *Disputà*.[35] Even without the explicit Romanism of Bramante, which disappeared as the Rochester building developed (as in Saint Peter's Basilica itself), Kahn's beautiful church would echo modern works such as a remarkable brick church by Lutyens (more on him later), not to mention such an actual, ancient Roman Christian church building as the beautiful brick Basilica of Trier, in Germany.

Wright was the Emerson of American architecture, the first who could supposedly do completely without tradition and nonetheless aspire to canonical greatness – as if to wish that Unity Temple might *not* resemble the Raphael-Bramante Saint Peter's pier. This naive (and vain) American sense of originality, which can only obstruct the construction of authentic tradition, was already wearing thin in the 1960s.

Notwithstanding apparent stylistic incongruity, the facade of the Performing Arts Theater in an arts complex that Kahn designed and built for Fort Wayne, Indiana, between 1959 and 1973, demands to be compared with the precocious and notorious "postmodern" facade of Guild House (Friends' Housing for the Elderly), in Philadelphia, of 1960–3, by Robert Venturi, who had worked in Kahn's office in 1956 with John Rauch. Alike in fixing on a spinelike central axis, these two facades could stand as representative of competing parties, high modernist-poetic and early, wised-up postmodern. Above the little curved central entrance marquee – with "GUILD HOUSE" in "Roxy" capitals – rise four stories of paired, set-back balconies, these topped by a notably wide segmental window split down the center, on axis. (The wide segmental or semicircular opening over a narrower portal is a late Roman motif, e.g., the Porta Aurea, the north gate to Diocletian's palace at Split, circa A.D. 300.) If Venturi and Rauch's Guild House looked almost embarrassingly pop-patronizing when new, like some halfhearted *pro bono* legal case, Kahn's theater entrance would have looked "tastefully," understatedly arch, *rich*. Here, also against brick, a hefty (ferroconcrete?) lintel with central pier resting oddly upon it defines an entrance underneath, as well as a split segmental window, with two even wider and more low-slung segmental windows to either side, overhead.

Apart from Venturi, where has such a strange conjunction of forms appeared before? Shallow segmental curves occur in engineering studies by Delorme, but also in Italian mannerist architecture. Ultrashallow elongations or otherwise extremist forms of segmental pediments, including the hefty split and reversed, "inside-out" segmental pediment with its "end" points at the middle, are seen over the Porta delle Suppliche of Vasari's Uffizi (1560–74), in Florence, and, at least as significantly, in Michelangelo's Porta Pia (1561–5), in Rome. The Porta Pia sports not only a flat-arch lintel under a split segmental pediment (which stands, in turn, under a triangular one) but, more tellingly vis-à-vis Kahn's theatrical *grand portail,* has a semicircular tympanum split vertically down the middle.

In Ackerman's *Architecture of Michelangelo,* which merited wide attention on its appearance in 1961, the Porta Pia is approached in an essentially scenographic way that would have recommended it to Kahn even as its ostensible mannerism (a term Ackerman tends to reserve) would have recommended it as "groovy" to Venturi. "Michelangelo's gate belongs more to the street than to the [city] walls," says Ackerman, adding, "It was pure urban scenography," and that "the role of the gate as street scenery made the portal and attic the heart of the design."[36] If calling the ornamentation of the Porta Pia "the most complex architectural detail of the era" is potentially Venturian, Ackerman's sense of the portal's structural rationality, whereby a relieving arch over a flat-arch lintel serves an engineering purpose, nevertheless has its aptness before Kahn's theater facade.[37]

Venturi had not yet published *Complexity and Contradiction* (1966) when he built Guild House, but the book was out when Kahn's design for the theater facade "took shape... in 1968."[38] Soon after mentioning Bramante's "layered walls" of the Belvedere Courtyard, and quoting Louis Kahn on "ruins... [*sic*] wrapped around buildings" in relation to his Salk Institute, Venturi devotes an entire paragraph to analyzing the Porta Pia.[39] Otherwise, segmental openings such as those that look so "formal" in the theater facade, unexpectedly akin to the supposedly antiformal big front window of the Guild House, recur furthermore as a leitmotiv in Kahn's Indian Institute of Management, Ahmedabad, begun in 1962.

Kahn started and finished during the same years Eleanor Donnelley Erdman Hall of 1960–5, at Bryn Mawr College, in Pennsylvania. Its chunky square pavilions link at their interpenetrating corners, three boxes along a continuous diagonal, whose zigzagging is picturesque, even abstractly crenellated-castellated (not unlike a nearby Victorian infirmary, among other collegiate Gothic buildings) from its two-story campus front, and appear sculpturesque in a more contemporary (minimalist) way at the three-story rear.[40] The principal public spaces, a sitting room and a dining room, one at the core of either end block, have their corners mightily broken through, hence are somewhat ambiguous as to mass and void. With poured concrete walls and square-coffered concrete ceilings, these cubic rooms have an abstract formality rather decorated with brutalist dotting of the wall slabs by their concrete forms (a finer detail: the angular junction of a concrete wall with the plaster wall of a hallway). The exterior is clad in slate panels set within a grid of thinner horizontal floor bands and thicker stone for vertical framing, as Kahn would do later at the Yale British Art Center.

The Fisher House, at Hatboro, Pennsylvania, on which Kahn worked from 1960 to 1967, is one of the architect's gems, not only in plan but in its fluctuating elevations and its kinetically sculpturesque interior space. Basically, the plan consists of two skewed and slightly interpenetrating squares. A case of "Complexity and Contradiction," this? Perhaps, but not without modernist artistic precedent. The suprematist vitalism of Malevich's 1915 *Suprematist Painting: Black and Red Square* (Museum of Modern Art) might be adduced, while the plasticity of Kahn's conception may be underscored by further reference to a touchstone of contemporary "postminimal" sculpture of obvious architectural interest – itself related to Malevich's composition – made by Bruce Nauman as Kahn's Fisher House was nearing completion: *Platform Made Up of the Space Between Two Rectilinear Boxes on the Floor* (1966). It would seem pedantic to rehearse what the building might owe to then-historical modernists; it is enough to say that this is an instance of some Alvar Aalto influence seeming evident in Kahn. The relaxation of axial overdetermination so notable here flowered in Kahn's concurrent designs for an unexecuted Dominican Mother House of Saint Catherine de Ricci in Media, Pennsylvania.

Kahn worked on an important unexecuted Philadelphia project from 1961 to 1972, Mikveh Israel Synagogue. Here, in a way, the work developed oppositely to the Rochester Unitarian Church. From within a sequence of plain rectangular blocks there emerged during 1962 something much more like a Renaissance sacred space on central plan. In a 1963 design for the complex, regularizing order becomes interestingly transparent, most obviously in the deliberately sublime sanctuary space, an elongated octagon with mightily formed but thinly walled cylindrical turrets, massively shadowed as well as dramatically light-admitting, at the corners, and as such a rigid gestalt or "form-structure." This sanctuary form has suggested the cabalistic Tree of Life;[41] it might also be likened to August Kekulé's semiconsciously discovered extended hexagonal benzene ring of organic chemistry, with its own structural mystique.[42]

In the overall plan of the synagogue complex, a congregational school looks to be (if this were possible) an equal and opposite term to regularity itself. Reading out along the axis of the sanctuary, one encounters two smaller, regular, square-plan elements – the first an antechamber of the main building, its counterpart freestanding – and, offside, a wall-less shed two still smaller squares long (this a *sukkah,* or bower, frame, for celebration of Sukkoth, the Feast of Tabernacles). In the asymmetrical courtyard one could go no farther without shifting from the processional continuity of the prime sanctuary axis to the stressed informality of a door centered in the wall, but at the extreme edge of the shedded space. Finally, one would have encountered an L-shaped "secular" building, whose spaces and voids, cylinders and cubic volumes, at least in one design, play in interesting compensations that are no more forced as asymmetrical-relational than they are as axial.

Although Kahn's famous concern with monumentality would fulfill itself in his designs for the Indian Institute of Management, Ahmedabad, and, even more, at Dhaka, Bangladesh, with the long-term project known as Sher-e-Bangla Nagar, also begun in 1962, during the decade of these Asian projects some of their features developed elsewhere, or vice versa.

One such case shows a way in which Kahn might be accused of formalism, for recycling an idea by turning it inside out.[43] While large circular (and rotated segmental) holes in the exterior walls of cubic (and at Dhaka, cylindrical) elements are conspicuous and satisfying elements of the Subcontinental schemes, a large inside cube with four big holes in the sides, at the center of the library of Phillips Exeter Academy in Exeter, New Hampshire, 1965–72, looks arty. I no doubt violate consensus further in saying that the exterior of the Exeter library suffers from weakly negated corners, where floors are obviously present, only hiding. It might, however, be interesting to think of this negation of mass in relation to the pursuit of volume instead of mass in contemporary minimalist sculpture. Curiously enough, the library rises from a ground plan, square with chamfered corners, rather like one of Lethaby's sacral examples (a temple of reason?), yet the built result is rather sculpturesque within while graphically gridded (by windows) without.

As the turn of the 1960s approached, Kahn, increasingly renowned, divided his attention among an unlikely variety of commissions. Between 1965 and 1969 he worked on the Saint Catherine's convent in Media, Pennsylvania, one of his most engaging smaller projects. A plan of June or July 1966 shows experimentation with some Mikveh Israel Synagogue thinking, especially in its centrally planned square chapel with large cylinders – again, light-wells? – at the corners. Unique, however, and not unlike Philibert Delorme's demonstration of the pre-Renaissance courtyard *regularized,* is a chain of four dormitories forming an enclosure on one side. In extended, and sympathetic discussions with the nuns, who eventually had to back out for lack of resources and declining membership, Kahn produced some of his subtlest conjunctions of blocks, in designs that might almost have been drawn by El Lissitzky, as inspired are they in their intuitive angling of block to block.

Even while spiritually attuned to the convent project, Kahn had another on the tables, this at an opposite extreme of nuts-and-bolts functionalism. Between 1966 and 1970 he designed and built the sprawling one-story Olivetti-Underwood Factory near Harrisburg, Pennsylvania, where large, single-footed umbrella-like units have clerestory skylights in abutting corners. One wonders if this building of Kahn's is overlooked not because it is a purely utilitarian site of production but because it is in a sense merely a vast space shed, so exclusively a light-vented roof. Despite its clever concrete umbrella-columns, the Olivetti-Underwood plant smothers its flat site with uniform square bays, like a project in mathematical stacking theory. While the interior has interest in extension of the tradition of the American multistory "daylight" factory[44] – as a single-story daylight factory with the daylight coming from above, instead of from the sides – there is hardly any "exterior" to speak of, except for a trivial opening of the first few bays for an entrance corner.[45]

Concurrently, however, and as if in triangulation between idealist, materialist, and realist projects, Louis Kahn was devoting himself to a veritable *ars poetica,* the 1966–72 Kimbell Art Museum in Fort Worth, Texas, a building widely known in art circles (Figure 15). The concern with daylight at Olivetti-Underwood extends to the Kimbell's ranks of shallow segmental vaults slit and baffled at the joints to admit sunlight indirectly. In merely formal terms, the grandly corrugated roof finds "leisure-time" precedent in a *petit maison de weekend,* roofed with a triplet of segmental bulges and topped with real grass(!), designed by Le Corbusier in 1935, but also in more elegant Corbusian precedents in the segmental vaulting of the Maison Taoul, at Neuilly, 1952, and the Sarabhai House, Ahmedabad, 1954–6, the latter finished ten years before Kahn's Kimbell was begun. How American of Kahn to take the idea of the palatial museumesque peristyle (as in Perrault's pre-museological Louvre, as well as in Schinkel's Altes Museum), and convert it into a "front" porch, accessed sideways from one end, while negating the very essence of the peri-

15. Louis I. Kahn, Kimbell Art Museum, Fort Worth, Texas, 1966–72. Photograph by Grant Mudford courtesy of the Philadelphia Museum of Art.

style by supporting it only at the extremities. The porch was even rather hacienda-like at an earlier stage. Of course, Fort Worth is not Paris or Berlin, and doing a merely transliterated peristyle here on former grazing land might have risked something like the "Parthenon" of Nashville.

More pertinent to Kahn's deeper historical aspect is the question of abstract Palladianism in the flush travertine infilling of the Kimbell's long blind wall. This consists of wide suppressed-arched tympana under the roof vaults, separated by narrow, flat-topped units, which together, though blind and defined only by vertical strips, inevitably recall the ultra-neo-Palladianism of the so-called Palladian motif. First, Palladio did not invent the device, which was transmitted through Serlio's books (1537–75). It has often been referred to Palladio's Basilica at Vicenza, where, according to Wittkower in the *Architectural Principles,* "Palladio monumentalized . . . a conception common in Bramante's circle and later popularized through Serlio's fourth book on Architecture. . . . He regarded his own building as an adaptation of the antique basilica type for modern usage. The classical forms as interpreted by Bramante were the medium through which he accomplished this revival."[46]

As Serlian, the motif was taken to resemble a triumphal arch, or, as here, an overlapping series of triumphal arches, like those also of the blind (but rusticated) wall of Bramante's Belvedere Courtyard of the Vatican, a prime source for the motif. Although one can manage to take the Fort Worth wall this way, its squat tympana under "arches" only show up the fact that the basic concept more fundamentally concerns coupled columns or pilasters as framing the wider intercolumniation; thus it traces back through the Venice of Sansovino and Palladio to the Roman work of Giuliano da Sangallo and Bramante, circa 1500.[47] (By the turn of the eighteenth century, the "Palladian," or "Serlian," but really Bramantesque, motif could even present itself in designs for classy Parisian shop fronts.)[48] Yet at the least because it reads in overlapping triads – now this segmental unit flanked by rectangular panels, now the next one claiming the same side panel – the motif has a mannerist potential for ambiguity likely to be activated in doing Bramante over anew. Any "Palladianism" in the Kimbell Museum also bears analogy with the mannerism in Palladio's own output. In our time Kahn, precisely in assuming a Bramantesque formal absolute, certainly produced a Palladio-mannerism truer to the historical experience of style than the philistine pseudo-Palladian architectural affectations of repressive merchant-banker taste in the 1980s – with which, unfortunately, simplistic revisionists are likely to confuse such masterworks of his as this.

Whatever the struggle, that such a building has attained classical standing of its own is evident in its still being extolled despite the *fin-de-moderne* doubt that came on its heels. In a lecture at Yale in 1983 the minimalist sculptor Don Judd held up the example of the Kimbell Art Museum in the face of a general demoralization in the field of architecture. Judd's historical sense is critically flawed – quite grossly for likening prevailing "ignorance and decline" to "late Hellenistic art and . . . subsequent Early Christian art" (!). Nevertheless he says:

> A good building, such as the Kimbell Museum, looks the way a Greek temple in a new colony must have looked among the huts. It looks the way the Roman temple, now a church, looks among the ordinary medieval buildings of Assisi. The temple looks like civilization. The Kimbell is civilization in the wasteland of Fort Worth and Dallas. The Seagram Building is that in New York. These few good buildings are and represent enlightenment in as simple a way as any survey tells you the first buildings of the Renaissance did.[49]

The Yale Center for British Art, built across Chapel Street from his Yale Art Gallery between 1969 and 1974, when Kahn died, is really his Albertian city palace. As such, it deserves to signal to American architecture an end to the hopelessly suburban (and too British) idea that, basically, everything nice should evoke the country, with at least a bit of lawn around it. True, most of Kahn's major work stands in what we Americans call "campus" (i.e., field) settings, and Kahn had some manifest interest in "planning." The theoretical problem runs deeper, given Alberti's notion of monumentality as pertaining essentially to the freestanding building. Nevertheless, the author of the Palazzo

Ruccelai, in Florence, would himself have been pleased by the British Art Center, whose flanks are geometrically articulated with beautifully thin, shallow, graphic relief – including the undisguised linear pattern of adjoining panels. Had this pattern been suppressed, the result would have been yet another behemoth in a city of once-architecturally fashionable (thanks, ironically, partly to Kahn) but spiritually callous brutalist parking garages. Even the inclusion of a row of shops at street level sustains Italian Renaissance urban precedent.

Speaking of city planning: Inner Harbor, a project for Baltimore, from 1969 to 1973, was far better conceived in its uncompromised modernity than so many "Rouse"-type speculative developments, with diddly, Whiggish, yuppie-Palladian touches, on the waterfronts of Anyharbour, USA, or now, even, abroad (why travel at all?).[50] At Inner Harbor (one imagines this urbane architect cringing at the tasteful-sportswear name) Kahn proposed a spatially interesting, distinctly citified handling of massive towers with shifting ground levels beneath them. Where a grand but not grandiloquent stairway narrows up into the complex, one is even reminded of the stairs up the Capitoline Hill in Rome, the righthand flight leading up to Michelangelo's Piazza del Campidoglio.

The great executed "plan," however, is essentially one of building-art, if only because, alarmingly like a hundred *luxe*-suburban corporate headquarters in plan, it looks to be splendid as actually built. This is Sher-e-Bangla Nagar (named after a statesman), Kahn's capital complex at Dhaka, Bangladesh, begun in 1962 and completed posthumously in 1983. Before it, Hegel might have launched off on Oriental despotism, but then he would have been wrong. How many fascistic projects for business and institutional complexes look ostensibly like plans or models of Sher-e-Bangla Nagar, whereas how humanely civic and magnificent, here, is the casual nobility of Kahn's result.

At last Kahn's penchant for cylindrical corners or entire pavilions, which tended toward the oversized, justly fulfills itself on a scale grand enough to call up the American grain elevators that had inspired classic European modernists.[51] And if a model of about 1964 of the National Assembly, with a ring of cylindrical niches running inside its enclosing wall, reminds one of such late Roman architecture as Santa Costanza (which had stimulated Aloïs Riegl on the opticality of late Roman structure as akin to the opticality of modern painting, in 1900) the great regular geometric holes cut through the walls, curved or right-angled, of the finished building most summon up Riegl on the Temple of Minerva Medica: "The pre-condition for the installation of windows in monumental art was . . . the *fernsichtig*[e] [farsighted in the literal sense] perception which made the shadowy hollows with their rhythmic change (symmetry of sequence) and the bright part of the wall in between them appear on the same plane as coherent optical units."[52]

At Dhaka, Kahn was obviously aiming, not for another Brasilia, that folly of Detroit styling set down in the jungle (somehow supposed by reactionaries to be an orthodox modernist notion), but rather for another Chandigarh, which is to say, an array of approachably dignified civic statements worthy of the twentieth century. Sometimes Kahn's larger walls, curved or straight, whether of brick, masonry or cast concrete, seem a bit flimsy, as if blown up from cardboard or balsawood, but such is not the case with Sher-e-Bangla Nagar. For one thing, the detailing at once entails distant (great geometric cutouts through outside walls) and closer-up scales – especially an astute plaid of light verticals and slightly wider horizontal bands, on the huge concrete "capitol" proper of the legislature – not to mention textural finesse, all the more remarkable in such an oceanic context, in the brickwork of subsidiary hostel structures.

The ultimate challenge at Dhaka may well have been a more literally Roman-classically modern than theatrically modernistic capital, like Brasilia, namely, Edwin Lutyens's New Delhi, including the famous Viceroy's House that Hitchcock, the original "International Style" apologist, begrudged in 1958 as "a *tour de force* for which, from the Queen Anne, the Neo-Georgian and the Palladian, Lutyens lifted his sights to a Roman scale."[53] (Perhaps especially Kahnian, there, is a superb small stone church of plain brick.) Today, the growing historical reappreciation of Lutyens's work at the Indian imperial capital may owe something, in turn, to the artistic impact of Louis Kahn's architecture, including the graciously light, humane splendor of Sher-e-Bangla Nagar.[54]

Aldo Rossi claimed that Kahn's "Roman-ness" and later classicism is shallow, unsystematic, and uncritical. Manfredo Tafuri has responded that Kahn may have been a step ahead. Undetained by analysis of the "contaminated architectual *systems*" with which he dealt, he may nevertheless have "already achieved his task through the transience of his historiographical data." Kahn was not "trying to accentuate, polemically, the dehistoricization of modern art through the *pastiche,* or . . . to fix, unequivocally, a new code," so that, "one begins to suspect that the misty and variable inconsistency of the Kahnian poetic might be, after all, entirely coherent with its purposes." Thus this Marxist historian accords Kahn the pursuit of "a *new objectivity*" in which "history is only an *ingredient* to be manipulated. He uses it to justify choices already made or to shed semantic light . . . on values that aspire towards the symbol and the institution" – openly, without credulousness. If "the historicism of the Kahnian school harks back to the European myth of Reason," at least that enables it to become "a phenomenon opposed to the pragmatist American tradition, balanced, by now, between a fun-fair irrationality and a guilty cynicism";[55] and even Kahn's eclecticism is something very different from that "banal a-historicism" of the International Style that made possible the "equally a-historical compromise . . . of the worst American eclecticism, from Yamasaki to Stone. . . ."[56]

The Dhaka Capitol, in particular, strikes Tafuri as hermetic, self-involved, too aloof from life to engage what Walter Benjaman called absent-minded attention.[57] Such works, he believes, ought to be more self-critical about their standing as "new symbolic object[s]" in a period of critical crisis.[58] Yet it is noteworthy, here, that Tafuri associates the "critical restorations" of "Kahn's

140

last work" with "the exasperated articulation of a theme originally taken as absolute" in "late-Gothic and Mannerist typological *inventions*,"[59] and remarks on Kahn's fixation on the late antique of Hadrian's Villa, with its "disarticulation of the spatial successions."[60] Shrewdly, Tafuri detects a certain far-fetchedness in ostensible formalist purity not only in the work of Paul Rudolph and others, but even in Kahn's, where even *that* I tend to take as historically manneristic.[61]

There is, in its own right, the theoretical problem of monumentality. Kahn did design actual monuments, in the sense of structures whose only function is memorial. In a principal version of the Memorial to the Six Million Jewish Martyrs (1966–72), for Battery Park on New York Harbor, the logic of a simple-looking "minimalist" set of seven cubic elements spaced out on a grid is more complex than it would seem. Take out your graph paper again, and fill in what will be the central square. A plinth will extend three squares out in each direction, with the outside ring, seven squares long on each side, clear. Along what will be the transverse axis, skip one square from the center and fill the next (i.e., third) on either side, producing (counting the blank border), one complete alternating sequence of blanks and solids; in the other direction, leaving only the central square of the longitudinal axis solid, make the knight's move of skipping to the next row in each opposite direction and filling in only the second square left and right. The resultant "checker" arrangement of volumes and voids manages to seem in different ways: fourfold, sixfold, sevenfold and ninefold, with a Star of David of six "points" implicit. (Not to be discounted, historically, however, in terms of a seeming ninefold square, is a possible allusion to the Palace and Temple of Solomon, which in the influential Ezekielesque Renaissance reconstruction of the Spanish Jesuit Villalpando, published in 1596, was set on a nine-square plan.)[62]

Another monument for New York, to Franklin Delano Roosevelt, on the southern end of Welfare (now Roosevelt) Island in the East River, and dating from 1973–4, was to consist of an acute angle of shallow-angled riverside ramps lined formally with trees. Saying that it may be better that neither of these monuments has been built will not, I trust, affront the memory of the Holocaust victims or of FDR. Not every space should be ceremonialized, especially not every prominent space. Perhaps one cannot live in a sanctuary without inevitable sacrilege; also, every generation has a right to possess the earth, even the citified earth, as not entirely assigned and programmed. It is no fault of Kahn's that both of these projects belonged to a time when encouragement was given to a pseudoradical idea of public art that invades private thought with notions playful or solemn. (Renaming Welfare Island after him was a better memorial to Roosevelt than the rendering "designed" and permanently visually earmarked, of the tip of that island, as even Kahn's monument would have done; and as for the Holocaust monument, what with Battery Park already starting to look like the municipal trophy collection, a grove of fine cedars would be better anyway, especially there.)

Actually, with Kahn the question of monumentality – already posed by

Summerson during World War II[63] – might be less urgent than a certain generalized "architecture-as-ritual" thematic of his work strikes me as ideologically defective if not dangerous, issuing as it has in the corporate imperiousness of I. M. Pei, who seems to think he is the "next" Louis Kahn, not to speak of those who wish they could be the next I. M. Pei. Kahn's own metaphysical touchstone of "light" is partly classical-Corbusian; but in the writings it is either a bit "potty" (a "paraphysics" of light) or else all too seriously gnostical. Who, believer or not, ever said that the mere air or aura of divinity was what was wanted anyway? These things may be difficult to articulate in such a secularized culture as ours, but what could be worse than the "power of God" with God quite out of the picture? Kahn himself cared about the real thing, but in the big league of American capitalist building that seems to be allowed only on sabbaths. Besides, there is *ceremony* without grandiloquence.

I wish we New Yorkers could say of Louis Kahn, "If you seek his monument, look around you," but only Philadelphians (how Greek that sounds) or dwellers in the vicinity can make anything like such a claim, Kahn never having built anything here. When he died in our Pennsylvania Station in 1974, it hadn't really been Penn Station for a decade. It was not McKim, Mead, and White's stupendous edifice, that greatest neo-Roman building in this hemisphere, as memorialized in Walker Evans's last full-dress photographs of the building on the eve of its destruction, including loving details of coffered classical barrel vaults as well as doctrinally modernist exposed steelwork. Thirtieth-Street Station, in Kahn's home town, is almost sheerly monumental enough to make the rest of that city seem like a distant afterthought. Staring high up at the crisp, square-cast twentieth-century coffers – trying to be so Greek – of its cityside portico, one senses Kahn's longing for a deeper classicism, and the genuine anxieties of producing it in our time.

10

Crystalline Form, Worringer, and the Minimalism of Tony Smith

ONE chief interest – and pleasure – of art history concerns the dialectic of continuity and change. That dialectic has lately flattened out, along with the sense of historicity that makes it possible. Aloïs Riegl, Wilhelm Worringer, and other great early modern art historians sustained a kind of stereoptic, or at least bifocal, attention to recent art along with art of the distant, and also the unorthodox, past. At this end of their century, most of the fun seems gone from the game. The barren antiquarian needlepoint of reactionaries persists even as a dreary, quite unspectacular, nihilistic "spectacle" of antihistoricism plays itself out.

If two formally similar works of art, ancient and modern, are juxtaposed – say, one just nearly classical Greek, the other American high abstract[1] – there are still, believe it or not, many who will construe the earlier work as a Newtonian cause or "source," direct if possible, of the later. Meanwhile, others will have dismissed the whole setup as hopelessly aestheticizing – as if all I were doing were extending beyond representational art a Winckelmannian sense that the ancient piece in question is still too "early" and, well, chubby, whereas at least the abstract one has the (later antique) *Apollo Belvedere* to thank for its elegant, would-be classical poise. Well, Wilhem Worringer was not looking for elegant poise and neither am I, though I imagine him, who in preparing the way for Kandinsky prepared the wider way for abstract art, wondering before my hypothetical comparison about the persistence of an ultimately classical sense of geometric form, now only more blatant in unalloyed abstraction.

After all, a great deal of abstract painting and sculpture on the geometric or constructivist, if not the ostensibly expressionist side, does offer essentially classical form and structure denuded of classical representation. The noble nude is stripped down beyond even pose to sheer structural disposition and the undraped forces of pure "composition." So too, one entire aspect of "ab-

stract" modernist architecture extends essentially classical, preeminently geometric, conceptions of form and composition. This fascinating matter of classical underpinnings in modern architecture arises in such varied forms
throughout the polemical as well as the historical literature that one might be
pardoned the simplification of thinking it the destiny of modern architecture,
over and against pedantries old or new, to inherit the most venerable form
problems of this singular plastic art that has always been "abstract."[2]

Ironically – because we can only see this in a modern light that emanates
partly from him – Worringer presents the already convinced modern reader
with a difficulty. Basically, he has to assume that you assume (as Jacques
Derrida, for one, patently still does) that art is essentially pictorializing. He
wants to convince you otherwise, so his filling in on crucial preclassical,
antinaturalistic – I would say, essentially Neolithic[3] – stylization *precisely as
abstract* is supposed to come as a surprise. Art was already ("abstractly") stylized
long before it was classically empathetic-naturalistic. Prehistoric (Neolithic)
stylization was itself the antithesis of still earlier, primeval (Paleolithic) naturalism. Given the thrust of Worringer's argument, why else would he say
"abstraction" first, and only then "empathy," especially since the implication,
in 1908, is: here comes abstraction *again*. Consequently, those of us who,
thanks partly to Worringer, take abstraction as a rule, with any naturalism
after the Paleolithic (particularly that of the nineteenth century) as a fly-by-
night exception, may find ourselves stumbling anew over his polemical terms.
Looking back to *Abstraction and Empathy* across eighty years of abstract art and
modern architecture, the compounded surprise that always strikes me, as one
who grew up devoted to modernity and seeing the premodern as much as
possible in a modern way, is not that the naturalistic Greeks felt at home in
the world, but rather, that the alternative, a sublimating distancing from nature
(especially when there was seemingly something wrong with the world), was
supposed to engender German expressionism instead of an opposite, geometric
constructivism (including architecture).

All of which concerns me in a Worringerian way because minimalist sculpture, which despite the American desire to be unbegotten descended in the
constructivist tradition, defining itself against the specifically "expressionist"
art (specifically painting) of the New York School, was to me and my generation what otherwise antithetical expressionism was to Worringer and his –
radically reactive and revisionist. While abstract expressionism in relation to
earlier German expressionism is a subject unto itself, it is hardly wrongheaded,
for instance, to think today of Jackson Pollock when, in that other classic of
his, *Form Problems of the Gothic* (1911), Worringer speaks of "the Gothic line"
as "essentially abstract and at the same time of very strong vitality."[4]

Needless to say, there was as yet no such thing as constructivism when
Worringer wrote *Abstraction and Empathy: A Contribution to the Psychology of
Style*. Insofar as the debut of cubism can be dated to November 9, 1908, when
Braque exhibited paintings from the previous year,[5] Worringer could not have
seen anything from which constructivism would in turn proceed when he
wrote, two months before, the preface to the book. Indeed, his crucial en-

counter with tribal art at the Trocadéro in the company of Georg Simmel (recalled in his 1948 preface), before he had even settled on this, his academic dissertation project, which was accepted as such in 1907, must have predated Picasso's equally revelatory visit to the same collection of tribal art in May or June of the same year.[6]

Most Western geometric art traces back readily through a great deal of Italianate, classicizing European painting, sculpture, and architecture – confusingly enough, if you try to hold to Worringer on this – to "empathetic" Greek art itself. As Wölfflin puts it, whoever goes from the North to Italy is likely to notice, "How plain and easy to grasp are the planes and cubes!"[7] But that, in a way, is exactly what Worringer challenges. To understand the original expressionist frame of mind we must see that it embraces the Gothic as "its" own opposite, Germanic analogue, necessarily ad hoc, to codified geometric classicism – a notion that goes back beyond Goethe,[8] but that now subsumes in an affirmative way the formerly disadvantaged formalist distinction of Northern versus Italianate art that Wöllflin absorbed from his teacher Jacob Burckhardt.[9] We must also see, more problematically, that this alternative system *is* indeed a system of sorts, and that as such it comprehends geometric form, even "classical" geometry.

In critical practice it was possible to stretch the notion of expression far enough to cover an updated classicism, at least in architecture. To take a period example: in 1917 the expressionistically sympathetic art historian Fritz Burger compared two recent and in one way or another modernist German buildings: Paul Bonatz and F. E. Scholer's Stuttgart railway station, 1911–14 (resumed 1919–27), with its loggia of plain, lightly Doricizing square piers; and Peter Behrens's 1911–12 German embassy in Saint Petersburg, also known as the Botschafter Palace (of which the young Mies van der Rohe happens to have supervised the construction), having an " 'industrially' stylized"[10] engaged Doric order. Faced with the (one might have thought) obvious fact that the great Behrens here seems to fall back on a traditionalist classicism whereas Bonatz's building makes do with demythologized square piers, Burger opts to count both buildings as expressively astute. He reads the sheer restraint of Bonatz's station as empathetic-expressive, while what might have been mere conservatism in Behrens's embassy Burger accommodates as an appropriately different, specifically ambassadorial expressive statement, namely, a willfully decorous aloofness and an elegant sophistication in which even a certain "concession" to classicism finds place.[11] Were rationalization required, I would instead have sought to stress Behrens's Doric order as formally abstract, possibly even as crystalline; but Burger stands by a broad linguistic of expression.

After all, the main argument for geometric abstract form is still the rationalist one, which has a much easier "logocentric" time laying claim to the Platonic solids, the Parthenon, Euclid, Vitruvius, Raphael, Poussin, whatever. Now, for instance, one can easily look at two English bridges of the late eighteenth century, built within a few years of each other, and see in the protofunctional Coalbrookdale Bridge (1777–9), by Abraham Darby III (with T. F. Pritchard), a directness that is not altogether estranged from the classical ornamental geometry of an Adamesque neoclassical canal bridge at Pulteney (1769–72 or 1797). To call both bridges loosely "classical" does mean something more than merely saying they are "classics."

Nor need one necessarily know the ancient Tower of the Winds in Athens, so often quoted in post-Renaissance European architecture (especially in steeples), to sense in front of Tony Smith's sculpture *Tower of the Winds,* 1962, a foursquare and abstractly "classical" structural aplomb. From about the same time, too, dates a sheet, *Untitled (No Stars),* on which Smith has sketched out simple and complex geometric solids, from "tet," "hex," "oct," and "dodeca" onward.[12] Yet the question within expressionism of crystalline geometry as classicizing or else anticlassical anticipates the question within latter-day minimalism, including Tony Smith's, of crystalline geometry as formal or anti-formal, antiexpressive or pointedly neutral.

Since Worringer himself was by no means oblivious to the Burckhardtian North–South distinction, it may help in establishing the ambiguous standing of crystalline form in latter-day minimalism to compare a cube drawn by Dürer with a well-known 1962 piece by Tony Smith called *Die.* Dürer's drawing, from his Dresden sketchbook (fol. 168v), dates from the 1520s, after he had spent more than two years in Italy on two visits. It shows a cube like a box with its top lifted off, the "box" transparent enough to reveal two intersecting inner diagonals, yet opaque enough, owing to horizontal hatching on the front and diagonal hatching on the side, to cast a shadow.[13] As transparently crystalline as it presents itself, Dürer's drawn cube is also rigid and earthbound, crystalline in the sense of quartz. No one would call Smith's *Die* "light and airy," but opaque as it looks, Smith's hollow steel cube hovers, slightly propped on two slats, as if definitively demonstrating the contemporary sculptural distinction – equivalently doctrinal in the realm of modernist architecture – between volume and mass. Not that the ideal of volume without mass was without its poetry; to quote a passage from Joyce that describes a blind man's negotiation of the three-dimensional world, in Tony Smith's beloved *Ulysses:* "How on earth did he know that van was there? Must have felt it. See things in their foreheads perhaps. Kind of sense of volume. Weight. Would he feel it if something was removed? Feel a gap."[14]

Even a natural crystal of iron pyrite seems almost privileged in a quasi-classical way as some marvelous exception to the irregularities (Romantically charming or not) of nature: in its cubicality it might as well have been designed by a cool neoclassical artist of the late eighteenth century, or equally, I am suggesting, by any cool minimalist sculptor of the 1960s or 1970s – not only the Smith of *Die* but also, perhaps, the Ruth Vollmer of *Heptahedron,* cast in acrylic in 1970. That minimalism was deeply apathetic in the strict, neutral sense, usually comes down on the classical side as cool – anti-pathetic as the movement was toward the emotional indulgences of abstract expressionism, and then to the embarrassing binge of hedonistic lyrical painting that formalist critics next anointed. The marked inertness of minimalism is widely manifest in a recourse to crystalline forms as generated systematically and without inflection, hence supposedly affect-free as well as formally self-evident. So I call minimalism apathetic with a cordial neutrality, much as the critic Charles Henry mobilized the concept of "anaesthesia" as opposite of the aesthetically enervated state on behalf of a new anti-impressionist art in the 1880s.[15] If this seems remote from Worringer, who would no doubt have preferred the art of the abstract expressionists anyway, it could probably not have been said, at least this way, but for *Abstraction and Empathy*.

Before considering the speculative background to the crystalline imagery of Worringer and Aloïs Riegl, let me make two suggestions. First, in Rieglian terms, Worringer's appeal to the very word "abstraktion," Latinate as that is, can only confirm an underlying and abiding, by no means defunct but innately protomodern, late Latinity – like Riegl's own deeply grounded philosophical appeal to Saint Augustine as perfectly, vitally late antique, and rightly spiritual as such, in the Holy Roman Empire of Vienna in 1901.[16] This puts the shoe on the other foot, leaving the etymologically Germanic "Einfühlung" (and the prevailing contemporary naturalistic aesthetic) in a defensive, by comparison very bodily, roughly physical, even "barbarian," position.

Second, Worringer was so concerned with contemporary psychology – mistakenly, Goldwater thought[17] – that I wonder how concerned he may also have been with other departments of contemporary science. Of course, the legacy of *Naturphilosophie* would remain available even in pre–World War II German culture, almost as if Goethe had still been watching, ever since the summer of 1787 in Italy, bursting pine kernels "[throwing] off their hood and reveal[ing] the rudiments of their destined form."[18] It is worth considering that the understanding of specifically organic structure as crypto-crystalline on even the molecular level was established only with August Kekulé's hypothetical hexagon of the benzene ring of organic chemistry, during Worringer's childhood. What, after all, in the entire universe, is more literally organic than the metaphorically crystalline benzene ring of chemical notation?

In the address of 1890 in which Kekulé recounted his *invenzione* of the spatially hexagonal benzene ring, which made modern organic chemistry possible – an address best known, ironically, as a rather surrealist case of inspiration through dream – Kekulé testifies that his mind was well prepared when the "idea-seed" of this essentially crystalline structural metaphor fell to it. He had discovered in high school special aptitudes for both mathematics and drawing that led his father to encourage him toward architecture even as this flowering of his structural imagination inspired an interest in the historical development of chemistry.[19] (In the same spirit of childhood imagination one might wonder how much subsequent popular comprehension of atomic structure is owed to the children's "Tinker Toy," dating from 1914 and in some sense derivative of Kekuléan molecular thought.)

Aesthetic speculation concerning regular structure as (finally) organic-crystalline-classical, frequent in the nineteenth century, culminated soon after Kekulé in the work of Aloïs Riegl.

Riegl is referenced at so many points in *Abstraction and Empathy* that I will simply put into extreme closeup, as he himself liked to do in visual description, one or two passages of his *Spätrömische Kunstindustrie* (1901; 1927) for a fresh sense of what must have attracted Worringer. In one place Riegl considers the faceted antique gemstone as classical and not yet, for his purposes, protoimpressionistically modern: "Classical art did not want to see the stone just for its optical-colorful value, but predominantly for its bodily shape value (*körperlichen Formwert*) and . . . therefore it gave the stone on one side its crystalline shape broken into clearly divided partial planes (*eine kristallinische, in klar geschiedene Teilebenen gebrochene Form*)."[20] In another passage, however, the crystalline connotes an immobile stasis, as Riegl notes in a late-antique bronze bird "a particular mixture between the observation of . . . animated organic nature and a tendency toward crystalline immotion (*kristallinische Ruhe*)."[21]

Evidently, Riegl's and Worringer's essentially active and sequential – I would say linguistically "asymmetric" – critical polarities owe much to the Apollonian and Dionysian terms of *The Birth of Tragedy* (1872). In the same way, Nietzsche owes some impetus, and says so, to Schiller's *On Naive and Sentimental Poetry* (1795–6). Again, if Worringer meant simply to shift from a happy Greek classical naturalism to an anxious modern distancing and "stylization," he could have called his book *Empathy and Abstraction*. Worringer owes his dialectical sense of filling in with background that reverses the foreground most profoundly to Nietzsche's great modernist attack on uncritical classicism in *The Birth of Tragedy*.

With Nietzsche, the light-cavalry elegance of early nineteenth-century Prussian classicism gives way to a violently Hellenic infantry action that undercuts all classicism of "mere appearance" in order to deepen it. In the "Attempt at Self-Criticism" prefixed to his 1886 reissue of *The Birth of Tragedy*, Nietzsche sarcastically regrets not having resorted to "an individual language" of his own, since some readers have obviously missed the point of his having "tried laboriously to express by means of Schopenhauerian and Kantian formulas strange and new valuations which were basically at odds with Kant's and Schopenhauer's spirit and taste"[22] – as if he didn't know!

"It is in Doric art that [the] majestically *rejecting* attitude of Apollo is immortalized," Nietzsche says early on in *Birth* (sect. 2),[23] as he initiates a great new rejection of that rejection, it having become "necessary to level the artistic structure of the *Apollonian culture,* as it were, *stone by stone,* till the foundations on which it rests become visible" (sect. 3).[24] "For to me the *Doric* state and Doric art are explicable only as a permanent military encampment of the Apollonian" (sect. 4).[25] When he says, in a practically crystalline image, "Everything that comes to the surface in the Apollonian part of Greek tragedy, in the dialogue, looks simple, transparent and beautiful" (sect. 9),[26] Nietzsche truly means that it only *looks* simple. This is peace only after war. And what Worringer owes above all else to Nietzsche is this sense that the direct, but far from superficial, appeal of crystalline form is grounded in and founded upon deep-set, chthonic struggle. (By the time Nietzsche and Worringer, alike, finish with them, key terms take on more adequate senses, if with newly opposite valences than they apparently had to begin with.)

An aside: Worringer seems to make something of a historical, as well as Nietzschean, mistake, in making a theoretical point, when he states too simply that "art does not begin with naturalistic constructs (*naturalistischen Gebilden*), but with ornamental-abstract ones."[27] That stance could only be maintained by dismissing the Old Stone Age as preartistic (and in a sense, Worringer does still confuse tribal with prehistoric art); but to leave paleolithic people in the position of *Naturvölker* risks projecting upon them a romanticized idea of the Old Stone Age.[28] That might start art history off once more on the wrong foot, winding up yet again with classicism, in an extended sense, as good news. This, however, is easy to say only because, thanks to both thinkers, we can understand paleolithic naturalism as "Dionysian" and neolithic stylization as (only) subsequently "Apollonian"; Worringer was worried about a later succession anyway. Otherwise, complex enough to count as a tour de force is his more vitally expressionist argument that whereas the classical Greek temple offers "organic life . . . substituted for matter . . . in the [protoexpressionist] Gothic cathedral, on the contrary, matter lives solely on its own mechanical laws" – "but these laws," he hastens to add, "despite their fundamentally abstract character, have become living, i.e. they have acquired expression."[29]

At its base, this idea of Gothic mechanics has its own protomodern French rationalist history, but for his own Germanic modernist reasons Worringer has to make a point of handling it his way. In that his distinctly more Northerly way also concerns nineteenth-century Gothicism as erecting itself like an ideological barricade against further circulation of official classical doctrine, we would do well to turn aside briefly to two principal midcentury Gothicists, French and English, and then return through important Germanic speculations of which Worringer would have been aware.

Eugène Emmanuel Viollet-le-Duc's *Dictionnaire raisonné de l'architecture française du XIᵉ au XVIᵉ siècle* (1854–68) was not so long ago still well known as a kind of old testament to twentieth-century functionalist architectural theory. In it this Gothic-modernist admires the "inflexible logic" of nature at her structural work, extrapolating from an equilateral triangle inscribed in a circle, to a tetrahedron in a sphere, higher and higher crystalline complexities. In one diagram Viollet juxtaposes rhombohedrons of granite crystals with hexagonal crystals of volcanic basalt "derived from the rhombohedral form." I will resist the temptation to tackle the implicit metaphysics by simply pointing out that in selecting this discussion for their analytical edition of selections from the *Dictionnaire,* Viollet's modern editors flag this passage with every appropriate tag: "reason," "geometry," "nature," "epistemology," "crystallization," "system," "organicism," "principles."[30]

In England, between Ruskin's *Seven Lamps of Architecture* (1849) and his *Stones of Venice* (1853), enthusiasm for the crystalline form on the part of this, the world's greatest despiser of classical regularity, had detectably increased. In the chapter titled "The Lamp of Beauty" in the *Seven Lamps,* even the geologist in Ruskin seems to object that the straight line is at odds with nature, hence with beauty: "To find right lines in nature at all, we may be compelled to do violence to her finished work, break through the sculptured and colored surfaces of her crags, and examine the processes of their crystallization" (4.6).[31] But in *The Stones of Venice,* four years later, under "The Material of Ornament," is a more affirmative paragraph on "Forms of Earth (Crystals)," stating that although a sculptor cannot hope to imitate either the scale of mountains or all the "steps of . . . [nature's] fury" in rock and mountain fractures, "crystalline form" now deserves admiration as "the completely systematised natural structure of the earth" (Chap. 11).[32]

Germanistically speaking, however, probably nothing is more pressing in this retrospection than Schopenhauer's *World as Will and Representation,* wherein crystalline metaphor of an utterly chemical enthusiasm is consistently prominent in conveying how phenomena snap ever in and out of stable organization only to assume another condition. Of many appropriate passages in the first volume (1819), where the crystalline even has its place in the Platonic musical unity of the organic and inorganic realms (1.52),[33] two can be singled out. First, as a stable aggregate, the crystal is taken as the only individuality in inorganic nature, at least provisionally holding its own as thing in itself, "Just as" – amazing analogy – "the tree is an aggregate from the individual shooting fibre showing itself in every rib of the leaf, in every leaf, in every branch" (1.26).[34] Schopenhauer's figure even entails the immortalizing finality of much cubical imagery in memorial art: "The crystal has only one manifestation of life, namely its formation, which afterwards has its fully adequate and exhaustive expression in the coagulated form, in the corpse of that momentary life" (1.28).[35]

In the second volume (1844), an extended and in some sense more romantic gloss on the first, three passages vie for Worringerian attention. Considering that "our knowledge consists only in the *framing of representations* by means of subjective forms," Schopenhauer's crystal connotes not microsublime simplicity but ultimately inscrutable complication: "For not merely do the highest productions of nature, namely, living beings, or the *complicated* phenomena of the inorganic world remain inscrutable to us, but even every rock-crystal, even iron pyrites, are, by virtue of their crystallographical, optical, chemical and electrical properties, an abyss of incomprehensibilities and mysteries for our searching consideration and investigation" (2.18).[36] Next, a passage that Riegl would surely have liked: "With the *organic* body . . . its life, in other words its existence as something organic, consists simply in the constant change of the *material* with persistence of the *form;* thus its essence and identity lie in the form alone. Therefore the *inorganic* body has its continued existence through *repose* and isolation from external influences. . . . " (2.23).[37] Finally, there is also an extended passage, too long to quote, criticizing Gothic architecture and crystal imagery as applied to it, but which would have concerned Riegl and Worringer for its dubious art history alone (2.35).[38]

Certainly Schopenhauer knew that to his hated Hegel, in the 1820s, the crystal connoted freedom, insofar as matter assumes its own pure form rather than having form imposed from without. It is a surprisingly short step in the same paragraph – one cannot help thinking, in the German modernist direction

– from there to "a similar activity of immanent formation" in the living human body and "its movement and the expression of feelings," whereby "inner activity . . . emerges vitally"[39] – even if, in the regular and symmetrical forms of crystals, "abstractions alone are active as determinants."[40] In his treatment of architecture, where the Egyptian pyramids – which a century later would fascinate Worringer and the German expressionist architects – are as yet pre-classically "just simple crystals," Hegel takes architecture itself as an "inorganic nature built by human hands."[41] Yet such "architecture as a mere enclosure and as inorganic nature (nature not in itself individualized and animated by its indwelling spirit) can be shaped only in a way external to itself, though the external form is not organic but abstract and mathematical."[42]

By the time Hegel preached his aesthetics, Friedrich Schiller's "naive and sentimental" distinction was a generation old. Now it is not only when aphoristic – "Our feeling for nature is like the feeling of an invalid for health,"[43] nor in tone (because the naive poet perceives a "dry truth [*trockene Wahrheit*]" he may seem to deal insensitively with his object)[44] – that Schiller adumbrates Nietzsche, who diputes him, but with a firm handshake. There is a similarly antinomian sense that, dissociated from the "artificial world," the poet can reattain to nature within, "exempt," then, "from all laws by which a corrupted heart is protected against itself."[45] Nietzsche might have disputed the terms of Schiller's distinction between "actual nature (*wirkliche Natur*)," which is commonplace, and "true nature (*wahre Natur*)," to which "belongs an inner necessity of existence (*eine innere Notwendigkeit des Daseins*)";[46] but as for the question of why we "cling" to nature "and embrace even the inanimate world with the warmest sensibility," both Nietzsche and then Worringer would have applauded Schiller's answer: "It is *because* nature in us has disappeared from humanity and we rediscover her in her truth only outside it, in the inanimate world."[47]

An early point in the *Birth of Tragedy* near which Worringer seems to hover is also the point at which Nietzsche most depends on Schiller for negation: "This harmony which is contemplated with such longing by modern man, in fact this oneness of man with nature (for which Schiller introduced the technical term 'naive'), is by no means a simple condition that comes into being naturally and as if inevitably. . . . Where we encounter the 'naive' in art, we should recognize the highest effect of Apollonian culture – which . . . must have triumphed over an abysmal and terrifying view of the world and the keenest susceptibility to suffering through recourse to the most forceful and pleasurable illusions" (sect. 3).[48] Our own later American abstract expressionists would have applauded Schiller's sense that "genius delineates its own thoughts at a single felicitous stroke of the brush (*mit einem einzigen glücklichen Pinselstrich*) . . . " while "to genius, language springs as if by some inner necessity (*durch innere Notwendigkeit*) out of thought, and is so at one with it that even beneath the corporeal frame the spirit appears as if laid bare." On the side of all art termed sentimental, meaning worked at, contrived, "the sign (*das Zeichen*) remains forever heterogenous and alien to the thing signified (*dem Bezeichneten*)."[49]

After all of this, it will seem like a letdown to quote Kant, against whose sense of the *Ding an sicht* Schopenhauer actually sharpened his crystalline imagery. In the *Critique of Judgment* (1790) Kant does sound like an unshakable classicist, maintaining that we admire perfect, regular geometrical figures for their (objective) availability to "all kinds of cognitive uses" rather than for a (subjective) aesthetic, even an "intellectual," beauty (sect. 62).[50] Let us turn forward, however, toward 1910 and 1960 by way of certain marginal but telling eighteenth-century works of art.

All the more because Worringer was not a rationalist type, and because academic classicism was the enemy in 1908, the problem of cubic and crystalline form in the eighteenth century holds Worringerean as well as minimalist interest. On the second page of *Abstraction and Empathy* – the Meridian paperback of which appeared during the burgeoning of American minimalism, in 1967 – the new law is laid down: "Just as the urge to empathy as a pre-assumption of aesthetic experience finds its gratification in the beauty of the organic, so the urge to abstraction finds its beauty in the life-denying inorganic, in the crystalline (*im Kristallinischen*) or, in general terms, in all abstract law and necessity."[51] These are Worringer's own words, even though he sometimes borrows "crystalline" from Riegl (and "cubic" from Adolf von Hildebrand).

To the annoyance of ahistorically minded artists and others, occasional neoclassical precedents for minimalist crystalline form do appear in the eighteenth century. (Indeed, sometimes minimalism begins to look like a replay of eighteenth-century Whiggish nouveau-bourgeois culture, beyond the obvious American attempt to efface historical complexity.) One such adumbration I have already entertained, apropos of a supposed stylelessness in minimalism: a Bible illustration by Johann August Corvinus (1683–1738) showing a plain, empty, open-topped cubic box under a loggia, this with a landscape beyond.[52] What can Corvinus's empty cube set in pictorial space have illustrated? The statement in Genesis 18:6 that Abraham told Sarah to run and get specifically *three seahs* of flour, to make rolls (three seahs equaling one *ephah,* or about half a bushel) – in other words, a pure, massless *volume,* not grain *in* that amount, at all.

More art historically urgent is an illustration published by the eighteenth-century classicizing, neo-Palladian architect Robert Morris in his *Lectures on Architecture* (1734–6), in which the pure proportions of potentially classical edifices are built up from neutral unit cubes, like children's blocks uniform (except for a half-block) in size. Wittkower, who discussed Morris's essentially proportional thinking in 1944 only to be disputed by Emil Kaufmann in 1955, returned to the matter in a lecture of 1966.[53] To Kaufmann, in Morris's "cubic" method, as he calls it, the Morrisonian "IDEA" was more important than specific proportions,[54] as many a minimalist has claimed. Now Rykwert adds that the "Ideal Beauty" at which Morris aims in architecture "is very like what [Francis] Hutcheson describes as 'Original and Absolute Beauty': in which the element of imitation is wholly absent. Yet Hutcheson explicitly, Morris by implication, recognize their difference from earlier Neoplatonic thinking. The beauty, even the harmony, is not something which is a property of the object: it is an idea in the mind, an idea which relates to the primary qualities of an object . . . "[55] Note that another rubric for minimalist sculpture, when it first appeared, was "primary forms."

As sparely as he conceived the exteriors of his cubical buildings (typically country houses), this Robert Morris actively allowed for contrastingly ornamented, even quasi-Rococo, interiors.[56] Admitting obvious differences (rural versus urban; gentry versus petit bourgeois), this Morris might thus be said to anticipate by a century Walter Benjamin's claimed origin for the "interior" of the "private citizen" in the age of Louis Philippe.[57] A hundred years after that, in the time of Worringer, we encounter the essentially urban, and utterly urbane, domestic architecture of the Viennese Adolf Loos, who sought as early as 1898 to establish "inside the historically determined city . . . a *wohnlichen Raum*," a closed, "protected" space "in which the individual can find 'shelter.' " This is quite the opposite of expressionist *Glasarchitektur*,[58] and in our time newly appealing in a minimalist way, like the crystalline expressionist "glass architecture," mostly of fantasy, itself.[59]

The eighteenth-century Morris's cube clusters would probably have been noticed in our time only by a sculptor interested in architecture, such as Tony Smith, author of *Die,* perhaps the single most famous minimalist cube sculpture. However, one eighteenth-century sculpturesque work, by the poet Goethe, was widely noticed when it appeared illustrated, in 1967, in Robert Rosenblum's *Transformations in Late Eighteenth-Century Art.* This is Goethe's so-called Altar of Good Fortune, dating from 1777, in the park at Weimar, a symbolic as well as elementally formal work alluding to the sphere of Fortune as resting unstably upon the cube of Virtue. While Rosenblum calls it "more of an exercise in symbolic geometry than a creative work of sculpture or architecture," he also notes, "It was characteristic of the late eighteenth century that these symbolic forms [i.e., sphere and cube] could be pushed to so absolute a reduction that they almost appear unrelated to a particular historical epoch."[60] Even with its funereal tinge, the cubic element of Goethe's monument will remind a modernist of Smith's *Die,* first executed in 1962, then again in 1967 (*Die II*), whose title plays not only on death but on the fateful throw of dice.

The Morris cubes were illustrated in Emil Kaufmann's *Architecture in the Age of Reason* (1955), which was reprinted in paperback in 1968,[61] two years after minimalist sculptor Carl Andre had begun to exhibit neat low stacks of firebricks in rectilinear disposition on the gallery floor.[62] (The British government purchase of one such piece for the Tate Gallery produced a scandal in which the English obviously forgot their old Robert Morris.) According to Wittkower, Morris's cube clusters were orthodox classical in their essential proportionality,[63] whereas the art of Andre and other minimalists stands against composed form per se; but if their placement on the floor is nonrelational, it is also rectilinear, far from arbitrary, and at least neutrally constructivistic.

From the eighteenth-century Robert Morris (there is an American minimalist by the same name) through early functionalist interest in the "Taylorism" of the famous American efficiency expert,[64] the cube or bricklike block has served as an elemental architectonic unit. Looking not unlike Morris's stacked cubes, but with an innate severity of cubical massing serving an expressive purpose of spiritual gravity, is Adolf Loos's 1921 project for a black granite mausoleum. Planned to have interior frescoes by the expressionist Oskar Kokoschka, this was to be built to the memory of the great Czech Viennese art historian and friend of the expressionists, Max Dvořák; to it, a line from Georg Trakl has been related: "Our silence is a black cavern."[65] Among the antiexpressive American minimalists, however, Andre's brick stacks make even the old Morris's diagram seem nuanced: their stubborn Emersonian plod away from all European "composing" has a stolidity of its own. If cubic and prismatic form is indeed generally counterexpressive, inexpressivity can be tantamount to expression; impassiveness, to affect.

Beginning in Germany in 1911, when Worringer's Gothic book appeared, Walter Gropius had begun to broadcast an enthusiasm for new American industrial architecture combined with an Egyptian enthusiasm, already influenced by *Abstraction and Empathy,* that in turn would influence Worringer's own *Agyptische Kunst* (1927); Gropius also praised Peter Behrens's new German industrial buildings as "commanding their surroundings with truly classical grandeur."[66] Ironically, when an "Authorized American Edition" of Worringer's *Form Problems of the Gothic* appeared (in 1920?), "For Which the [anonymous] Translator Has Selected Illustrative Material Chiefly from American Collections,"[67] a photograph of Cass Gilbert's new but neo-Gothic Woolworth Building of 1913, was included – not one of the more functionalistic industrial structures.[68]

By the time Loos designed the Moller House, in Vienna, of 1928, where the wall of a stairwell is pierced by a rectangular opening to leave a continuous square-cornered sequence of rising, crossing, descending and then low right-angled horizontal elements (Figure 16), he, too, was aware of the type of the American concrete-framed "daylight" factory with its gridded walls, built from 1903 onward. On a visit to this country at the turn of the century the radically restrained, antiornamental Loos, like the more wildly expressionist Erich Mendelsohn two decades later, already found American industrial architecture inspiring.[69] We may tend to think of such forms as belonging to a type of building so utilitarian as to be utterly materialist; but as with the minimalist sculpture yet to be, there was the possibility of a kind of chaste ultimacy even in that. Loos would claim in 1932, in the spirit of Le Corbusier's *Vers une architecture* a decade earlier, that these "engineers are our Hellenes."[70]

Certainly under the new minimalist impassiveness Loos looked peculiarly interesting all over again, as a juxtaposition of the Moller House stairway with Tony Smith's *Free Ride,* of 1962 (New York, Museum of Modern Art), suggests. And setting *Free Ride* beside David Smith's *Cubi XXIII,* 1964 (Los Angeles County Museum) might only make the rigorous abstraction of the piece by the more famous Smith seem traditionally compositional, what with the syncopated crossing of its twin right angles and its supporting but also

16. Adolf Loos, Moller House, Vienna, 1928. Interior staircase. Photograph by
Roberto Schezen, courtesy of the photographer.

formally inflecting pole at one end and footed terminus on the other. Sol
LeWitt's minimal modular lattices are more to the point, though LeWitt didn't
start making them until two years later. Tony Smith's *Free Ride* also predates
"our" contemporary Robert Morris's *Untitled (L-Beams)*, of 1965, by three
years. Twelve years after *Free Ride* LeWitt began his even more similar *Incomplete Open Cubes*, in 1974, while *Free Ride* itself relates to experiments in
cubical stereotomy in Smith's drawings from around the same time, such as
one from December 16, 1962.[71]

With the spatially squared square of *Die*, which at six by six by six feet
was designed so that the average person could not look over it, Smith is known

17. Josef Chochol, Block of flats in Neklanova Street, Prague, 1912. After *Architectural Review*, March 1966.

to have been inspired by Leonardo da Vinci's famous drawing of the Vitruvian man, of c. 1485–90, this as "reproduced on the cover of a paperback." Recalling that moment, it seems more than likely that the book in question was the Anchor paper edition of Geoffrey Scott's antimodernist *The Architecture of Humanism* (1914), in which, it happens, the Gothic is dismissed under "The Romantic Fallacy." This Scott, a classy Edwardian classical apologist, says that the Gothic "lose[s] architecture in sculpture," and "admits its deep indifference to ordered form."[72] Tony Smith's cube certainly doesn't look Gothic, but in a sense that Scott could not have anticipated it displays its own minimalist "indifference to ordered form." When Smith reiterated *Die* as *Die II* in 1967, the sheer interchangeability, if never absolute identity, of the two pieces became a minimalist statement with modernist architectural overtones of its own (akin to certain modernist architects' demystifying openness to prefabrication).

18. Tony Smith, *Smoke,* 1967. Wooden mock-up, 24 × 34 × 48 feet (as installed in the Corcoran Gallery of Art, Washington, D.C.). Photograph courtesy of the Paula Cooper Gallery.

The whole *Die* project, however, also relates back indirectly to the Worringerean distancing of much geometric constructivist art, in that fabrication was directed by Smith over the telephone, without even making a drawing. The constructivist artist László Moholy-Nagy had already had a group of five paintings executed by telephone, using graph paper and a commercial paint chart, in 1922, as Smith could easily have known from a supplement to the second edition of Moholy-Nagy's *The New Vision* (1949), or else from Reyner Banham's classic *Theory and Design in the First Machine Age* (1960), even if he had managed not to learn of this while studying under Moholy himself in Chicago, in 1937–8.

Born in 1912, Smith went from the Art Students League of New York (1931–6) to the "New Bauhaus," in Chicago, with a special interest in architecture. From 1938 to 1940 he worked as a *capomastro* for Frank Lloyd Wright. Architectural practice extended from 1940 into the 1960s, but the years 1953 to 1955 he spent in Germany, where he "began to develop his artwork based [on] modular units," especially in a series of paintings and with architectural projects.[73] Since it was soon after his return that he began to produce his sculptures, one wonders, despite the season in Wright's Thoreauesque all-American entourage, about this minimalist founding father's exposure to German modernism. Because he never held an architect's license, Smith's own buildings had to be executed in collaboration with someone else, which function sometimes devolved upon his brother Thomas, who had studied, at Tony's suggestion, under Ludwig Mies van der Rohe in Chicago.[74]

Tony Smith did, however, practice architecture, producing "about two dozen" buildings, "mostly private homes,"[75] between 1940 and the early 1960s. This firsthand architectural work, neither as extensive nor as remarkable as the sculpture that grew out of it, includes a 1943–4 house that extends a clearly Wrightean hexagonal cellular structure along three 60-degree axes of unequal length; an interesting project for a Catholic church on Long Island consisting of irregularly clustered hexagonal cells on *pilotis* (this might have had windows directly dripped by his friend Jackson Pollock);[76] and a 1950 house for the abstract expressionist painter Theodore Stamos, at East Marion, Long Island, this rectangular in plan but related to the church design by its elevation's expressing the hexagononal unit in vertical wooden trusses (influenced by bridge construction) on stilts.[77] Also prismatic – with a slight torque, and as such quite like such a sculpture by Smith as *For D.C.,* 1969, while somewhat Corbusian in its openwork facade – is a model for a small museum. (In museum architecture Smith has seemed perhaps most conspicuously influential upon practicing latter-day architects, especially I. M. Pei.)[78]

Considering his literally architectural work, I have for years thought that the chamfered, angular faceting of the post and lintel elements of Smith's larger lattice sculptures, such as the enormous plywood mock-up of *Smoke*, erected in the Corcoran Gallery of Art, Washington, in 1967 (Figure 18) and later related works, share with such faceting in contemporary "brutalist" architecture a source in earlier, so-called cubist, central European architecture. I re-

19. Bruno Taut, *Crystal House in the Mountains*. Ink drawing; after Taut, *Die Au-flösung der Städte; oder auch, Die Ende eine gute Wohnung; oder auch, Die Weg zur Alpinen Architektur* (Hagen in Westfalien, 1920).

member how interesting one particular architectural article looked at the moment of its appearance in 1966, Jaroslav Vokoun's "Czech Cubism." Although not the only publication on the subject at the time, even this article's dated headline typeface displays a chamfering that looks similar to the memorable illustration of an apartment house in Neklanova Street, Prague, of 1912, by Josef Chochol – who had studied under Otto Wagner in Vienna – as Vokoun published it in *Architectural Review* in March 1966 (Figure 17),[79] which is to say, less than a year earlier than Smith built *Smoke,* the "piers" and "lintels" of which are taperingly chamfered much in the manner of the totally faceted Prague facade.

In her engrossing study of the occult roots of crystal imagery in German expressionist architecture, Rosemary Bletter reproduces two very different designs published by Bruno Taut, in 1919 and 1920, for a "Crystal House in the Mountains," of which the second, published in 1920 (Figure 19), has "sharp faceted excrescences."[80] Now, with its harlequin diagonal faceting, Smith's sturdily prismatic *Atlanta* (Figure 20), cast in bronze in 1980, the year of the artist's death, stands not so far, after all, from such a once hopelessly farfetched expressionist project in three dimensions as Bruno Taut's mountain house. Before this, one of the last works of Tony Smith, I would add to Bletter's survey of the early spiritual literature something

159

20. Tony Smith, *Atlanta,* 1980. Bronze (ed. of 6), 48 × 31 × 24 inches. Photograph © 1989 by Geoffrey Clements courtesy of the Paula Cooper Gallery.

from dialogues of the seventeenth-century mystic Jacob Boehme: to a student's inquiry, "in what *materia* of form" our bodies are to be resurrected, a master replies that, as with the individual human body, "When the visible world passes away ... only a heavenly, crystalline matter and form of the world remains" (6.46–7).[81]

Tony Smith developed in a latter-day expressionist artistic context as an architect of essentially prismatic-geometric tendency, and went on to produce freestandingly prismatic or crystalline sculptures. That the origins of his crystalline architectonic structures are rooted, despite superficial stylistics, in the spiritual subsoil of expressionism itself, is no mere paradox but a fruitful contradiction. "The evolutionary history of art is as spherical as the universe," Worringer says, "and no pole exists that does not have its counter-pole. . . . Only at the moment when we reach the pole itself do our eyes become opened, and we perceive the great beyond, that urges us toward the other pole."[82]

11

Form Behind Concept
The Bechers' Imaging of Industrial Architecture

For A.A.

IN 1972, the minimalist sculptor Carl Andre published an article introducing the collaborative photographic work of two German artists, Bernd and Hilla Becher.[1] This body of work came into being when a painter, Bernd (or Bernhard) Becher gave up painting (a topos in itself) in order to record photographically with Hilla Becher an intriguing category of structures that had initially concerned him as a painting motif, namely, industrial buildings. Andre's sympathy for his fellow artists was encouraging; but what one artist takes as fresh food for thought is not always so to others, sometimes not even problematic. Surely it has been a creative function of art history to draw on the memory banks of culture and claim for contemporary artists traditions to which they may, knowingly or not, contribute by bringing timely historical material to light.

I find problematic Hilla Becher's statement that what the pair does may not be "art," and that whether it is or not doesn't matter. But not to recognize the pictured structures themselves as possible artworks could only tend more to obscure than to reveal them as prior works of others, however anonymous. Items like the Bechers' blankly imaged gas tanks and water towers may be waiting in art-historical limbo for the chance to manifest contemporary pertinence. As conceptual photography, or rather photoconceptualism, the Bechers' work claims its own attention now.

I want to sketch out some evidence that not only the choice of material, but also the "project," of these two German artists is *fortunately* not "original," and that it is surely "art" enough to appear in a stylistic light. Here Andre's obliviousness to history may itself be typical, if all the more remarkable in an artist of sophistication.

What exactly do the Bechers do? They take, mount in rigorous grids, and exhibit photographs of anonymous, mostly industrial architecture (Figure 21). Andre's comment that "photography . . . makes it easier to compare the pro-

21. Bernd Becher and Hilla Becher, *Typology of Framework Houses*, 1959–74. Mounted photographs, 59¼ × 43¼ inches. Photograph courtesy of the Sonnabend Gallery.

portions of similar structures of unequal size" is as pregnant as it is astute, because what is at the very center of the Bechers' method is the morphological (and taxonomic) procedure of classical art history.[2] The approach is essentially typological, as must be all art history, at least until it has control of enough relevant data and iconography. Once the types, ways of meaning, and range of "content" are known, visual beholding can reengage attention, as it did in the initial stages of fresh but ignorant perception. The Bechers thus proceed in a way that is barely distinguishable from how they would do so if they were producing an art-historical monograph on the material they "take" to classify, except that there is none but visual "text."

Even their three-way shots of *Two Pithead Gears,* showing flank, three-quarter, and end views, resemble both the visualization procedures done before a structure is built (or, in painting, works like Philippe de Champaigne's three-way portrait study of Richelieu), and also standard study angles for recording a building, scupture, or object for historical study. In other words, the method calls into play an established technique of both art and art history for recording formal and structural facts when a work is still a project or else when it is the object of historical recovery.

Andre's admiration for the way the Bechers' procedure negates or suspends scale is important. For art historians, the comparison of two photographs or slides often rightly carries anxiety over the canceling of scale. At the same time, the procedure is helpful because it encourages grounding of analysis in the evidence of internal, including reciprocal, relations, such as proportion. Thus two juxtaposed slides, one of the Piazza of Saint Peter's and the other of the approach to the Manhattan Bridge, reveal as a useful consequence of the violation of scale that the later, smaller structure has some vital and intrinsic relation to the other (and also, if one cares to notice, that it is architecturally inferior). It is no accident that the pedagogical system whereby two adjacent projection screens encourage a steady stream of formal comparisons – the legacy of Heinrich Wölfflin's pedagogy at the University of Munich – is an orthodox formalist device. Ironically, just such a system, in other circumstances understandably criticized by contemporary artists, here stands almost as the subject matter of a nondiscursive but analytical art instituted by two artists in Germany and confirmed by another in New York.

To a formalist, even a plain-Jane building can lend a painter, more than a mere motif, the materials of an operational image structure. Consider Roger Fry, describing a painting by the youthful Corot of a hulking, workaday building in his essay "Some Questions in Aesthetics" (the point concerns a gift for "finding" artistic possibility): "Asked to paint the portrait – one can call it nothing else – of a huge, bleak, ugly, factory-like building," with "dull square windows," Corot "gave fully every architectural commonplace" but in so doing "found an entirely unexpected and exquisite harmony of colour . . . [and] disposed the cast shadow in the foreground and chose the proportions of everything relatively to his canvas so adroitly that he created a moving spiritual reality out of an incredibly boring suburban scene."[3]

The poetic content in the Bechers' series of photographs is traditional (they might say that they don't construct it, but they do let it install itself). It belongs to a specifically Romantic tradition that began when the grime had hardly settled on the major early industrial buildings of England. Take, for instance, T. H. Hair's *A Series of Views of the Collieries in the Counties of Northumberland and Durham,* of 1844 (the year of Engels's famous social study), with which the Bechers' various *Pithead Gears* would readily compare (and note that Hair was already concerned with a typological "series").

Inescapable in the Bechers' project is a sense of the picturesque as radically stretched to cover many large-scale industrial structures that were or are sublime simply for exceeding, or supposedly violating, old-fashioned picturesqueness. Rural-industrial as the emphasis is, their project's sociological prehistory concerns an earlier, indirect impact of the industrial revolution on the countryside, with the displacement of rural life that provoked subjects "worthy of the pencil of Hobbema." Thus in an advertisement to a suite of rural prints, with commentary, by George Cuitt the Younger (dated, it happens, May 1, 1848); the printer, M. A. Nattali, offering such subjects as "the bold outline of Welsh Hovels and Water-Mills," appeals not only to "a strong relish of the Picturesque, traces of which are evidenced in every plate," but to "a love of Archaeology." And according to Cuitt, the artist, "The picturesque effect of the scenery of Wales is greatly enhanced by the singular construction of the hovels and farm buildings of the peasantry," especially for the contrast of "their bold outline in the foreground with the Romantic Scenery."[4] Do not rather handsome derelict industrial structures of the Ruhr or the Saarland now represent but a later, rust-belt phase of the same historical phenomenon?

In the twentieth century an enthusiasm for industrial architecture as "picturesque" subject matter conveying a modern "Wonder of Work" is manifest on the threshold of World War I in the graphic art of the Whistler disciple Joseph Pennell. Apropos of his own print *Flour Mills, Minneapolis,* Pennell noted in 1916, "The mills of Minneapolis are as impressive as the cathedrals of France"; and, "The beauty of the flour mills is the beauty of use – they carry out William Morris's theory that 'everything useful should be beautiful' – but I don't know what he would have said to them."[5] Ironically, the very newness of such structures, in type but also in fact, appealed to this conservative artist, whereas before long an enthusiasm for industrial architecture inclusive of even quite charmingly derelict older examples would comprise a kind of nostalgic accompaniment to the buildings and theory of the International Style. Here Andre's general hunches – "structures built to serve the same purpose," "conglomerations of machine and structure," "structures with the same function" – are appropriate but by 1972 almost fascinatingly traditional.

To call upon functionalist ideas this way is, at the least, the architectural equivalent of treating synthetic cubism or constructivism as news. Actually, a major turning point in popular American acceptance of a heavy-industrial constructivist or functionalist aesthetic had already occurred in New York in 1931, with the embrace of the "unfinished" George Washington Bridge. This structure, by O. H. Amman, engineer, was designed (from 1927 on) to have its towers encased in masonry by Cass Gilbert, architect, but just before it opened, unadorned, the *New York Times* toasted it as "a symbol of man's mastery over matter" and of "this machine age." For Amman's purely engineered design itself was by no means "brutally utilitarian," the bridge having from the start been "built also – like the Brooklyn Bridge – for beauty."[6]

Also, Charles Sheeler's job photographing the Ford plant at River Rouge, Michigan, in 1927, moved him to paint in a now obviously dated modernistic, romantic-rationalist mode, then a matter of conviction for Le Corbusier. And it was precisely as appealingly industrial-structural that the George Washington Bridge appears as a motif in his photography. Sheeler also took finely formalizing photographs of optimistically *moderne* industrial architecture, from about 1939; but he also chose more obviously Becheresque motifs, as for his painting *Ballardvale,* 1946, which derives from his own photograph of an old brick industrial mill in Massachusetts.[7]

The Bechers went in the other direction, perhaps in realizing that the tradition they were observing was not only self-evidently formidable but dying and deserving of documentation. Their work allies even more with these historical realms when one thinks of it in terms of the publications of the art historian Sigfried Giedion, a disciple of Wölfflin: *Space, Time, and Architecture: The Growth of a New Tradition* (1941) and *Mechanization Takes Command* (1948), the latter subtitled, significantly for the Bechers' project, "A Contribution to Anonymous History" (1948).

It is also similar to the International Style–inspired antiquarianism of J. M. Richards's *The Functional Tradition in Early Industrial Buildings,* with easygoing photographs by Eric de Maré (1958). Richards had already written and published *An Introduction to Modern Architecture* (1940), an early Penguin paperback, during World War II. Indeed, since the 1950s, tracking down Becher-type material has been a not-uncommon hobby in Britain, and handy guidebooks are published for devotees, such as the field guides of the British Archaeological Research Group. In the 1960s there was even a sixpenny promotional booklet put out by London Transport. What really distinguishes the Bechers' work is its emergence as functionalism itself lost architectural conviction.

Among other American minimalist sculptors, Don Judd was not alone in exercising a taste for simply built, not ostensibly fine-art, architectonic structures. Judd himself opens a 1964 review of an exhibition, "Twentieth-Century Engineering," at the Museum of Modern Art, with a comment that might still have seemed daring despite the museum's ongoing crusade for "good design," but which in another sense merely extended an already obsolescent enthusiasm of the architectural functionalists: "Dams, roads, bridges, tunnels, storage buildings and various other useful structures comprise the bulk of the best visible things made in this century." Judd concedes that most people would be prepared to agree in theory, and he seconds Arthur Drexler's curatorial notion that engineering itself is in part an aesthetic enterprise, though with such structures, "utility" rather than "looks" "seems much more important."[8] While establishment modern architects aspire to a "puerile" elegance, "Much . . . engineering is better architecture than most architecture." "It's well known," Judd states, "that Buckminster Fuller's domes cannot be architecture. His lenticular Union Tank Car Rebuilding plant (1959) in Baton Rouge is an interesting building, and that's architecture."[9] One begins to suspect that industrial beauty might never have been categorically disreputable to observers of unprejudiced aesthetic awareness.

It is not surprising that Judd should admire the McMath Telescope, at the Kitt Peak Solar Observatory (Arizona), 1962–3, which I have already related to ramplike contemporary minimalist sculptures, including Robert Grosvenor's *To panga,* of 1965.[10] It is more surprising that he should call it "probably . . . [the] best structure" by the (Miesian) firm of Skidmore, Owings and Merrill (architects and engineers).[11] The antihistoricism of minimal art could only have encouraged the pretense or delusion of freshly discovering such forthright, unarty virtues, since even an antiquarian connoisseurship of industrial structures was already under way in the generation before minimalism.

Obviously, the minimalist Bechers have no desire to construct any but the most baldly documentary, unfinessed image, distinguished all but trivially (or subtly?) from other structures of a given type. Minimalism itself, however, is often a highly structural art even when markedly void as to form. The Bechers' *Typology of Framework Houses,* 1959–74 (Figure 21), is a photo grid of nine old *fachwerk* (more correctly translated as "half-timbered," *Fachwerk* being "half-timbering") buildings: a distinctly earthy type of timelessly traditional North European architecture in which there still echoes a quite early medieval, dark-against-light, angular-linear grille structure. With its own typological subtleties, the category is all the more interesting for upholding postpicturesque reminiscences in any "Coketown."[12]

In America, Dan Graham's minimalist architectural photographs of cheap American suburban row houses still under construction are an important counterpart going as it were in the other direction.[13] And the contemporary abstract painters Ellsworth Kelly and Robert Mangold, whose work is sometimes referred to minimalism in sculpture, have both drawn, by way of photography, on inert architectural forms for highly "concrete" abstract images in painting.[14] Mangold's *Barn Doors,* 1976, a mounted row of photographs, documents his own typological approach to such neglected utilitarian architecture, admittedly of an American-nostalgic sort, which also recalls Charles Sheeler and Georgia O'Keeffe.

When Bernd and Hilla Becher exhibited their photographs at the "Neue Sammlung" of the Staatliches Museum für Angewandte Kunst, in Munich, in 1967, they had already published photos in *Werk und Zeit, Bauwelt,* and *Architectural Review.* In his introduction to the catalog of the exhibition, straightforwardly entitled "Industriebauten: Eine fotografische Dokumentation," Wend Fischer takes a somewhat dubious, if not dissembling, stance: "For the presentation to be taken as monument-preservation is absurd; nothing here purports to be an artistic monument." Not even in a "Museum of Applied Art"? Or, again: "Therefore we have not troubled ourselves to pass aesthetic judgments in the selection of objects, but to search out characteristic trends (*Zügen*)." And yet Fischer himself cannot escape the fact that the photographs, singly and in series, offer a distinctly aesthetic experience, all the more as swept

22. Bernd Becher and Hilla Becher, *Lagerhaus im "Prince-Albert-Dock," Liverpool, 1845,* photograph. After B. and H. Becher, *Industriebauten 1830: Eine fotographische Dokumentation* (Munich, 1967).

(minimalistically) free of incident: "The pure, precise reproduction of objects is obscured by nothing: no clouds in the sky, no shadows from the sun, no smoke from the chimneys, no people, no vehicles, nothing but the absolute fixity of the objects which any extension through movement could disturb."[5]

Fischer contradicts himself by exhibiting these photographs and denying their artistic substance in a pseudo-avant-garde way on one page, only in effect to assert it on the next. Carl Andre's own minimalist reticence, in writing on the Bechers' photos, saves him from falling into any such trap. And I myself had collected the Munich catalog at the time just for its architectural content, not yet familiar with the names of the artists.

Naturally the Bechers' work has distinct stylistic features that mark its identity within the tradition of industrial-archaeological photography; which provides even more evidence that it is art. For example, their presentation of the Albert Dock at Liverpool, in the same 1967 exhibition (Figure 22), compares with the Albert Dock as photographed by de Maré and published in Richards's *Functional Tradition* (Figure 23). The Bechers identify the structure merely as "Lagerhaus im 'Prince-Albert-Dock,' Liverpool, 1845," and show what is a blunt, mute, head-on view of the end of one block, whereas de Maré and Richards also show more spatial, picturesque views of the handsome flanks

23. Jesse Hartley, Warehouse, Albert Dock, Liverpool, 1845. After J. M. Richards, *The Functional Tradition in Early Industrial Buildings,* photographs by Eric de Maré (London, 1958).

of the warehouse complex enclosing the harbor basin, and supplying the following (characteristically narrative) information: "It was built, in 1845, by Jesse Hartley, who was the dock surveyor of Liverpool from 1824–60."[16] In other words, the art of the Bechers is so much after an anonymity of effect that in avoiding all possible picturesqueness it deliberately ignores the authorship of its subject materials, when the date and the name of the designer of a work are known to history, as well as the visual historiography of its representation.

The art of the Bechers has its deliberately few and controlled levels of reference, which are, however, apparent. As "conceptual art," it employs clinically direct approach (as such, stylistic), to a medium (photography) dealing with the subject matter of another art (architecture), and relying, for all its "conceptual" antiformalism, on a system of classification well known to formalist art history. In terms of a recognizable aesthetic attitude (romanticism) it is concerned with outmoded rationalistic and utilitarian materials. But even on that score it shares in a specifically German tradition of "hard," or puritanical, supposedly uningratiating romanticism, that traces back at least to the eighteenth century.

12

Classical Sass

Notes on Soft Postmodernism

For A.C.D. and B.W.

B Y the mid-1980s an advertisement had appeared on subway billboards in
Latino neighborhoods of New York. A bottle of Dewar's White Label
whisky appeared atop the capital of a gravely drawn Doric column whose
abacus was inscribed with the Spanish for "the Classic Scotch." Graphically,
the poster extended an old convention of identifying claims of abiding quality
with the classic orders of architecture, in this case the traditionally masculine
Doric. In the free-for-all money culture of the time, in which the most superficial classical pastiches circulated under an otherwise critical rubric of architectural postmodernism, capitalizing on a critical withdrawal into theory,
much was connoted by this appeal to New York *caballeros* by means of the
endorsement *classico* and its invitation to buy into a desirable bourgeois ex-
clusivity.

At the same time, Judy Rifka was advancing a very different, suavely raucous processing of the image of the Parthenon, that preeminent Doric architectural image of the classical absolute. Within painting, her new-wavy project
constitutes, I think, a "hard," critical double to a phenomenon I would call
"soft," antimodernist postmodernism in architecture – as distinct from actively
critical or revisionist "hard" postmodernism. This other postmodernism entails an easy fraternization with "the vernacular," versus anything as de-
mandingly grammatical as classical Latin or Greek, that is sometimes referable
to pop art, in then-recent architecture. The very rendering of the poster was
antimodern (one does not buy a Rolls Royce in order to look avant-garde),
whereas Rifka's essentially postmodern Parthenon paintings are artistically
knowing to the point of being fed up as well as wised up. Typically, in her
painting *Museum Wallpaper*, 1982 (Figure 24), the casually repeating, silk-
screened Parthenon motif is for Rifka at once detached and available, as classic
text, modernist pretext, and postmodern, willing absurdity.

As to classical text: the Winckelmann who emblazoned the title page of his

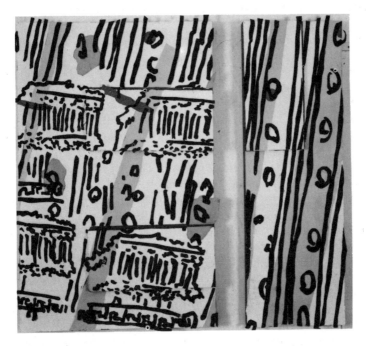

24. Judy Rifka, *Museum Wallpaper*, 1982. Oil on linen; two panels: 72 × 47 inches, 72 × 24 inches. Photograph by Pelka/Noble; courtesy of the Brooke Alexander Gallery.

Remarks on Ancient Art (1763) with a classical columnar capital was himself also an upstart of sorts, a zealous acolyte of hierarchy who would have wanted only the best unblended scotch. The very success of his pursuit of a highly idealized Greek classical truth, however, inevitably had to undermine the canonically Roman basis of established authority.

The column of the advertisement was different, its purpose being to sell established taste as is, a toe-the-line tip on what is top of the line in the real world of getting and spending, including the traditionalistic marmoreal whiteness (spoiled around 1830 by Hittorff's discovery, still resisted, of the original polychromy of the Greek temples) that attaches to the White Label brand name, as indeed to Scottish, as definitively Gringo, nationality. Even on a more spiritual plane the poster's addressee was being encouraged to drop any ethnic Romanism and conform to the higher Calvinist ideals of the average president of the United States.

When the modern falls away, presumably the dismissed classical ideal reappears. Now that it does, however, the shopworn Parthenon, like a tenth-generation Xerox, is no more ideal than Ciriaco d'Ancona's now amusingly overconfident little sketch of the temple – and a hilariously cruder copy of it from later in the fifteenth century (Codex Manzoni) – with which the classicists' cult of the Parthenon once stumbled to begin.[1] Beyond Greece, Rifka further intimates a defunct Egypt and even a jivey primevalism beyond that: or rather, all three coincident pasts in the same virtual space of the constructed and utterly concocted image. In a painted construction, *Wall,* 1983, deracinated images of Athena's Parthenon and Queen Hatshetsup's temple skid indiscriminately together over a joggled flotilla of canvas planes – like the boggled faces of the shifted ashlar blocks of the Acropolis itself, as Rifka has commented. The architectural images come and go insubstantially but demystifyingly, as perfectly suits equally disoriented, pseudoprehistoric human forms also careening like hunters in a cave painting. History backs up, piles up, as stylishly mannered style proceeds.

Not that Rifka has been alone in countering a fashion of illiterate trivialization of classical ornamental forms.[2] Different, but also implicating architectural classicism (this time in its romanticization around 1800), is the project of John Miller, which is perhaps as easily affiliated with literature as is Rifka's with rock 'n' roll. His novel of sorts, *Contamination* (1982), is illustrated with some of his drawings (the fattish brush line of which also evokes Picabia, and others, in the 1920s), including one of a freestanding memorial column (1981). In the book, a Corinthian column is at one point addressed mock-archaically: "Column, column, column, what vestiges of antiquity spring from thy brow? You impenetrable one. You who know more than me. You of geometric perfection. You who refuse to shave." This is followed by the preclichéd musing, "(It is clearly a product of a bygone era)."[3] One might well think of the architect Robert Venturi's dictum "I am a monument."

Such recent, knowingly dubious classicizing in the realm of painting can only stimulate one to notice soft postmodernism in architecture, whether in unrigorous, ungrammatical appeal to classical ornamentation or in campy, folkloric vernacular retreat. Various historical factors are implicated in the emergence of such architecture, including (a) the detached postromantic experience of classical forms as sheerly visual, overlooking the caesura between the old and new except to indulge romantic nostalgia; (b) the phenomenon of sixteenth-century mannerism as just such a caesura, noticed sympathetically in modern time; (c) a passively conservative nonmodernist classicism that went underground with the emergence of modern architecture and resurfaced with its supposed demise; and (d) an explicitly vernacular elastic clause opened by pop art, especially as concerns the partying junk architecture of the "strip." Then there is the matter of the fate of an abstract classical value that modernism, more integrally than traditionalist, conservative architecture, may have preserved.

Even serious romantic classicism may play into an emphasis on surface artifice. The same Chateaubriand who in the *Génie du christianisme* (1802) praises the imagined temples for slapping their columns against the sky (5.4) is delighted in the real Greece of 1806 to be shown his sculpture-bedecked quarters: "What a pleasure for me to be put up in Athens in a room full of plaster casts from the Parthenon!"[4]

Against the drift of ancient Greece's familiarization under Romantic classicism, post-Napoleonic Egypt became something of an "unspoiled" hyper-Greece, but also an anticlassical and orientalizing, not to mention older, primitivizing destination. Here, it happens, photographic demystification began even before photography with the *camera lucida,* which Frederick Catherwood used in Egypt around 1830 – and later with John Lloyd Stephens in the Yucatan, as if for only more of the same – to record archaeologic sites in decentered, atomized detail. For all their topographical precision, Catherwood's *camera lucida* drawings proffer a thought-effacing mechanical equalization of intensities that yields a brittle thinness, crisply disengaged and artificial.[5]

Flaubert's visit to Egypt with the photographer Maxime du Camp, at midcentury, was a case of hot orientalism arm in arm with cool science. Du Camp's pursuit of archaeological facticity bored his literary friend, whose accounts of the trip concern a boundless erotic realm refreshingly removed from European conventionality. Flaubert, from sheer historical detachment drunk on this safely irrelevant Egypt of the moment, wrote to his mother in April of 1850 in terms evoking the surfer-sky euphoria, the parfait palette and even the interperforated color layers, as well as of the exotic as immediate, in Rifka's paintings: "Gods with heads of ibises and crocodiles are painted on walls white with the droppings of the birds of prey that nest between the stones. We walk among the columns, . . . we stir up this old dust; through holes in the temple walls we see the incredibly blue sky. . . . *This is the essence of Egypt. . . .* We are always dazzled in the towns . . . the white, yellow or blue clothes stand out in the transparent air – blatant tones that would make any painter faint away."[6]

Focillon recalled in 1934 that (surrealistically enough) Flaubert had described the Parthenon as "black as ebony."[7] However, in a passage added to the second edition (1759) of his *Philosophical Enquiry into the Origin of Our Ideas of the Sublime and Beautiful* Edmund Burke had already observed how Milton "describes the light and glory which flows from the divine presence; a light which by its very excess is converted into a species of darkness": "Dark *with excessive light thy skirts appear*" (*Paradise Lost,* 3.380; misquoted, Burke's modern editor has noticed). "Here is an idea," Burke says, "not only poetical in an high degree, but strictly and philosophically just. Extreme light, by overcoming the organs of sight, obliterates all objects, so as in its effect exactly to resemble darkness." He considers the black afterimages of the sun to note, "Thus are two ideas as opposite as can be imagined reconciled in the extremes of both; and both in spite of their opposite nature brought to concur in producing the sublime" (2.14).[8] Immediately follows a section (15) on "Light in Building," in which, because "to make an object very striking, we should make it as different as possible from the objects with which we have been immediately conversant," a dark interior will be all the more impressive on entering from sunlight (likewise a brightly lighted interior at night).[9] Burke's specifically architectural thought here underlies Flaubert's (and Focillon's), and perhaps even Rifka's own sense of Parthenonian overload.

One can perhaps too confidently assume formal inheritance and historical continuity from the old classical to a new modern tradition, ignoring a Nietzschean rupture that had to occur before something worthy to become classic could begin again. Well before Nietzsche, Marx (also a lover of Greek antiquity), remarked on the brutal demythologization of classical culture under impact of modern industrialism: "What chance," he says in a notebook of 1857–8, "has Vulcan against Roberts & Co., Jupiter against the lightning rod, and Hermes against the Crédit Mobilier?"[10] How happy, then, can one have been expected to be to hear from Theo van Doesburg, in 1921, that "The spirit that conceived the Parthenon is no longer the same spirit that creates a Hall of Turbines, a Larkin Building, or a modern cottage"?[11] Certainly Le Corbusier's *Vers une architecture,* of 1923, was nothing if not an attempt to summon up on behalf of future Halls of Turbines, Larkin Buildings, and modern dwellings, an at least architectural equivalent to the "spirit" that had once, miraculously enough, conceived the Parthenon.

Within the development of modern European art, however, the question of anticlassicism inevitably concerns the twentieth-century senses, even more than the sixteenth-century facts, of mannerism as an anticlassicism devolving from the High Renaissance itself. As a style of cultural crisis mannerism has held more than revivalistic interest in the inescapable crisis of postmodernism in contemporary culture. Despite attempts, notably John Shearman's, to confine it to whatever the sixteenth century itself said about what it was up to (the "intentional fallacy" on period scale?), mannerism itself, all of it and in all its implications, has been an essentially modern *problem,* and one in which architecture has been especially problematic.

The general (modern) issue of mannerism was framed during a crisis in painting, but only as modernist architecture took off. When Max Dvořák's wartime (1918) lecture on El Greco was published in 1924, Corbusier's *Vers une architecture* had just appeared, but modernist painting was threatened with outright retrenchment.[12] Pevsner, to become one of the most important modernist architectural historians, had just finished a dissertation on baroque architecture when he published his early contribution to the cultural, historical, and specifically "spiritual" understanding of mannerism in painting, "The Counter-Reformation and Mannerism" (1925). Later, a significant new architectural historian, Manfredo Tafuri, would publish *L'architettura del manierismo* (1967), contemporaneously with Shearman's study. This was already a year after Venturi's *Complexity and Contradiction in Architecture* (1966), with its cordial entertaining of mannerist forms and structures, just as the historiography of mannerism and latter-day modernist architecture exhausted themselves in a kind of supernova flare.[13]

In 1925 Pevsner used Giulio Romano's painted fantasies of the crashing collapse of once-grave classical architecture in the Hall of Giants of Giulio's Pallazo del Te, in Mantua, to generalize on "a new, complex and even confused pictorial form combined with an exaggeration of the details of the previous [classical] style." His claim, "Everywhere there was a reaction against the anthropocentric and harmonious ideal of the Renaissance,"[14] sounds almost like a latter-day deconstructive negation of the rationalist humanist sense of order as repressive. Vasari, himself a sophisticated mannerist artist, had liked the irony by which this painted architecture of about 1530 could only seem chaotic thanks to Giulio's cool perspectival control. The early modern formalist Wölfflin might have had to hold off delight in Giulio's murals, affronted by the spectacle of form's collapse but also apparently disturbed by a "pleasure found in treating matter with violence."[15] Nevertheless, in 1967 John Shearman pointed to a period gloss by Francesco Luisino on Horace's *Ars poetica:* because Horace frowned on anything too fantastic, Luisino siezed his chance to stress just that affirmative fictive character in poetry or art that makes the Hall of Giants a tour de force, not so much of deceptive illusion as of manifest artifice. Thus Shearman can imagine Giulio's contemporaries standing before the great anticlassical architectural paintings "unmoved, except," importantly enough, "for a *frisson* of delight in a particular kind of beauty."[16]

The Giulio Romano case is telling, for one would have to see his Hall of the Giants architectural murals either as stimulating an experience of the jaded charm of wreckage, or as projecting deep disenchantment by horrific images of destroyed perfection – with obvious analogies to the embrace or rejection of postmodern architecture's iconoclasm toward modernist architecture as "classical" statement. In a 1972 overview of the historiography of mannerism, Henri Zerner takes Shearman to task for neglecting historical complexity in favor of a single mannerism of ultrasophistication, finding "today's art" in a "comparable situation" to that of the sixteenth century insofar as an abstract painting by Ellsworth Kelly requires contextualizing "knowledge of its place in the historical development of art" if it is not to appear as "senseless surfaces of flat colors."[17] But by the time of C. Ray Smith's book entitled *Superman-nerism: New Attitudes in Post-Modern Architecture,* in 1977, one could quite simplistically employ the Palazzo del Te to license postmodernism as the next packaged style, as if much of the hoopla over that masterpiece of mannerist architecture and painting had not itself been a phenomenon of the 1960s.[18]

Almost by definition worse than mannerist anticlassicism, some of which has always exercised a bravado of confident belief (and which in any case has its distinguished premodern history), is a kind of blasphemy against any further possibility of worthy modern art or architecture. It is because even the effete blasphemies of mannerism were (ultra)aestheticizing that the historical precedent of mannerism, not merely manneristic versus more orthodox-classical forms, has had urgency.

Philip Johnson's desperate stylishness could only have advanced the new attitude of soft, unrigorously aestheticizing neomannerism, and might count almost before the blatant fact as soft postmodern. To think of Johnson as a disciple of Ludwig Mies van der Rohe is to see his productions of the pop-*zeit* and after as practically oedipally reactive. The real issue here is an inverted innocence that cannot be completely hidden behind, nor simply discharged as irony under the rubric of camp. It is intimated already in the strange, glitzy tackiness of Johnson's New York State Theater, 1964 – home to the New York City Ballet, which under George Balanchine's geometric-classical direction functioned as an aesthetic home away from home to many an abstract painter – a building that from the start has appeared at once inhibited and indulged, and is only by shaky rationalization excusable "theatrically."

Johnson's AT&T Headquarters, of 1978–82, is made of such dreamy stuff, but in a fantasy of morbid permanence whose every concrete inflection, perhaps inevitably imperfect, disappoints close up. Louis Kahn once defined the city as "a place where a small boy, as he walks through it, may see something that will tell him what he wants to do his whole life." That is nice, but Johnson gave us a too-literalized mock-up version of the boy's-eye spectacle that I remember well from the New York of around 1950: the masonry grandeur of giant doorways with huge billowing flags high above, along with Léger-esque workmen; whistle-blowing cops in brass-buttoned, doublebreasted mel-ton; spiffy red fire engines, à la Demuth, with real, mechanically whining, Varèsean sirens; sailors in snappily folded (inside-out) real cotton whites – all this, and lunch at the Taft Hotel, with Vincent Lopez, at the piano. Here was indeed a world that seemed, especially in maternal company, larger than life, fantastically real for any boy, and which the AT&T building reconstitutes in a gigantic toylikeness of manneristic exaggeration.

Much soft postmodernism is indeed marked by a kind of deco-rococo infa-tuation with out-of-scale classical detail archly, if not ignorantly, disengaged from the classical grammar. I believe that this tendency traces back to a clubby, wimpy, Corinthianism (vs. tough Doricism) in turn-of-the-century America, a specifically plutocratic ultraclassiness that in encounter with modernity could only react with the philistinism of mere good taste. In her writing on interior decor in 1897 (with Ogden Codman), the upper-class novelist Edith Wharton represented, believe it or not, a progressive, quasi-formalist wing of this class taste. Here can be found the obliviousness to linguistic or grammatical integrity that proudly marked American postmodernist architects in our time: "It mat-ters not if the connection between base and cornice be maintained by actual pilasters or mouldings, or by their painted or woven imitations. The line, not the substance, is what the eye demands."[19] (After that, Jean Baudrillard on the subject of baroque stucco can only read like an infuriated modernist.)

A pertinent period example of the taste, scrupulously curated, is Beauport, a house at Gloucester, Massachusetts, started soon after 1900 with quaint, actual transatlantic architectural elements to which sympathetic new construc-tion was fused. The structural conglomeration, as Wallace-Nutting pictur-esque, is not remarkable; what is, is the utter domination of the whole by a fastidious decorator's sense that renders visible and specific a usually trans-parent class taste. This taste entails the painting of woodwork, room by room, in the fruity colors familiar today from postmodern buildings, classicizing or not. An enthusiast's description of one of these fanatically "unified" period rooms at Beauport makes the point unwittingly: "Paneled walls are vibrant with the dark color of eggplant... Delicate blood-red lines delineate doors and windows and give accent and refinement to this amazing room."[20]

As later under conservative postmodernism in the 1920s and 1930s, one finds outlandish inflations of historicizing architectural ornamentation in otherwise vacantly "modernistic," often overscaled, contexts – most conspicuously, in the giant pseudoclassical and white-plume deco-rococo plasterwork of 1930s movie sets – but also in real ensembles, even after World War II.

Also, the arch-WASP cult of the so-called Williamsburg (Virginia) restoration, begun on behalf of national morale during the Great Depression, can only have instituted a Whiggish neo-Palladian "colonialism" that would reemerge in a great deal of yuppie-speculator, "soft" postmodernist building in the 1980s. Notwithstanding the supreme contradiction, the Rockefeller family pursued this project even as, to a different audience at the Museum of Modern Art in New York, it advanced the cause of modernist architecture. It was, indeed, a 1931 exhibition at the Modern that engendered Henry-Russell Hitchcock and Philip Johnson's authorizing account, *The International Style: Architecture since 1922* (1932), in which they note that "by the mid-thirties the Style was effectively rivaled – or rejected – both by older and by younger architects during just those years when it was also spreading most widely through the western world."[21]

Simultaneously, the Williamsburg site was being cleared of stylistically extraneous structures. According to one of the chief Williamsburg architects, "The fortunate thing is that American history (the revolutionary part of it) was enacted in the Georgian scene. It is reasonably certain that Mr. Rockefeller would not have felt the interest which led him to include the Restoration of Williamsburg among his many educational philanthropies, had not the important events of our history taken place in Williamsburg during the premierships of Pitt, Fox and North rather than during those of Disraeli and Gladstone."[22] Also: "Nowhere in the English Colonies did the transplanted cutting from the mother tree of the later Renaissance [*sic!*] flourish more vigorously than in Virginia."[23] By rules of the Board of Advisory Architects, the site was purged of all but "Colonial tradition," with special discretion to be used in demolishing anything else that could be saved as "Classical Tradition." In contrast to actual preservation, the object of the whole "restoration" was defined by the board of architects as "the recovery of the old form by new work."[24] Here, then, begins the yuppie Republican architectural Disneyland.[25]

Halfway between cinema fantasy and the one-note neo-neo-Palladianism of bankers of the mid–1980s stands an important unsung transitional monument in what would become conservative, or soft, postmodernism in architecture. I refer to Evelyn Waugh's library in his Combe Florey House, at Taunton, Somerset,[26] probably outfitted around 1956. This remarkable room boasted gushily tapering pilasterettes with capitals, these stuck onto the ends of bookstacks running edgewise, as a portrait photograph of the novelist standing in it, by Karsh of Ottawa, testifies (Figure 25). The whole, including plain rectilinear wall panels, was apparently done in a natty dark-green-and-white color scheme. Waugh, by the way, reportedly "loved the architecture of every age except the twentieth century."[27]

Such a "soft" postmodern building as Robert Stern's Lang Residence in Connecticut, of 1973–4,[28] is close to Waugh's weirdly dated "custom" library

25. Yousuf Karsh, *Mr. Evelyn Waugh*, 1964. Photograph © 1964 Yousuf Karsh.

in its employment of detached classicizing detail on behalf of conservatively tasteful novelty. The Lang Residence sports a manicured casualness that in a Veblensque way bespeaks excessive maintenance, in particular for its fancy polychrome paint job.

In *The Language of Post-Modern Architecture* (1977) Charles Jencks drew on the Venturian concept of the "decorated shed" (as opposed to the modernist "duck" of a building, with its claims to semiotic self-evidence),[29] and proposed – in semiobvious allusion to both Greek pedimental sculpture and Greek poly-chromy – that the Greek temple be kept with "its geometric architecture of elegantly fluted columns" down below, with "a riotous billboard of struggling giants above." Interestingly enough, however, he quotes C. R. Cockerell's terse comment on the terrace houses of John Nash in Regency London, which deserves more than superficially "semantic" fascination: " 'Greek bedevilled ... scenographic tricks hastily thought, hastily executed.' The indictment may have its point, but still Nash's willingness to change to the appropriate semantic system has its greater point."[30]

But James Wines is right to retrieve Robert Venturi, Denise Scott Brown and John Rauch, together, from such enthusiastically embraced superficiality, seeing their buildings instead as "brilliant and understated inversions of popular iconography, as opposed to . . . decorative and stylish architectural allusions"; he finds their work "unlike the more recent Post-Modernist spin-offs, with their ersatz historicism and chic polychromed decoration."[31] Venturi was not a kitsch architect, despite his architecture's only passive, though not quite coquettish, resistance to kitsch reading. His work in the 1960s shares both unpretentious pop taste for the vernacular and also minimalism's radical understatement of formal articulation, even if the latter has taken longer to recognize as subtly refined over and against commonplace speculative building.

As to Venturian theory (which was amalgamated, like it or not, with the cult of kitsch, even in the literary sphere): in a tradition older than modernism, the architect's writings could only have served as publicity for his practice – theory being a traditional way for architects to develop a clientele. Nevertheless, Venturi's catholicity did feed into a broad trend encouraging the regressive sense of premodern (and subnoble) forms as "innocent, accessible, immediate, and popular," a regression "robbing these forms of their depth and significance," so that "architecture became taxidermy."[32] Again, what is difficult to understand against a lingering inertia of 1980s artistic entrepreneurialism is that such influence and even consequent fame (no mere notoriety) were not the "real" project. Already the refinement of actual works outlives the coarseness of vulgarized Venturianism.

Whereas with high academicism, McKim, Mead, and White had upheld American "Corinthianism" – a theoretical milestone of which was Morris Hicky Morgan's 1914 translation of Vitruvius's *Ten Books of Architecture,* still in print – spectacularly enough with their big-boned Italian Renaissance campuses for Columbia and University College of New York University (now Bronx Community College), it was actually at McKim's Columbia that the young Robert A. M. Stern would pick up the torch, only to pass on a dimmed flame. Stern's 1980 renovation there of the lounge in Ferris Booth Hall offers a sort of do-it-yourself, plywood, Levittown classicism, a cheap version of Waugh's uppity library ornament, said by the architect to be "restating the classical language of the campus in contemporary terms." Since this cannot mean that in 1900 one had on hand the actual Italian Renaissance, it must mean that the special task of 1980 is, as it were, to render indicative the subjunctive of 1900, presenting with newly literal falseness what once carried poetic truth. Stern's pseudo-Corbusian office trademark, a stylized frontal humanoid cutout, owes more to Léger's exotic Africanesque stage decor for *La création du monde,* 1923, than to Le Corbusier's revisionist-humanist "Modulor Man." Tellingly, Stern says he doesn't mind being considered an interior decorator, insofar as Stanford White was one.[33] Thus his spurious contextualism at Columbia willingly diluted even White's turn-of-the-century, upper-class classicism to a middle-class suburban standard, simply meeting it halfway *down.*

By the mid-1980s, things reached a point where a creative eclecticism busy within history – James Stirling's actual "contextualist" buildings, for instance, even if his notions of architectural "representation" and of a bottomless contextuality are troublesome in theory[34] – might have distinguished itself from necromaniac variety as well as from any false, historically oblivious "originality." Otherwise, as Leopold Eidlitz already remarked a century ago, the fashionable architect, essentially a businessman rather than an artist, momentarily "startles the world by his bold combinations of architecturel bric-a-brac," these only to be "quickly appreciated and admired and as quickly cast aside."[35]

Anyone looking directly at Rifka's paintings of Parthenon motifs would have thought of pop art before any of the foregoing; but insofar as they relate to soft postmodernism, that, too, I have suggested, has its architectural prehistory. So does pop in painting, which had a direct effect on the pursuit of architectural vernacularism.

Neither those who in the 1960s dismissed pop art categorically as kitsch, nor those anxious to embrace it precisely as such, were prepared to assess the precedent, considerable all over again with Rifka, of Fernand Léger among "high-"cultural artists. Léger had managed radically to undercut Renaissance humanist idealization of the figure while reestablishing for it a Brechtian aesthetic as well as moral value. He transformed expired, if not phony, bourgeois-humanist nobility into the accessible but not debased dignity of ordinary healthy proletarians happy with their sleek new purist seltzer bottles. Léger's equanimity actually accomplished what Stalinist socialist realism claimed to seek in painting, and compared with the (perennially French) classicality of that accomplishment, soft postmodernism stands oddly akin to the misplaced classical rhetoric of antimodern Soviet architecture.

Léger was French even in America during World War II. However, it was in Britain, struggling to recover after the war, that in the 1950s the first pop artists initiated the cult of American material bounty and mindless, lowbrow enjoyment of life with the definitive Independent Group, which was actively aware of architecture.

Not without reason does one think of Venturi and Brown's architecture in relation to pop art, but the matter has a certain historical complexity because the founding architectural members of the Independent Group, who produced the important 1953 exhibition, "Parallel of Life and Art," at London's Institute of Contemporary Art, were actually Reyner Banham, eventual advocate of a "New Brutalism" much less ostensibly pop, and Alison and Peter Smithson, who, though clearly concerned with the everyday, hardly stand apart from "high" modernist architectural tradition.[36] As formalist as well as Marxist critics have thought of pop art's supposed criticality, Venturi's exaltation of ambiguity seems stimulating only at first: "Only after realising that his historical analyses, tensions, contradictions, and complexities become critical parameters *bons à tout faire* [that is, expediently] . . . one sees that the adoption of the concept of 'ambiguity' in the work of art, borrowed from the analytical texts of [William] Empson and [T. S.] Eliot, is aimed at justifying personal planning choices rather more equivocal than ambiguous." Thus Tafuri can commend "the great modesty of Venturi's designs and realisations" without approving either his "failed historicisation of architectural ambiguity that becomes . . . an *a priori* category with only generic meanings," or the "historio-graphical flattening" that facilitates his artistic choices.[37]

Within American popular culture itself, no other postwar event can have had greater cultural consequence than the building of Television City in Hollywood rather than in New York, the high-cultural capital, in the mid-1950s, as California flowered into a new populist version of Flaubert's hedonistic Egypt as well as of Léger's livable vision (not dismissible as "utopian") of socialist bonhomie. Here was the cheerful, sunny place where everything was at least OK, that fascinated the English painter David Hockney and even New Yorkers. Inevitably, Californian attitude and affect extended to architecture, before long licensed as early stirrings of what would be termed postmodernism.

In fact, the whole aesthetic of the Las Vegas "strip" is merely an offshoot of California pop, including Los Angeles's Sunset Strip. Ed Ruscha's "artist's-book" taxonomies of (extra good) deadpan documentary photographs of ordinary speculative buildings, notably *Twenty-six Gasoline Stations* (1962) and the very Hockneyesque *Some Los Angeles Apartments* (1965), purveyed in minimalist documentary structure a wryly vacuous, self-evidently pop content. Ruscha's photo books were an art-world setup for the Vegas punch line in architecture. What Venturi and Denise Scott Brown did, in effect, was take the architectural critic Peter Blake's *God's Own Junkyard* (1964), a still interesting photocritique of the new trashiness of suburbanized postwar America by an apologist of orthodox modernism, and show it a wet blanket, countering Blake's taste with, as it were, "Hey, wait a minute; some of this stuff is nifty." The wonder, in retrospect, is that their new reading of the Strip was not itself patronizing, even if it would facilitate camp.

Contemporaneous with *God's Own Junkyard* in 1964 were Richard Artschwager's deadpan grisaille paintings on cheap Celotex wallboard of junk architecture, both urban – *High Rise Apartment* (Philip Johnson's gift to the Smith College Museum) – and suburban – *Tract Home*. Soon Ruscha's 1966 picture book, *Every Building on the Sunset Strip,* whose format recapitulates long streetscape engravings of the seventeenth century,[38] fit right in with Venturi's various studies culminating in the influential *Learning from Las Vegas* (1972). Tom Wolfe published journalistic belles lettres on Las Vegas as early as 1966, writing that only confirms the Angelino essence of the Vegas Strip cult. How different this pop architectural vernacularism was from a sometimes patronizing but earnest connoisseurship of the tasteful folkloric vernacular, as counterpart to functionalism, that includes the writings on American cultural history of John A. Kouwenhoven (*Made in America,* 1948) as well as Sibyl Moholy-Nagy's fascinating *Native Genius in Anonymous Architecture of North America* (1957).

A year before *Learning from Las Vegas* appeared, produced by Venturi in collaboration with Denise Scott Brown and Steven Izenour, the British "Independent Group" architectural historian Reyner Banham had already published *Los Angeles: The Architecture of Four Ecologies* (in London), in 1971. In a review by the art critic Peter Plagens, aware also of Venturi, the temper of the moment comes through in a contrast between the harmless indulgence of a 1972 article by Ray Bradbury in *Esquire,* "Los Angeles Is the Best Place in America," and Plagens's response that "when you get into architecture it's big casino, real people's real lives, and the Pop artiness of Banham and Venturi greases the slide into the moneymen's pockets... (*sic*) and here we go with another strangling round of McDonald's, freeways, and confectioners' culture palaces." To the eyes of Plagens, who knew the territory, the Englishman, at least, was slumming: "an ostensibly perceptive specialist takes a look at this obvious dung-heap and pronounces it a groove."[39] A decade later, the same critic would liken such postmodern architects' work as Venturi's, Peter Eisenman's ("harder," I would say), Michael Graves's, and Philip Johnson's, to the interestingly farfetched productions of a Czech cubist architecture of the 1920s,[40] and likewise admirable only insofar as they at least "go for it" out of crazy fervor.[41]

The most abiding problem of soft postmodernism in architecture is that the very vernacularism that seemed to offer an easy connection with the reality principle, as a tempting alternative to highbrow demands of criticality, has only facilitated the digitalizing desubstantialization of everything. If spiritual value once seemed a heavy demand, one now has to search even for material significance in the face of a generic formalism oblivious even to material qualities, what with cheap prefabrication raising ramshackle structures oblivious to the promise of decent modular proportion that once advanced the case for prefabrication. All about us rise stand-ins for architecture, hardly buildings at all, that, dolled up classically or not, cannot make a point of either their inadvertent complexity or their simplicity. Even the most willful reference to classical tradition is now just a peculiarly classy fetish notation, more like the fetishized Dewar's column than Rifka's defetishized Parthenon, inscribed on the billboard of a "decorated shed."

Fredric Jameson has called attention to a scene in Godard's *Les Carabiniers* (1963) in which "new world conquerors exhibit their spoils," consisting of famous works of ancient monumental architecture. Unlike Alexander the Great, however, "they merely own the images of everything, and triumphantly display their photos of the Colisseum, the pyramids, Wall Street, Angkor Wat, like so many dirty pictures." Jameson expands this principle to encompass a categorical "American tourist" snap-shooting a common landscape and thereby "graphically transforming space into its own material image."[42] The *Carabiniers* sequence, however, as Jameson's own telling shows, seems also to concern the readiness of typed monuments, such as the Parthenon, to serve as fetishizing regalia. How Roman after all (and perhaps only American insofar as American hegemony itself seems Roman) is this symbolic concession that the stock exchange is a kind of throne room, or that if you could but *take* the Parthenon, photographically if not militarily, you would thereby *have* Greece. On the other hand, such processing of the potentially reified image as Rifka's can advance the polysemous, so that in Jameson's terms – unlike the conservative resort to classicizing ornament in soft postmodernist architecture – it need not offer itself in acquiescent or conniving, readily consumable fashion, as just another commodity.

This, which is not as simple as the notion that photography negates imagic aura (of which we have heard so much), far from implying simple commandeering of the Parthenon, just might mean liberating it from more manipulative arrogation. Pop Parthenons by Lichtenstein, for instance, are high-styled productions, businesslike in facture, rationalistic in their smoothly oiled wit, mechanically graphical even in a sense of being published; whereas Rifka's, precisely as outworn motifs, still manage to connote something that must always be fine in the abiding myth of Greece, floating on the surface like so many pieces of Adriatic seaweed, thin and strong, translucently rubbery, virtually natural in their proliferate fertility.

Conservatives will continue to invoke the Parthenon, but only those daring to live in their own age deserve it. In a beautiful essay called "Summer in Algiers" (1936) the now unfashionable Camus speaks of an Algerian "haste to live that borders on waste," whereby "everything is given to be taken away." Camus is getting at a Dionysian, wildflower classicism that doesn't even need the term, in which bodily beauty itself is ennobled in its very squandering, by people who have "wagered on the flesh, but knowing they were going to lose" – which reminds him of the very origin of the Doric order of the Parthenon itself: for if such creatures have the luxury of living for a few years in the present "without myths, without solace," they have, just so, such "haste to live" that "if art were to be born here it would obey that hatred of permanence that made the Dorians fashion their first column in wood."[43] Maybe only such a noble recklessness can engender anything worthy to stand beside actual classical art and architecture – which most "classicists" have only helplessly desired.

13

Tired Tropes

Cathedral versus Bicycle Shed; "Duck" versus "Decorated Shed"

For M.W.

In the postwar promulgation of architectural modernism and then of post-modernism, and of modern and postmodern senses of architecture in general, two pairs of categories in self-contained binary opposition have stood duty in turn as tropes. The first, that of the cathedral and the bicycle shed, was more casually framed by a modernist setting out to survey the history of Western European architecture from its native, which is to say, medieval *antiquité* onward: it concerned the limits of architecture as against mere building. The second, of the "duck" versus the "decorated shed," was polemical from its more recent inception, and concerned a distinction between an increasingly historical modernist expressivity of structure and a new, ostensibly semiotic, emphasis in buildings, whether culturally high or low. The first trope underlay the second, but the second had its own business to do.

What is architecture? Or rather, what makes one building mere construction and not architecture? Le Corbusier's conviction in architecture as irreducible art is manifest in his remark "The purpose of construction is TO MAKE THINGS HOLD TOGETHER; of architecture, TO MOVE US."[1] In actually defining architecture, nonarchitectural construction or building has for him no determining role: "Architecture is the masterly, correct and magnificent play of masses brought together in light"; again, "Architecture is the skillful, accurate and magnificent play of masses seen in light"; further, "The elements of architecture are light and shade, walls and space."[2] If this seems like an airy way for the supposed hero of a utilitarianism of function to conceive of his enterprise, what are we to make of the fact that in the sense and phraseology of the modernist Le Corbusier there echoes a French theoretical tradition long underwritten by the royal academy?

Le Corbusier himself by no means stands outside that tradition. In fact he admits one of its founding fathers, François Blondel, to his revisionist anti-academic *Vers une architecture* (1923), in image as well as in word.[3] Le Corbusier would surely have found certain of Blondel's notions interesting, such as – given the modernist questioning of the old rhetoric of the facade, and advocacy of flat roofs – Blondel's speculation that the ornamentally heightened front or face developed as a consequence of the gable (2.7.1).[4] In a sense, he was Le Corbusier's kind of guy, "an engineer and a mathematician . . . [whose] energies were mainly directed towards theory."[5] A century later, he could have found himself in the polytechnic setting, where he might, however, have suited the twentieth-century modernist's dialectic less ably. For Blondel opens his own *Cours d'architecture* (1675) with an academic-classical definition of architecture as the art of "*bien bâtir*," that is, "well-building," or building well (1.1),[6] an idealist standard that often since Alberti, in the Renaissance, has posed for moderns a problematic two-step conception of first the pragmatic and then, resources permitting, the ornamental.

Etienne-Louis Boullée, who stood chronologically midway between Le Corbusier and Blondel, taught in the new engineering schools at the turn of the eighteenth century but was also a member of the academy. Engaging the ultimately Vitruvian notion of *l'art de bâtir*, he shifts its emphasis. In *Architecture: An Essay on Art* (written between 1770 and 1784), Boullée asks, concerning architecture, "Shall I define it, with Vitruvius, the art of building? No, this definition contains a gross error. Vitruvius takes the effect for the cause." The Vitruvian "art of building" is only a "secondary art . . . the scientific (*scientifique*) part of architecture."[7] Architecture proper is "a process of the spirit," a "creation," that deserves to be defined as "the art of producing and of bringing to perfection [N.B.] every kind of edifice."[8] Reviving Perrault's critique of Blondel from the century before, Boullée reiterates Perrault's denial that architecture springs from nature: it is "an art of fantasy (*fantastique*) and pure invention."[9] But what can this mean, one wonders, besides the mere "dreams" of a Piranesi? Something rightly called a "poetry of architecture," which is called for above all in one particular "species of production," namely, the funeral monument or cenotaph (with its immortalizing demand for spare, unfrivolous eloquence). "This interesting poetry" is what Boullée seeks more broadly to convey.[10]

By the turn of the eighteenth century, engineering was asserting new claims to *building* in the sense of what Boullée called the (mere) "science of architecture." Within the orbit of Boullée, whose work certainly has its own protofunctional aspect, Claude Nicolas Ledoux, in the account of his project for a country house for a "*mecanicien*" – which it is fair to translate as "mechanical engineer" – salutes engineering: "Nothing is foreign to this precious art which the futility of the century appears to disdain."[11] Describing a house for two cabinetmakers, he writes that some have wanted "the arts that they qualify as liberal, considered as a luxury, not to be available to everybody," wishing "those arts which they call mechanical" to suffer debasement in order to satisfy their own vanity; whereas everybody who designs and executes – take note, architects and other artists – is an "*ouvrier*" (workman): "The ordinary man is an *artiste ouvrier,* the distinguished man, an *ouvrier* become artist."[12] Ledoux thought the intellectual had much to learn from such operatives and their sometimes marvelous works, notably, again, in his allusion to a "tall ship" that anticipates the excitement Le Corbusier took in modern maritime design: "What builder would not experience utter transport if one told him of an edifice three hundred feet tall, erected in the middle of a stormy sea?"[13] But the rivalry of engineering only put a new twist in the problem of what is and is not architecture, while the British protomodernists of the second half of the nineteenth century, not only Ruskin but the more radical William Morris, tended to shrink back from the new spectacles of engineering construction in their times as the fruit of an evil system.

In *Vers une architecture* Le Corbusier embraces modern engineering *by way of analogy,* precisely in order to surpass within fine-art architecture its challenging accomplishments. As he was aware, once there developed, at first in France, an institutional alternative to the official, full-dress "architecture" of the fine arts academy, the question of what architecture *is* necessitated a more specific question of what architecture is *not,* in respect to engineering and all forms of purely (or merely) utilitarian construction, whether elegant, efficient, or not. Thus there comes inevitably into view the matter of the fine art of architecture itself, over and against the satisfaction of utility, and the question of what this might mean in modern circumstances.

A modern formula that by now has some classic standing is that with which Nikolaus Pevsner opens the introduction to his still widely read *Outline of European Architecture* (1942): "A bicycle shed is a building; Lincoln cathedral is a piece of architecture."[14] Note, already, an inevitable awkwardness in the phrase *"piece of* architecture," as Pevsner defers from the questionably singular building to the comprehensive singularity[15] of the fine art as circumscribed by its Latinate abstract noun. But it is to the question of the art of architecture in that sense that we have to turn first.

To reinvoke the traditional definition of architecture as the *art of building* seems hardly more helpful today than to speak of an "ideal of the real." Historically, the rather unphilosophical ancient Roman treatise of Vitruvius, *The Ten Books of Architecture,* which held almost scriptural standing for Renaissance and later classicisms, categorizes building as one of three departments of architecture, but alongside clock making and the construction of machinery (1.3.1).[16] Vitruvius mantled the architect in a noble mystique, and his thought implies something of the ambitious nineteenth-century engineer concerned to effect dignified appearances. For centuries the theory, practice and history of Western architecture had to abide a deep foundational inadequacy due to Vitruvius's *allzurömische* (and rather "American") metaphysical obliviousness.

In religious terms, the question of what counts as a house for purposes of Jewish law arises in the Talmud in respect to the temporary *Sukkah* erected for the Feast of Tabernacles. Apropos simple magnitude – thinking of the bicycle shed as too small to matter, beside Lincoln Cathedral – it is interesting that legalities of observance concerning houses apply only to a structure at least four cubits square. More qualitative considerations serve to define in both sacred and pragmatic terms something like what the modern philosopher Heidegger would ground in the verb "to dwell." Thus, concerning any structure too negligible to count as a house: one would not "return on its account from the array of war." As well, a house is "a permanent abode," that is, "people dwell therein . . ." (*Sukkah*, 1.3a–3b).[17] The status of an "outpost," meaning a tower standing permanently outside city walls, but only for a night's temporary lodging, is interestingly affirmed: "Outposts are suitable for their purpose. . . ."[18] No building not conceived as a substantially permanent dwelling will do.[19] Only the purposiveness of dwelling justifies any house meeting (the small) size requirement, but not even, say, a large porter's lodge – let alone a bicycle shed, where one might if necessary sleep, but not specifically dwell.

It was Descartes who framed what Heidegger calls the modern world picture, Descartes whose dualism dissociated emotion from its physical expression. However, his contemporary, the Jansenist Arnauld, turned to a protomodernist architectural figure in pursuing the nature of expression. In a letter to Gottfried Wilhelm Leibniz in 1687, Arnauld employs as a trope a principle that resounds through modern architectural theory: "One thing *expresses* another (in my terminology) when there exists a constant and fixed relationship between what can be said of one and of the other. This is the way that a perspectival projection expresses its ground-plan."[20] Here is a seed of the modernist doctrine of the determining role of the plan as propounded out of a characteristic Cartesianism by Le Corbusier in *Vers une architecture*.[21]

Already in the title of the protofunctionalist Abbé Cordemoy's *Nouveau traité de tout l'architecture; ou, l'art de bastir; utile aux entrepreneurs et aux ouvriers* (1714), some threat to the classical (and class-affiliated) convention of considering architecture the art of *bien bâtir* may be detectible as much in what is not said – *bien* – as in what is – the almost petit-bourgeois, entrepreneurial appeal. Charles Etienne Briseux's *Architecture moderne; ou, l'art de bien bâtir pour toutes sortes de personnes, tant pour les maisons des particuliers que pour les palais* (1728) insinuates a "concession" of extending *architecture* to the middle class as a possible intermediate step toward a "modern architecture" for every class. Too, from the English Whig neo-Palladian movement with its own doctrinal classicism, come the first publications to extend down, if not break through, social hierarchy by according serious architectural consideration to the houses of the lower orders, at least in the country: first Daniel Garrett's *Designs and Estimates for Farm Houses* (1747), then Robert Morris's *Rural Architecture; Consisting of Regular Designs . . . in Which the Purity and Simplicity of the Art of Designing are Variously Exemplified* (1750), and others, including John Wood the Younger's later *Series of Plans for Cottages or Habitations of the Labourer* (1781).[22]

Piranesi's character Didascalo says, in the *Parare* (1765), "Architects are normally called in when one intends to build a beautiful building. . . . But when one does not have such a concern, it is the patrons themselves who are the architects, and it is enough for them to find someone merely to throw up the walls. All the rest of architecture, other than ornamentation, is of so little importance and of so little little glory for architects that few of them are proud of it."[23] If somebody thought to throw up unornamented walls in such a way as to make an extra-fine bicycle shed, that might only show up vanity as the determining requirement; or at least it might exercise a finer vanity.

Since in Boullée's view, architecture begins – like all the arts of *disegno* in Renaissance art theory – with an essentially intellectual *conception,* an idea in the mind, then even "our earliest ancestors could only have built their huts (*cabanes*) after having conceived their image."[24] If Boullée's "poetry of architecture" does not seem vivid enough to be definitive, Ledoux's analogy with poetry may be more useful: "Architecture is to stone construction (*la maçonnerie*) what poetry is to belles lettres, the dramatic enthusiasm (*enthousiasme dramatique*) of the métier" – "Art without eloquence" being "like love without virility."[25] And we come close to Pevsner's hypothetical bicycle shed with a suburban refreshment stand – a *guinguette* – projected by Ledoux for his ideal city of Chaux: "The magnificence of the *guinguette* and the palace will both present themselves; not that *égalité morale* will suffer, either, since those of superior *esprit* and talent will be all the more pleased."[26]

As professor specifically of architecture at the new Ecole polytechnique, Boullée's student J. N. Durand takes the object of that discipline to be "the composition and execution of edifices, public and private alike." Durand entertains the Abbé Marc-Antoine Laugier's primeval hut as the origin of architecture, only to decide that neither was Laugier's *cabane* a natural production, with its supposed tree-trunk shafts as protocolumns (the hypothetical hut could only have been shaken by the sensational renown, in 1800, of an adolescent *enfant sauvage* who had lived without shelter in the forest, and to whom any indoor living seemed only confinement, imprisonment); nor could the classical ornamental orders be the essence of architecture – which, he says, some think is workaday building (*batisse*) in the trade (*métier*) sense. If anything, Roman classical ornament associates in Durand's mind with *parvenus,* whereas the Greeks were "bien moins opulens." Aware of the contradiction of representing architecture per se in this new antithetical setting, he allows that this *art* whose object is composition and execution has, after all, *un genre propre,* though he has to wonder, what with "engineers being in charge, more likely than not, of raising important buildings," how to recommend the study of architecture to Polytechnique students "and at the same time give them the means to engage in it with success."[27] Basically, Durand is prepared to assert general juristiction, taking the task of architecture in an "economical," utilitarian way. Military architecture already stood as a special category in which engineering had, since the Renaissance, been dignified as a matter of state; now at the militarily instituted Polytechnique the prerogative of architecture was to be extended in a kind of universal suffrage, with at least major useful buildings eligible, as it were, for senatorial rank (it being difficult to imagine such a leveling before the industrial revolution enabled the tycoon to rival the nobleman in civil life).

Ledoux says, notably in his *L'architecture* (1804), apropos of a design for a modest, orderless, if not diminutive, country house for a Besançon merchant:

> You see, by this little edifice that there is not as much difference as is supposed in respective fitnesses (*convenances*). Art presides over the quarters of the ant and of the elephant. If all animals had understanding, if they could speak, they would ascribe to their species all the enjoyments (*jouissances*) it is possible to muster; but the force of nature is so great that it gives to each what suits it (*convient*), . . . the superfluous (*superflu*) is not [appropriately] commodious (*incommode*).[28]

Here as generally in classical theory, social *convenance* is pretty much self-regulating, if only because ostentation will reprove itself to sophisticated eyes.

Napoleon, himself of course a princified commoner as well as a military man who valued military – and the new civil – engineering, was evidently of the same leveling persuasion. He is reported to have said, in an 1812 conversation, "Even in the mere collier's hut (*cabane d'un charbonnier*) you can have architecture." The emperor was dicussing public urban architecure with an architect who had just said, among other things, "Every edifice must have a distinct character. Utility must everywhere justify (*motiver*) decoration." In context, his remark is perhaps subtler than it might seem: "I know very well that one had no pretense of making a palace facade, but only that of a barracks . . . It doesn't matter! Even in the mere collier's hut one can have architecture."[29]

Not really, according to Hegel's *Aesthetics,* which says that "the special purpose (*Bestimmung*) of architecture (*Architektur*)" is "to furnish . . . enclosure merely (*blosse Umschliessung*)."[30] Hegel framed this special purposiveness to distinguish from "independent symbolic buildings" in Egypt, something else that could be considered pure architecture – a distinction that the modernist Loos would as much as reverse, polemically, a century later.[31] The Hegelian historical outline proceeds from "Independent or Symbolic" to "Classical" architecture, under which fall "Subservience to a Specific End" and "the Building's Fitness to Purpose." Finally comes the historical Gothic, or as he classes it, "Romantic," architecture, which begins with the "pre-Gothic" Romanesque – as in fact did Lincoln Cathedral itself[32] – and includes the theme of "the Form of the Exterior and the Interior." Thus by the place in Hegel's system where one could arrive at Lincoln Cathedral it might seem absurd to be detained by a case of "symbolic," as well as space-enclosing, triviality, with the bicycle shed.

Without reviewing Hegel's entire chapter (Pt. 3, I.3), it is noteworthy that its opening section affirms that in the Gothic, "The architecture which is independent is united with that which serves a purpose," in that "enclosure provides the fundamental type to a greater extent than is the case in Greek temple-building, while, on the other hand, mere utility (*Dienstbarkeit* = servitude) and adaption to an end is transcended all the same and the house (*Haus*) [i.e., of God] is erected freely, independently, and on its own account. Thus these buildings and houses of God do prove . . . to be entirely suitable for worship and other uses, but their real character lies precisely in the fact that

they transcend (*fortzugehen* = exceed) any specific end and, as perfect in themselves, stand there on their own account." Even a feature serving what we
would call an engineering purpose "disappears again" into the transcendent
whole. "No one thing completely exhausts a building like this . . . It has and
displays a definite purpose; but in its grandeur and sublime peace it is lifted
above anything purely utilitarian (*Zweckdienliche* = serviceable) into an infinity
in itself."[33]

Schopenhauer sought to quarantine "*architecture* as a fine art . . . from its
provision for useful purposes, in which it serves the will and not pure knowledge, and thus is no longer art in our sense." Here, in the first volume (1819)
of *The World as Will and Representation,* the philosopher is pleased to snub the
material aspect of even fine-art architecture: besides light, only the abstract
"conflict between gravity and rigidity" concerns him as "the sole aesthetic
material" of the art. True architectural beauty, which is a visual, superphysical
assurance of "stability," is free of the "outward arbitrary purpose of man (to
this extent the work belongs to practical architecture)"; then, more classically,
it can be considered a function of designed "suitability" of parts to the visually
stable whole (3.43).[34]

Ruskin, however, could be utterly passionate toward the material, whereas
Schopenhauer was almost indifferent, superior. To Ruskin the very stones of
building offered live connections, through the cultural past – style, craft tradition, social life – to the very earth in its own geologic historicity. Pevsner's
mention of an English cathedral is inescapably Ruskinian, but Ruskin's own
reverence for medieval building construction on every scale from humble-
Christian to church-triumphant would imply some respect for the bicycle shed
or its equivalent. He would have appreciated the remarks of an American
retracing the steps of the poet Cowper and observing the disappearence of an
old peasant architecture in the early nineteenth century:

> I reached a whitened dwelling-house that had been once the "Peasant's
> Nest." But nowhere else in the course of my walk had the hand of
> improvement misimproved so sadly. For the cottage, "Environed with
> a ring of branchy elms / That overhung the thatch," I found a modern
> hard-cast farm-house, with a square of offices attached, all exceedingly
> utilitarian, well kept, stiff, and disagreeable. It was sad enough to find
> an erection that a journeyman bricklayer could have produced in a single
> month, substituted for the "peaceful covert" Cowper had so often wished
> his own, and which he had so frequently and fondly visited.[35]

The same writer offers a constructional metaphor in the spirit of Constable's
Boat-Building Near Flatford Mill, 1815, praising Cowper for "taking the most
stubborn and intractable words in the language, and bending them with all
ease round his thinking, so as to fit its every indentation and outline, as the
ship-carpenter adjusts the stubborn planking, grown flexible in his hand, to
the exact mould of his vessel."[36] Here, then, the romance of the peasant makes
of the older humble elm-vaulted "nest," as now displaced by its modern and
hard-cast utilitarian equivalent, something of a nostalgic minicathedral. Would

a bicycle shed, as a modest structure, compare with the first, or would it as housing for something as newfangled as the bicycle connote the second?

What about a Gothic bicycle shed – which, at best, would have to mean a new type of shed simply in Gothic style? Ruskin tended to despise the actual, hardheaded materialist productions of the new age of iron architecture, if not the idea of a new architecture somehow extending the Gothic into modern circumstances. On the other hand, he could not have despised the simple utility shed categorically, unless for possible deprivation of craftsmanly scope; for in itself, no honest, one-person utility could be ignoble. Nevertheless, what could be called spiritual utility – presumable with Lincoln Cathedral, more problematic with the shed – is an important qualification for architectural standing on Ruskin's terms. In Chapter 1 ("The Lamp of Sacrifice") in *The Seven Lamps of Architecture* (1849), Ruskin defines architecture itself as "the art which so disposes and adorns the edifices raised by man for whatsoever uses, that the sight of them contributes to his mental health, power and pleasure."[37] This definition constitutes paragraph one in its entirety; next, "It is very necessary, at he outset of all inquiry, to distinguish carefully between Architecture and Building," and insofar as it is *utilitarian,* the building of a church no less than a ship "ceases to be one of the fine arts."[38] (The Protestant Ruskin implicitly plays down liturgical utility.)

This is no simple distinction of high and low. What qualifies an otherwise incidental structure as architecture is some transcendentally or "sacrificially" useless, unnecessary, extra consideration, ornamentally expressed. Important, however, is a certain "craft" argument, from Ruskin through William Morris and down at least to John Dewey and Nikolaus Pevsner himself, which emphasizes fine art as rooted in and growing out of lowlier artistic practice. For Ruskin as much as claims that fine Gothic cathedrals depended on a firm tradition of building such things as bicycle sheds when he says, "All good architecture rises out of good and simple domestic work; and . . . therefore, before you attempt to build great churches and palaces, you must build good house doors and garret windows."[39]

Ruskin's terms here may reflect the sense of William Whewell, in his historical survey of "The Inductive Sciences," that just as Gothic structural developments such as the flying buttress and the groin vault occurred first empirically in building craft, and only later in theory, so something similarly marvelous in the new industrial age (1837) was the "skew arch" used in railway bridges.[40] If so, however, Ruskin forgot or rejected Whewell's exciting new example, as he rejected what of the new railroad construction he himself saw, preferring to take his examples from the homier realm of one-man carpentry. Actual bicycle sheds are moot because the modern bicycle was not common until late in Ruskin's life; but under "The Lamp of Beauty," in *Seven Lamps,* a new (yet already conventional) railway architecture is condemned as materialist and wasteful instead of spiritual and sacrificial: "Railroad architecture has or would have a dignity of its own if it were only left to its own work" (4.21).[41] Several times, Ruskin censured the secular-spectacular, bare-bones Crystal Palace of 1851, as merely an overblown greenhouse, and as such grossly unarchitectural. This was in the first volume (1851) of *The Stones of Venice,* with further attacks in "The Opening of the Crystal Palace" (1854) and *The Two Paths* (1859). Why then, or how, might Ruskin ever have defended the bicycle shed? For its likely unpretentious humility, it seems, versus the more vainglorious Victorian railway constructions as false cathedrals that entailed all too painful "sacrifice," to secular values at that.

Despite a reputation as a protofunctionalist hero that is by no means un-warranted given his happy obsession with modern industrial materials and new construction techniques, the modernist-Gothicist Viollet-le-Duc may be said to stand, in at least one significant place, against Pevsner in the matter of the bicycle shed. In his novella-like *Histoire d'une maison* (1873), he raises the pointed question of whether, if truthfulness and simplicity be all that ultimately matter in architecture, a barn ought to be considered "a work of art." The reply is, "Certainly; if it is so constructed as to offer a suitable shelter for what it is intended to hold."[42] Admittedly, that is not a very serviceable definition of a work of architecture, let alone of a work of art in general; but since, Viollet adds, a barn might well prove "more admirable" than some overde-corated but "inconvenient palace," the point he is really out to establish is the initial, negative one that a barn's lack of ornamental rhetoric (and so its de-tachment from decorous social qualification) is not enough to rule out its being a true work of art. By the same token, Pevsner's antinomy falls back on the cultural repute, including historically codified ornamental traits, of Lincoln Cathedral, by assuming that such a structure is not a work of architecture just because, lacking historical birthright, the credentials committee, as it were, of social convention could not supply stud papers for it.

Many have come to assume that any building is a possible occasion for a work of architecture. Too many assume so, according to the early formalist theoretician Conrad Fiedler, who complains in *On Judging Works of Visual Art* (1876) that historians survey all sorts of structures indiscriminately before considering which buildings even deserve to be approached as architecture, which is to say, as art. Fiedler insists that one first distinguish "between building construction and architecture as an art (*zwischen Bauen und Baukunst*)," isolating worthy "artistic achievement" from any "nonartistic demands" (2.5).[43] But how, except by empty fiat of connoisseurship? Compared with that, the spiritual utility demanded in Ruskin's moral interrogation of buildings seems quite workable in praxis.

Ruskin hated the traditionally Roman architectural orthodoxy and the equally Roman passion for engineering, though in his beloved Gothic he respected the basic engineering of the arch and its spatial projection, the vault. More reactively, the architect Giles Gilbert Scott dismissed the Roman arch system as "mere construction," and not essentially architectural, in the second of his *Lectures on the Rise and Development of Mediaeval Architecture* (1879).[44] Actually, it is thanks substantially to the writings of Nikolaus Pevsner that Ruskin and William Morris belong to the critical prehistory of modernism in architecture, though a simplistic, rather Emersonian, functionalism advanced especially in America would rend apart Ruskin's "disposing" and "adorning,"

Calvinistically discarding the latter and reducing the former to a semiautomatic projection of the program into buildable structure. Not unlike Freud's *geistlich,* rendered all too cooly as "mental" in the official English "Standard Edition,"[45] Ruskin's working concern with spiritual value, developed by Morris into a socialist theory of unalienated work, has fallen into neglect.

We approximate a case of a "bicycle shed" with a medieval barn (at Great Coxwell, Berks.) that Morris loved, Frederick Evans photographed, and Morris's architect friend Philip Webb – who by the way was not so opposed to the eighteenth century as Ruskin and Morris – remarked for its "nice precision of building," calling it "as beautiful as a cathedral, with no ostentation of building whatsoever: a perfectly suitable barn and nothing else."[46] (To the extent that Webb's comment implies a hierarchy from architecture to building and down to not-even-building, with rejection, possibly, of only the middle term, it suggests a sometimes patronizing antibourgeois idealization of the lower classes in modern culture.) Interestingly, the poet Coventry Patmore actually played the "ostentation" card affirmatively, in line with Ruskin's conceit of sacrifice: decrying the "scamped modern tenement," Patmore advocates a "modest ostentation of extreme substantiality" by which "a labourer's cottage or the smallest village church" that goes the extra Ruskinian mile can be "an artistic and rightly architectural work; and the nobleman's mansion or cathedral which wants it is not."[47]

Notably, however, on the subject of modern bridge construction, Morris held in practice to Ruskin's path, as in some sense Nikolaus Pevsner himself would manage to do. "Every improvement in machinery being uglier and uglier," Morris said, taking the Firth of Forth Bridge, 1883–9, as "the supremest specimen of all ugliness." As it happened, Benjamin Baker, the bridge's designer, had insisted that only for aesthetic reasons had he given the bridge anything like an arched form at all, and had sought clear visual distinction between thick tubular forms for compressive members and thin ones for tension.[48] At the turn of the century, despite confessing architecture's general relation to utility, and promising that "we may have a new architecture when we have new problems to be solved, and insight brought to bear upon them," an aesthetician still equivocates: "There is a real problem in the use of iron; but, while they may be engineering feats, neither the Crystal Palace nor the Forth Bridge is architecture."[49] To the American Montgomery Schuyler in 1896, however, the Forth Bridge is an obvious example of a major new form finding "its basis and motive in the laws of organic structure."[50] And, aware of the discussion of the bridge in Fidler's *Treatise on Bridge Construction* under "The Comparative Anatomy of Bridges,"[51] D'Arcy Thompson favorably likens it to botanical and zoological structures[52] in his modernist-influential *On Growth and Form* (1917).[53]

The modernist case of John Roebling's Brooklyn Bridge, finished as the Forth Bridge was begun, would be different, though Morris could surely have accepted the bicycle shed, at least, as akin to the barn he is known to have loved. Even before it was finished, the Brooklyn Bridge was being admired as an engineering wonder in France, thanks to a lavish French government report on American public works, published in 1873, in which the bridge is hailed as "un ouvrage d'une importance exceptionnelle, même pour l'Amérique, au double point de vue de la circulation qu'il doit desservir et des difficultés techniques du programme auquel il doit satisfaire."[54] Its transatlantic literary career, in a *modernolatria* that includes even Mayakovsky, is well known.[55]

Schuyler's criticism, beginning with the Brooklyn Bridge when it was new, seeks to distinguish between the modern engineering and traditional architectural aspects of bridge design; indeed, these are kept as if socially apart, though the former is allowed an aesthetic of its own within its parameters. Architecture is treated as a matter of nonutilitarian beauty, while engineering, which is not architecture but is utilitarian (though capable of beauty), is confined between negations. It might be fair to say that knightly honors are bestowed on worthy engineering if it does not presume too much to the nobility of architectural rhetoric. Of the Brooklyn Bridge itself, whose masonry its designer, John Roebling, implicitly considered art, and the steel work, engineering,[56] Schuyler writes, "The utilitarian treatment of our monument is as striking and as characteristic a mark of the period as its utilitarian purpose. It is a noble work of engineering; it is not a work of architecture."[57]

Like Le Corbusier before the Brooklyn Bridge – unbelievably, hardly a generation later – Schuyler takes engineering impressiveness as Roman, in an essay of the turn of the century: "A modern metallic structure, 'mathematically conceived,' may ... attain a result more than Roman in power and more than Roman in beauty." He also wishes that "engineers were trained to regard the expression, or the expressibility, of the primary forms of their bridges as an element in the choice of constructions, instead of confining themselves to the points of stability and economy; if, as Mr. Russell Sturgis has reminded the American Society of Civil Engineers, instead of concentrating their attention upon whether their works would stand, they would direct some of it to the question of whether they were fit to stand." Why should "the primary form of a great work of engineering ... [determine] its artistic success"? "If the general form does not in itself appeal to the sense of beauty, it is quite futile for the engineer to attempt any subsequent beautification, either by his own efforts or by invoking the aid of architects"; hence, "The scientific designer of a work of engineering must be the artistic designer also, if it is to be a work of art." More problematic, in light of eventual constructivist architecture and art, is the claim that "it is the choice of a construction that primarily determines the artistic result."[58] If that is saying more, or trying to, than simply that worthy bridges have nothing superfluous and express their essentials,[59] it already begins to pose the problem of an untranscendental less-as-more.

But the American locus classicus of stunned enchantment by the machine, as well as by the new heavy industrial construction, remains Henry Adams's encounter with the dynamo at the Paris exposition of 1900. Before, at the 1867 Universal Exposition in Paris, the realist painter Thomas Eakins had been thrilled by the machinery, and above all by an American locomotive: "By the finest there," he wrote in a letter. "I can't tell you how mean the best English,

French and Belgian ones are alongside it"[60] (shades of Fernand Léger's enthusiasm for the Salon de la Locomotion Aérienne in 1912).

In his own account, comprising the famous chapter "The Dynamo and the Virgin" in his third-person *Education of Henry Adams* (1907), written in 1905 as a sequel to that famous celebration of the Gothic, his *Mont-Saint-Michel and Chartres* (1904), Adams first confesses to knowing neither how to apply his study of Karl Marx nor "how to look at the art exhibits of 1900."[61] Ironically, had he pursued the art as well, he might have been stimulated by an American painting of the Brooklyn Bridge just then and there singled out for praise by French critics, namely Harry W. Ranger's *Pont de Brooklyn*.[62] In New York, the art critic Sadakichi Hartmann wrote in 1900 that "a large majority" would not share his sense "that there is an imposing grandeur in the Brooklyn Bridge," nor "acknowledge the beauty of the large sweeping curves in the new [Harlem River] Speedway, which would set a Munich Secessionist wild."[63] Indeed, when, not long after, Hartmann showed the conservative painter George de Forest Brush a portfolio of contemporary photographs, the artist said, "These are queer times. Perhaps we shall have to accept new ideals of beauty. Maybe the East River bridges will be aesthetically attractive to the man of the coming generation as the Parthenon appeared all-sufficient to our forefathers."[64]

"To him," writes Adams of himself, "the dynamo was but an ingenious channel for conveying somewhere the heat latent in a few tons of pure coal hidden in a dirty engine-house carefully kept out of sight; but to Adams the dynamo became a symbol of infinity. As he grew accustomed to the great gallery of machines, he began to feel the forty-foot dynamo as a moral force, much as the early Christians felt the Cross." It also concerned a distinctly modern *expressivity* of focused force: "Among the thousand symbols of ultimate energy, the dynamo was not so human as some, but it was the most expressive."[65] According to Adams, the symbolic power of the Virgin had long since disappeared among "the German and English stock": the sculptor (Augustus) "St. Gaudens[66] at Amiens was hardly less sensitive to the force of the female energy than Matthew Arnold at the Grande Chartreuse. Neither of them felt goddesses as power – only as reflected emotion, human expression, beauty, purity, taste, scarcely even as sympathy. They felt a railway train as power; yet they, and all other artists, constantly complained that the power embodied in a railway train could never be embodied in art."[67] To just this hint of neopagan, mechanical animism, as it were, the modern poet Auden would object: "Actually, Venus is the Dynamo in disguise, a symbol for an impersonal natural force, and Adams' nostalgic preference for Chartres to Chicago was nothing but aestheticism; he thought the disguise was prettier than the reality, but it was the Dynamo he worshipped, not the Virgin."[68] For better or worse, to Adams the dynamo was the modern analogue of Chartres, if not Lincoln, Cathedral, with, if necessary, the "dirty engine-house carefully kept out of sight" as not impossibly like the bicycle shed.

The relation of architecture proper, whatever that now ought to mean, to mere building, probably including the new industrial construction, was an inevitable preoccupation of founding modernist architects of the turn of the century. Significantly, after Otto Wagner's book *Moderne Architektur* was first published in Vienna in 1896, it was the suggestion of Hermann Muthesius that "the German words *moderne* and *Architektur* no longer be used, the former for its linguistic association with the German word *Mode* (fashion), the latter because of its corruption through nineteenth-century efforts at style making." *Baukunst* (the art of building) was recommended instead. So Wagner retitled the fourth edition (1914) *Die Baukunst unserer Zeit* (literally, The Building-Art in Our Time).[69] Also in Vienna, Adolf Loos developed his sense of a nobly useless (even funereal) architecture over and against mundane and artless building, not to mention his notorious notion of ornament as "crime."

Pevsner's problematic statement notwithstanding, his larger project helped to open to aesthetic regard some plain building, including industrial architecture, that inevitably deepened the vernacular category. If that doesn't sound like much, one should remember that in Bannister Fletcher's standard *A History of Architecture on the Comparative Method* (1896; endless subsequent editions), all noncanonical architecture is simply dismissed as "non-historical." "Vernacular" is a good term, too, considering that Latinate abstraction *Architektur*. The late Gert Schiff called attention, within art history, to Julius von Schlosser's working distinction, in regard to medieval architecture, between fine art as equivalent to literature, and an equivalent to mere "language," with "dialects" at that.[70] (While Schiff rightly thought of the aesthetician Croce as relevant for his sense that only the extraordinarily worthy production counts as "art," in the problem at hand Lincoln Cathedral is more than a peculiarly inspired bicycle shed, and the bicycle shed is less than an uninspired cathedral.) It is in an essay, "On the Historiography of Art Historiography: The Gothic" (1910), that Schlosser writes, "Profane architecture is older than the true work of art, the temple; for the art of building precludes [*sic*] a knowledge of carpentry, and the former evolved out of the latter." What is more, "Art was formative long before it was beautiful."[71]

Not to be overlooked as too obvious is a social distinction between Lincoln Cathedral, as emblematic of the establishment, and the common workaday bicycle shed. Ironically, the secularization of twentieth-century society began to let any old buildings stand vaguely sacrosanct, as sheer longevity qualified for an "establishment" aside from any intrinsic merit. In response to an objection by the *Times* of London, about 1913, to the tearing down of old buildings in Regent Street, the formalist art critic Roger Fry had to counter, "The Kodak building in Kingsway... puts all its [old] neighbours to shame by sheer reasonableness and good sense, for it has what they lack – essential dignity of style."[72] Yet one also observes a plain-talking acquiescence to class distinction in another remark of Fry's, in an article in *Vogue* rather hesitatingly entitled "A Possible Domestic Architecture" (1918), that "Houses are either builders' houses or architects' houses."[73] And speaking of Coventry Patmore's positive *ostentatio:* Fry had then only recently commented on what struck him as the "hypocrisy" of a "peculiar style of ostentatious simplicity" in Cistercian architecture.[74]

Toward the end of Joyce's *Ulysses* (1922), written between 1914 and 1921, Bloom and Stephen enter "the cabman's shelter, an unpretentious wooden structure," a small all-night workmen's café of pointedly basic aesthetic conceit whose furnishings include, to Bloom's eye and mind, "a blunt hornhandled knife with nothing particularly Roman or antique about it to the lay eye." The entire mise-en-scène entails subtle aesthetic ambiguity as to the architectural standing of the structure itself: a parenthetical thought of theatrical verisimilitude (itself reminiscent of a statement by Roger Fry) occurs to Bloom ("ships of any sort, phantom or the reverse, on the stage usually fell a bit flat as also did trains"), who also reflects on photography as not an art, even as the author surreptitiously speculates on the soiling and surface crinkling of a photographic print. But then the shelter is called – more impermanently and disreputably – a "shanty," this only to be succeeded by "shelter or shanty," with Joyce himself thereby conveying indecision as to nuance.[75]

Quite challenging on behalf of the bicycle shed, at Fry's British moment, is a recollection from the front in World War I by the Welsh poet David Jones in his autobiographical *In Parenthesis* (1937), this under the headline "I Built a Shit-House for Artaxerxes." The writer recalls being told by a fellow soldier on latrine duty, "the army of Artaxerxes was utterly destroyed for lack of sanitation."[76] The on-with-it, soldierly humor of Jones – who one day would be quoted approvingly in Robert Venturi's *Complexity and Contradiction* (1966), on the artistic importance of building practice[77] – covers an aesthetic of rigor in necessity that recalls Napoleon on the architecture of the barracks and the collier's hut.

At an opposite extreme, cathedral-evocative, mystically crystalline structures (in one sense redemptions of the Crystal Palace and in another, direct expressionist resurrections of the Gothic) were projected by those German architects who corresponded as the "Crystal Chain" at the war's end. In one of these letters (May 30, 1920) Hans Luckhardt writes, "Pure form is that form which, released from all embellishment, is freely composed out of the basic elements of straight line, curve and irregular form, and can serve any expressive purpose, be it for a religious building or a factory."[78] Under the pseudonym "Glas," Bruno Taut muses rather mystically in an essay, "My World-Picture," dated October 19, 1920, "The slope of the kennel roof, the cubic form of the most humble living-room, and every color too – all derive from the rays of the 'astral' crystal. In the final analysis nothing is formless – right to the limits of the Universal Nothingness."[79] Note the abstraction of Taut's operative terms – the slope rather than the roof itself, for example, – which is how, in this case, the fact of a kennel seems so incidental, even though its earthy humility is here to the point.

In their definitive study of *The International Style: Architecture Since 1922* (1932), Henry-Russell Hitchcock and Philip Johnson comment, "Some modern critics and groups of architects both in Europe and in America deny that the aesthetic element in architecture is important, or even that it exists. . . . This new conception, that building is science and not art, developed as an exaggeration of the idea of functionalism."[80] Special blame for this is laid at the doorsteps of the historian Sigfried Giedion and the Bauhaus architect Hannes Meyer (later at Harvard) as being antiaesthetic, materialist functionalists.[81] And in chapter 8, devoted to the very problem of "Architecture and Building," Hitchcock and Johnson affirm that even under the modernist reform there will still be "architecture: that is, edifices consciously raised over the level of mere building."[82] It may not be easy even for such well-meaning American modernists to defend the transcendental, but where some extra potential seems to inhere in specifically public buildings they come close to doing so: "Because of their greater scale it is possible to give them a more architectural character than the ordinary surrounding buildings. Emphasized by the idiosyncrasies of their function, they [N.B.] symbolize group activities."[83]

Ruskin's distinction between architecture and mere building is recalled in a chapter on "Engineering and Architecture in the Nineteenth Century" in Pevsner's own earlier *Pioneers of the Modern Movement* (1936; since retitled *Pioneers of Modern Design*). Pevsner quotes it with the elaboration that this "separates architecture from a wasp's nest, a rat hole or a railway station."[84] Within the *Outline,* Pevsner accepts the structural appeal of the Gothic cathedral, but in the second sentence of the introduction the Ruskinian moral subtlety of "sacrifice" becomes embarrassingly epicurean, if not hopelessly cosmetic: "Nearly everything that encloses space on a scale sufficient for a human being to move in, is a building; the term architecture applies only to buildings designed with a view to aesthetic appeal."[85] The obvious question is, Why not an especially beautiful bicycle shed? – and why necessarily an inappropriately *luxurious* bicycle shed at that?[86]

Out of speculation that began in the late 1920s, Roman Ingarden published, after World War II, an extended essay titled "The Architectural Work." This begins by ranking some major structures – "Notre Dame, St. Peter's Basilica, the Parthenon" and civic equivalents – as "undoubtedly works of art," products of human work that possess (in scrupulous redefinition of the usual je ne sais quois) "certain properties that are not indispensable . . . for the fulfilling of . . . religio-social functions, but which confer . . . certain aesthetically qualitative characteristics, by virtue of which . . . [they are] treasured as . . . 'great art.' "[87] Even taking the Paris cathedral as a "building," however, already implies for Ingarden some sort of cultural articulation beyond just so many stones put together. That as architecture Notre Dame is also more than a "building" here importantly entails its literal consecration. For such an "act of consciousness" is no simple projection of intention by imposition of individual will, but a collective deference toward the intentionality of its special object.

Where Ingarden claims that "one time" such an act "might have as its object a splendid building, another time a wretched hut or nothing more than a grove of trees, which from then on is a 'sacred' grove,"[88] a problem may arise, given the linkage between the twin (but not symmetrically interdependent) aspects of the "two-sided ontic relativity"[89] that obtains between building and architecture. It might be supposed that a certain episcopal decision in about 1175 was a simple act of will by one peculiarly and powerfully placed to channel (if not project) the future architectural intentionality of what we now point to as Notre Dame, as if the bishop in question could arbitrarily have determined any structure to be the Cathedral of Paris. But even a consecrating bishop will have had to know some principle of suitability.[90] Should the archbishop of Paris (or Lincoln) have chosen to place his *cathedra* (chair of authority) in a pointedly humble building, perhaps even a "wretched hut,"[91] thereby legally establishing *it* the Cathedral of Paris, the same authority would still have intentionally decided on the intrinsic suitability of some particular, ready-made building in consecrationally elevating it (thenceforth a very qualified "wretched hut") to the standing of architecture.[92] Ingarden tends to play down whatever (subjective) intention may have preceded, enablingly, the (objective) intentionality of the architectural work; the more difficult task of highlighting the latter occupies him. If this line of thought seems at all inconclusive, it has nevertheless carried us further than we might have thought we could go, since it is now clear at least how "a determinately ordered heap of building materials is just what a 'church' is not."[93]

For Ingarden, then, the "real building" is but the basis of the work of architecture as an essentially "cultural object."[94] He gives the example of the Cathedral of Rheims, which *building,* was severely damaged by bombing in 1914, and could never, as building, be "resurrected"; nonetheless, insofar as reconstruction was accurate, the same "architectural work of art" can indeed be seen again today, since this architectural entity has had restored to it whatever it needed from the material world to reestablish itself.[95] In accordance with architecture's "ontic relativity," all sensible qualities pass over from the material of which the building is composed into the work of architecture for which the material building is the occasion. It is because the qualities of materials attach, out of suspension as it were, to the realization of an artistic idea, that any structure which "falls short of the artistic goal . . . is something that could be a work of art, but that *de facto* is only a building, that fulfills its practical purposes, but is artistically incomplete."[96]

What Pevsner, too, means by a mere building has no such conditional double, nothing (else) to bring to appearance, whereas every essentially architectural object is real enough on its own terms to be "embodied in several different real buildings, which might be of different durability depending on the material used . . . "[97] (Long-destroyed early Christian churches and countless projects never built or even intended to be built have important places in the history of *architecture.*) Especially significant for the problem of the bicycle shed and functionalism is a sense of architecture's intentionality as unimpeded or compromised by utilitarian intention: "All purely technical or practical fittings and determinacies . . . should either be concealed or made unnoticeable to the viewer of the work (for example, the pipes for central heating, etc.), or else should be so chosen that those of their determinacies accessible to the viewer can function as a harmonious component of the whole of the work of art."[98]

So, in light of Ingarden, it might be possible, after all, to begin to allow for a hypothetical bicycle shed so well articulated in its necessities as to be tantamount to a work of architectural art. It might then have to be settled whether or not extraordinary executional attention, artisanal or artistic, would suffice as an "act of consciousness" to dignify or celebrate the bicycle housing function. This condition would probably be more readily met, or else more readily avoided in circumstances exceptionally high – an Olympic, national (like all the People's Bicycle Sheds of China) or academic-idealistic "*team bicycle shed*" – or low – a privately recreational or commercial bicycle shed – than under simple workaday necessity (in an unidealized sense, the bicycle sheds of China).

Lincoln Cathedral is easy to defend as architecture by Ingarden's argument, thanks especially to its formal, legal consecration (specifically to the Virgin), which Pevsner in his general modernist secularism chose to ignore, preferring to attempt to take the church, for his *Outline of European Architecture*, as a simple C-major of architectural self-evidence.[99] Ingarden, however, allows for a large gray area wherein analysis is obligatory. While many buildings stand apart from architecture, including, in our time, "many utilitarian structures lacking all charm,"[100] it is at least as true in modern times that "purely ar-chitectural works of art, buildings that serve no sort of practical purpose whatever, are very rare."[101] Usually – if not in a Gothic cathedral – pragmatics dominate the disposition of interiors, while (notwithstanding conventional types) the architect's freedom "can either take a direction such that the exterior form harmonizes with the configuration of the interior and is, within certain limits, subordinated to it, or else can take him in the opposite direction, so that the development of the exterior form is made as independent as possible of the inner composition and thus conceals to a certain extent the practical purpose of the building," even to the point of a conflict that violates its unity as a work.[102] (He didn't say it would be a *good* work of art.)

At the latter extreme is a problem familiar to functionalism:

> The exterior is not founded in the inner structure and in no way results from it; the aesthetic values that it perhaps brings to appearance are deprived of their foundation, and thereby lose the character of authen-ticity or earnestness and become mere external ornamentation lacking an inner ground. Ultimately, the principle of architecture as such – the principle of the work's inner logic – is violated.[103]

Ingarden is grateful to modernism for exposing, not only by simplification of construction and massing but by "the receding of the essentially nonarchitec-tural decorative moment," a definitive architecturality arising from architecture itself,[104] in light of which all worthy architecture appears as "a manifestation of humanity's victory over matter" and an affirmation of the human capacity for imposing "on lifeless matter" intellectually and emotionally satisfying forms.[105] Not that this produces, at last, a "pure" architecture, which, among the arts, is a unique impossibility according to Ingarden.[106]

All in all, every work of architecture, even that to which we refer as Lincoln Cathedral, has as its necessary occasion or basis (host?) a mere building, even if few mere buildings are so blessed. In the scheme of Ingarden there is no reason why some remarkable bicycle shed could not transcend itself and become, like a poem made out of otherwise mundane words and phrases, a genuine work of architectural art.[107] In the meantime, all the standing bicycle sheds of the world are no worse off, categorically, than all its many other unarchitectural buildings, no matter how large or vainglorious.

Pevsner's opening statement has always stood in need of illumination, seeming as it does to beg its own basic question. John Dewey might have helped if one considers how "instrumentality" has come to be paired against "expressivity" (in some studies of gender, the former as conventionally masculine and the latter feminine). Instrumentality is favorably supposed to connote the negotiation of practical tasks, a straightforward accomplishment of things. But as it might apply even in my writing of this sentence, the flexibly stronger instrumentality of Dewey could begin as far back as the satisfaction of needs of which I am unaware, and extend continuously through the task of getting something consciously across (entailing vocabulary and syntax, affect and nuance), and beyond, to its efficacy for the reader (with his or her spiritual as well as utilitarian needs). Inseparably, any writerly "expressivity" of mine affects my instrumentality, and although one can overindulge expressivity, there is no writerly instrumentality without expression. Every execution of a task or negotiation of a problem, including even Dewey's and Pevsner's, is also a kind of performance,[108] and connotation belongs as much to the science of language as does denotation.

From closer to Pevsner's adopted English home come some related but more penetrating contemporary remarks of the 1940s, in which Wittgenstein distinguished between building and architecture.[109] First (in 1942), drawing upon a bodily analogy, the point is expressive significance as against mere instrumentality, though it would be easy for a mere embellisher of sheds to suppress an implicit figurativeness in the following statement (including an italicization to stress a metaphor) and (mis)take this as simplistically linguistic, as a semiotic sense of mere indication of purpose by means however crude: "Architecture (*Architektur*) is a *gesture (Geste)*. Not every purposive movement of the human body is a gesture. And no more is every building designed for a purpose (*zweckmässige Gebaude* [which seems more Kantian in the original]) architecture."[110] Later (about 1947–8) there is the more transcendental, indeed, surprisingly Ruskinian, statement, "Architecture (*Architektur*) immortalizes and glorifies something. Hence there can be no architecture where there is nothing to glorify."[111] Note also in the former instance the resort to the concept of the *Geste* – from the Latin *res gestae,* that is, "things done," meaning significant deeds (often the decisive deeds of important individuals, as against a more run-on continuum of *historia*).

Beyond the introduction to the *Outline,* the first line of Pevsner's text proper, which depends on empathy theory to tell something of what he means by "aesthetic appeal," amounts to an endorsement of traditional humanist classicism that is practically immoralist on Ruskin's terms: "The Greek temple is the most perfect example ever achieved of architecture finding fulfilment in bodily beauty."[112] In a sense, Pevsner's initial "cathedral" proves an oddly cast or oddly costumed stand-in in summing up an essentially classical epic tradition of what "architecture" is supposed to mean, for the special benefit of the English, whose national *antiquité* is not classical but Gothic (an equivalent historical analogy has its own textual history in France).

To have said more revisionistically, "Lincoln Cathedral is a piece of architecture; a bicycle shed is a *real building*," however, could have muddled the issue from the start. What keeps Pevsner's larger meaning under control is the bicycle shed as a purely rhetorical setup for the cathedral, which also, if necessary, allows the cathedral lightly to connote, for those in the know, "Gothic engineering" as protomodern. But let's not overlook, either, how down to earth, almost squirish, it must have been for this emigrant, Herr Professor Pevsner, to preach to the English about architecture by breaking the ice in such a sporty, and almost Churchillian, manner, pointing to a fine old English medieval building at that, which also, conveniently for Tory readers, happens to be a cathedral of the Church of England (cf. Churchill's quip: "I consider myself a buttress of the Church, supporting it from without"). How many, after all, including architects, have been encouraged by Pevsner's introductory remark to think that it puts a very big question to rest. But if "architecture" is simply a privileged subcategory of "building," the case for modern architecture might not lean so safely on the utilitarian bicycle shed.

In the same year as Schlosser's vernacularizing "Historiography" essay, 1910, Frank Lloyd Wright had written in a rather less cosmopolitan spirit, under the title "The Sovereignty of the Individual," "The true basis for any serious study of the art of Architecture still lies in those indigenous, more humble buildings everywhere that are to architecture what folklore is to literature or folk song to music and with which academic architects were seldom concerned." These very words were emblazoned on the dedication page of a classic and still inspiring study of vernacular architecture, published only a few years before Pevsner's *Outline: Native Genius in Anonymous Architecture of North America* (1937), by the émigrée Bauhaus modernist Sibyl Moholy-Nagy.[113] Meanwhile, from Prague School linguistic theory, came the notion of *aktualisace*, translated as "foregrounding" (why not "actualization"?), to describe how ordinary language is thrust forward, activated by deviation from normal usage. By analogy,

> The *poetic* identity of a building depends not on its stability, on its function, or on the efficiency of the means of its production but on the way in which all the above have been limited, bent and subordinated by purely formal requirements. What distinguishes a classical building as a poetic object from ordinary buildings is there, on the surface, in its formal organization. But beyond this formal veil lies the act of foregrounding through which selected aspects from the reality of a building are recast into formal patterns.[114]

Ludwig Mies van der Rohe made a number of recorded remarks against formalism (form for form's sake alone), especially in the 1920s – that is, contemporaneously with the coming into authority of simplistic functionalism. Unlike vulgar functionalists, his claim to reject formalism represents an aspiration to attain a truer if still elusive sense of form. When Mies – whose own supposedly too-neutral chapel at the Illinois Institute of Technology, by the way, is properly styled the "Robert F. Carr Memorial Chapel of Saint Saviour" – says, apropos of his great work at Illinois Tech during World War II, that he is after *beinahe nichts,* "almost nothing," the *beinahe* is at least as important as the *nichts;* likewise his ideal of an "absence of architecture" in the interest of *Baukunst,* the "art of building," far from abolishing the aesthetic, leaves architecture sounding artificial but building-art perhaps more aesthetic than ever.[115] Later, in 1961, Mies is reported to have said, "I must make it clear that in the English language you call everything structured. In Europe we don't. We call a shack a shack and not a structure. By structure we have a philosophical idea. The structure is the whole from top to bottom, to the last detail – with the same idea. That is what we call structure."[116] Of course, the question then becomes whether one could have (or sustain) a "philosophical idea" of a sufficiently "structured" shack, from top to bottom, so to speak, or whether nothing justifiably considered a shack could be worth the trouble. It is certainly possible to imagine Mies devoting enough metaphysical regard to a bicycle shed to take it out of the basically profane shack category by a kind of consecration of the ordinary. Owing to Mies's known difficulty with English (at I.I.T. he had to be ordered by the dean to speak it), his choice of the word "shack" in this context may or may not be pejorative; nevertheless, it permits him to sharpen his thought on all building above shack level, even if, to the extent that a bicycle shed is a "shack," it would seem to confirm Pevsner's distinction.

Not to be underestimated is the distinct secularist edge that Pevsner's remark carries, even if the self-evident "piece of architecture" appealed to is not a nineteenth-century railway station (as new, internationalist beginning) but a Gothic cathedral (as old English beginning). Nowhere in his and John Harvey's extensive discussion of Lincoln Cathedral, in their *Lincolnshire* volume (1964) of the Buildings of England series, is the building's dedicatory title acknowledged, namely, the "Cathedral Church of Saint Mary, Lincoln." This is all the more glaring in view of Pevsner's attempt, at the end of the *Outline,* to applaud modernism as the fitting expression of a new social harmony reinstated, or supposedly about to be, immediately after World War II. There Pevsner celebrates "Cubism and then abstract art" as "the most architectural art that had existed since the Middle Ages"; and if for the time being society seems a bit disharmonious, well, what can one expect? At least "the Modern Movement is a genuine and independent style"; so, he hopes, "Can we not take it then that the recovery of a true style in the visual arts, one in which once again building rules, and painting and sculpture serve, and one in which form is obviously representation of character, indicates the return of unity in society too?"[117] But was ever a falser hope placed in a style of art? And just where have we ever heard something like such a claim before? In the proto-modern Gothic Revival, reformist tradition, of course: the tradition of Pugin, and Ruskin, and Morris – *minus,* however (one must now notice) the socialism of Morris as much as the social-organic Catholicism of Pugin, who would have been very happy to celebrate the identification of this exemplar of great architecture with the incarnationally Blessed Virgin Mary. At least we can say that with this withering away, if not aggressive pruning back, of its own spiritual and ideological roots, Pevsner's historicism modern was hopelessly weakened in its capability for defending its transcendental claim.

The notion of architecture as *bien bâtir* (building well) persisted in at least one modernist attempt to coin something like a usage "beau building," in the sense of beaux arts. I refer to a British wartime text concerned with good industrial design and humane mass housing as well as discrete International Style structures, namely, Maxwell Fry's *Fine Building* (1944), where architecture implies a "significant form of shelter for human life."[118] This critic subscribes to a frankly libidinal "spiritual" function for architecture, disbelieving in the cult of progress of which early modernists are now sweepingly accused.[119] Unusual in tempering his modernist enthusiasm for increasingly venerable engineering works with consideration of their human cost during the industrial revolution,[120] he enjoys sharing with engineering the glory of the classic art of architecture. Juxtaposing the neo-Palladian front of Kedleston Hall, c. 1757, by James Paine (not identified), "to illustrate the grand idea of living in times past," with the (contemporaneous?) Milford Mill, also in Derbyshire, the latter as "fine building in the early Industrial Age," this Fry praises "the work of the great civil engineers," who

> saw themselves very much as modern architects do to-day, as serving society directly and responsibly. They worked to standards of knowledge and integrity foreign to most industrialists, and were aware of the scale of the undertaking. Like monuments their works stood out from the thick lava-like spread of the towns, structures and works of art where all else was unintegrated and without meaning.[121]

It has been a long time since there was any problem of acknowledging as architectural, vernacular buildings of at least ornamentally tasteful, undisqualifying restraint, despite possible condescension toward work of collective authorship. But on the theoretical plane, such material may qualify only for an elementary Esperanto of formal beauty, inevitably confirming a dehistoricized sense that what the modern artist, in this case the architect, really does (as any commonsensical person could have said), is solve problems in an economic way. A more challenging call to take seriously not only charmingly humble buildings previously unentitled to historical suffrage, but even recent examples of an enormous but overlooked governmental institutional vernacular, came from Bruce Allsopp at the end of the 1960s. In taking this position a generation ago, Allsopp could already see the new problem of dissolving art history into something else: "It may be easy to assent in principle to the idea of studying art history, including the history of architecture in relation to social history, but the effect would be to change the character of art history as a discipline because we should have to concern ourselves not only with 'good art' but with *all* art."[122] Perhaps that would not necessarily be disadvantageous, for a while.

But it ought to be possible to face up to the critical component of all art-historical study – something too easily overlooked in regard to all those periods, remote in time, from which surviving humble work has rewarded the attention of even the more conservative historians attracted to such fields. Narrow-minded functionalism, however, always has its dangers, including the promise of a world full of bicycle sheds, with no cathedrals.

According to an important revisionist architect who emerged in the 1970s, there opened up a dichotomy in practice, as the building business expanded after World War II, between a "general," that is, a generic or general-purpose, and a specific architecture: "Specific architecture . . . will include buildings of prestige, as a kind of alibi: thus architects preserved for themselves some of their old territory. And so the architecture of 1950 is perpetuated with a little cosmetic treatment."[123] This offhand point of Lucien Kroll, who is equally opposed to the modernism of rationalization and the superficially reformist postmodernism that merely dresses up the same "underlying procedures and techniques,"[124] concerns more than the external sociology of architecture. The widespread popular loss of faith in modern culture can only have been confirmed by an international glut of buildings of both types that is hardly the responsibility of modern architecture, even where these have been designed by licensed architects academically trained in modern, or at least postclassical, building. The real sociological question is how the profession conceded general loss of respect for aesthetic authority, access to commissions allowing artistic latitude now being in practice as restricted to its socially privileged members as a hundred years ago.

Sometimes the artist works for himself, and sometimes that produces a true *ars poetica* of architecture. The underlying current of thought in *The Most Beautiful House in the World* (1989), by Witold Rybczynski, comprising reflections on the planning, construction, and continuous revision of a small boathouse for his own use, runs more or less explicitly against Pevsner. This Canadian teacher of architecture recalls having himself questioned Pevsner's dictum as a student: "I had no quarrel about the significance of Gothic cathedrals . . . but I liked sheds too. Were the two really so different? What was it, exactly, that made a cathedral, and not a bicycle shed – or here a boatshed – architecture?"[125] Considering the formidable thirteenth-century stone barn at Great Coxwell, Berkshire, vis-à-vis the Galilee Porch of Lincoln Cathedral as a gabled *shelter,* and the cathedral's timber roof as barnlike, Rybczynski muses rather casually, "in many ways a cathedral resembles a great embellished barn, which is why the interior of a barn, with its tall posts and streaks of light, recalls the dignified gravity of a Gothic nave."[126]

Although, thanks to the dominant North American secularism, it is doubtful if Rybczynski could appreciate Ingarden's elucidation of the spiritual matter of consecration as germane to the case of the cathedral, he nevertheless devotes seven pages, and more, to a divination system of ancient Chinese ancestor worship, pooh-poohing nineteenth-century Protestant missionaries' antipathy toward it (they considered it superstitious and pagan).[127] Tellingly, Rybczynski tries to enlist Alberti on his apostate Western side, never giving the original title of Alberti's *De re aedificatoria* but rendering it *Of Built Things,* which of course discards connotations of the noble edifice, even of edification. The Jesuit motto "To the Greater Glory of God" he is happy to level to the ordinary handshake in its "almost certainly magical" origins, this by way of introduction to an otherwise moving description of the worshipful foundation of the city of Montreal. That, in turn, is compensated for with themes of architectural soothsaying in Ghana and sheep-liver divining in Babylon (no thought of the metaphorical "Agnus Dei" of Montreal's founding Mass observed).[128] Even Rybczynski's willingness to make do with a jerry-built phenomenology of architecture ("A recreational vehicle in the rain is just a wet metal box; a screened porch with wide, sheltering eaves is a place to *experience* the rain")[129] advances a typically North American foreclosure on anything more "metaphysical" than the Chinese *feng-shui* (wind and water) geomancy caper.

I hope that in making this point on general attitude it does not seem that I place myself above the mere architect in some garret of ideal theory. If anything, *The Most Beautiful House in the World* appeals most happily to me as one who myself once built, with my own hands and those of a friend, a certain fishing cabin to which I still resort. At that, we followed the plans and guidelines of an official publication titled *Canadian Wood-Frame House Construction,* discovered (I date myself) in *The Last Whole Earth Catalog.*

My cabin is the only construction I know of from any period that I might delude myself into classifying as styleless. At a certain point in *his* project, after abandoning the look of a "romantic Victorian boathouse," it seems to have struck Rybczynski that a "functional" result might be as stylistic as anything else: "It looked . . . [sic] well, 'functional' was a kind description – like one of those buildings one sees beside a railroad track, housing switching equipment or spare parts."[130] Is this not dissembling, insofar as the railroad shack is simply asked to serve as the next "fall guy" – as if we pretended to solve our whole problem by restating it, "A railroad shack is a building; a bicycle shed is a piece of architecture" (then why not, "A newsstand is a building; a railroad shack is a piece of architecture," etc.?).

With Pevsner's general problem concerning the implicit cultural, let alone architectural, "historylessness" of undignified – versus categorically noble – town building types, Rybczynski is wise to delve more deeply into the architectural repute of that definitive unsung rural type, in a chapter entitled "Just a Barn," confessing: "After almost two years and two full sketchbooks, I was going to build . . . [sic] a barn. Not even a bicycle shed – a cowshed."[131] The parade of post-Renaissance barns is quite remarkable: ignoring some in classical livery, the more relevantly nonrhetorical examples include a sixteen-sided barn by George Washington; examples by two Canadians, Casimir Stanislaus Gzowski, a civil engineer, and Edward Maxwell, architect; a projected icehouse as well as a built barn, both by H. H. Richardson; and Frank Lloyd Wright's barn at Taliesin. "Obviously," Rybczynski says, none of these designers "had felt that it was beneath him to design a barn,"[132] which is a more solid claim than, "The designers of common farm buildings, who were usually the farmers themselves, were no less inventive than trained architects. After all, someone had to introduce the changes that transformed the barn from one time and place to another, and which produced distinctive regional variations of the 'ordinary' barn."[133] One need not invoke Lamarck to say that whoever reacts to changed circumstances by adapting custom is only extending *like* custom; adaptation is precisely *not* invention. Regarding cabins: more cozily domestic examples were built by the likes of Jefferson and even Le Corbusier,[134] though there are also the writing cabins, meant for escape from domestic life, of Mark Twain (octagonal; probably architect-designed) and Shaw ("The Shelter," designed by himself to rotate to catch the sun, which didn't work).[135]

As it metamorphosed from a hypothetical boat shed into an actual dwelling, Mrs. Rybczynski took increasing interest in this architect's project and its implications, which were of theoretical interest to Mr. Rybczynski in terms of typology: "A shed was all right for boatbuilding, but...she expected something more of a *home*."[136] It is not easy to explain all that "home" connotes in English, except that that becomes a cliché whenever we overlook the like connotativeness of *das Heim*.[137]

More worthwhile, ultimately, is Rybczynski's struggle to account for one Ramón Castrejón's caring and resourceful self-building of his poor family's house in present-day Mexico, a "house – most people would call it a shack – ...not without artistry."[138] But while everyone can applaud Rybczynski's enthusiasm, even the modest Casa Castrejón does not put to rest the theoretical problem of Pevsner's bicycle shed. Rybczynski accords the house special, transcendental standing, speaking of "the moving loveliness of human occupation, of a place transformed," and of a house's "collective image," only to fade out with the generalization that the "expression and recreation" of such a collective image "was once a commonplace event, so ordinary it escaped the attention of historians – hence the lack of interest in 'sheds.' "[139]

If fifty years ago Nikolaus Pevsner's conjunction of the bicycle shed with Lincoln Cathedral seemed like simple common sense – just about all the metaphysics of architecture anybody should need – that is even less escapably problematic now than it was twenty-five years ago in Robert Venturi's 1960s. Genially enough, Pevsner's dictum served authoritarian as well as authorial purpose. Even its tropic complexity was underplayed, since Lincoln is an actual and specific building, or rather, "piece" (!) of architecture, whereas if the bicycle shed is generic, it's hardly too hypothetical, because every (British) child knows what one looks like. (Stimulated by Venturi in the later 1970s there was also generalized vernacularist speculation among American architects on "The 'House' as Any Child Would Draw It.")[140]

Robert Venturi's new metaphorical, concretized symbolism of a caricatural modernist architectural "duck" – any building expressing either its supposed functionalist purpose, or (indiscriminately) its idealized tectonics – was defined in negation by the literalized semiotic of a "decorated shed" that impinges on, without coinciding with, the undecorated shed of Pevsner's duality. Venturi's dual figure can only point up the disguised metaphorical function of Pevsner's specific cathedral even as it leads into a duplicity of architecture eschewing "well-building" itself in favor of a socially realistic play of graphically literal, billboard-like signs. Pevner's figure was at once popularly light and donnishly freighted; Venturi's, populistically antimodernist and simplistically collegiate. The "duck" inherits by default the (now foolish) transcendental hope of a modernism whereby the bicycle shed might have aspired to stand beside the cathedral as akin in structural forthrightness, if otherwise content with its historically insignificant lot. So in some sense, the semiotically decorated shed does take, all too happily, the position of the neglected "bicycle shed," but as conceptually dolled up, while the duck is "sent down" to join the Gothic cathedral as Gothic-engineering obsolete.

Halfway between then and now, the new project (in practice as well as theory) of Robert Venturi and Denise Scott Brown, despite its independent aesthetic merit, was contextually akin, indeed at first relegated, to pop art. It tended to strike those unsympathetic to pop as so antiformal as to be philistine, though the Venturis' early buildings are still underestimated in their formal sophistication, their very artful interest in both "vernacular" and ultrasophis-ticated mannerist architecture.[141] The Venturis had, by and large, to wait half a generation for their work, supposedly "postmodern" (but both early and abiding), to register not merely as some literalized rhetorical "semiotic" *about* architecture but also as innately architectural. As with pop art, the new aesthetic (some would still say, antiaesthetic) did entail an extended epiphany of the commonplace, with much of what modernist taste had overlooked or looked down on in common visual "culture" turning out to be not half bad. Should this potential somehow reach masterpiece pitch, the Pevsnerean bicycle shed might at last match up to the cathedral; but this would be unlikely, given the antitriumphalism of the embrace of the ordinary.

Sometimes architectural postmodernism seems to be hiding its own shame about its lucrative commissions for mere buildings – in Pevsner's sense, big "sheds" putting on ornamental airs. In a sense this is but an old class-related problem of the practice of architecture as a trade, with dual but not usually equally urgent concerns for construction *and then* ornamentation. It surfaces in the first English book on architecture (1563), where John Shute, addressing "that which the Greeks named architectonica, and of the Latins, architectura (I think not altogether unfit nor unaptly by me termed in English the art and trade *to raise up and make excellent* edifices and buildings),"[142] significantly apologizes for his own book's prose as unsophisticated by speaking (disin-genuously?) of "the thing not being garnished as it ought to be," in the same sense as the ornamental application of "measures, proportions and garnish-ments," above all the classical architectural orders, to buildings.[143]

Architecture, in Shute's and others' Renaissance sense understood as a so-cially special affair, did not impinge on the lives of ordinary people living in ordinary houses, only on their participation in institutional life. Not, that is, until full-scale industrialization made Pugin, Ruskin, and Morris social as well as architectural critics. Insofar as it accommodated to industrialism, architec-tural modernism assumed some culpability, specifically for a glorification of the commercial and corporate that has long since exceeded Sullivan's humane, rather post-Hanseatic, sense of the dignity of business.[144] Heavy industry and ever more immense corporate bureaucracies offering occasions for an applied aesthetic of efficiency to a small élite of fine-art architects tended to eclipse small-scale manufacture and commerce, by and large neglected as commonplace and unprofitable. Certain interesting small-scale exceptions do, however, occur among the loftiest modernists, such as a gas station by Wright[145] and projects not only for a gas station but for Joe Cantor's Drive-In Restaurant, in Indianapolis, by the aesthetic patrician Mies van der Rohe.[146]

When in *God's Own Junkyard: The Planned Deterioration of America's Landscape* (1964) the modernist historian Peter Blake illustrated the visual junk and aesthetic junk food of the postwar American landscape, his point was to show up outright vulgarity. This was not unlike F. Scott Fitzgerald's literary point of the billboard with the big "eyes of Doctor T. J. Eckleberg" looking out over "the solemn dumping ground" (of Flushing Meadow), in Queens, in *The Great Gatsby* (1925; chap. 2). But when American pop art came to bloom, the English Amerophiles of the Independent Group had already been positively obsessed with American postwar vulgarity, especially consumer advertising, for a good decade. Even observers outside the precocious London group associated with the Institute of Contemporary Art were now indulging a slumming fascination with American vulgarity – including even the "upscale" American cultural cult of Williamsburg, in Virginia. As Wilfred Sheed would recall:

> We foreign-born America-fanciers (if I may invent a group to stuff some generalizations into) occasionally ran to a taste for streamlined trash: we would not have liked an America as pure as the native radicals wanted. The worst of us were not even embarrassed by salesmen named "Elmer," although we could do without historians named Chauncey Thruslow Adams, Jr. The authentic tended to put us to sleep, but swing and country music revived us. We liked, when it slunk onto the scene, Las Vegas much better than Williamsburg. Americans believed we were putting them on, or down.[147]

Ironically, in 1927, the year in which Le Corbusier's *Vers une architecture* appeared in English translation, there began the Rockefeller "restoration," as it is still institutionally named, of "Colonial Williamsburg," which has its historical relevance for American "soft" postmodernism in the 1980s.[148]

A monkey wrench was thrown into Peter Blake's modernist-motivated project when the Venturis became rather more than naughtily fascinated by his supposedly bad-taste examples, even the jerry-built outlet stores that sold the shiny new toys of the pop life. Blake's photograph of an Esso gas station was first commandeered by Robert Venturi for his 1966 *Complexity and Contradiction in Architecture,* that learned and intellectually lively revisionist call – published by the Museum of Modern Art itself – for poetic ambiguity and richness (as opposed to phoniness and superficiality). Like so much else, this treatise would apparently have to get flattened out for wider dissemination, but for the time being Venturi parenthetically explained his mobilization: "If in *God's Own Junkyard* Peter Blake had chosen examples of roadside landscape for his book which were less extremely 'bad,' his point, at least involving the banality of roadside architecture, would ironically have been stronger."[149] (Note the rather Warholian transvaluation of the aesthetically "bad.")

This gas station photo borrowed from Blake was to yield the definitive postmodern "decorated shed," in opposition to a certain "duck" that Venturi would also subvert from its role as a photoillustration to Blake's text. Venturi's wife, Denise Scott Brown, wrote an article, "On Ducks and Decoration," for the October 1968 issue of *Architecture Canada,* and in 1972 she, Venturi and Steven Izenour published a book much more widely read than *Complexity and Contradiction* (and a much faster read, at that): *Learning from Las Vegas: The Forgotten Symbolism of Architectural Form* (2d edition, 1977). The book certified that it was OK to like the Las Vegas "Strip" or even, by extension, almost the whole of Los Angeles.

Just before *God's Own Junkyard* itself, and within the sphere of California pop, Ed Ruscha had painted what is still his most famous painting, *Standard Station, Amarillo, Texas,* in 1963. Of this image – which would become known as a fine-art print as well as in widespread reproduction – it was written in 1966: "A huge painting of an isolated gas station with sharply delineated perspectives into airless lunar space and engineer simpifications reminds one of Charles Sheeler and, by extension, of the Immaculates, painters whose semi-abstract distillations of the industrial American landscape are not unrelated to the current Pop mythicizing of mass-media America."[150] Peter Plagens would make a point more relevant to the importance of signage to the notion of the "decorated shed," that by virtue of its STANDARD logotype the gas station motif was part of a series of "word-paintings" leading by "cross-media free-association" to this and related works as "whole environments for words."[151] Meanwhile, Ruscha's very "L.A.," pop-conceptual productions included the textless photo book *Some Los Angeles Apartments* (1965), clearly related to the in-the-swim California pool paintings of the Englishman David Hockney; and then came Ruscha's important fold-out print or artist's photographic book, *Every Building on the Sunset Strip* (1966). The *Standard Station* was spiffy-keen, but then again Venturi himself thought, by 1966, of "less extremely 'bad' . . . examples."

The gas station's necessary antithesis was to be found in another Blake photo, this time of a Long Island highway stand for the selling of ducks – real ducks for cooking – itself built in the shape of a huge duck, which became the canonical source of a new "duck" trope to stand for the self-proclaiming expressivity of purpose of the modernist building, since (if this sounds un-believably simpleminded, it is not my fault) the little hut was *actually shaped like what it "was for."* For that sort of thing, there was French eighteenth-century precedent in the category of *l'architecture parlante* (speaking architecture) – though it does happen that Ledoux was struck by how the frivolous of his day loved to gape at a certain mechanical "duck."[152] Now, against a new, absurdly self-representational, caricature "duck," the "decorated shed" would emblematize an intellectually raucous, coolly inexpressive but semiotically crackling, jazzy type of structure – which, all too conveniently for too many speculative architects of the next two decades, supposedly obviated the formal obligations – showed up the "abstract art" – of highbrow architecture.

The actual duck stand with which all this began survives: in the late 1980s it was moved out of the way of a condominium development from its original site on Flanders Road, in Flanders, on the East End of Long Island, and given to Suffolk County for a museum. After being parked four miles down the same road, it was at last report destined to be installed permanently nearby. In *Learning from Las Vegas* this original "Long Island Duckling" stand of Blake's book appears on a left-hand page, with an amusingly didactic diagram version in line, and inscribed "Duck," given below (Figure 26). To the right in the same graphic (and mock-Corbusian?) spread the "Decorated Shed" also appears in mock-schoolish line drawing under the other photo from Blake's book, that of the bleak, heavily billboarded gas station landscape, now drolly called a "Road Scene," of the tattered urban fringe. In juxtaposition with the semiotic duck, the lettered signage of the gas station appeared all the more telling – not only its big, official ESSO[153] sign but also a more pathetic, hand-lettered "Last Stop Before Phila. Bridge" and others. Billboards themselves, after all, were anathema to orthodox International Style modernism, in the terms of which they connoted trashy, disposable superficiality as well as art-lessness: "If architecture is not to resemble billboards, color should be both technically and psychologically permanent," Hitchcock and Johnson had proclaimed in 1932.[154]

An unbuilt project from as early as 1967 for a National Football Hall of Fame shows the Venturis putting their sense of semiotic, versus constructive-expressive, architecture to work (or into play). A contemporary essay on this project by Venturi alone characterizes the "ideological" program of the official (i.e. commercial) organization as knowingly fetishistic, even quasi-religious, and at once introduces and deliberately underplays modernist analogues for the building from works by Le Corbusier and Alvar Aalto.[155] In retrospect, it seems that Venturi and Denise Scott Brown's "original idea" was, conflict-edly, of a kind of semiotic "duck" posing as the first so-designed "decorated shed," all the more since the architects first thought "to make the building the shape of a football [i.e. American, pointed oval style] on the outside."

It was because "limitations on cubage in the program precluded a sculptural outer shape which did not conform closely to the inside architectural space," that Venturi and Brown "devised a sign instead of a sculpture: an essentially two-dimensional billboard, big in size but economical in cubage, which is also a building." Already in 1967, then, this "buildingboard," a decorated shed if there ever was one, stood to negate "that too subtle kind of expression which is derived from pure architectural elements." In other words, here was a counter, *avant le lettre,* to the modernist "duck" of task-manifesting "pure architecture." A rationale or a rationalization: "Space, form, and structure," the traditional architectural elements, "mean little in the vast parking spaces

that are the context of this building and most other buildings that architects
can't force into their megastructural fantasies. You just can't see space, form,
and structure across a teeming parking lot without a mixture of other media"
(a desperately functionalistic expedient, this latter claim?). "From nearby," the
apology continues portentously, "the building corresponds to the largely false
west facade of a Gothic cathedral, especially an Italian one like Orvieto, teeming
with glittering mosaics and niched statues, whose main function is to com-

26. Diagrams of "Duck" and "Decorated Shed." From Robert Venturi, Denise Scott Brown, and Steven Izenour, *Learning from Las Vegas* (Cambridge, Mass.: MIT Press, 1977), 88–9.

municate information toward the piazza. From a distance, the analogy with the billboard on the highway is obvious."[156]

Very well, but isn't that like, say, considering the Iconoclast controversy while oblivious to the problem of true or false imagery?[157] In an essay of a decade later Venturi declares the photograph of the sanctuary, with white marble furniture, of the basilica of Santa Maria in Cosmedin, as presented in *Vers une architecture,* "symbolically wrong if formally right" for Le Corbusier's own art, relative to his photos of grain elevators and such (which indulges a kind of formalism of format). Now Venturi appropriates for himself the type of the ancient basilica (at the time a serious preoccupation of art history), distinctly de-iconologized, for his own, purportedly "symbolic," semantic purpose: "The source for our fancy architecture is in the conventions of the commercial strip. Its prototype is not the spatial Baroque monument, but the Early Christian basilica, *that plain barn smothered in frescoes, the decorated shed par excellence.*"[158]

The forms of works of art, however, sustain intentionalities independently of their creators' personal intents. Because the rear of the Football Hall of Fame offers an actual (lateral) built-on grandstand, as well as the billboard in which Venturi invests his critical attention, the project poses an opposition between the sheerly pictorial and the physically space-displacing, or between passively optical and actively bodily spectatorship. Like it or not, this attached grandstand, simple as it is, also raises a historical question of the type of the stadium as monument, not so much of Albert Speer's huge Nazi "Zeppelinfeld" stadium at Nuremberg as of that itself as innocently adumbrated by the Belgian Henry Van de Velde's project, aborted by World War I, for a Nietzsche Monument at Weimar, with large, U-shaped stadium facing a "temple."[159] The ultramonumentalizing Zeppelinfeld, planned in pure, heavy masonry to one day stand as a noble ruin, projected the Nazis' own vulgarization of Nietzsche's will to power in architectural terms. In view of the most cynical criticism of the 1980s, "radical" at any cost to truth, it should be noticed that Venturi and Brown's buildingboard-cum-grandstand is no more obliged to the Zeppelinfeld than the frustrated and suffering Van de Velde was responsible for it to begin with: the Football Hall of Fame project looks, if anything, antimonumental, like something polyester and casual, almost sloppy, even as writ large and loud. In that pop time, a still reliably democratic, otherwise outright *lumpen* vulgarity might still hold a harmless charm.

The later 1978 essay, "A Definition of Architecture as Shelter with Decoration on It, and Another Plea for a Symbolism of the Ordinary in Architecture" (a title itself populistically tinged with mock Victorianism as to theory), deserves closer reading, in part for a parallel it sets up between modernist (abstract?) architecture and abstract painting. The account is by no means eccentric in maintaining that as orthodox modernist painting succumbed to its own worst threat, namely, decoration, much the same happened in late-modernist architecture of the 1960s: pure "articulation," forbidding itself ornamental statement, went wild in a "fundamentally more irresponsible" breakdown into nothing but generalized – allover? – ornamentalism; thus, "Structure protrudes rhythmically, functions protrude sensitively, clerestories pulsate on the roof."[160] Actually, the crisis of doctrinaire formalist painting was also producing, even as Venturi wrote, new, more theoretically astute, varieties of abstraction that continue into the present; so one can only wonder where this now leaves (pop-) Venturian theory vis-à-vis any ongoing modernist architecture.

"Elaborating . . . on a main theme" of *Learning from Las Vegas* in specifically "high" and "low" terms, Venturi compares the Roman piazza and the Vegas Strip to the iconoclastic advantage (of course) of the Strip, as more semiotically lively. No one seemed to mind that the Venturian ideal looked (even) better in the dark: "And when you see no buildings at all, at night when virtually only the illuminated signs are visible, you see the Strip in its pure state."[161] Neither did it matter that such an, in a sense, anesthetic, rather Warholian, claim was also as aestheticizing as Whistler's 1885 "Ten O'Clock Lecture": "And when . . . the poor buildings lose themselves in the dim sky, and the tall chimneys become campanili, and the warehouses are palaces in the night . . ."[162] Nor, we are assured, is the aesthetic sex appeal of the Strip "necessarily more promotional" than, in corporate high design,

> the "masterly, correct, and magnificent play of masses" [Le Corbusier, but significantly omitting his final term, ". . . in light"] . . . now that big business has taken over the "progressive" symbolism of orthodox Modern architecture. We ourselves often feel less uncomfortable with the crass commercial advertising on the roadside than we do with some of the subtle and tasteful persuasion inherent in the Modern formalist symbolism that pervades corporate architecture, including that of the military-industrial complex.[163]

"Why not admit," this erstwhile apprentice of Louis Kahn asks, "the impossibility of maintaining pure functionalism in architecture and the almost inevitable contradictions between functional and aesthetic requirements in the same building, and then let function and decoration go their own separate ways so that functional requirements need not be distorted for unadmitted decorative aims."[164] Wait a minute! At least we might be entitled to suppose that where the *id* was, there might the art of architecture be. Yet Mies van der Rohe himself is cast as the draggy "industrial" modernist straight man to the folksy, good-sport gagsterism of the McDonald's logotypic arch. Perhaps surprisingly, in retrospect, Venturi is better prepared than many of his fans to access the (modernist) high-cultural historicity of the McDonald's hamburger-stand motif: Freyssinet's hangars at Orly, Le Corbusier's Palace of the Soviets project, Eero Saarinen's Saint Louis arch. However, in the rush to package a fast-lane American-style idea that a hundred thousand students will be able to absorb in fifteen minutes before setting out on lifetimes of designing "semiotically" dolled-up junk buildings, the straight man is cut short. Mies, who we know was not above designing a drive-in fast-food restaurant, was no simple adapter of an "industrial vernacular." To say so is not only crude but also oddly formalistic – going by materials and gross shape alone.

A major problem of Venturian cultural critique occurs in the section of the same essay headed "Plain and Fancy Architecture." Now the major American plain/fancy distinction derives definitively from the Mennonites and other quietists among whom the "fancy" pertains to the vanities of the fallen world, with the "plain" signifying a saving humility in withdrawal from that world. Correctly speaking, the Seagram Building itself would count as perilously "fancy" for its blatant elegance alone. The Las Vegas Strip is only the same worldliness with its hair down. In light of the plain/fancy distinction, it is already problematic for Venturi to begin by announcing that "there is room for high design and popular art in the architecture of our communities." But while suggesting that most contemporary buildings ought to be "plain" – meaning calm, no big rhetorical deal, and if anything understatedly modernist by default – he advocates employing for the special fanciness of extraordinary buildings – what? Precisely the vulgarity of the Strip. Not only is anything like a modernism of high statement effectively eliminated; but despite the catholicity of the opening claim, high design is asked either to assume all (and only) workaday tasks, or else to bow out altogether, leaving architecture a matter of popular art.[165]

Art historically, the Venturian duck did not come out of nowhere any more than did the pseudosemiotic decorated shed. Even as the duck posed, hilariously primped, seemingly AWOL from historical seriousness, it was really little more than a secondhand pun, a *trouvé* backyard counterpart of the *architecture parlante* – such as Ledoux's "Oikema," or Temple of Love, of the 1770s,[166] on the plan of erect male genitalia[167] – in which new interest was flourishing among pop-attuned intellectuals by the later 1960s. Actually, the duck quite particularly calls to mind Jean-Jacques Lequeu's project (!) for a cow stable in the shape of, *mais oui*, a giant "cow," shown in the influential traveling exhibition, originating in France, "Visionary Architects: Boullée, Ledoux, Lequeu," of 1967–8, in which Lequeu could only become the 1968 freak "lightening-up" the 1800-into-functionalist orthodoxy.[168] In the catalog, Louis Kahn says, in a poem beginning "Spirit in will to express..." that "Boullée is / Ledoux is / Thus architecture is."[169] I notice Kahn does *not* say "Lequeu is," perhaps because Lequeu's cow was already fraternizing with the first Venturian "ducks." Anyway, the point, the *only* point, would be the duck as expressivist – simplistically enough, of *purpose* (!), which for Lequeu would at least have signified duck breeding, here on the East End of Long Island.

As for the decorated shed: especially as a modernist heresy, it has somewhat obvious precedent in that nineteenth-century movement against which modernism had defined itself, eclecticism. We still tend to think of eclecticism as mere miscellaneous stylistic happenstance, the just reward for thinking of architectural history as a stylistic cafeteria. But as Peter Collins pointed out a generation ago, the beginning of a more markedly eclectic position can be dated to 1861, when in a lecture at the Architectural Exhibition, London, J. L. Petit argued that the Gothic Revival had not fulfilled its promise of extending deeper Gothic *principles* and recommended instead "our ordinary and vernacular architecture" (which notion Collins says may derive from Scott's *Remarks on Gothic Architecture*, 1858). Petit witnessed the vernacular buildings of Queen Anne's reign for their supposedly nonstylistic practicality as "simply vernacular buildings plus ornamentation of a very appropriate kind" (Collins), thus introducing "the idea that 'vernacular' forms should constitute the basis of all architectural design." His ideas undermined the classical grammatical sense, and the very fine-arts affiliation of architecture, in which the

question of ornament is systematic and pertinent to the entire body of a building. Though Petit himself was a clergyman, he also tended to play down
temples and churches as definitive types. He instead promoted a sense of
architecture as direct, unrhetorical speech: "Just as speech is composed by
selecting from a vocabulary of naturally evolved words, so architecture should
be composed by selecting from a vocabulary of naturally evolved tectonic
elements, all established by purely practical criteria, and articulated in accordance with the requirements of functional needs" (Collins). Not only for this
semantic (rather than grammatical) emphasis, but also for its favoring of the
"artisan mannerism" of Queen Anne buildings, Petit's position deserves more
recognition than it has as proto-Venturian, especially in Collins's articulation
of it in 1965.[170]

In an influential book still in print, *The Language of Post-Modern Architecture*
(1977), Charles Jencks reproduced the paired Venturi diagrams, handing them
over to a new generation. One wonders how seriously he took Venturi's actual
drawing, since he gives it in negative, white on black (in ye olde "blueprint"
manner, or in the playfulness of children's "chalk talk"?). Jencks is in such a
hurry to the land of simulacra, where phoniness is the only truth, that he calls
the duck stand "a bird-shaped building selling duck decoys,"[171] this despite
clear *signs,* plainly visible in Venturi's reprinting of Blake's photograph, ad-
vertising real fresh ducks as well as turkeys and Cornish game hens.

Restating Venturi's visual trope, Jencks comments in *Post-Modern Architecture,* "The duck is, in semiotic terms, an *iconic* sign, because the signifier (form)
has certain aspects in common with the signified (content). The decorated shed
depends on learned meanings – writing or decoration – which are *symbolic*
signs."[172] The sheer naïveté of this, as it were, hobbyist application of C. S.
Peirce's semiotics makes it difficult to do critical justice to the claim; it will
do to say that "having . . . aspects in common" can be symbolic, but that the
fact that Jencks can't quite get his simplistic formula to stay put is a symptom
of the deeper problem. Jencks is thinking in such a pre-Saussurean way that
he does not even understand the play of terms by which his essentially un-
reformed "form" and "content" relate to the concrete world by means of
concept. Moreover, while semiotics itself assents that "a church strikes one as
different from a factory,"[173] two differently decorated sheds (or "boxes," as
is sometimes given) do not strike one with anywhere near such architecturally
sufficient difference.

True, in some measure the problem of let's say a puritanically decorated
box was built into the official line in postwar modernist polemic. After a
literally Vitruvian fanfare – "2000 years ago the Roman architect VITRUVIUS
said: ARCHITECTURE should meet three requirements: utility, strength,
beauty"[174] – *What Is Modern Architecture?,* a booklet published by the Museum
of Modern Art in 1946 to accompany a traveling exhibition, passes in rational
outline form to "beauty." For the curious, means to beauty here include
obvious International Style prescriptions, "the open plan" for "the new spa-
ciousness," "volume instead of mass," and, of course, (a nonpicturesque?)
"asymmetry." On the matter of ornament, first comes its declared absence;

then the consolation that "structural forms can be ornamental." Penultimately to "free forms of nature," however, comes the item "materials instead of ornament," where the only intoxicant still permitted is as foolish as sub-alcoholic beer: "For further interest and variety the architect relies upon the texture, color and pattern of the many materials at his disposal. . . . In recent years architects have come more and more to delight in the richer, more varied surfaces of wood, brick and stone, materials as old as architecture itself."[175]

Is it possible that the metaphorical duck was turning into a nonmetaphor-ically, "abstractly" decorated shed of its own accord? Was not the dumbest possible form of a dubious idea more than catching on, namely, just to give up on the modernist "duck" and go realistically for a "decorated shed" hardly different from the cosmeticized boxes that the speculators, with less patience for theory than for "styling," had been busy building all along?

It is unfortunate that the title of a book by Klaus Herdeg, *The Decorated Diagram* (1983), plays to the antimodernists, because what Herdeg articulately critiques in the interest of a profounder modernity is a too narrow, but all too influential, essentially positivist *and* altogether suburbanizing strain in latter-day American modernist architecture (with its equivalent in painting) that never deserved to dominate the modernist field to begin with. It seems that under Gropius and Breuer, at Harvard between 1937 and 1953, a whole school of architects absorbed Hannes Meyer's 1930 Bauhaus codification of an orig-inally more plastic Corbusian idea – how "The Plan Calculates Itself" – and developed the notion that modern architecture consists exclusively of trans-lating the program into a plan, projecting it upwards into space, and then simply treating its surfaces with texture and other abstract but trivial visual incident.[176] Here, before the fact, was a paltry but firm theoretical perch on which could alight postmodern obliviousness to spatial form as well as that particular schizoid disconnection between the structural and the essentially ornamental that by the 1970s had opened the door wide to a mere appliqué of superficial "semiotic."

Addressing the special, ideological reductivism of postmodernist architec-ture, specifically Venturi's graphic, "billboard" demotion of building function, Michael Hollander has maintained:

> The powerful unsettling connotations of the prototype are, of course, not those denoted in the "billboard" itself, as Venturi almost perversely suggests, but rather in the complicated, ironic relation between the su-perficial and elaborately rhetorical messages of the façade and the "hon-est" meanings intrinsic in the very shapes of the complementary enclosures. The caustic dualism, overt in the dissociated façade and ar-chitectural shell of the building, is a potent symbolic construct, because it is a metaphor for so many troubling perceptions and experiences of the present world. The duality itself conveys a profound cynicism re-garding the incongruence, in commercial and political public relations, between projected images and concealed, innate realities; on the other hand, the crisply graphic conventional symbols, considered indepen-

dently, are like models of logical behavior, and, in the skeptical ambience of recent years, *seem* refreshingly clear, frank and efficient, far preferable to the highly emotive and empathetic abstract images characteristic of Modernism, and so often identified with the liberal sentiments with which Modernism may be depreciatively associated.[177]

"A building is a work of art," according to the aesthetician Nelson Goodman, "only insofar as it signifies, means, refers, symbolizes in some way." Without some substantial exemplification, however, even signification is not enough for architectural qualification, since "even when a building does mean, that may have nothing to do with its architecture." Neither, in itself, does even the purest form; for what matter are not "formal properties that the building merely possesses but . . . properties it exemplifies." No "purely formal," essentially nonsignifying building counts as architecture by inertness alone, but only, on the contrary, insofar as it nonetheless "exemplifies certain of its properties, and only so distinguishes itself from buildings that are not works of art at all."[178] At least all "ducks" strive to exemplify (and such striving itself might count as exemplification), whereas most "decorated sheds" – including, now, all upscale boxes decorated only with tastefully "abstract," sarcastically meaningless classical ornamentation – rest content with their literally and merely superficial signification.

In the world of Ronald Reagan and Margaret Thatcher it became the case that "form follows profit," since "the horizons of stockbrokers and accountants do not extend to posterity"; hence, "The architect's vocation has been reduced to designing 'machines for making investments in,' and short-term investments at that."[179] These are the words of Richard Rogers, who with Renzo Piano designed the Centre Pompidou, 1971–7, in Paris.[180] Rogers accuses postmodernism of being "obsessed with money and fashion" along with "the aesthetics of prettiness and the heritage industry."[181] (Half a century before, partisans of the "International Style" had found American architects, in particular, too "ready . . . to deface their building with bad architectural design if the client demands it.")[182] In Rogers's view, "The buildings of the future will be more like robots than temples. Like chameleons, they will adapt to their environment." He imagines an architecture that will be "non-mechanical . . . fluid, seamless" and – in a word that threatens to concede too much in a Benthamite, utilitarian way – "self-regulating."[183]

Unless we are to be forced to make do, in effect, with billboards instead of buildings, Rogers is calling for some new form of "duck," if not of "Lincoln Cathedral," and his Pompidou building may be the major duck or "cathedral" of recent times. In a section of *Learning from Las Vegas* (1972) headed "the Cathedral as Duck and Shed," Venturi, Brown, and Steven Izenour claimed contemporaneously that an actual Gothic cathedral is "a decorated shed *and* a duck": Amiens, for (their) example, is a billboard [or "two-dimensional screen for propaganda"] with a building behind it, while the "shed" behind has "the shape of a cross."[184] Now, a good generation later, Arata Isozaki declines identification with postmodernism because his newer work ("still collage-like") has been "moving away from direct quotations and toward abstract forms – toward buildings that embrace fiction," whereas architects of the postmodern persuasion "use historical elements to make a pastiche, which, in some cases, is nothing more than a decorated shed."[185]

Hasn't there been a situation like this before? I am thinking of the strange way the Woolworth Building, famous as New York's first true skyscraper, has sometimes seemed modern and sometimes not.

Cass Gilbert's rather too literally ornamentally Gothic Woolworth Building, finished in 1913, makes an apparently unremarked photographic appearance in an early "authorized" American edition (c. 1918–20?) of Wilhelm Worringer's expressionist treatise *Form Problems of the Gothic* (1911). The only contemporary building illustrated, it is keyed to the text at this point: "Only modern steel construction has brought back a certain understanding of the Gothic. For in it people have been confronted again with an architectural form in which artistic expression is supplied by the method of construction itself."

Worringer, however, who in the Weimar period grew to hate American culture, was also disappointed that this undeniably formidable piece of architecture had not really risen to its spiritual occasion. His general terms as much as criticize Gilbert's soon to be world famous structure presenting itself in all too literally historicizing Gothic ornamental style instead of in some newly direct and thoroughgoing form of metaphorically "Gothic" structurality:

> In the modern case . . . the material itself . . . directly encourages . . . structural one-sidedness, while the Gothic arrived at such ideas [as expression advanced through construction], not by means of the material, but in spite of the material, in spite of the stone. In other words, underlying the artistic appearance of modern buildings of steel construction is no form will that, for definite reasons, emphasizes structure, but only a new material. One may go as far as to say, perhaps, that it is an atavistic echo of that old Gothic form will which prompts modern northern man to artistic emphasis of this material and even allows the hope of a new architectural style to hang on its appropriate employment.[186]

Although Worringer himself could not yet have been picturing the Woolworth Building as he actually wrote these words, others, including the artists Joseph Pennell and John Marin, discovered in its naked steelwork genuine modern interest. As an artist, Pennell – some of whose European drypoints (views of Puy and Toledo) are praised by Apollinaire in a review of 1911 – was a pioneer in his recourse to heavyweight construction as artistic motif. He was doing New York architecture in etchings and lithographs as early as 1908–9, although, not unlike Cass Gilbert himself, he has been convicted of dressing his structures "in a romantic garb more fitting for Gothic cathedrals."[187]

If his visual sense of the Woolworth Building is less exciting than Marin's, he visited the Panama Canal while it was still under construction, in 1912, and produced a suite of lithographs of this quite Saint-Simonian "Wonder of

Work." Calling the canal, "From my point of view ... the most wonderful thing in the world," his comments on the specifically unfinished construction even anticipate Robert Smithson, the latter-day "earthworks" artist: "I have tried to express this in my drawings at the moment before it was opened, for when it was opened, and the water turned in, half the amazing masses of masonry will be beneath the waters on one side and filled in with earth on the other, and the picturesqueness will have vanished."[188] Today, as an architect, Frank Gehry is among those who have turned to such a newly architectural version of a rather Michelangesque, *"non-finito"* thought.[189]

Then too, apropos of his own print, *Flour Mills, Minneapolis,* which obviously relates to the early European modernist interest in the grain elevators of the American Midwest, Pennell noted as early as 1916, "The mills of Minneapolis are as impressive as the cathedrals of France"; and in the same breath, "The beauty of the flour mills is the beauty of use – they carry out William Morris's theory that 'everything useful should be beautiful' – but I don't know what he would have said to them."[190]

John Marin, who had worked as an architectural draftsman after a year at the Stevens Institute of Technology in Hoboken, had his etching of the (Gothic and later) *Cathedral of Meaux* published in the *Gazette des Beaux-Arts* in 1908.[191] Later, back home, he produced not only "Woolworth Building" watercolors and etchings, but also numerous fine etchings of the Brooklyn Bridge (with its more integrally "Gothic Revival" towers) and the Woolworth Building, too, in the excitement of its ongoing construction, in 1912–13 (also later).

Some would now say that the Pompidou Center looks *non-finito,* unfinished – as if that were such a bad thing – though Worringer (and Nelson Goodman) could be much more pleased by the beautiful way it visibly puts steel to work than by the Woolworth Building, finished or not. Yet even in its conservative metaphorical ornamentation as the "Cathedral of Commerce" Gilbert's skyscraper earned some modernist symbolic repute in its own right. *Sans* late Gothic ornament, but with its tower recognizably in smokestack-front, tugboatlike position, it is the discernible prototype of Picasso's big architectural costume of the "Manager from New York" for the ballet *Parade* (1917).

Finally, now that the entire cult of the New York skyscraper has lately been taken as falsely progressivist,[192] one can only wonder where that leaves such early antimodern reaction as Lord Balfour's, repeated with delight by a distinguished medievalist: told on a visit to the site that the Woolworth Building was "fireproof from top to bottom," Balfour responded, " 'What a pity!' "[193] Differently, at the start of *Finnegans Wake* (1939) Joyce salutes a punning but nonmetaphorical erection (or, in context, metaphorical nonerection) as "a waalworth of a skyerscape of most eyeful hoyth entowerly."[194] Perhaps, like the Woolworth Building as Worringer might have had it in 1910, modern architecture by no means fulfilled itself; and perhaps what Umberto Eco calls the decided "openness" of Joyce's work bespeaks its (ever) unfinished business.

Notes

Introduction

1. Ernest Klein, *A Comprehensive Etymological Dictionary of the English Language,* 2 vols. (Amsterdam, 1966), vol. 1, 500, col. 2.

2. Martin Heidegger, "Building Dwelling Thinking" (1951–4), in his *Poetry, Language, Thought,* trans. Albert Hofstadter (New York, 1971), 145–61. Although Heidegger's antitechnologism is a specialist's problem (see "The Question Concerning Technology" [1949–55], trans. William Lovitt in his ed. *The Question Concerning Technology and Other Essays* [New York, 1977], 3–35), in my brief and inexpert opinion, given only in order to place myself, the status of a mere thing vis-à-vis an artwork, in "The Origin of the Work of Art" (1935–60; *Poetry,* 17–87), develops affirmatively enough in "The Thing" (1949–51; *Poetry,* 165–82) to find in certain technical constructions a Heideggerean beauty that Heidegger himself might or might not have approved.

3. Walter Benjamin, "The Work of Art in the Age of Mechanical Reproduction," in his *Illuminations,* ed. Hannah Arendt, trans. Harry Zohn (New York, 1969), 217–51, here 222–3.

4. Aloïs Riegl, *Spätrömische Kunstindustrie,* 3d ed. (Darmstadt, 1964), 349; trans. Rolf Winkes, *Late Roman Art Industry,* Archaeologica, no. 36 (Rome, 1985), 198, uses the, in English, more ambiguous "moving . . . tendrils," a small point, but one worth making here. Actually, the figure may have a considerable history. A learned humanist of the fourth century, Saint Gregory of Nyssa, describing in a letter a ridge of leafy oaks, used the notably Homeric phrase "far seen with quivering leaves": Gervase Mathew, "The Aesthetic Theories of Gregory of Nyssa," in *Studies in Memory of David Talbot Rice,* ed. Giles Robertson and George Henderson (Edinburgh: Edinburgh University Press, 1975), 217–22, here 219.

5. John Herman Randall, Jr., *How Philosophy Uses Its Past* (New York, 1963), 54–5, 80–4, esp. 82, quoting Bertrand Russell, *Wisdom of the West* (Garden City, N.Y., 1959), 5.

6. This and the following quotations from Paul Fussell, *BAD; or, The Dumbing of America* (New York, 1991), 34.

1. Bentham's Panopticon

1. Michel Foucault, *Discipline and Punish: The Birth of the Prison,* trans. Alan Sheridan (New York, 1977), esp. chap. 3, "Panopticism," 195–228. Studies of the Panopticon, more of which will be mentioned, include Robert (i.e., Robin?) Evans, "Panopticon," *Controspazio,* 2, no. 10 (October 1970), 4–18; Robin Evans, "Bentham's Panopticon: An Incident in the Social History of Architecture," *AAQ: Architectural Association Quarterly,* 3, no. 2 (April–June 1971), 21–37. See now also Donald Preziosi, *Rethinking Art History: Meditations on a Coy Science* (New Haven, Conn., 1989), chap. 3, "The Panoptic Gaze and the Anamorphic Archive," 54–79, esp. 62–7.

2. Bentham intended to revise his texts on the project into a unity, but settled under pressure of time for publishing an original epistolary 1787 text with a long two-part "Postscript," in 1791. In the present discussion references to *Panopticon* pertain to the successive texts in *The Works of Jeremy Bentham,* ed. John Bowring (London, 1838–43; repr. New York, 1962), vol. 4 (1843): "Panopticon; or, the Inspection-House: Containing the Idea of a New Principle of Construction Applicable to Any Sort of Establishment in Which Persons of any Description are to be Kept under Inspection; and in Particular to Penitentiary-Houses . . . " (37–66); "Postscript, Part 1: Containing Further Particulars and Alterations Relative to the Plan of Construction Originally Proposed, Principally Adapted to the Purpose of a Panopticon Penitentiary-House" (67–121); and "Postscript, Part 2: Principles and Plan of Management" (121–72, plus two further plates); I ignore the "Panopticon *versus* New South Wales; or, the Panopticon Penitentiary System and the Penal Colonization System Compared," which comes next.

3. Bentham, *Panoptique: Mémoire sur un nouveau principe pour construire des maisons d'inspection et nommément des maisons de force* (Paris, 1791); not listed in Charles Alfred Rochedieu, *Bibliography of French Translations of English Works, 1700–1800* (Chicago, 1948), 21–2, where, however, French editions of Bentham's 1787 *Defence of Usury* (two of 1790) and 1778 *View of the Hard Labour Bill* (1797) are detailed, the latter published together with Beccaria's *Traité des délits et des peines* by the press of the *Journal d'Economie Publique.*

4. W. Carbys Zimmerman, "The Circular Prison and Jail Plan: A Discussion of Its Merits as Exemplified in the New Illinois State Penitentiary," *Brickbuilder,* 23, no. 8 (August 1914), 189–90.

5. Gertrude Himmelfarb, "The Haunted House of Jeremy Bentham," in *Ideas in History: Essays Presented to Louis Gottschalk by His Former Students,* ed. Richard Herr and Harold T. Parker (Durham, N.C., 1965), 199–238, esp. 209.

6. Niall McCullough and Valerie Mulvin, *A Lost Tradition: The Nature of Architecture in Ireland* (Dublin, 1987), 110–15, with illus. of the buildings mentioned. Manfredo Tafuri, *Theories and History of Architecture* (1968; 4th ed., 1976), trans. Giorgio Verrecchia (New York, 1980), illustrates (pl. 63 on p. 294), without discussion, a panopticon prison projected in 1824 for Padua by Giuseppe Jappelli.

7. McCullough and Mulvin, *Lost Tradition;* also, "the workhouse was the flagship of that experiment in social legislation – partly dictated by a desire to try out new ideas in social management before implementing them in England – which made Ireland the first of the world's welfare states" (115). On workhouses, see also Frank Jackman, "Buildings for Health and Welfare, 1839–1989," in Royal Institute of

the Architects of Ireland, *150 Years of Architecture in Ireland: RIAI, 1939–1989,* ed. John Graby (Dublin, 1989), 88–91, esp. 88.

8. See the excellent article by Bruno Foucart and Véronique Noël-Bouton, "Une prison cellulaire de plan circulaire au XIXe siècle: La prison d'Autun," *L'Information d'Histoire de l'Art,* 16, no. 1 (January–February 1971), 11–24, here 19 n. 44, 20 n. 48, with refs.; also, Bruno Foucart, "Architecture carcérale et architectes fonctionnalistes en France au XIXᵉ siècle," *Revue de l'Art,* no. 32 (1976), 37–56, especially for prison architecture by N. Hourou-Romain and his son in the midnineteenth century; and on the last point, especially: Walter A. Lunden, "The Rotary Jail, or Human Squirrel Cage," *Journal of the Society of Architectural Historians,* 18 (1959), 149–57, here 152. The State Prison as built at Statesville, Illinois (1919), remains a classic Benthamite example.

9. Foucart and Noël-Bouton, "Prison cellulaire," 19.

10. Ibid., 20 n. 48.

11. Rudolf Wittkower, *Art and Architecture in Italy, 1600 to 1750,* Pelican History of Art, 2nd ed. (Harmondsworth, 1965), 122, mentioning this as "an 'industrial' work" with "three large halls of impressive austerity," refers to H. Brauer and Wittkower, *Die Zeichnungen des Gianlorenzo Bernini* (Berlin, 1931), 126, and A. Busiri Vici in *Palladio,* 6 (1956), 127.

12. Foucault, *Discipline,* 203, with ref. to G. Loisel, *Histoire des ménageries,* vol. 2 (Paris, 1912), 104–7; see also Fiske Kimball, in *Gazette des Beaux-Arts* (1938).

13. Ibid., 22–3, with fig. 9 on p. 23. In 1788 Pierre L'Enfant, the military engineer known for his city plan of Washington (1791), with its strong axial lines of sight, designed a temporary banquet pavilion for celebrating the ratification of the United States Constitution in New York; a bird's eye watercolor view by David Grim (c. 1800; New-York Historical Society) shows ten long tables arranged semipanoptically in respect to the dais. Cf. also round barns, below, p. 55.

14. Question: inasmuch as the Panopticon ought to run itself as a social device, should guards rendered redundant by it be exempted, if only for the sake of morale, from being sent to panoptic workhouses themselves? On the Panopticon and the latter type, see Anna Dickens, "The Architect and the Workhouse," *Architectural Review,* 160, no. 958 (December 1976), 345–52.

15. Augustine Welby Norchmore Pugin, *Contrasts* (1836), 2d ed. (1841), repr., The Victorian Library (New York, 1969), unnumbered plate.

16. S. Lang, "The Principles of the Gothic Revival in England," *Journal of the Society of Architectural Historians,* 25 (1966), 240–67.

17. "Philosophy is never more worthily occupied than when affording her assistances to the economy of common life: benefits of which mankind in general are partakers, being thus superadded to whatever gratification is to be reaped from researchers purely speculative. It is a vain and false philosophy which conceives its dignity to be debased by use": Bentham, *Panopticon,* 117n.

18. Edward Robert de Zurko, *Origins of Functionalist Theory* (New York, 1957). At the same moment of late functionalism, Richard Adams traced back to Coleridge the idea that form should arise naturally from within the work rather than be applied from without. In "Architecture and the Romantic Tradition; Coleridge to Wright," *American Quarterly,* 9 (1957), 46–52.

19. The *Encyclopédie* itself having begun as a translation of the *Encyclopaedia Britannica* (1771), composed by Scottish rationalists, the text of which opens with the very word "utility."

20. Charles Everett, *Jeremy Bentham* (New York, 1966), 20.

21. J. B. Bury, *The Idea of Progress: An Inquiry into Its Origins and Growth* (1932; ed. New York, 1955), 162.

22. For pedagogical purposes, that is, to test his idea that anyone can be taught anything; Bentham, *Panopticon,* 65.

23. In economics, a decade before Bentham's *Introduction,* a principle of automatic adaptation to changing circumstances figured prominently in Adam Smith's *An Inquiry into the Nature and Causes of the Wealth of Nations* (1776), which served to qualify the physiocrats' sense of the "natural order" as given; Charles Alfred Rochedieu, *Bibliography of French Translations of English Works, 1700–1800* (Chicago, 1948), 304, lists eight translations of the *Wealth of Nations* between 1778 and 1800.

24. According to Benjamin Nelson, *The Idea of Usury: From Tribal Brotherhood to Universal Otherhood,* 2d ed. (Chicago, 1969), 98, 123–4, Bentham's rationale for usury (one after all might as well write a *Defense of Drug-Pushing*) shows the influence of Locke and also of the Anglican archdeacon William Paley.

25. On which see Monroe C. Beardsley, "The Concept of Economy in Art," *Journal of Aesthetics and Art Criticism,* 14 (1955–6), 370–5.

26. "Froude, I think, was disgusted with the whole Tract, and accused me of *economy* in publishing it. It is principally through Mr. Froude's *Remains* that this word has got into our language": John Henry Newman, *Apologia pro Vita Sua: Being a History of His Religious Opinions* (1864ff.; ed. London 1908), 45–6. Edmund Burke had spoken with memorable disparagement, but restrictedly, of "economists and calculators" in his *Reflections on the Revolution in France* (1790).

27. Bentham, *Panopticon,* 39; repeated at the end of the first proposal, 66.

28. Leon Battista Alberti, *On the Art of Building in Ten Books,* trans. Joseph Rykwert, Neil Leach, and Robert Tavernor (Cambridge, Mass., 1988), 138.

29. Ibid., 139.

30. Ibid. A further paragraph gives practical suggestions, including general disposition, with debtors "in separate cells" behind a "more restricted prison" for minor criminals and an "innermost section" for capital criminals; 140.

31. Emil Kaufmann, *Architecture in the Age of Reason: Baroque and Post-Baroque in England, Italy and France* (Cambridge, Mass., 1955; repr. New York, 1968), 96, 97; on Lodoli, see also Edgar Kaufmann, Jr., "Memmo's Lodoli," *Art Bulletin,* 46 (1964), 159–75, also 589.

32. Ibid., 104; possibly the indignity this provoked was at least partly due to implication of Luther's castigation of Rome as "sink of abominations." The present-day Belgian architect Lucien Kroll criticizes the general tendency to hierarchical ordering, in design and planning (instead of equalizing, overall networks) as "architecture cloaque" and "urbanisme cloaque"; see his *An Architecture of Complexity* (originally *Composants,* 1983), trans. Peter Blundell Jones (Cambridge, Mass., 1987), 5, 77 with n. 1, 79 (gloss). One can project as antiutilitarian Kroll's claim that, freeing itself from a sense of industrial domination, architecture might pursue "a distinction . . . between the form which an intelligent organisation of work produces spontaneously, expressing an inherent complexity, and that born of cultural paralysis, with its rigid alignments, its identical elements, its complicity with [Frederick] Taylor's system which splinters work into unrelated fragments" (31).

33. Tafuri, *The Sphere and the Labyrinth: Avant-Gardes and Architecture from Piranesi to the 1970s* (1980), trans. Pellegrino d'Acierno and Robert Connolly (Cambridge, Mass., 1987), 312 n. 16. Jansenism has some relevance in the matter of surveillance, for, notwithstanding a claim of John Hubbel Weiss, *The Making of Technological Man: The Social Origins of French Engineering Education* (Cambridge, Mass., 1982),

264 n. 9, relying on Georges Synders, *La pédagogie en France aux XVIIe et XVIIIe siècles* (Paris, 1965), 31–56, that "round-the-clock 'guidance' " had characterized Jesuit education, the Jansenists actually criticized Jesuit schools for lax discipline: "It was probably [the Jansenist Abbé de] St. Cyran's view of human nature which made him lay down the principle that no boy must be out of sight of his instructors for a single moment"; Ronald A. Knox, *Enthusiasm: A Chapter in the History of Religion; With Special Reference to the XVII and XVIII Centuries* (Oxford, 1960; repr. New York, 1961), 205, with refs.

34. Tafuri, *Sphere*, 43.

35. Francesco Milizia, *Dizionario delle arti del disegno, estratto in gran parte dall'Enciclopedia metodica* (Bassano, 1797), vol. 1, chap. 7; quoted in Kaufmann, *Architecture*, 102.

36. Marguerite Yourcenar, "The Dark Brain of Piranesi," in *The Dark Brain of Piranesi and Other Essays* (1962), trans. Richard Howard (New York, 1984), 88–128, here 109, 111, 112, 115, 119.

37. Milizia, *Principi di architettura civile*, 3rd Milanese ed., ed. Luigi Maseri (Milan, 1853), this edition so "functionalistically" up-to-date that it includes an appendix on railroad engineering. Pellegrino d'Acierno kindly helped with the Italian.

38. Kaufmann, *Architecture*, 102–3.

39. Milizia, *Principi*, part 2, book 3, chap. 10, sect. 3, p. 300. Even the radical antiornamentalist Adolf Loos, in the early twentieth century, offers, "Architecture arouses feelings in people. The task of the architect is therefore, to define what the feelings should be.... The court-house must make a threatening impression on the furtive criminal"; "Architecture" (written 1910; various eds. to 1931), trans. Tim and Charlotte Benton, in *Architecture and Design, 1890–1939: An International Anthology of Original Articles*, Whitney Library of Design (New York, 1975), 41–5, here 45. Thanks to Joan Ockman for this reference.

40. In the mid-eighteenth century the category of the useful was opened in aesthetic rivalry with conventional beauty, that is, not as the unbeautiful or the ugly but as an alternative beauty. Thus in 1756 Alexander Gerard saw utility itself not merely as "the fitness of things for answering to their ends" but as "contributing another species of beauty distinct from that of figure" – which is as much as to say, a more *abstract* species: Peter Collins, *Changing Ideals in Modern Architecture, 1750–1950* (London, 1965), 218.

41. I follow here Ledoux's *Architecture Considered in Relation to Art, Mores and Legislation* (1804), as excerpted and translated in Elizabeth Gilmore Holt, ed., *From the Classicists to the Impressionists: A Documentary History of Art and Architecture in the Nineteenth Century*, A Documentary History of Art, vol. 3 (Garden City, 1966), 229–42, 311–13, 418–21, here 237. Cf. Klaus Herdeg's pessimistic application of the basic idea to Philip Johnson's 1001 Fifth Avenue apartment house, in New York, of 1979: "Perhaps...the presumably wealthy tenants...might interpret architectural impudence as personal flattery"; *The Decorated Diagram: Harvard Architecture and the Failure of the Bauhaus Legacy* (Cambridge, Mass., 1983), 23.

42. Ibid., 235.

43. Quoted in Dickens, "Architect and Workhouse," 352, from *The Builder*, 1868, p. 827.

44. But see also Helen Rosenau, "The Functional and the Ideal in Late Eighteenth-Century French Architecture," *Architectural Review*, 140 (October 1966), 253–8.

45. Milizia, *Principi*, quoted in Kaufmann, *Architecture*, 103, with 245 n. 228.

46. C. N. Ledoux, *L'architecture considérée sous le rapport de l'art, des moeurs et de la législation* (Paris, 1804; repr. Nördlingen, 1981), 135.

47. Ananda K. Coomaraswamy, "Ornament," *Art Bulletin*, 21 (1939), 375–82.

48. Rosenau, "Functional and Ideal," 253, quoting Helvetius's *De l'homme* (1773) as well as Diderot and d'Alembert's sense, in the *Encyclopédie*, of *caractère* as "la manière qui ... est propre," which eliminates *le superflu*. This *caractère*, however, is surely a modernization of the classical and Renaissance *decorum*. In this interesting article, which more or less aligns the style of 1800 with contemporary style, Rosenau speaks of the architect Petit's "utilitarian explanation" of a hospital design. Note that in *Vers une architecture* (1923), Le Corbusier quotes from the 1920 program of *L'Esprit Nouveau* a like application of the same distinction to artistic style: "It is in general artistic production that the style of an epoch is found and not, as is too often supposed, in certain productions of an ornamental kind, mere superfluities which overload the system of thought [that] alone furnishes the elements of a style"; Charles-Édouard Jeanneret (called Le Corbusier), *Towards a New Architecture*, trans. Frederick Etchells (1927), 2nd ed. (London, 1946; repr. 1965), 83.

49. Nikolaus Pevsner, *Pioneers of Modern Design from William Morris to Walter Gropius* (originally *Pioneers of the Modern Movement, 1936*), 4th ed. (Harmondsworth, 1975). In a seventeenth-century "Christianopolis" on a square plan (with *columnar* loggie protecting the public walkways from rain), "No one need be surprised at the rather cramped quarters; for there ... is ... need for ... very little furniture. Other people who house vanity, extravagance and a family of that sort, and who heap up baggage of iniquity, can never live spaciously enough" (chap. 12). Yet already here, two centuries before *News from Nowhere*, craftsmen make things "not always because necessity demands, but for the purpose of a competition among the mechanics, in order that the human soul may have some means by which it and the highest prerogative of the mind may unfold themselves through different sorts of machinery, or by which, rather, the little spark of divinity remaining in us, may shine brightly in the material offered" (chap. 13). Johann Valentin Andreae, *Christianopolis: An Ideal State of the Seventeenth Century*, trans. and ed. Felix Emil Held (New York, 1916), 156, 157–8, respectively.

50. Amédée Ozenfant, in his *Foundations of Modern Art* (1928), trans. John Rodker (ed. New York, 1952), 140; emphasis added.

51. Ibid., 200.

52. Jean Jacques Rousseau, "Discours 'Si le rétablissement des sciences et des arts a contribué à épurer les moeurs' " (1750), in his *Les rêveries du promeneur solitaire...* (Garden City, N.Y. 1961), 5–39, here 12.

53. Denis Diderot, "Pensées détachées sur la peinture, sculpture et la poésie pour servir de suite aux Salons" (1775), in his *Oeuvres esthétiques*, ed. Paul Vernière (Paris, 1961), 743–840, here 815 (to see under the skin of *another*, being the moral point); Diderot here discourages the study of the *écorché*, or skinned model of bodily musculature, as also in the essay "My Bizarre Thoughts on Drawing." I have discussed this as anticipating Oscar Wilde in an essay, "Plastic Art and General Culture" (1980–1), reprinted in my *Historical Present: Essays of the 1970s* (Ann Arbor, 1984), 281–8, esp. 285. The idea has its prehistory, including Lomazzo's remark of 1584, "Let the painter beware, not to do as Michelangelo did, who, wishing to show how to be a master at anatomy, gave all his figures those muscles that the anatomist alone is able to see through dissection." This follows a 1513–14 note by Leonardo da Vinci: "O anatomical painter beware, lest in the attempt to make your nudes display all their emotions by a too strong indication of bones, sinews and muscles, you become a wooden painter." Both quotations from Carlo Pedretti, *Leonardo: A Study in Chronology and Style* (1973; repr. New York, 1982), 165. The

modern sculptor Giacometti is said by Mercedes Matter, *Alberti Giacometti Photographed by Herbert Matter* (New York, 1987), 214 (ref. lacking) to have remarked, "I have enough trouble with the outside without bothering about the inside."

A distinguished civil engineer, struggling against a simplistic, positivist sense of truth to materials, wrote in 1952, "It is not possible to avoid, nor is there reason to regret, hidden, load-bearing structural parts. In particular, reinforced concrete hides its own reinforcing. . . . It is necessary not to deceive, though without going to the extreme of painting the reinforcement on the surface (so that the observer could know what is inside). We have learned to have a feeling for the human skeleton, which we do not see, and do not wish to see, under the expressive softness of the flesh." Further: "In our time . . . [the] correlation between form and function is considered a virtue, whereas other symbolic ambitions are cut short. As regards the functional expressiveness of the structure as such . . . a proof that the artist now seeks after the very root of aesthetic quality, is his disdain for ornament. . . . This could not be justified merely on the ground of economy. . . . At most it is part of an intimate desire to attain to a complete solution to the total aesthetic problem." Eduardo Torroja y Miret, *Philosophy of Structures* (originally titled *Razón y ser de los tipos estructurales*), trans. J. J. Polivka and Milos Polivka (Berkeley, 1967), chap. 17, "The Beauty of Structures," 268–89, here 276, 279.

54. *Boullée's Treatise on Architecture,* ed. Helen Rosenau (London, 1953), 80. The remark may seem confusing if, as a modern, one limits the skeletal analogy to framed structure.

55. As above, at n. 46.

56. Georgi Valentinovich Plekhanov, *Art and Social Life* (London, 1953), 162–3; Plekhanov's source was the Goncourts' discussion of the Salon of 1793.

57. Kaufmann, *Von Ledoux bis Le Corbusier: Ursprung und Entwicklung der Autonomen Architektur* (Vienna, 1933), 50–3.

58. To give a single example: an armadillo-like fossil creature captioned "Architecture naturelle," followed by the pairing in one plate – captioned "Analogies" – of a dinosaur skeleton and the fuselage of a zeppelin under construction, in Elie Faure's *Histoire de l'art,* vol. 5, *L'esprit des formes* (Paris, 1927), figs. 150 on p. 307, 151 on p. 309, respectively. Here Faure's enthusiasm had been wildly stimulated by Lamarck's protoevolutionist *L'introduction à l'étude des animaux sans vertèbres* (1801) and *La philosophie zoologique;* Paul Desanges, *Elie Faure,* Classiques du XXᵉ Siècle (Paris, 1966), 22, identifying several premodern structures as *architecture utilitaire* and reserving to modern functionalist works *architecture industrielle.*

59. For purposes of cultural history it is worth remembering how new this is: "ecology" was still a specialized scientific term until G. E. Hutchinson published *The Ecological Theater and the Evolutionary Play* (New Haven, Conn. 1965).

60. Kenneth Burke, *A Grammar of Motives* (1945), in *A Grammar of Motives and a Rhetoric of Motives* (New York, 1962), 285, referring to Bentham's *Table of the Springs of Action;* see also idem, "Terministic Screens" (1965), in his *Language as Symbolic Action: Essays on Life, Literature and Method* (Berkeley, Calif., 1968), 44–62, esp. 46–7, and idem, "I, Eye, Ay: Concerning Emerson's Early Essay, 'Nature' and the Machinery of Transcendence" (1966), 186–200, esp. 196.

61. Leo Tolstoy, *Anna Karenina,* trans. David Magarshack (New York, 1961), 93.

62. Ledoux, *Architecture,* in Holt, *Classicists to Impressionists,* 233.

63. Ibid., 235.

64. Bentham, *Introduction to the Principles of Morals and Legislation,* in *The Utilitarians* (Garden City, N.Y., 1961), preface.

65. Speaking of the means of giving school instruction in the Panopticon, Bentham suggests (*Panopticon,* 162n) that, if unlikely necessity requires, a restraining bar might be laid across the laps of seated inmates, such as a "Mr. Blackburne" had devised: "Mechanics and anatomy contributed each their share in the production of this simple and ingenious contrivance..."

66. Thomas L. Hankins, "Malebrance on Mechanics," *Journal of the History of Ideas,* 28 (1967), 193–210. "The conservation laws of Descartes and Leibniz would allow the universe to leave the hand of the creator and exist independently of him. But this is not true of the Principle of Least Action. Action is always produced anew and created at each instant with the greatest possible economy" (205). On Nicolas de Malebranche's influence, see A. A. Luce, *Berkeley and Malebranche: A Study in the Origins of Berkeley's Thought* (Oxford, 1934; repr., 1967).

67. W. K. Wimsatt, "Organic Form: Some Questions About a Metaphor," in G. S. Rousseau, *Organic Form: The Life of an Idea* (London, 1972), 61–81, here 69, with specific credit to G. N. Giordamo Orsisi obscured by an error in the notes. Kant speaks of the product of nature as "an *organized* and *self-organizing* being" in sect. 65: Immanuel Kant, *Critique of Judgment,* trans. J. H. Bernard (New York, 1951), 220 (emphases in original).

68. Thomas Malthus, *An Essay on the Principle of Population,* 8th ed. (London, 1878), 6–7.

69. John Wesley, *A Plain Account of the People Called Methodists* (London, 1816), 3. Himmelfarb, "Haunted House," 201, noticing Bentham's rather odd reference to God as all-seeing in Psalm 139:2–3 (especially in the Authorized Version, "Thou art...about my bed: and spiest out all my ways"), suggests that the Panopticon "was not so much to provide a maximum amount of human control, as to transcend the human and give the illusion of the divine." Her larger point concerns deep-set contradiction in the professed radicalism of Bentham, who managed to think not in terms of human "rights" at all but only of impersonal "interests," and to posit himself the unselfish contractor of his proposed establishment.

70. Himmelfarb, "Haunted House," 209, quoting Lazare Carnot, "Essai sur les machines en général," in his *Principes fondamentaux de l'équilibre et du mouvement* (Paris, 1803) (11.16).

71. Edward Young, *Conjectures on Original Composition in a Letter to the Author of "Sir Charles Grandison"* (London, 1759), in H. A. Needham, ed., *Taste and Criticism in the Eighteenth Century: A Selection of Texts Illustrating the Evolution of Taste and the Development of Critical Theory* (London, 1952), 93–4.

72. Diderot, "Sur le Génie," in his *Oeuvres complètes,* ed. J. Assézat and Maurice Tourneaux, 20 vols. (Paris, 1875–7), vol. 4 (1875), 26–7.

73. Somehow the editors felt this belonged with the more serviceable modern *génies,* since for "Génie en peinture" one is referred separately to the entry on painting.

74. Charles François Viel de Saint-Maux, *Lettres sur l'architecture des anciens et celles des modernes; dans lesquelles se trouve développé le génie symbolique qui présida aux monumens de l'antiquité* (Paris, 1787).

75. Nicolas Le Camus de Mézièrs, *Le génie de l'architecture; ou, l'analogie de cet art avec nos sensations* (Paris, 1780).

76. Here I translate directly from Rosenau, *Boullée's Treatise,* 83.

77. Rousseau, "Discours," 37 (emphasis added).

78. Paul Robert, *Dictionnaire alphabétique et analogique de la langue française: Les mots et les associations d'idées,* vol. 3 (Paris, 1960), 279.

79. André Félibien, *Des principes de l'architecture, de la sculpture et de la peinture et des*

autres arts qui en dépendent (Paris, 1699; repr. Farnborough, Hants, 1966), 63–4. Already in the 1670s, Louis XIV was pleased by the beauty and low cost of new military construction; see Charles Perrault, *Memoirs of My Life,* ed. and trans. Jeanne Morgan Zarucchi (Columbia, Mo., 1989), 110–11.

80. For this institutional history, see Weiss, *Making of Technological Man,* esp. foreword and chap. 1. On the engineering aspect of architecture beforehand, there is Roland J. Maidstone, "Structural Theory and Design Before 1742," *Architectural Review,* 143, no. 854 (April 1968), 303–10.

81. Weiss, *Making of Technological Man,* 29–31.

82. Ledoux, *L'architecture,* 83.

83. A brief, useful bibliography on antique, medieval, and Renaissance engineering can be found in Frank D. Prager and Gustina Scaglia, *Mariano Taccola and His Book "De Ingeneis"* (Cambridge, Mass., 1972), 218–221; also of interest is C. St. C. B. Davison's catalogue of an exhibition at the Science Library, *Historic Books on Machines* (London, 1953; repr., 1963).

84. On which see Hans Straub, *A History of Civil Engineering,* trans. Ernest Rockwell (Cambridge, Mass., 1964), esp. chap. 5, "The Advent of Civil Engineering," and chap. 6, "The Origins of Structural Analysis in France (1750–1850)."

85. Ibid., 122. On the giving way of specifically Palladian aesthetic precedent to direct engineering in early-eighteenth-century design theory, see the book-review essay by Reyner Banham, "Voyeurs des Ponts et Chaussées," *Journal of the Society of Architectural Historians,* 39 (1980), 152–3.

86. Which in 1802 would acquire a protomodern iron and glass roof by F. T. Bélanger when the original timber dome burned; Rosenau, "Functional and Ideal," 254.

87. A Renaissance antetype for this can be adduced: Raffaele Riario's paneled "stumpy" square piers with "plain capitals" like heavy moldings, these connoting "strength and simplicity [as] attributes of status," in S. Lorenzo in Damaso, Rome, built after 1486; John Onians, *Bearers of Meaning: The Classical Orders in Antiquity, the Middle Ages and the Renaissance* (Princeton, N. J., 1988), 203–4, with fig. 114 on p. 203.

88. For a modernist reading of which, see Pierre Francastel, "L'Architecture de Versailles: fonction et décor," in *Urbanisme et architecture* (Paris, 1954), 119–26.

89. Douglas Phillips-Birt, *Ships and Boats: The Nature of Their Design* (London, 1966), 24–6.

90. Ibid., 34.

91. Quoted, ibid., 33.

92. Ibid., 97.

93. Ibid., 37.

94. Horatio Greenough, *Form and Function: Remarks on Art,* ed. Harold A. Small (Berkeley, Calif., 1947); N. Wynne and B. Newhall had already published "Horatio Greenough: Herald of Functionalism," *Magazine of Art,* 22 (1939), 12–15.

95. Wassily Kandinsky, *Point and Line to Plane,* trans. Howard Dearstyne and Hilla Rebay (New York, 1947; repr., 1979), figs. 65 on p. 102, 67 on p. 103.

96. J. N. L. Durand, *Précis des leçons d'architecture données à l'Ecole polytechnique* (Paris, 1802–5) as excerpted and trans. in Holt, *Classicists to Impressionists,* 203–12, here 203, 208, respectively.

97. Durand, *Précis des leçons d'architecture données à l'Ecole royale polytechnique* (1809), 2 vols. (Paris, 1819, 1817; repr. Nördlingen, 1981), vol. 1, 98.

98. Ibid., vol. 1, 3.

99. Ibid., 6.

100. Ibid., 8, 9.
101. Ibid., 11, 16.
102. Ibid., 17.
103. Ibid., 19. In our time, the Princeton civil engineer David P. Billington, important as a scholar of the matter "from the other side" (e.g., "Structures Implicit and Explicit," *Via*, 2 [1973], 29–39) who does worry about beauty, runs out of steam toward the end of his essay, "An Example of Structural Art: The Salginatobel Bridge of Robert Maillart," in *Journal of the Society of Architectural Historians*, 33 (1974), 61–72, arguing almost by punning that what Maillart or any other engineer renders up is as "representational" of the play of natural forces as a portrait (by Leonardo, at that!), rather than "abstract." James S. Ackerman makes a subtler argument that Palladio's buildings are more "naturalistically" antique than those of the more manneristically inventive Vignola in "The Tuscan/Rustic Order: A Study in the Metaphorical Language of Architecture," in the same *Journal*, 42 (1983), 15–34, esp. 22. Insofar as engineering represents (or better, *embodies*) anything, what is represented is not "nature" but some (already abstract, conventional) mathematical prerepresentation of a play of forces.
104. Ibid., 21.
105. Ibid., 23.
106. Quoted in Collins, *Changing Ideals*, 231; see also 230. Baltard's book was "inspired by John Howard's famous *State of Prisons* published in 1777."
107. Foucault, *Discipline*, 319 n. 13, quoting L. Baltard, *Architectonographie des prisons* (1829), 18, but dropping the phrase claiming that the English have "perfected" the art of mechanics.
108. Ibid., 205. Later in the nineteenth century, society itself might be likened to a building: witness the anonymous book by a native of Feldbach, in Styria, exiled to England from France for leftist activities in 1849, *Social Architecture; or, Reasons and Means for the Demolition and Reconstruction of the Social Edifice* (London, 1876).
109. J. B. Treilhard, *Motifs du code d'instruction criminelle* (Paris, 1808), 14, as quoted, ibid., 217.
110. Kenneth Burke, again, has written, apropos of Bentham's "programmatic dislike and distrust of metaphor," of "symbolic motives behind the thinking of that crabbed old bachelor, Jeremy Bentham, who propounded the philosophy of Utilitarianism, and who visited upon himself a kind of symbolic castration in his plans for a 'neutral' scientific vocabulary for avoiding the 'censorious' terms of rhetoric and poetry. His utilitarian theory of language reduced purpose to agency by seeking the *interests* that correspond to *ideals* (another word for the purposive)": *Grammar of Motives*, 284–5; see also, in his *Language as Symbolic Action*, "What Are the Signs of What? (A Theory of 'Entitlement')" (1962), 359–79, esp. 371n, 375–76.
111. Foucault, *Discipline*, 317 n. 4, mentioning "the Panoramas that Barker was constructing ... (the first of which seems to have dated from 1787) ... in which ... the visitors occupied exactly the place of the sovereign gaze." The devices of this Barker, an Irish artist, and his son Henry Aston Barker, in London, belong to a kind of ultragadgetry in the field of contemporary landscape painting. On Philip de Loutherbourg's especially tricky, illuminated "Eidophusikon" set up in London in 1781–2, see Austin Dobson, "Loutherbourg, R. A.," in his *"At Prior Park" and Other Papers* (Oxford, n.d.), 94–127, esp. 111ff. Of such Jack Lindsay, *J. M. W. Turner: His Life and Work: A Critical Biography* (New York, 1966), 51, says, "Many of the constructions or machines that were devised were mere toys or

novelties, but in a wider view we can see how they link with a general search for deeper insight into, and greater control of, the natural phenomena that most concerned the artist."

112. *Sunday Times Magazine* (London), October 29, 1967, 7.

113. August Strindberg, *Du hasard dans la production artistique* (repr. from *Revue des Revues,* 1894) (Paris, 1990), 25; also according to orig. MS., 36.

114. "Overlooked"? Foucault's recurrent references to an observational "tower" are somewhat misleading in view of the actual section, which shows a circular pit admitting light to the low "inspector's lodge" occupying the same height as and giving a view of only the first two floors of cells. Whether this means observation of the upper stories would have had to be more conventional, or whether this feature was seriously modified, is hard to glean from the wordy promotional text; but there is certainly no tall "tower" in the center of the space of the published section.

115. Cf. Meyer Schapiro, "Architect's Utopia" (review of Baker Brownell and Frank Lloyd Wright, *Architecture and Modern Life*), *Partisan Review,* 4, no. 4 (March 1938), 42-7, here 43; regarding "social well-being" as "not simply an architectural problem," and the importance of "the economic conditions that determine freedom and a decent living": "A prison may be a work of art and a triumph of ingenuity."

116. Quoted in George H. Weitzman, "The Utilitarians and the Houses of Parliament," *Journal of the Society of Architectural Historians,* 20 (1961), 99-107, here 106. Weitzman explains that even before the disastrous fire (painted memorably by Turner) that necessitated a new Parliament building, Joseph Hume, Liberal M.P., was in the forefront of a utilitarian caucus (including Henry Cole) demanding a new House answering to *utility* rather than to sentimental "Gothic or Elizabethan" sentiment. While traditionalists specifically opposed anything like "a semicircular theatrical edifice" (99), Hume interrogated the architect Sir John Soane as to acoustics: "Is it not probable that you will be more successful in having a good sound by having a round end than by having a square?" (100). Weitzman does not say so, but Bentham's Panopticon, probably specifically his semicircular-*looking* published half-plan, seems implicated. Cf. below, p. 239 n. 44.

117. Thomas Carlyle, "The Hero as Man of Letters," in his *On Heroes and Hero-Worship and the Heroic in History* (1841), The World's Classics (Oxford, 1935, repr., 1974), 224-5.

118. Ibid., 226-7. Mill's 1838 essay "Bentham" (John Stuart Mill, *On Bentham and Coleridge* [New York, 1962], 39-98) attacks the man as a seriously limited moral philosopher before praising his contribution to legal thought. Without mentioning the Pantopticon, the critique employs relevant imagery, of building construction as well as optical viewpoint: "He . . . reconstructs all philosophy *ab initio* . . . But to build either a philosophy or anything else, there must be materials. . . . Bentham failed in deriving light from other minds" (57-8); "But, from points of view different from his, different things are perceptible; and none are more likely to have seen what he does not see, than those who do not see what he sees" (60); "He had never been made alive to the unseen influences which were acting upon himself, nor consequently on his fellow-creatures. . . . He saw accordingly in man little but what the vulgarest eye can see" (63); "The bad part of his writing is his resolute denial of all that he does not see" (64); plus this tantalizing inconsistency: "The field of Bentham's labours was like the space between two parallel lines; narrow to excess in one direction, in another it reached to infinity" (75). On the

legal hand, Mill comes up with a figure differently entailing design, praising Bentham as it were functionalistically in saying that previous, piecemeal legal reforms had "much the same effect as if... the plough could only be introduced by making it look like a spade; or as if, when the primeval practice of ploughing by the horse's tail gave way to the innovation of the harness, the tail, for form's sake, had still remained attached to the plough" (77–8).

119. Maurice Denis, "Definition of Neotraditionism" (1890), trans. in Hershel B. Chipp, ed., *Theories of Modern Art: A Source Book by Artists and Critics,* California Studies in the History of Art, 11 (Berkeley, Calif., 1970), 94–105, here 104.

120. Carlyle, *Past and Present,* The World's Classics (London, 1960), e.g., 277, 299; thanks to Steven Marcus here for a tip.

121. Hence, since the mid-nineteenth century, the dubious but unflagging belief in art museums as defensibly "educational" in the sense of personal "improvement" vis-à-vis the world, instead of supposedly indefensibly "elevating" in any sense of spirit.

122. Tolstoy, *Anna Karenina,* 23; cf., among other places, part 3, chap. 3, 251–6.

123. Ibid., 628.

124. Aldous Huxley, *Prisons; with the "Carceri" Etchings by G. B. Piranesi; Critical Study by Jean Adhemar* (London, 1949), essay, 1–26; here, 13, 15, respectively.

125. Tolstoy, *War and Peace,* trans. Rosemary Edmonds, 2 vols. (Baltimore, 1957, repr. 1969), vol. 2, 1142.

126. Huxley, *Prisons,* 24.

127. Ibid., 15.

128. Cf. "From a definition a mathematician can normally deduce only a single property of the object defined; to know several properties he must introduce new points of view..."; Gilles Deleuze, *Expressionism in Philosophy: Spinoza,* trans. Martin Joughin (New York, 1990), 20. Relevant to my distinction between living and geometric bodies, as commonly understood, is chap. 14, "What Can a Body Do?" (217–34). I am aware that my discussion will provoke some to welcome Bentham's project as an "indexical" architecture, in simplistic application of the linguistic terminology of C. S. Peirce. It would be easier and more intellectually *useful* to consider it godless architecture.

129. In comparing two opposed European office buildings (and tendencies) of 1974 – Herman Hertzberger's Central Beheer, at Apeldoorn, and (Norman) Foster Associates' Willis-Faber & Dumas, Ipswich – Kenneth Frampton sees the warren of floating tiers of the first as critically antifunctionalist; whereas, paraphrasing Manfredo Tafuri's argument that the architect ought to "master" prevailing means of production "so as to be able to participate in the production of meaning," the clear, open ordering of the latter constitutes "a natural successor to Bentham's Panopticon of 1791"; Frampton, *Modern Architecture: A Critical History* (New York, 1980), 292–5, esp. 295.

130. Bentham, *Panopticon,* 63. Although the initial inspiration for the Panopticon thus derived, and was first written up "in the year 1787, from Crecheff in White Russia to a Friend in England" (37), Samuel's reported larger attempt at social planning, a completely organized and industrialized agricultural community at Zadobras in the Ukraine, started for Catherine the Great, struck Jeremy as "little better than a madhouse": Everett, *Bentham,* 37–9.

131. Illus., ibid., gatefold pl. opp. p. 39.

132. Reyner Banham, *A Concrete Atlantis: U.S. Industrial Building and European Modern Architecture, 1900–1925* (Cambridge, Mass., 1986); for my review of which, see

"Temples to the Dynamo: The 'Daylight' Factory and the Grain Elevator," in Joseph Masheck, *Modernities: Art-Matters in the Present* (University Park, Pa., 1993), 51–6.

133. Pevsner, *Pioneers*, 122, 124, with fig. 63 on p. 124; refs., 232 n. 10.

134. Bentham, *Panopticon*, 43; illus., gatefold after 172.

135. Ibid., 95 (emphasis in original).

136. And Wesley's "Method" itself, cutting through conventions and offering access to self-fulfilling grace, may not be irrelevant background to the otherwise irreligious Bentham.

137. See Damie Stillman, "Church Architecture in Neoclassical England," *Journal of the Society of Architectrural Historians*, 38 (1979), 103–19, figs. 12 on p. 110 and 24 on p. 115, respectively; thanks to Tom Nozkowski for a copy of this article.

138. That everything came to a halt in 1813 is curious, considering the British government's contemporary activity building cylindrical "martello" towers for (optically radial) defense against French coastal attack, such as the one James Joyce would inhabit a century later at Sandycove Point, outside Dublin, and in which *Ulysses* fictionally opens.

139. Bentham, *Panopticon*, 78n.

140. H. M. Colvin, *A Biographical Dictionary of English Architects, 1660–1840* (London, 1954), 492–3, here 493.

141. Wittkower, "Inigo Jones: Architect and Man of Letters" (1953), in his *Palladio and Palladianism*, ed. Margot Wittkower (New York, 1974), 49–64, with fig. 100 (Palladio after Barbaro) on p. 63.

142. See next chapter, "Politics of Style: Dublin Pro-Cathedral in the Greek Revival."

143. Illus., Sigfried Giedion, *Architecture and the Phenomena of Transition; The Three Space Conceptions in Architecture* (Cambridge, Mass., 1971), fig. 91 on p. 118.

144. Bentham, *Panopticon*, 77.

145. Ibid., 83n, 98n, respectively.

146. Ibid., 43.

147. The present essay has grown out of a study of Bentham's Panopticon and the architecture of 1800 for Dorothea Nyberg's Columbia seminar in the spring of 1967. It may not be obvious that twenty-five years ago this sort of topic was not something most art historians liked their graduate students to pursue, but that was not the case with this exceptional teacher.

2. Politics of Style

1. Henry-Russell Hitchcock, *Architecture: Nineteenth and Twentieth Centuries*, 2d ed. (Harmondsworth, 1963), 439 n. 1, claims that the term was first used by Sigfried Giedion in 1922, and first used in English by Fiske Kimball in 1944; but as I have noted (*Studio International*, March 1969, 148), George Santayana arrived at the concept in his 1915 essay "Hints of Egotism in Goethe" with the remark, "Nothing . . . was more romantic in Goethe than his classicism." The present essay derives from my 1973 Columbia dissertation *Irish Church-Building from the Treaty of Limerick to the Great Famine*. This work began long ago when I was working under my mentor, Rudolf Wittkower, in London, and affiliated with Trinity College, Dublin, as a research student under Anne Crookshank. In the 1960s, my concern with international affinities and even my modest cultural revisionism must have seemed as eccentric as my ignorance of local history was acute, though

art history has since been unveiling such contradictions. Edward McParland, now at Trinity, read a penultimate draft of the present essay.

2. Henry-Russell Hitchcock and Philip Johnson, *The International Style* (1932), 2d ed. (New York, 1966), 24.

3. James M. Osborn, "Travel Literature and the Rise of Neo-Hellenism in England," *Bulletin of the New York Public Library*, 67 (1963), 279–300.

4. Frederick M. Jones, *The Counter-Reformation*, A History of Irish Catholicism, vol. 3, fasc. 3 (Dublin, 1967), 48.

5. J. Mordaunt Crook, *The Greek Revival*, R.I.B.A. Drawings Series (Feltham, 1968) is a short book, but long enough to make more than a single mention of the Greek war (13), in one sentence that also includes Byron, Keats, Shelley, Landor, Flaxman, Thorvaldsen, Hamilton, and Playfair.

6. Apropos of Berkeley's independence: Wittkower never tired of stressing the pertinence to Burlington's project of "A Letter Concerning Design" (1713), written by Anthony Ashley Cooper, the (Whig) Third Earl of Shaftesbury, in Naples in 1712 (e.g., "English Neo-Classicism, the Landscape Garden, China and the Enlightenment" [1969], in his *Palladio and Palladianism* [New York, 1974], 176–90; also, "Classical Theory and Eighteenth-Century Sensibility" [1966], 192–204). But Berkeley's "An Essay Towards Preventing the Ruin of Great Britain" (1721) is anti-Shaftesburean (and Tory), if in places Shaftesbury shows through; and Berkeley's "The Theory of Vision... Vindicated and Explained" (1733) attacks Shaftesbury's deism.

7. *The Works of George Berkeley, Bishop of Cloyne*, ed. A. A. Luce and T. E. Jessop, vol. 7, ed. Luce (Edinburgh, 1955; repr., 1964), 279, observation of May 24, 1717, on the Doric order.

8. In a letter of July 28, 1718, to John Percival, as noticed by Benjamin Rand, *Berkeley and Percival* (Cambridge, 1916), 172; here quoted from Joseph Rykwert, *The First Moderns: The Architects of the Eighteenth Century* (Cambridge, Mass., 1980), 224 n. 211; emphasis added.

9. Edward Chaney, "George Berkeley in the Veneto," *Bolletino del Centro Interuniversitario di Ricerche sul "Vaggio in Italia"* (Turin), 1, no. 2 (July–December 1980), 82–8. Thanks to McParland for stressing Berkeley's relevance and for pointing me toward Chaney's researches, here and in note 17.

10. Dora Wiebenson, *Sources of Greek Revival Architecture* (London, 1969), 21 n. 9.

11. We cannot know if the Doric colonnade was especially Greek, that, starting in 1758, Bishop Pococke built at St. Canice's Cathedral, Kilkenny, to link his bishop's house to the old (thirteenth-century) cathedral, and it was soon subjected to "Gothick" restoration; see James Graves and John G. Augustus Prim, *The History, Architecture and Antiquities of the Cathedral Church of St. Canice, Kilkenny* (Dublin, 1857), 56–7. These rather Ruskinian authors approve of neither the Gothic renovations nor the effect of the colonnade, which was already observed in G. N. Wright, *Scenes in Ireland, with Historical Illustrations, Legends and Biographical Notices* (London, 1834), 133, and may have been dismantled by 1868: Mark Bence-Jones, "Kilkenny, I: Irish Gentility and Urbanity," *Country Life*, 139 (1966), 1254–7.

12. Conyngham twice represented Irish constituencies in Parliament; the *Promenade d'un français dans l'Irlande* (1792) of Jacques-Louis de Bougrenet, Chevalier de Latocnaye, is dedicated to him, at least in the translation of "an Irishman," *Rambles Through Ireland* (Cork, 1798).

13. Wiebenson, *Sources*, 23 n. 15. Also along was one "Scott," not impossibly (?) John "Copperfaced Jack" Scott (1739–98), the notorious Earl of Clonmell who swindled Catholics out of their lands and built Clonmell House, c. 1777–8, in Dublin (Lord Killanin and Michael V. Duignan, *The Shell Guide to Ireland,* 2d ed. [London, 1967], 225); he would only have been a boy, his father's name being uncertain (*DNB*). The all-Irishness of the party was remarked on by Maurice James Craig, *The Volunteer Earl; Being the Life and Times of James Caulfield, First Earl of Charlemont* (London, 1948), 44, noting that the members had met in Italy. From Charlemont's papers, Craig outlines the itinerary (chaps. 2–3, pp. 38–75): after study at the Turin academy in 1747–8 (with David Hume there), Charlemont was, in 1748–9, in Rome, Naples, Constantinople, and then the Greek islands (Robert Wood may already have reached the Eastern Mediterranean prior to, or earlier in, 1749; see 55 n. 6); late in 1749 he toured Athens and other Greek sites, departing early in 1750. Himself more concerned with ethnographical, and some archaeological, rather than architectural, observation, Charlemont avoided noting even major architectural monuments except, prompted by Wren on the subject, for the Mausoleum of Halicarnassus (69–70, with 75 n. 24); otherwise unfortunate are his various anti-Catholic comments.

14. Albert Carré, *L'influence des Huguenots français en Irlande aux XVIIe et XVIIIe siècles,* thesis, Faculté des lettres, University of Paris (Paris, 1937), 120.

15. I rely on the excellent essay of Michael McCarthy, "Paestum and Ireland," in the catalog for the National Academy of Design venue of Joselita Raspi Serra's Centro Di (Florence) exhibition *Paestum and the Doric Revival (1750–1830): Essential Outlines of an Approach* (New York, 1986) (which also has a fine preface by Giulio Carlo Argan), 161–3; also, H. M. Colvin, *A Biographical Dictionary of English Architects, 1660–1840* (London, 1954), q.v. Mylne. See also Nikolas Pevsner and S. Lang, "The Doric Revival" (1948), in Pevsner's *Studies in Art, Architecture and Design,* 2 vols. (London, 1968), vol. 1, *From Mannerism to Romanticism,* 195–211; and, especially, Suzanne Lang's "Early Publications of the Temples at Paestum," *Journal of the Warburg and Courtauld Institutes,* 13 (1950), 48–64. To think of Francis Johnston around the turn of the century in Ireland (on whom see McParland, "Francis Johnston, Irish Architect," *Quarterly Bulletin of the Irish Georgian Society,* 12 [1969], 61–139) as knowledgable in the establishment neo-Palladianism that once rested so firmly on a Roman base, while also aware so early of modern Doricism (not to mention a growing sympathy for the Gothic), is perhaps to think of that distinguished architect as having stood in the eye of a theoretical or ideological hurricane.

16. Maurice Craig and the Knight of Glin, *Ireland Observed* (Cork, 1970), 85, with illustrations.

17. Chaney, "The Grand Tour and Beyond: British and American Travellers in Southern Italy, 1545–1960," in *Oxford, China and Italy: Writings in Honour of Sir Harold Acton,* ed. Chaney and Neil Ritchie (London, 1984), 151–60, esp. 154 and 132 n. 2.

18. Osborn, "Travel Literature," 286.

19. Craig and Glin, *Ireland,* 19.

20. Latocnaye, *Rambles,* vol. 2, 28.

21. Thomas Wood, *An Inquiry Concerning the Primitive Inhabitants of Ireland, Illustrated by Ptolemy's Map of Erin, Corrected by the Aid of Bardic History* (London, 1821), 14.

22. In Berkeley, "A Word to the Wise; or, an Exhortation to the Roman Catholic clergy of Ireland," *Works,* vol. 6, ed. Jessup (London, 1953), 235–49.

23. John Savage, *Picturesque Ireland* (New York, 1884), 562–3, relying on an 1812 ed. of Isaac Weld's *Illustrations of the Scenery of Killarney and Surrounding Country* (London, 1807); for an early nineteenth-century view, see Lady Chatterton, *Rambles Through the South of Ireland During the Year 1838* (London, 1839), vol. 2, pl. 8.

24. Wood, *Inquiry*, 251.

25. Jean-Gabriel Cappot [pseud., Capot de Feuillide], *L'Irlande*, vol. 1 (Paris, 1839), 336, as quoted in Marie-Hélène Pauly, *Les voyageurs français en Irlande au temps du romantisme*, thesis, Faculté des lettres, University of Paris (Paris, 1939), 205. One of the more unusual modern Hiberno-Hellenic connections during the Greek War of Independence concerns an actual Greek refugee, Basil Patras Zula, who arrived in Dublin in 1827, became a Moravian minister at Kilwarlin(?), County Down, and there constructed a garden landscape modeled on Thermopylae!; W. B. Stanford, *Ireland and the Classical Tradition* (Dublin, 1976), 119–20, with detailed description.

26. Henry Grattan, "Roman Catholic Bill" (February 22, 1793), in *The Speeches of the Right Honourable Henry Grattan in the Irish and in the Imperial Parliament*, ed. his son, vol. 3 (London, 1822), 43–6. It was of course in order to prevent Irish seminarians from being exposed to republican thought while studying in France that St. Patrick's College, Maynooth, was set up in 1795. (At the outbreak of the United Irish uprising of 1798 Wolfe Tone was in France, where Robert Emmett, expelled from Trinity College for nationalism in 1798, and other exiled United Irishmen fled in 1800–2.)

27. Quoted, Osborn, "Travel Literature," 297 n. 27. Although Byron finds the Turks more courageous than the Greeks, his politics were clear.

28. Alvin Redman, *The House of Hanover* (New York, 1968), 277.

29. Alexis de Tocqueville, *Journeys in England and Ireland*, trans. George Lawrence and K. P. Mayer, ed. J. P. Mayer (Garden City, N.Y., 1968), 133, emphasis added. The bishop's thankfulness is not extreme: in 1793, with initial suffrage, Catholics were led to believe that their support of the Union would lead to full religious liberty. To the delight of Unionists, George III left them stranded.

30. Cappot, as quoted in Pauly, *Voyageurs*, 197.

31. Michael Petzet, *Soufflots Sainte-Geneviève und der französische Kirchenbau des 18. Jahrhunderts* (Berlin, 1961); Wolfgang Hermann, *Laugier and Eighteenth-Century French Theory* (London, 1962); R. D. Middleton, "The Abbé Cordemoy and the Greco-Gothic Ideal," *Journal of the Warburg and Courtauld Institutes*, 25 (1962), 278–320, and 26 (1963), 90–123; and my teacher Dorothea Nyberg's " 'La Sainte Antiquité': Focus of an Eighteenth-Century Architectural Debate," in *Essays in the History of Architecture Presented to Rudolf Wittkower* (London, 1967), 159–69, and other writings by her. The possible influence of Berkeley's *Alciphron; or, The Minute Philosopher* (1732), written in America, on this Continental line of thought is disputed, though with his textual and grammatical dedication to Roman precedent and tradition, Chambers had to stand against Berkeley and also Hogarth, both of whom " 'favoured' in no uncertain terms the [immediate, noncitational] identification of fitness and beauty"; Hermann, *Laugier*, 166 n. 63, 177; on the affirmative side, in the matter of protofunctionalism, see Marcus Whiffen, "Bishop Berkeley," *Architectural Review*, 123 (1958), 91–3.

32. Middleton, "Cordemoy," 100 n. 2.

33. Nyberg, " 'Sainte Antiquité.' " The phrase "sainte antiquité" had been used in the mid-seventeenth century with respect to Roman art and thought: see Karl Heinrich Rengstorf, "Antike und Christentum: Probleme und Aufgaben," *Arbeitsgemein-*

schaft für Forschung des Landes Nordrhein-Westfalen: Geisteswissenschaften, 17 (1953), 23–39, esp. 24–5 n. 3b.

34. In England, there is a Hawksmoor design of c. 1711–12 for a "Basilica after the Primitive Christians," with a notation on the "Manner of Building the Church – as it was in ye fourth century in ye purest times of Christianity": Kerry Downes, *Hawksmoor* (London, 1959), 163 with pl. 52a. See now also Pierre de la Ruffinière du Prey, "Hawksmoor's 'Basilica after the Primitive Christians': Architecture and Theology," *Journal of the Society of Architectural Historians,* 48 (1989), 38–52, reproducing (fig. 3 on 49) a plate in *Sacrum Antiochenum consilium* (Antwerp, 1681), by Emmanuel Schelstrate (like Allacci a Vatican librarian), showing ground plan as given in *De Templis,* and exploring the anti-Romanism in contemporary Anglican admiration for such Byzantine things.

35. Jacques-François Blondel, *Cours d'architecture; ou, traité de la décoration, distribution et construction des bâtiments,* (Paris, 1771), vol. 1, 410. Chambers is said to have studied under Blondel in Paris in 1749–50, i.e., too early to have been shaken in the crisis of Hellenism. Neither does it matter that Blondel spoke so absolutely of Greek forms, for his Greece was an ideal projected through Vitruvius, not something that could be seen and measured; see Rykwert, *First Moderns,* 113–15.

36. George Hersey, *The Lost Meaning of Classical Architecture: Speculations on Ornament from Vitruvius to Venturi* (Cambridge, Mass., 1988), 53.

37. As to designs, there are two unsigned drawings, a plan and a section; illustrating them in their catalog, *Irish Architectural Drawings: An Exhibition to Commemorate the 25th Anniversary of the Irish Architectural Records Association* (Dublin, Belfast, and London, 1965), nos. 90, 91, Craig and Glin note the authorship as "uncertain," mentioning several old attributions of the building.

    The windows in question are not true Roman thermal (from *thermae,* "baths") type because they are not divided by vertical mullions into three lights. In England, large thermal or "Diocletian" windows already occur transeptually as well as in the front wall of Joseph Bonomi's square-plan Great Packington Church, 1789–92, in Warwickshire, with hefty Greek Doric columns supporting the corners of the "crossing" vaults that constitute the nave: see Damie Stillman, "Church Architecture in Neo-Classical England," *Journal of the Society of Architectural Historians,* 38 (1979), 103–19, esp. for figs. 10 on p. 108, 21 on p. 114.

38. G. N. Wright, *An Historical Guide to Ancient and Modern Dublin, Illustrated by Engravings After Designs by George Petrie, Esq.* (London, 1821), 175.

39. M. McCarthy, "Paestum," discusses Johnston's own early adoptions of the baseless Doric order; for Johnston's drawing of the Nelson Pillar, in the National Library, see Craig and Glin, *Irish Architectural Drawings,* cat. no. 16, with plate. It was also in 1808 that a Doric north porch was added to the lord lieutenant's house, now Áras an Uachtaráin, in the Phoenix Park, Dublin, to be followed by the addition of Francis Johnston's Ionic south porch in 1815–16; Killanin and Duignan, *Shell Guide,* 259.

40. According to Anthony Cutler, in the introduction to his edition of Leo Allatios, *The Newer Temples of the Greeks* (University Park, Pa., 1969), 19, while in Ottoman Greece churches could be built by tending bribes, "the Christian dome or tower might not compete with a minaret, although there is no body of legislation in which to find such a restriction."

41. Article 7 provided that "no benefits of this act shall extend . . . to any popish ecclesiastic who shall officiate in any church or chapel with a steeple or bell"; "An

Act for the Further Relief of His Majesty's Subjects of this Kingdom Professing the Popish Religion," in Edmund Curtis and R. B. McDowell, *Irish Historical Documents* (London, 1942), 196–8. The same act also prohibited Catholics from using any symbol or title. To my knowledge the only scholar who has noticed the prohibition against steeples is Alphons Bellesheim, *Geschichte der katholischen Kirche in Irland,* vol. 3 (Mainz, 1891), 56, 132, 731, and even he does not draw the architectural inference. In a letter of April 17, 1977, Patrik Reutersward wrote me on this point: "I wonder if 'steeple' stands for church tower in general, and that the law prohibited Catholics from having church towers in general with bells – in the same sense as the Catholics in Holland during the 17th and 18th centuries were forbidden to have visible churches at all."

42. It is ironic that a Scottish (crypto-)Catholic, James Gibbs, should have designed the neo-Palladian Saint Martin-in-the-Fields, London (1721–6), in America and elsewhere in the former British Empire (until the Oxford Movement) the proto-typical Anglican church, with steeple over pedimented temple-front.

43. See Joseph Masheck, "Irish Gothic Theory Before Pugin," *Studies* (Dublin), 70, nos. 228–9 (Summer–Autumn 1981), 206–19, esp. 212–15.

44. According to J. M. Frew, "Gothic is English: John Carter and the Revival of the Gothic as England's National Style," *Art Bulletin,* 64 (1982), 315–19, after Walpole suggested (from 1762) that Gothic, lacking in "simplicity and proportion," had otherwise improved upon classical architecture, Carter, as draftsman and coauthor in *Builder's Magazine,* in 1775–8, cautioned not to "condemn . . . Gothic entirely, but as occasion serves and the subject requires, give preference to it" – obviously, for associative affect, in churches. James Essex thought (1777) Gothic masons "had a taste well adapted to the religion and genius of the age in which they lived." Carter, anti-French and antirepublican, suggested in 1801 that "English" substitute for "Gothic"; and when George Whittington showed the French origins of Gothic, *Historical Survey of the Ecclesiastical Antiquities of France* (1809), Carter accused him of "travelled prejudice," "blind delusion," "dark deviation," "Gallic scientific presumption." Cf. Engels, *Condition of the Working Class in England* (1845) on new "elisabetheischen" villas as, to Gothic, what Anglicanism is to "the apostolic Roman Catholic religion" (chap. 3).

45. John Milner, *An Inquiry into Certain Vulgar Opinions Concerning the Catholic Inhabitants and the Antiquities of Ireland* (London, 1808), 264n.

46. Ibid., 260.

47. Brian Little, *Catholic Churches Since 1623: A Study of Roman Catholic Churches in England and Wales from Penal Times to the Present Day* (London, 1966), 54; the architect was Joseph Ireland.

48. See Cutler, "A Baroque Account of Byzantine Architecture: Leone Allacci's *De Templis Graecorum recentioribus,*" *Journal of the Society of Architectural Historians,* 25 (1966), 79–89, as well as his ed. of Allatios (note 40).

49. University of Dublin, Trinity College, *Catalogus librorum impressorum,* (Dublin, 1864), vol. 1, 46–7; the catalog, begun in 1835, accounts for at least four copies of *De Templis* and some 40 other works and editions of Allacci.

50. The cornerstone was laid by the Dublin coadjutor, Daniel Murray, titular Archbishop of Hierapolis; Bellesheim, *Geschichte,* vol. 3, 350. Hierapolis is an important early Christian site in Turkey.

51. Dermod McCarthy, *Saint Mary's Pro-Cathedral, Dublin,* Irish Heritage Series, 60 (Dublin, 1988), unpaginated, votes for Sweetman after further complicating the

issue by claiming (without reference), "A more likely opinion is that...the architect was...Louis Hippolyte leBas, whose Parisian church of Notre Dame de Lorette closely resembles St. Mary's." While it is not wrongheaded to think of Le Bas (or Lebas; 1782–1867), owing to the Paris church's strongly early Christian basilican aspect, nevertheless Notre-Dame-de-Lorette, built after the Pro-Cathedral between 1832 and 1836, has a Corinthian porch and a flat, coffered ceiling over the nave; see Bernard Violle, *Paris: Son église et ses églises: histoire, art, foi*, 2 vols. (Paris, 1982), vol. 2, 328–9, with illus. Le Bas was the teacher of two famous architects, Labrouste and Garnier; for the Lorette porch he used drawings of the Corinthian order by the former, otherwise known as a protomodernist: Pierre Saddy, *Henri Labrouste, architecte, 1801–1875* (Paris, 1977), 14, with illus.

52. McParland, "Who Was P?" *Architectural Review*, 157, no. 935 (January 1975), 71–3 with illus. of the building, the early drawings for it and the giant model.

53. Craig, *The Architecture of Ireland from the Earliest Times to 1880* (London, 1982), 188, 254.

54. M. McCarthy, "Paestum," 161. Troy is briefly mentioned near the end of the "Laestrygonians" episode of Joyce's *Ulysses* (1922), curiously enough just before a mistaken but telling thought of Greek Revival architecture. According to Don Gifford and Robert J. Seidman, *Ulysses Annotated: Notes for James Joyce's "Ulysses"* (Berkeley, Calif., 1988), 187, the phrase "Solemn as Troy" occurring there negatively memorializes him in the popular mind for having condemned the 1798 rebellion and supported the Act of Union. Apart from the question of what choices Troy had, this tends to flatten a contextual Joycean irony, for Bloom is actually likening a self-important *Freemason* to the famous archbishop: "Sir Frederick Falkiner going into the freemasons' hall. Solemn as Troy. After his good lunch in Earlsfort terrace. Old legal cronies attacking a magnum..." (*Ulysses*, The Modern Library, [New York, 1961] 182). As Bloom approaches the National Library and thinks, "Sir Thomas Deane was the Greek architecture" (*Ulysses*, 183), pedantic concern with correcting the authorship of that all too Roman building (as by Sir Thomas [Newenham] Deane II) risks obscuring the more remarkable fact that the Greek Revival is something Leopold Bloom did think about.

55. Craig, *Architecture*, 261. To complain that in this great church as executed the "giant lunettes...[span] three bays in a pendentive-and-dome arrangement in no way prepared-for by any inflection of the Doric colonnade below" might even reflect on such a happy conjunction of giant ultra-Roman lunettes over (straight Corinthian) colonnades as in Soufflot's great Ste. Geneviève.

56. If I exaggerate at all, it is to compensate for the superficial sense of styles, revived styles all the more, as merely so many flavors.

57. Even eighteenth-century Hellenism may have carried political overtones: at least two of the early British travelers to study Greek architecture were known Jacobites, one of them, James Dalkins, exiled from England; Wiebenson, *Sources*, 55. Henry, the last Stuart pretender, who thirty years later would have a medal struck identifying himself as King Henry IX of England, "not by the grace of man, but of God," was in 1758 consecrated titular Archbishop of Corinth by Pope Clement XIII; Alice Shield, *Henry Stuart, Cardinal of York, and His Times* (London, 1908), 170.

58. Peter Augustine Baines, *An Inquiry into the Nature, Object and Obligations of the Religion of Christ; with a Comparison of the Ancient and Modern Christianity of England* (Bath, 1824), 51, 61.

59. Baines, *Outlines of Christianity; Being the Substance of Six Lectures Delivered in the Catholic Chapel, Pierrepont Place, Bath, During the Sundays in Lent, 1839* (Bath, 1839), 24.

60. Denis Gwynn, *Lord Shrewsbury, Pugin and the Gothic Revival* (London, 1946), 54–5.

61. Arthur Schopenhauer, *The World as Will and Representation*, trans. E. F. J. Payne (Indian Hills, Colo., 1958), vol. 2, 339.

62. Hermann, Fürst von Pückler-Muskau, *Tour in England, Ireland and France in the Years 1826, 1827, 1828, and 1829* (Philadelphia, 1833), 422.

63. Schopenhauer, *World*, vol. 2, 413.

64. James MacCaffrey, *History of the Catholic Church in the Nineteenth Century (1798–1908)*, 2d ed. (Dublin, 1910), vol. 1, 287.

65. The personal closeness of the Bavarian crown prince Maximilian to his uncle by marriage, Friedrich Wilhelm, crown prince of Prussia, led to a major project by the Berlin architect Schinkel for a more ambitious royal palace integrated with the ancient buildings of the Acropolis. Klenze, Schinkel's Munich counterpart, planned to restore the actual Parthenon, proceeding as far as a cornerstone-laying by the new king in 1831. See Rand Carter, "Karl Friedrich Schinkel's Project for a Royal Palace on the Acropolis," *Journal of the Society of Architectural Historians*, 38 (1979), 34–46.

66. He turned down an invitation to visit Greece with C. R. Cockerell (and also decided not to visit America), concerned as he was to build a reputation in Britain; Klaus Eggert, *Friedrich von Gärtner: der Baumeister König Ludwigs I* (Munich, 1963), 147.

67. "Ionische Kirche mit kleinen Thurmkuppeln, gewölbten Fenstern an den Seitenfronten, Balustern und ohne Mittelthür": Karl Friedrich Schinkel, *Aus Schinkel's Nachlass: Reisetagebücher, Briefe und Aphorismen*, ed. Alfred von Wolzogen (Berlin, 1863), 116.

68. Hitchcock, *Architecture*, 70.

69. MacCaffrey, *History*, vol. 2, 43.

70. On the philhellenism of Ludwig as crown prince, and of Frederick Tiersch, and on the Munich Greek community, see Emmanuel Turczynski, *Die deutschgreichischen Kulturbeziehungen bis zur Berufung König Ottos*, Südeuropäische Arbeiten, 47 (Munich, 1959), 245–50; also, on German concern for the Orthodox Church under Turkish rule, 164–78.

71. MacCaffrey, *History*, vol. 1, 109. A revival of Catholic liturgical music, too, finds a mid-nineteenth-century Irish parallel, since the Dublin Pro-Cathedral was soon endowed with a special choir to sing plainchant and polyphony; ibid., vol. 2, 489.

72. Leo von Klenze, *Anweisung zur Architektur des christlichen Kultus* (Munich, 1834), 22. Oswald Herderer, *Leo von Klenze: Persönlichkeit und Werke* (Munich, 1964), 387, gives 1833 as the date of the first edition, while a copy in the Avery Memorial Architectural Library of Columbia University carries the date 1822.

73. According to D. McCarthy, *Saint Mary's*, the Cathedral Street entrance peristyle was walled up in 1928. Its von Klenzean, propylean aspect was only highlighted thereby.

74. George Davie, "The Scottish Enlightenment" (1981), in his *The Scottish Enlightenment and Other Essays* (Edinburgh, 1991), 1–50, esp. 39–43.

75. Graham Law, "Greek Thomson," *Architectural Review*, 115 (1954), 307–16.

76. Masheck, *Irish Church-Building*, 154–7, with pls. 100, 103.

77. With this last element, one thinks of the Greek temple tower of Patrick Byrne's

Franciscan Church, Merchant's Quay, Dublin, of c. 1830 and after. The church, known as "Adam and Eve's" from a pub sign of penal times, has the distinction of being mentioned in the first line of Joyce's *Finnegans Wake*.

78. In the Dublin church Pückler-Muskau admired the "excellent alto-relievo" of the *Ascension* in the apse, over the altar; *Tour*.

79. On which see Robert Rosenblum, *Transformations in Late Eighteenth-Century Art* (Princeton, N.J., 1970), 29, 40, 79ff., 95.

80. Henry Hatfield, *Aesthetic Paganism in German Literature from Winckelmann to the Death of Goethe* (Cambridge, Mass., 1964), 142–81.

81. Crook, *Greek Revival*, 23, denying that there was "a native Greek Revival tradition" in Ireland, likens the country to Wales. If anything, Scotland, with an important Greek Revival architecture and also its own strong Jacobite political tradition, could furnish a more telling parallel.

82. Jeanne Sheehy, "The Nineteenth and Twentieth Centuries," in Peter Harbison, Homan Potterton and Jeanne Sheehy, *Irish Art and Architecture from Prehistory to the Present* (London, 1978), 189, 191–3; see also Brian de Breffny and George Mott, *The Churches and Abbeys of Ireland* (New York, 1976), 142–3.

83. Illus., ibid., fig. 201 (Portaferry) on 193.

84. Matthew J. McDermott and Aodhagán Brioscú, *Dublin's Architectural Development, 1800–1925* (Dublin, 1988).

85. Craig, *Architecture*, chap. 16, esp. 257–63.

3. An American Utopian Schoolhouse Design

1. Barbara Wriston, "The Use of Architectural Handbooks in the Design of School-houses from 1840–1860," *Journal of the Society of Architectural Historians*, 22 (1963), 155–60.

2. Ibid., figs. 4, 5 on p. 157.

3. Although both projects are said to have been reprinted in "the many editions of Barnard's *School Architecture*" (ibid., 156), I do not find them in the second edition (New York, 1854) of Henry Barnard, *Practical Illustrations of the Principles of School Architecture*. One undated edition, possibly an 1850 reprint, shows a Westerly, R.I., version of the rectangular school (Wriston, "Architectural Handbooks," 156 n. 4) but does not show the octagonal school.

4. Alonzo Potter and George B. Emerson, *The School and the Schoolmaster* (New York, 1842), 549.

5. New-York Historical Society, A. J. Davis, Misc. manuscripts.

6. Avery Architectural and Fine Arts Library, Columbia University, New York, Davis Collection, R2–30a, 30b, 30c.

7. Potter and Emerson, *School*, 527–8.

8. Ibid., 526. *Convenient*, here, is an important word, for the French *convenance* carries the implication of Vitruvian *decorum*, of socially significant dignity.

9. *Henry Barnard's School Architecture*, ed. Jean and Robert McClintock, Classics in Education, 42 (New York, 1970), "Plan, &c., of an Octagonal School-House Furnished for the *School and Schoolmaster* by Messrs. Town and Davis," 135–42, with figs. 11–14, here 136–7, 135, respectively.

10. Victor Cousin, *Oeuvres*, vol. 3 (Brussels, 1841): pl. 1, "Maison d'école de campagne pour une petite commune"; pl. 2, "Maison d'école communale de moyenne gran-deur"; pl. 3, "Maison d'école pour 40 enfans, avec logement de l'instituteur"; pl.

4, "Maison d'école à 2 classes pour 60 élèves chacune, avec logemens pour 2 instituteurs"; pl. 5, "Maison d'école à 2 classes pour 100 enfans chacune, avec logemens pour 2 instituteurs"; pl. 6, "Maison d'école à 3 classes de 50 élèves chacune, avec logemens pour 3 instituteurs"; pl. 7, "Maison d'école à 3 classes de 30 élèves chacune, avec le logement pour l'instituteur."

11. Vincent-Augustin Fribault, "Dissertation sur la métaphysique de la géometrie," in Cousin, *Fragments philosophiques*, 3d ed. (Paris, 1838), vol. 1, 376–410.

12. Bertha-Maria Marenholtz-Bülow, *Woman's Educational Mission; Being an Explanation of Friedrich Froebel's System of Infant Gardens* (London, 1855), 55.

13. Frank Lloyd Wright, *An Autobiography* (London, 1933), 11 (emphasis in original). For the considerable bibliography on sometimes conflicting interpretations of the Froebel "gifts," see Edgar Kaufmann, Jr., " '*Form* Became *Feeling*': A New View of Froebel and Wright," *Journal of the Society of Architectural Historians,* 40 (1981), 130–7. Kaufmann points out that the blocks could not have inspired any sense of space: they were solids, not meant for building walls to be roofed over, and were to be reassembled after play into a solid cubical mass. Helpfully, he discusses the reception of the Froebelian "kindergarten" in America before the Philadelphia Centennial Exposition of 1876, reproducing two entire chapters from Nina C. Vandewalker's *The Kindergarten in American Education* (New York, 1908) (133–7). It is now clearer what the early dissemination of the kindergarten ideal owed to German-Americans of the Midwest (with their liberal and leftist refugee heritage of 1848, not discussed by Kaufmann); while on the Anglo-American side, Henry Barnard had been impressed hearing Froebel's disciple Marenholz-Bülow speak in London in 1854, and Edna D. Cheney and Anna Q. T. Parsons, also stimulated by Marenholz-Bülow, published an article on the kindergarten in the *Christian Examiner* in 1859. Kaufmann has also written on "Frank Lloyd Wright's Mementos of Childhood," in the same *Journal* (41 [1982], 232–7); there too Jeanne S. Rubin has since published "The Froebel-Wright Kindergarten Connection: A New Perspective" (48 [1989], 24ff.), pointing out that before taking up pedagogy Froebel himself had attained eminence in crystallography, and suggesting how a fascination with helical crystal dislocation may well extend through the Froebel "gift" blocks to the plans of even late Wright projects.

14. Marenholtz-Bülow, *Woman's Educational Mission,* 59 (emphasis mine).

15. Friedrich Froebel, *The Education of Man,* trans. Josephine Jarvis (New York, 1885), 5. Significantly, when Froebel speaks out against models "in form" rather than "in nature" (1.10), he carefully confines his remarks to models of behavior: he is not speaking generally against models "in form." Anyway, imagery of this sort, German Romantic in origin, will reappear in the thought of expressionist architects in the early twentieth century; see below, Chapter 10.

16. There is hint of a possible psychological predisposition on Froebel's part for a school at least freestanding, if not centrally planned: "A notable influence upon the development and formation of my character was . . . exercised by the position of my parents' house. It was closely surrounded by other buildings, walls, hedges, fences, and was further enclosed by an outer courtyard, a paddock, and a kitchen-garden. Beyond these latter I was strictly forbidden to pass. The dwelling had no other outlook than on to the buildings to right and left, the big church in front, and at the back the sloping fields stretching up a high hill. For a long time I remained thus deprived of any distant view . . . my perceptions were in this manner limited to the nearest objects." Froebel, *Autobiography,* trans. and ed. Emile Mi-

chaelis and H. Keatley Moore, 12th ed. (London, 1915), 6. For a picture of Froebel's own school at Keilhau, see Arnold H. Heinemann, ed., *Froebel Letters* (Boston, 1893), 60.

17. Froebel, *Education*, 205. This section is entitled, significantly, "Exercise in and for Outward Corporeal Representation in Space, Advancing According to Rule and Law from the Simple to the Compound."

18. Thieme-Becker, *Allgemeines Lexikon der Bildenden Künstler*, q.v. Furttenbach.

19. Marie Luise Gothein, *A History of Garden Art*, trans. Mrs. Archer-Hunt, ed. Walter P. Wright, 2 vols. (London, n. d.), vol. 2, fig. 373 on p. 26. I do not, however, find this plate in an edition of *Architectura civilis*, which is given as source here (vol. 1, p. ix) and in the original, *Geschichte der Gartenkunste* (Jena, 1914), vol. 1, 479.

20. Joseph Furttenbach, *Architectura universalis* (Ulm, 1635): pl. 16, "Erste Grundriss zu der Schul"; pl. 17, "Ander Grundriss zu der Schul."

21. Alexander Jackson Davis, *Rural Residences; Consisting of Designs, Original and Selected, for Cottages, Farm-Houses, Villas and Village Churches, with Brief Explanations, Estimates and a Specification of Materials, Construction etc.* (New York, 1837; repr., New York, 1980), unpaginated. Thanks to James S. Ackerman for recalling the *Rural Residences* design as churchlike.

22. See Georg Hermann, *Die protestantische Kirchenbau in der Schweiz von der Reformation bis zur Romantik* (Zurich, 1963), 25–39.

23. George W. Dolbey, *The Architectural Expression of Methodism: The First Hundred Years* (London, 1964), chap. 5, "The Octagonal Chapels," 97–115.

24. Elizabeth B. Mock's Museum of Modern art survey, *The Architecture of Bridges* (New York, 1949), 34, with illus.

25. Talbot Hamlin, *Greek Revival Architecture in America* (1944; repr. New York, 1964), 137–41.

26. Ibid., 324.

27. "There is a peculiar beauty in mechanical work of every kind, when well executed; no matter what is the object of the article, no matter how homely the purpose to which it is applied. . . . Many a man whose walks are in intellectual paths might learn a good lesson from this. How perfect . . . the machines! How beautiful the workmanship of everything! How admirable the finish! Here, indeed, we seem to have found perfection": "The First Exhibition and Fair of the Massachusetts Charitable Mechanics Association," *North American Review*, 46 (January 1838), 312–14; quoted in Elisabeth Fellows Andrus, *Measure and Design in American Painting, 1760–1860*, Ph.D. dissertation, Columbia University (New York, 1976).

28. Sigfried Giedion, *Architecture and the Phenomena of Transition: Three Space Conceptions in Architecture* (Cambridge, Mass., 1971), 80, where the implication, rather more subtle than vulgar functionalism allowed, is that in its very nonclassical resort to engineering, John Smeaton's lighthouse is, shall we say, *abstractly neo-Roman*. Ralph Waldo Emerson, "Thoughts on Art," reprinted from *Dial*, 1 no. 3 (January 1841), 367–78, in John W. McCoubrey, ed., *American Art, 1700–1960: Sources and Documents* (Englewood Cliffs. N.J., 1965), 71–80, here 71: "The conscious utterance of thought, by speech or action, to any end, is Art. From the [child's] . . . first pile of toys or chip bridge, to the masonry of Eddystone lighthouse or the Erie canal. . . . from the simplest expedient of private prudence to the American constitution. . . . Art is the spirit's voluntary use and combination of things to serve its end." (Maybe that, in its American way, is neo-Roman too?)

29. Johann Heinrich Pestalozzi, *Sämmtliche Schriften*, 15 vols. (Stuttgart, 1819–26).

30. See Froebel, *Autobiography*, 29, 31, 41, 45–52.

31. J. and R. McClintock, introd. to *Barnard's School Architecture*, 5 with n. 7.
32. Sibyl Moholy-Nagy, *Native Genius in Anonymous Architecture in North America* (New York, 1957; repr., 1976), 132–33 with illus. (Fort Edgecomb, Maine, as army-engineer designed, possibly stimulated by eighteenth-century octagonal Fort Erie), 120–21 with illus. (Circular Stone Barn, New Lebanon, N.Y.), respectively.
33. Carl Carmer, *My Kind of Country: Favorite Writings About New York* (New York, 1966), 145–8; thanks to Thomas Nozkowski for the reference.
34. Ward E. Hermann, *Spans of Time: Covered Bridges of Delaware County, New York* (Delhi, N.Y., 1974), 45. I am grateful to Wesley and Martha Burczak for this reference.
35. Barnard, *School Architecture*, 141.
36. Rudolf Wittkower, "English Literature on Architecture" (unpub. lecture, 1966), in his *Palladio and Palladianism*, ed. Margot Wittkower (New York, 1974), 93–112, esp. 108.
37. Louis H. Sullivan, *Kindergarten Chats and Other Writings*, rev. ed., ed. Isabella Athey (1918; New York, 1947, repr. 1979), 100.

4. Note on Sullivan and the Rarefaction of Bodily Beauty

1. Elizabeth Gilmore Holt, ed., *From the Classicists to the Impressionists: Art and Architecture in the 19th Century*, A Documentary History of Art, vol. 3 (New Haven, Conn., 1986), 200 (editorial comment).
2. Louis H. Sullivan, *The Autobiography of an Idea* (1924; ed. New York, 1956), 246, "He discerned that in truth the science of engineering is a science of *reaction*, while the science of architectural design – were such a thing to be presupposed – must be a science of *action*."
3. This was clear even in the sophisticated brazenness of his wisecracks against Whitman's beloved New York. Consider some thoughts entertained in the run-on dialogue of "Kindergarten Chats" (1901–2): on the Montgomery Ward Building, Chicago: "a rather rancid, New-Yorky flavor"; or on the Cathedral of Saint John the Divine: "there isn't anything divine about it; it seems more like a temple of Mammon." "Well – St. John or Mammon; it's all one in New York; and I am not sure that they are two elsewhere." Further: "I wish to inquire why New York with all its wealth, and, therefore, its great power to build, has not the best, as it should have, but, on the exact contrary, the most decadent, the most bumptious architecture in the country. I wish to ferret out the reason. That there is a fundamental crookedness of attitude is evident. Indeed it is something worse than that! It is akin to rapine. No chivalry, no scruple there!" Sullivan, *Kindergarten Chats and Other Writings* (1918), ed. Isabella Athey (New York, 1947, repr. 1979), 21, 75, 76, respectively.
4. E.g.: "That all this may be taken from the realms of the transcendental and brought into physical, tangible, even psychic reality, requires that the spirit of man breathe upon ideas the breath of his living powers that they stand forth, created in his image, in the image of his wish and will, as demonstrations of man's ego-power"; Sullivan, *A System of Architectural Ornament According with a Philosophy of Man's Powers* (New York, 1967), notes to pl. 5.
5. Evidence of "Schopenhauer in the Air" in turn-of-the-century American culture includes a pessimist short story under that title by the art critic Sadakichi Hartmann (collected in his *Schopenhauer in the Air: Seven Stories*, 1899). On Schopenhauer's influence on George Santayana's *Sense of Beauty* (1896), see Arthur C. Danto,

"Santayana's *The Sense of Beauty:* An Introduction," in Santayana, *The Sense of Beauty: Being the Outlines of Aesthetic Theory*, ed. William G. Holzberger and Herman J. Saatkamp, Jr. (*Works*, Critical Edition, vol. 2), (Cambridge, Mass., 1988), here xxii–xxiii.

6. Unable to find both quotations exactly in published texts of Wilde, I here follow Arthur Siegel, ed., *Chicago's Famous Buildings* (Chicago, 1965), 46. The larger American issue here is that of "The Virgin and the Dynamo," on which see Chapter 13, below.

7. On adumbrations of the Sullivanian notion of "form follows function" in Baudelaire as well as Ruskin and Viollet-le-Duc, see Peter Collins, *Changing Ideals in Modern Architecture, 1750–1950* (London, 1965), 155–6.

8. John Ruskin, *Modern Painters of Truth and Theoretic Faculties,* vol. 2 (Boston and New York, n.d.), 254.

9. Andrew Jackson Downing, *The Architecture of Country Houses* (New York, 1850), quoted in John A. Kouwenhoven, *Made in America* (1948), repr. as *The Artist in Modern American Civilization* (New York, 1967), 96.

10. Sullivan, "On Poetry," *Kindergarten Chats,* 158–61, here 160.

11. See Chapter 6, this volume.

12. Philip Steadman, *The Evolution of Designs: Biological Analogy in Architecture and the Applied Arts,* Cambridge Urban and Architectural Studies (Cambridge, 1979), chap. 3, 23–32.

13. Paolo Rossi, "The Nature-Art Relationship and the Machine of the World" (1962), in his *Philosophy, Technology, and the Arts in the Early Modern Era,* trans. Salvator Attanasio, ed. Benjamin Nelson (New York, 1970), 137–45, here 142, quoting Gassendi's *Syntagma philosophiae Epicuri* (1649).

14. Louis Agassiz, "Evolution and Permanence of Type," in *The Intelligence of Louis Agassiz: A Specimen Book of Scientific Writings,* ed. Guy Davenport (Boston, 1963), 215–32, here 228.

15. Sullivan, *System,* notes to pl. 2.

16. On which see Ananda K. Coomaraswamy, "Ornament," *Art Bulletin,* 21 (1939), 375–82.

17. Steadman, *Evolution,* 154–8; there is also Donald Drew Egbert, "The Idea of Organic Expression and American Architecture," in S. Persons, ed., *Evolutionary Thought in America* (New Haven, 1950).

18. Sullivan, *System,* note to pl. 4. On the seed trope, see Steadman, *Evolution,* 154, noting the likely influence of Sullivan's reading Edmund Beecher Wilson, *The Cell in Development and Inheritance* (1896) and repeatedly "redrawing Wilson's diagrams of the stages of mitosis from memory."

19. Collins, *Changing Ideals,* 115.

20. Ibid., 116.

21. In Joseph Masheck, "Irish Gothic Theory Before Pugin," *Studies* (Dublin), 70 (1981), 206–19, esp. 219 n. 50, I have instanced Ruskin's *two-page* rant against Catholic Emancipation, "Note 1" appended to *The Seven Lamps of Architecture* (1849), plus the following in *The Stones of Venice* (1851–3): an extended excerpt from a journalistic tirade published by his father in 1839 (vol. 1, Appendix 5); a wisecrack in the discussion of the quality of savageness (vol. 2, chap. 6, p. 15); and a highly prejudiced remark on Irish juries (vol. 2, chap. 8, p. 128).

22. Ruskin, "Lectures on Architecture and Painting," in his *Pre-Raphaelitism; Lectures on Architecture and Painting,* Everyman's Library (London and New York, 1907; repr. 1920), 98 with figs. 18, 17, respectively, on p. 99.

23. James F. O'Gorman, *Three American Architects: Richardson, Sullivan, and Wright* (Chicago, 1991), 87–8. On Sullivan and modernism: Michael Mostoller, "Louis Sullivan's Ornament," *Artforum*, 16, no. 2 (October 1977), 43–9. Sullivan's ornamental "sources" in European protomodern stylized vegetal ornament (*underpinnings* would be a better term) have been studied rather pedantically. Paul E. Sprague, "The European Sources of Louis Sullivan's Ornamental Style" (abstract of paper), *Journal of the Society of Architectural Historians*, 33 (1974), 167, concentrates, relevantly for the present discussion, on the late Gothic Revival stream, after 1860, within the British design movement (relying on a dubious notion of "originality"). Theodore Turak, "French and English Sources of Sullivan's Ornament and Doctrine," *Prairie School Review*, 11, no. 4 (1974), 5–28, 31, unconvincing in details, notices usefully Victor Ruprich-Robert's *Flore ornementale* (Paris, 1866) and his contributions to the *Révue Générale de l'Architecture et Travaux Publics* (1853, 1870), which Sullivan had. One wonders about the American's possible influence upon European modernists. Mostoller illustrates (48) a Sullivan-Wright drawing of the 1880s that anticipates the famous Central European art nouveau whiplash designs of an Olbrist wall hanging and of Endell's Studio Elivira facade, Munich. Some Sullivan ornament designs were published before the turn of the century in America (*Engineering Magazine*, August 1892; *Forms and Fantasies*, June 1898, with photos of his own roses; *Brush and Pencil*, April 1899).
24. Sullivan, *Autobiography*, 107.
25. J. B. Robinson, *Architectural Foliage Adapted from Nature*, (New York, 1868[?]); e.g. pl. 4, giving oak, fern, ivy, and snapdragon "crockets."
26. Paul E. Bolin, "The Massachusetts Drawing Act of 1870: Industrial Mandate or Democratic Maneuver?" in Donald Soucy and Mary Ann Stankiewicz, eds., *Framing the Past: Essays on Art Education* (Reston, Va., 1990), 58–86.
27. Sullivan, *Autobiography*, 165–6.
28. O'Gorman, *Three American Architects*, 74.
29. Bolin, "Massachusetts Drawing Act," 65.
30. Charles A. Barry, *Primer of Design* (Boston, 1878), fig. 1 in "Historical Ornament" plates at end. To Barry, natural and historical-artistic sources are effectively interchangeable; see chap. 7, "Progressive Steps in Elementary Design," 45, para. 37.
31. Willard Connely, *Louis Sullivan: The Shaping of American Architecture* (New York, 1960), chaps. 2–6.
32. Ibid., 44.
33. Ibid., 66.
34. Ibid., 73.
35. Ibid., 74; Sullivan, *Autobiography*, 207.
36. Quoted, ibid., 83.
37. W. H. Goodyear, *The Grammar of the Lotus: A New History of Classic Ornament as a Development of Sun Worship; with Observations on the "Bronze Culture" of Prehistoric Europe as Derived from Egypt; Based on the Study of Patterns* (London, 1891), 43–66.
38. Ibid., fig. 8 on p. 29, repeated large on p. 104. Apropos of the lotus cult in the 1890s: for the February 1896 issue of a cultural journal newly renamed *The Lotos* the Boston orientalist Ernest Fenollosa wrote on "The Symbolism of the Lotos" (a Buddhist motif rendered *symboliste*), emblematizing the opposition between Oriental and Western cultural mentalities with the flower and an architectural element – "the Lotos and the Arch." If he sounds Sullivanian likening the lotus "lift[ing] from the pool of sense . . . a perfect harmony of individually curved petals

in blossom" to "a self-determined, self-harmonious individual" (quoted in Lawrence W. Chisolm, *Fenollosa: The Far East and American Culture,* Yale Publications
in American Studies, 8 [New Haven, Conn., 1963], 122–6; quotation, 125), Sullivan
had already set the same pitch.

39. Lauren S. Weingarten, "Louis H. Sullivan: Investigation of a Second French Connection," *Journal of the Society of Architectural Historians,* 39 (1980), 297–303.

40. Sullivan, *Autobiography,* 240.

41. No incidental feature of Le Corbusier's work, nor of the problem of a new "academy," this topic has a considerable literature. I quote from Klaus Herdeg, *The
Decorated Diagram: Harvard Architecture and the Failure of the Bauhaus Legacy* (Cambridge, Mass., 1983), 18, a critique that stands apart from now commonplace
antimodern philistinism.

42. Arthur Drexler, ed., *The Architecture of the Ecole des Beaux-Arts* (New York, 1977),
pl. on p. 312, with unsigned caption. On the academic encouragement of concentric
mise au point du plan, the "centrifugal or peripherical organization around a point,"
as promulgated academically by Jules André and codified, with special graphic
conventions, in Gaudet, *Elements et théories de l'architecture* (1894), see Mohamed
Chaoui, *The Rhetoric of Composition in Julien Gaudet's Elements et Théories,* Ph.D.
dissertation, University of Pennsylvania, 1987, esp. 175–9, with ref. to Richard
A. Moore, "Academic Design Theory in France After the Reorganisation of 1863,"
Journal of the Society of Architectural Historians, 36 (1977), 145–74. In the last year
of his life (1965) Le Corbusier wrote an essay, published as a little book, *Mise au
point* (Paris, 1966).

43. Santayana, *Sense of Beauty,* 24–5.

44. Ibid., 102.

45. Masheck, "Santayana: A Sentimental Education" (1975), in my *Historical Present:
Essays of the 1970s* (Ann Arbor, Mich., 1984), 15–31.

46. Now partly translated in Gottfried Semper, *The Four Elements of Architecture
and Other Writings,* trans. Harry Francis Mallgrave and and Wolfgang Herrmann,
Res Monographs in Anthropology and Aesthetics (Cambridge, 1989); there is
also Hermann's *Gottfried Semper: In Search of Architecture* (Cambridge,
Mass., 1984).

47. Aloïs Riegl, *Spätrömische Kunstindustrie* (1901), 2d ed. (Vienna, 1927; repr. Darmstadt, 1964), 9.

48. Santayana, *Sense of Beauty,* 134.

49. Ibid., 103.

50. Ibid., 134–5.

51. Sullivan, "Ornament in Architecture" (1892), *Kindergarten Chats,* 187–90, here 188;
further: "The ornament, as a matter of fact, is applied in the sense of being cut in
or cut on, or otherwise done: yet it should appear, when completed, as though
by the outworking of some beneficent agency it had come forth from the very
substance of the material and was there by the same right that a flower appears
amid the leaves of its parent plant" (189).

52. Santayana, *Sense of Beauty,* commentary by Holzberger and Saatkamp, 194.

53. Sullivan, "The Tall Office Building Artistically Considered" (1896), *Kindergarten
Chats,* 202–13, here 202.

54. Ibid., 205–6.

55. Sullivan, "What Is an Architect?" *Kindergarten Chats,* 135–42, here 138.

56. Ibid., 139.

57. Ibid., 140 (emphasis in original).

58. Ibid., 141.

59. Theodor Adorno, *Aesthetic Theory,* Engl. trans. (London, 1984), 322, as quoted by Hans Belting, *The End of the History of Art?,* 2d ed., trans. Christopher S. Wood (Chicago, 1987), 101 n. 31. Cf. Thoreau, quoted epigrammatically at the start of W. H. Auden's lecture "Making, Knowing and Judging" (1956), in his *The Dyer's Hand and Other Essays* (New York, 1968), 31–60: "The art of life, of a poet's life, is, not having anything to do, to do something."

60. Sullivan, *Autobiography,* 211.

5. De Chirico's Pathos of Lost Antiquity

1. Giorgio de Chirico, *Hebdomeros: A Novel,* trans. Margaret Crosland (New York, 1988), 27.

2. Friedrich Engels, *The Condition of the Working Class in England,* trans. and ed. W. O. Henderson and W. H. Chaloner (London, 1958; repr. Stanford, Calif., 1968), 52.

3. I have not made a detailed comparison of her translation side-by-side with the Flammarion edition, but the almost completely unrelieved flatness of the simple past cannot have escaped the translator, Crosland's, notice.

4. It is no accident that I get to think this way about de Chirico, at one remove from an artist with whom I have never before been particularly concerned, on the repainting of a considerable body of the master's work by the "appropriationist" Mike Bidlo, thanks to whom de Chirico's work now acquires for me an, as it were, more pluperfect historical depth in (re)representation, a deeper "pastness" that I tend to think it wanted all along. Thus the present essay derives from "The Pluperfection of de Chirico," written for the catalogue *Bidlo (Not de Chirico)* (Paris 1990), pp. 31–8. I appreciate Bidlo's encouragement of my recentering of it for the present context.

5. On de Chirico and the classicizing Novecento movement, which from 1931 fed into Italian fascist architecture, see Kenneth Frampton, *Modern Architecture: A Critical History* (New York, 1980), 203, 214–16.

6. See Charles Jencks, *The Language of Post-Modern Architecture,* rev. ed. (New York, 1977), 20, 91, where (91) Jencks characterizes Rossi's 1971 Modena Cemetery project as "perfect for dead people and De Chirico." Rossi's own denial of a fascist reading of his Chiricesque forms pales today, when, with East Europeans preparing to entertain their technocapitalist suitors, one can only wonder, against the drone of nihilistic millionaire-Marxist American critics, if we will ever have a social-democratic alternative.

7. Manfredo Tafuri, *The Sphere and the Labyrinth: Avant-Gardes and Architecture from Piranesi to the 1970s,* trans. Pellegrino d'Acierno and Robert Connolloy (Cambridge, Mass., 1987), 273–4; see also 357–9, nn. 18–21.

8. In 1915 a noted Anglican mystic could say of Manet, Degas and Cézanne, "These have seized and woven into their pictures strands which never presented themselves to you; significant forms which elude you, tones and relations to which you are blind, living facts for which your conventional wisdom finds no place"; Evelyn Underhill, *Practical Mysticism* (New York, 1915, repr. 1960), 21.

9. Robert Goldwater, *Symbolism* (New York, 1979), 56–7: "The German artists do indeed proclaim that they are dealing with ideas, but there is nothing in the manner of their art which suggests that the visible world is a sign for any further reality. . . . Indeed Böcklin, admired as a thinker, proposed an art whose assump-

tions are the very opposite of those of symbolism. He sets out to make us believe in the physical existence of his very solid pagan creatures – to make them live, not in the fluid world of the imagination... but very much now and here on earth." (In a sense any "Bidlo-Böcklin" in Mike Bidlo's "new" de Chiricos is now at last distanced, orphaned from genealogical dispute.)

10. Heinrich von Geymüller, *Die Architektur der Renaissance in Toscana* (Munich, 1884–1908); idem, *Friedrich II. von Hohenstaufen und die Anfänge der Architektur der Renaissance in Italien* (Munich, 1908).

11. Namely, that of Johann David Passavant's *Views on the Visual Arts and the Description of Their Course in Tuscany* (1820), which claimed for Nothern Gothic a quasi-classical systematic; see Hans Belting, *The End of the History of Art?* trans. Christopher S. Wood (Chicago, 1987), 88–9.

12. In a manuscripts written in Paris between 1911 and 1915 (trans. in James Thrall Soby, *Giorgio de Chirico* [New York, 1955], as Appendix A, 244–50), de Chirico twice attacks the Gothic. In the "First Part" he says that when "the Gothic and Romantic disappear... in their stead appear measurements, line, forms of eternity and infinity. This is the feeling produced by Roman architecture. This is why I believe that Greek and Roman buildings, and all those which later were fashioned upon the same principles, even though somewhat transformed are what is most profound in *art*" (245); in the "Second Part: The Feeling of Prehistory" he says, "Some few modern artists, among them the cubists, have freed themselves from the stupid Gothicism of French impressionism and seek an art at once more solid and more spiritual; a *more Romanesque art*. This development is the reverse of that of the medieval architects. So much the better" (249; emphasis in original).

13. Soby, *De Chirico*, 108, 110.

14. Jacques Derrida, *Eperons: Les styles de Nietzsche/Spurs: Nietzsche's Styles,* trans. Barbara Harlow (Chicago, 1979), 87, 89; in the original: "...La distance – la femme – écarte la vérité – le philosophe, et donne l'idée. Qui s'éloigne, devient transcendante, inaccessible, séduisante, agit et montre le chemin à distance, *in die Ferne.* Ses voiles flottent au loin, le rêve de morte commence, c'est la femme" (86, 88).

15. Ibid., 87; in the French: "forment une histoire – l'histoire elle-même peut-être... que la philosophie ne peut à elle seule décrypter, y étant elle-même comprise" (86).

16. Joseph Masheck, "Magritte in an Imagist Light" (1974) in my *Historical Present: Essays of the 1970s* (Ann Arbor, Mich., 1984), 33–45.

17. As where Durkheim and Mauss speak, in 1903, of a certain tribal people to whom "with fire are connected eucalyptus branches, the red flowers of the Eremophilia, the sound of a horn, heat and love": Emile Durkheim and Marcel Mauss, *Primitive Classification,* trans. Rodney Needham (London, 1963), 37.

18. Samuel Johnson, "Abraham Cowley," in his *Lives of the English Poets,* 2 vols. (London, 1925), Vol. 1, p. 11.

19. T. S. Eliot, "The Metaphysical Poets," in his *Selected Essays,* 3d ed. (London, 1951), 287. Eliot's conjunctive imagist thought reverberates in the novel *Mrs. Dalloway* (1925; ed. New York, n.d.), in which Virginia Woolf writes "The cook whistled in the kitchen. She heard the click of the typewriter" and, soon after, "...like a faint scent or a violin next door" (42, 45).

20. On the wrongheadedness of charging such twentieth-century pictorial space to Leon Battista Alberti's Renaissance theory of painting, see Masheck, "Alberti's 'Win-

dow': Art-Historiographic Notes on an Anti-Modernist Misprision" (1989; 1991) in my *Modernities: Art-Matters in the Present* (University Park, Pa., 1993), 13–29.

21. De Chirico, *Hebdomeros*. Wagner, on the other hand, was sufficiently obsessed by the corners of rooms not to be able to compose until they had been covered with drapery.

22. Quotation in Soby, *De Chirico*, 30.

23. Down-bearing ceilings carry over from the expressionist cinematography of F. W. Murnau in the following decade into American film (John Ford). Although Orson Welles's *Citizen Kane* (1941) is sometimes wrongly claimed to be the first film to fit room sets with ceilings for expressive effect, the device could only have become more emphatic with the "deep focus" technique of the cameraman Gregg Toland, first for William Wyler and then for Welles, who did first use *full*-ceilinged sets; see Peter Cowie, "The Study of a Colossus," excerpted from his *The Cinema of Orson Welles* (London, 1965), in Ronald Gottesman, ed., *Focus on "Citizen Kane"* (Englewood Cliffs, N.J., 1971), 109–19. Thanks to the abstract painter Thomas Nozkowski for this information, all of which can only underscore de Chirico's otherwise *in*expressively even clarity of rendering, now transliterated by Bidlo.

24. De Chirico, *Hebdomeros*, 13.

25. Ibid., 70.

26. Ibid., 39–40; emphasis in original.

27. Ibid., 102–3.

28. David Frisby, *Fragments of Modernity: Theories of Modernity in the Work of Simmel, Kracauer and Benjamin* (Cambridge, Mass., 1986; repr. 1988), chap. 4, "Walter Benjamin: The Prehistory of Modernity," 187–265. See also Susan Buck-Morss, *The Dialectics of Seeing: Walter Benjamin and the Arcades Project* (Cambridge, Mass., 1989; repr. 1991), esp. 256–60.

29. Walter Benjamin, *Das Passagen-Werk,* ed. Rolf Tiedemann (*Gesammelte Schriften,* 5) (Frankfurt am Main, 1982), 584 (N5a, 2), quoted in Buck-Morss, *Dialectics,* 257.

30. Wilhelm Jensen, "Gradiva: A Pompeiian Fancy," trans. Helen M. Downey, in *Delusion and Dream and Other Essays by Sigmund Freud,* ed. Philip Rieff (Boston, 1956), 147–235, with Freud, "Delusion and Dream in Jensen's *Gradiva,*" trans. Harry Zohn, 25–121.

31. The modern edition that could have been available to de Chirico is *Le songe de Poliphile; ou, Hypnérotomachie de frère Francesco Colonna,* trans. and ed. Claudius Popelin (Paris, 1883); see Linda Fierz-David, *The Dream of Poliphilo Related and Interpreted,* trans. Mary Hottinger, Bollingen Series (New York, 1950).

32. De Chirico, *Hebdomeros*, 17–18.

33. Ernest Jones, *The Life and Work of Sigmund Freud,* 3 vols. (New York, 1953–7), vol. 1, *The Formative Years and the Great Discoveries, 1856–1900,* 111.

34. Ibid., vol. 2, *Years of Maturity, 1901–1919,* 341.

35. Ibid., vol. 2, 343.

36. See Donald B. Kuspit, "A Mighty Metaphor: The Analogy of Archaeology and Psychoanalysis," in Lynn Gamwell and Richard Wells, eds., *Sigmund Freud in Art: His Personal Collection of Antiquities* (Binghamton, N.Y., 1989), 133–51.

37. For instances of the debasement of modernist forms to suit a conservative "modernistic" taste, see Katherine Morrison Kahle, *Modern French Decoration* (New York, 1930).

38. Jones, *Freud,* vol. 2, 341.

6. Textual Life of the Living-Machine

1. *The Journal of Eugène Delacroix,* trans. Walter Pach (New York, 1961), 220.
2. Reyner Banham, *Theory and Design in the First Machine Age* (London, 1960), 220.
3. Marcus Vitruvius Pollio, *Architecture; ou, Art de bien bastir,* trans. Jean Martin (Paris, 1547; repr. Ridgewood, N.J., 1964); according to the appended "Declaration des noms propres et mots difficiles contenus en Vitruve" (unfoliated), q.v. *organes,* "Organs, instruments, and engines are all the same thing." In the present reading I am most grateful to David Murphy and Marie-Rose Logan for discussions, respectively, of the Latin and French texts.
4. Ibid., f. 135r. In support of the translation of "to move mechanically" as "with the ingenuity of art": to the delight of any Purist, in the same appended "Declaration des noms" the term *mecaniques* is defined as "industrious (*industrieux*) people who live by their art." By the way: Nietzsche, for one, would have liked the definition of *athletes* as "those who exercise themselves in grappling (wrestling) and other corporeal strengths; also sometimes, people who dispute one against the other, or do spiritual exercises against boredom."
5. Ibid., f. 135v (orthography modernized).
6. Ernest Klein, *A Comprehensive Etymological Dictionary of the English Language,* 2 vols. (Amsterdam, 1966–7), vol. 2, 1094.
7. "Of Building," in *Francis Bacon: A Selection of His Works,* ed. Sidney Warhaft, College Classics in English (Minneapolis, Minn., 1984), 159–63, here 159.
8. René Descartes, "Discourse on Method," in *Discourse on Method and Other Writings,* trans. Arthur Wollaston (Harmondsworth, 1960, repr. 1966), 44, 73, 75, 81, respectively, followed by "Meditations," ibid., 109, 111; the latter, in the original: *De la Méthode,* ed. Etienne Gilson (Paris, 1925), 249, 253 (and "esprit," 251).
9. Banham, *Theory and Design,* 223, quoting "Voici la machine à émouvoir" together with another phrase as translated by Frederick Etchells as examples from Parthenon captions in Le Corbusier's section "Architecture: Pure Creation of the Mind," does not seem to notice that this use of "Voici la machine à émouvoir" is suppressed in Etchells's standard English translation: Le Corbusier, *Towards a New Architecture* (London, 1927).
10. Charles-Edouard Jeanneret (called Le Corbusier), *Le voyage d'Orient* (Paris, 1966), 154.
11. Andre Félibien, *Des principes de l'architecture, de la sculpture, de la peinture et des autres arts qui en dépendent avec un dictionnaire des termes propres à chacun de ces arts* (Paris, 1699), 453.
12. I trust I do no violence, on this last, to the fine-grained account of G. N. Giordano Orsisi, "The Ancient Roots of a Modern Idea," in G. L. Rousseau, ed., *Organic Form: The Life of an Idea* (London, 1972), 7–23.
13. Charles Robin, "Recherches sur l'origine et le sens des termes organisme et organisation," *Journal de l'Anatomie et de la Physiologie,* 16 (1880), 1–55. In this critical survey of the scientific literature from the eighteenth century through Pasteur, the author insists that "organism" and "mechanism" are really "two opposed notions" designating "two orders of different, if not contrary, things": the source of activity in the one is internal, in the other, external. A contemporary physiological "organicism" is criticized for merely being a "mechanism" that fails to account for "intimate and immanent correlative activity of which each exterior organic manifestation is the expression" (44–5).

14. Julien Offray de La Mettrie, *Man a Machine,* ed. and trans. Gertrude Carman Bussey, Religion of Science Library (Chicago, 1912), 128, with French on 56.

15. Ibid., 131; French, 60.

16. See Thomas Puttfarken, *Roger de Piles' Theory of Art* (New Haven, 1985); reviewed by Joseph Masheck, *Art in America,* 75, no. 2 (February 1987), 29.

17. Paolo Rossi, "The Nature-Art Relationship and the Machine of the World" (1962), in his *Philosophy, Technology, and the Arts in the Early Modern Era,* trans. Salvator Attanasio, ed. Benjamin Nelson (New York, 1970), 137–45, here 142.

18. Rudolf Witkower, *Architectural Principles in the Age of Humanism* (1949), 3d ed. (London, 1962), 15–16.

19. Among them, Gabriel Fallopius's *Lectiones . . . de partibus similaribus humani corporis . . .* (1575), Felix Plater's *De corporis humani structura et usu* (1583) and also Archangelo Piccolomini's *Anatomicae praelectiones . . . explicantes mirificam corporis humani fabricam . . .* (1586).

20. See illus. from Galileo Galilei, *Dialogues Concerning Two New Sciences* (1638) reproduced in Charles Singer, *A Short History of Scientific Ideas to 1900* (Oxford, 1962), fig. 101 on p. 232; likewise in Philip Steadman, *The Evolution of Designs: Biological Analogy in Architecture and the Applied Arts* (Cambridge, 1979), fig. 10 on p. 51. Steadman treats Galileo's sense of varying proportionality as unlike that of the orders in their set proportions regardless of size, but neglects the simple codification of vertical sequence whereby a slenderer order of column surmounts a heftier one in the classical system.

21. *Boullée's Treatise on Architecture,* ed. Helen Rosenau (London, 1953), 36 (my translation). When, in 1888, Heinrich Wölfflin established his principle that "we judge every object by analogy with our own bodies," this in *Renaissance and Baroque,* trans. Kathryn Simon (London, 1964), 77, he was aware of Gottfried Semper's *Der Stil in den technischen und tektonischen Künsten* (vol. 2, Munich, 1878, 5; cited by Wölfflin, 167 n. 5) but mentioned no such precedent as this.

22. Erik Nordenskiöld, *The History of Biology,* trans. Leonard Bucknall Eyre (New York, 1935), 155; further, "In another connexion the halves of the heart are compared with the mechanism of a sluice-gate." See also André Hallays, *Les Perrault: Essais sur le XVIIᵉ siècle* (Paris, 1926), 112.

23. Harold Dorn and Robert Marck, "The Architecture of Christopher Wren," *Scientific American,* 245, no. 1 (July 1981), 160–8, 171–3.

24. Christopher Wren, Jr., comp., and Stephen Wren, ed., *Parentalia; or, Memoirs of the Family of Wrens* (London, 1750; repr. Farnborough, Hants, 1965), 227 (orthography modernized). On Wren's science: Dorothy Stimson, "Christopher Wren, F.R.S.," *Scientific Monthly* (New York), 53 (October 1941), 360–7; H. W. Jones, "Sir Christopher Wren and Natural Philosophy; with a Checklist of His Scientific Activities," *Notes and Records of the Wren Society,* 13 (1958), 19–37; John Summerson, "Sir Christopher Wren, P.R.S. (1632–1723)," ibid., 15 (1960), 99–105.

25. Which Picasso, among other artists, would illustrate.

26. Nordenskiöld, *History,* 221.

27. Emil Kaufmann, *Architecture in the Age of Reason: Baroque and Post-Baroque in England, Italy, and France* (Cambridge, Mass., 1955; repr. New York, 1968), 167.

28. J. Nardine, "The Concept of Homology in Biology," *British Journal for the Philosophy of Science,* 18 (1967), 125–39; Anthony Vidler, "The Idea of Type: The Transformation of the Academic Ideal, 1750–1830," *Oppositions* (Spring 1977), 94–115; Steadman, *Evolution of Designs,* 98–9 and passim.

29. Jean Baptiste de Lamarck, *Philosophie zoologique* (Paris, 1968). Regrettably, I have lost track of this exact citation; here, however, is another of Lamarck's many architectural figures: "The proportions and dispositions of parts of all the individuals that comprise a species or a race always appear the same" (77).

30. Ibid., 204–5.

31. Georges (Baron) Cuvier, *Leçons d'anatomie comparée,* 5 vols. (Paris, 1805), vol. 1 (1st ed. 1800), 18.

32. Madeleine Barthélemy-Madaule, *Lamarck the Mythical Precursor: A Study of the Relations Between Science and Ideology* (1979), trans. M. H. Shank (Cambridge, Mass., 1982), 26; important in this revisionist study is Baron Cuvier's authoritarian marginalization of the humble Lamarck.

33. Ibid., 25, 27.

34. Ibid., 49.

35. Quoted, ibid., 71.

36. Ibid., 76.

37. Ibid., 113.

38. Ibid., 86.

39. Ibid., 117, 125. During which time Ernst Haeckel's *History of Creation* (1868) mistook Lamarck's sense of mechanism as "fully and strictly mechanistic" (127), and at an opposite extreme the Catholic paleontologist Maximilien Begouën (*La création évolutive,* 1879; *La vibration vitale,* 1885) and his son developed "a spiritualist evolutionism" (133–5). A study of evolutionary theory, from the time of functionalism, reinstates "adaptation" as "an adjustment such that the living machine can first of all function, then endure, and finally reproduce itself. This term, which refers exclusively to life, contains the idea of fitness more than utility or necessity": ibid., 99, quoting Lucien Cuénot, *L'evolution biologique* (Paris, 1951), 311ff.

40. Ibid., 101 (emphasis added).

41. "As Bergson stated it, the word 'effort' then need only be taken 'in a more profound, more psychological sense . . . ' and the result is Bergson's metaphysics": ibid., 137, quoting Henri Bergson, *Creative Evolution,* trans. A. Mitchell (Westport, Conn., 1975), 86.

42. Louis Pasteur, "Recherches sur la dissymétrie moléculaire des produits organiques naturels (Leçons professées à la Société chimique de Paris le 20 janvier et le 3 février 1860)," Société chimique de Paris, *Leçons de chimie professées en 1860* (Paris, 1861), 1–48, here 27; see also 31–2, 38.

43. Charles Baudelaire, *Art in Paris, 1845–1862: Salons and Other Exhibitions,* trans. and ed. Jonathan Mayne (London, 1965), 57; in the orig., *Critique d'art,* ed. Claude Pichois, 2 vols. (Paris, 1965), vol. 1, 106.

44. Edgar Allan Poe, "The Philosophy of Composition" (1846), in his *Essays and Reviews* (New York, 1984), 13–25, here 20–1.

45. Baudelaire, *The Painter of Modern Life and Other Essays,* trans. and ed. Jonathan Mayne (London, 1965), 32; in the orig., *Critique,* vol. 2, 475.

46. Ibid., 40; in the original, *Critique,* vol. 2, 484–5.

47. Horatio Greenough, *Form and Function: Remarks on Art,* ed. Harold A. Small (Berkeley, Calif., 1947), 51–68, here 60–1; ed. note, 51n. "American Architecure" was collected in Henry T. Tuckerman's *Memorial of Horatio Greenough* (New York, 1853). John Ruskin's discussion of beauty in the second volume (1846) of *Modern Painters* includes a "Vital Beauty" defined as "the appearance of felicitous fulfilment of function in living things, more especially of the joyful and right exertion of

perfect life in man"; quoted in the excellent study of Raymond Williams, which shows the political conservatism of Ruskin's sense of the functional and the socially organic: *Culture and Society, 1780–1950* (Harmondsworth, 1963), 140–51, here 141. On Greenough, there is Theodore M. Brown, "Greenough, Paine, Emerson and the Organic Aesthetic," *Journal of Aesthetics and Art Criticism*, 14 (1955–6), 304–17.

Although *Navis*, the book of Alberti on "The Ship," is now lost from his architectural corpus (it was known to Leonardo da Vinci), in *De re aedificatoria* chapter 12 of book 5 deals with ship design, including the idea that "in building a ship, the ancients would use the lineaments of a fish; so that its back became the hull, its head the prow; the rudder would serve as its tail, the oars are its gills and fins": Leon Battista Alberti, *The Art of Building in Ten Books,* trans. Joseph Rykwert, Neil Leach, and Robert Tavernor (Cambridge, Mass., 1988), 136. Because Greenough was a sculptor, it is also worth mentioning the Corbusian remark of *De Statua* (c. 1464), para. 8: "Who would dare to claim to be a shipbuilder, if he did not know how many parts there are in a ship, or how one ship differs from another, and how the parts of any construction (*operis*) fit together?"; Alberti, *On Painting and On Sculpture: The Latin Texts of De Pictura and De Statua,* ed. and trans. Cecil Grayson (London, 1972), 129 (English), 128 (Latin), with 141n.

Baudelaire, a confessedly bored reader of Emerson, seems to register an influence from Greenough when, in reviewing "The Exposition Universelle" (1855; *Art in Paris,* 121–43), he writes of "those solitary wanderers who have lived for years in the heart of forests, in the midst of illimitable prairies, with no other companion than their gun – contemplating, dissecting, writing" – "They know the admirable, eternal and inevitable relation between form and function" (122).

48. W. T. Bandy, "New Light on Baudelaire and Poe," *Yale French Studies,* no. 10 (1953), as noted by Mayne, Introd. to Baudelaire, *Painter of Modern Life,* xviii.
49. Leo Tolstoy, *War and Peace,* trans. Rosemary Edmonds, 2 vols. (Baltimore, Md., 1969), vol. 2, 935.
50. Tolstoy, *Anna Karenina,* trans. David Magarshack (New York, 1961), 277.
51. Baudelaire, *Critique,* vol. 2, 295–378, here 316.
52. Mary McLeod, " 'Architecture or Revolution': Taylorism, Technocracy and Social Change," *Art Journal,* 43, no. 2 (Summer 1983), 132–47.
53. Tolstoy, *Anna Karenina,* 628–9.
54. Charles De Comberousse, "Cinqantenaire de l'Ecole centrale" (1879; MS. of lecture), quoted in John Hubbel Weiss, *The Making of Technological Man: The Social Origins of French Engineering Education* (Cambridge, Mass., 1982), 226; see also 150. Certain of Comberousse's own terms seem cryptoartistic: "Useful, convenient and least expensive" sounds like a utilitarianization of Vitruvian *utilitas, firmitas, venustas,* all the more so because in French architectural theory *convenence* signified a more aesthetic agreement of parts; even *ensemble* is a term far from innocent of French classical aesthetics. Some of the French engineer's pride may be compensatory, after the Franco-Prussian War: even the young Le Corbusier (identifying himself as "architecte" on the title page) wrote in his 1912 report on the vast progress of the industrial arts in modern Germany, "Mais voici 1870. *L'Allemagne triomphe!*"; Le Corbusier, *Etude sur le mouvement d'art décoratif en Allemagne* (Paris, 1912; repr. New York, 1968), 12.
55. Eugène Viollet-le-Duc, *Entretiens sur l'architecture,* 2 vols. (Paris, 1863, 1872; repr., Ridgewood, N.J., 1965), discourse 19, vol. 2, 353–88, here 388.
56. Alan Colquhoun, "Architecture and Engineering: Le Corbusier and the Paradox

of Reason" (1980–1), in his *Modernity and the Classical Tradition: Architectural Essays, 1980–1987* (Cambridge, Mass., 1989), 89–119, here 90, quoting Le Corbusier, *Vers une Architecture* (Paris, 1923), 15.

57. Ibid., 97–8.

58. Colquhoun, "The Significance of Le Corbusier" (1984), ibid. 163–91, here 164.

59. Colquhoun, "Postmodernism and Sructuralism: A Retrospective Glance" (1988), ibid., 243–55, here 249. These detached quotations cannot evoke the depth of thought in Colquhoun's stimulating book.

60. Arnold Bennett, *The Human Machine,* "Author's edition" (ed. New York, 1911), 23.

61. Ibid., 39.

62. Ibid., 44.

63. Ibid., 123.

64. Ibid.

65. On which, see Masheck, "Magritte in an Imagist Light" (1974), in *Historical Present* 33–45, esp. "Postscript," 44–5; also, Philip Steadman, *The Evolution of Designs: Biological Analogy in Architecture and the Applied Arts,* Cambridge Urban and Architectural Studies (Cambridge, 1979), 135.

66. Bennett, *Human Machine,* 13. *The Human Machine* does not appear to have been translated early on, but Bennett was in steady communication with Gide during the whole course of purism: *Correspondance André Gide–Arnold Bennett: Vingt ans d'amitié littéraire, 1911–1931,* ed. Linette F. Brugmans (Geneva, 1964).

67. See Erik Satie, "Memoirs of an Amnesiac, No. 7," in *The Writings of Erik Satie,* trans. and ed. Nigel Wilkins (London, 1980), 58; reference and quotation from Satie's *Le Coeur à Barbe,* no. 1 (April 1922), in "A Mammal's Notebook," 70, from Paul Zukofsky's Museum of Modern Art *Summergarden* program notes for the 1991 season (New York, 1991), unpaginated.

68. My account here derives from Alexandra Aldridge, *The Scientific World View in Dystopia,* Studies in Speculative Fiction (Ann Arbor, Mich., 1984).

69. Paul Westheim, "Architecture in France: Le Corbusier-Saugnier" (1922), excerpt trans. Hildegarde Hunt von Laue in Peter Serenyi, ed., *Le Corbusier in Perspective,* Artists in Perspective (Englewood Cliffs, N.J., 1975), 28–31. The reference is to T. W. Twyford (sanitary potter), *Twyford's Catalogue of Sanitary Specialities* (Hanley, Staffs., 1894).

70. Meaning Le Corbusier's *Etude sur le mouvement d'art décoratif en Allemagne* (La Chaux-de-Fonds, 1912; repr., New York, 1968).

71. Westheim, "Architecture," 30, without source.

72. Ibid., 30–1 (with quotation from Corbusier here excised).

73. Yevgeny Zamyatin, "Herbert Wells," in *A Soviet Heretic: Essays by Yevgeny Zamyatin,* trans. and ed. Mirra Ginsberg (Chicago, 1970), 259–90, p. 284, as quoted in Aldridge, *Scientific World View,* 26; on date of Wells's novel, see 84 n. 17.

74. As well as "in minutely calculated social organization, even in programmed sexual activity"; ibid., 40. Persona non grata in Stalinist Russia, Zamyatin lived in Paris from 1931 until his death in 1937 (34–5).

75. Moisei Ginzburg, *Style and Epoch,* trans. Anatole Senkevitch, Jr. (Cambridge, Mass., 1982), foreword by Kenneth Frampton, 8.

76. Ibid., 87.

77. Ibid., 89.

78. Ibid., 106.

79. Ibid., 107. Like Le Corbusier, Ginzburg enthusiastically illustrates the grain ele-

vators of Buffalo, N.Y.; cf. Reyner Banham, *A Concrete Atlantis: U.S. Industrial Building and European Modern Architecture, 1900–1925* (Cambridge, Mass., 1986), reviewed by Masheck, "Temples to the Dynamo: The 'Daylight' Factory and the Grain Elevator" (1987), in his *Modernities* (University Park, Pa., 1993), 51–6.

80. Le Corbusier, *New Architecture,* 89.

81. Le Corbusier, *Vers une architecture:* "Une maison est une machine à demeurer," 73; "La maison est une machine à habiter," 83; "machines à habiter," 100, caption; see below, p. 278 n.l.

82. I. A. Richards, *Principles of Literary Criticism* (New York, 1959), 1.

83. Given in booklet of a Paul Bennett Memorial Lecture: Paul Valéry et al., *Thoughts on Book Design* (New York, 1968).

84. Valéry, *Eupalinos; ou, l'architecte; précédé de "l'âme et la danse"* (Paris, 1924), 38.

85. Valéry, *Idée fixe,* trans. D. Paul, (New York, 1965), 27.

86. Hellmut Lehmann-Haupt, *Art Under a Dictatorship* (New York, 1956), 120.

87. Le Corbusier, *Aircraft* (London, 1935; repr. New York, 1988), 56.

88. Ibid., 33.

89. Ibid., 49. In "Plastic Art and Pure Plastic Art" (1937) Mondrian says that technical civilization has not made the abstract artist "a mechanic, but . . . a living machine, capable of realizing in a pure manner the essence of art"; in Herschel B. Chipp, ed., *Theories of Modern Art* (Berkeley, 1968), 362.

90. Ibid., 109.

91. Quoted, without source, by Yve Alain-Bois in his review of the Le Corbusier centennial exhibitions, "Report from Paris: Against Functionalism," *Art in America* (December 1988), 53–5, 57, 59, 61, 63; here, 61.

92. Le Corbusier, *Aircraft,* 8.

93. Le Corbusier, *When the Cathedrals Were White,* trans. Francis E. Hyslop, Jr. (1947; ed. New York, 1964), 50.

94. Jan Mukařovský, "On the Problem of Functions in Architecture" (1937–8), in his *Structure, Sign, and Function: Selected Essays,* trans. and ed. John Burbank and Peter Steiner (New Haven, Conn., 1978), 236–50, here 239.

95. Ibid., 241–3; on Mukařovský and "foregrounding" (*aktualisace,* in Czech) in respect to Victor Shlovsky, Brecht, also Aristotle: Alexander Tzonis and Liane Lefaivre, *Classical Architecture: The Poetics of Order* (Cambridge, Mass., 1986), 276–8.

96. Ibid., 244–5, with 245 n. 2.

97. Ibid., 246.

98. Ibid., 247.

99. Ibid., 249–50.

100. Ibid., 240.

101. Max Horkheimer and Theodore W. Adorno, *Dialectic of Enlightenment,* trans. John Cumming (New York, 1982), 57.

102. Denis de Rougemont, *Penser avec les mains* (ed. Paris, 1945), 163.

103. Roman Ingarden, "The Architectural Work" (1946), in his *Ontology of the Work of Art: The Musical Work; the Picture; the Architectural Work; the Film,* trans. Raymond Meyer with John T. Goldthwait, Series in Continental Thought (Athens, Ohio, 1989), 253–313, here 281–5. Even if one gave up "architecture" to the operations of a purely symbolic order, it would not "function" analogously.

104. Ibid., 285.

105. " . . . Not only do the corresponding parts of a given organism assume a somewhat different shape in different individuals (for example, the human ear or the lines

of the same part of the human skin), but the parts of one and the same organism which are of the same kind . . . deviate from one another somewhat in detail. That is 'normal' in what is organic. In architecture, however, it would be rather an anomaly . . . "; ibid., 285–6.

106. Ibid., 286.

107. Herbert Read, *The Grass Roots of Art: Four Lectures on Social Aspects of Art in an Industrial Age* (delivered in 1946), Problems of Contemporary Art, 2 (New York, 1947), Lecture 2, "The Social Basis of Great Architecture," 38–55, here 39.

108. Jean Charlot, "Mexican Heritage," in *An Artist on Art: Collected Essays of Jean Charlot* (Honolulu, 1972), Vol. 2, 69–73, here 71. The term *maison,* or "house," in Corbusier's formula does not necessarily imply a secularist-modern outlook, since there is Saint Thomas Aquinas's "often-cited definition of the church building" as *"Domus in quia sacramentum celebratur, ecclesiam significat et ecclesia nominatur.* 'The house in which the sacrament is celebrated signifies the Church and is called "church" ' " (*Summa theologicae,* III.83.3 ad 2m); Karsten Harries, *The Bavarian Rococo Church: Between Faith and Aestheticism* (New Haven, Conn. 1983), 8. Thanks to my former student Denise McColgan for calling my attention to Harries.

109. Aleksandr I. Solzhenitsyn, *The Frist Circle,* trans. Thomas P. Whitney (New York, 1968), 147; thanks here to Donald B. Kuspit for remembering this. In the broader matter of new (if in Russia no longer modernist) architecture in the service of modern despiritualization, the architectural reader will also be interested in chap. 68, "Civic Temples" (416–20).

110. Statements of the architect V. Shkvarikov, as quoted in Peter Blake, *Le Corbusier: Architecture and Form* (Baltimore, Md., 1966), 110.

111. "Embalmed Objects: Design at the Modern," *Artforum,* 12, no. 6 (February 1975), 49–55; "The Propeller and the *Bird in Space*" (1987), in my *Modernities,* 73–92.

112. Peter Collins, *Changing Ideals in Modern Architecture, 1750–1950* (London, 1965, repr. 1967), 231. On Bentham's Panopticon, see above, Chap. 1.

113. Kenneth Clark, "The Blot and the Diagram," *Encounter,* 20, no. 1 (January 1963), 28–36, here 31.

114. Alison and Peter Smithson, seminar statement at Technical University, Berlin, December 4–9, 1967, quoted in their *The Heroic Period of Modern Architecture* (New York, 1981), 13.

115. Masheck, "Living Modern: James Stirling's Sackler Museum" (1986), in his *Modernities,* 57–62.

116. André Malraux, "Funérailles de Le Corbusier," in his *Oraisons funèbres* (Paris, 1971), 103–14, here 107–8.

117. See Martin Heidegger, "Building Dwelling Thinking" (1951; 1952) and ". . . Poetically Man Dwells . . ." (1951; 1954), in his *Poetry, Language, Thought,* ed. and trans. Albert Hofstadter (New York, 1975), 145–61, 213–29, respectively.

118. On La Maison Médicale itself: Lucien Kroll, "The Soft Zone," *Architectural Association Quarterly* (London), 7, no. 4 (1975), 48–59.

119. Kroll, *An Architecture of Complexity* (originally *Composants,* 1983), trans. Peter Blundell Jones (Cambridge, Mass., 1987), 6.

120. Ibid., 8, 30, 31.

121. Ibid., 9.

122. Ibid., 30.

123. Ibid., 94.

124. Ibid., 106.

125. Ibid., 85.

126. Matei Calinescu, *Five Faces of Modernity: Modernism, Avant-Garde, Decadence, Kitsch, Postmodernism* (Durham, N.C., 1987), 130.

7. Reflections in Onyx on Mies van der Rohe

1. Henry-Russell Hitchcock, *Modern Architecture. Romanticism and Reintegration* (New York, 1929), 191.

2. Dorothea Nyberg, "Meissonnier: An Eighteenth-Century Maverick," introduction to *Oeuvre de Juste Aurèle Meissonnier* ([ca. 1750] New York, 1969), 20.

3. Cf. Joseph Masheck, "The Propeller and the *Bird in Space*" (1987), in his *Modernities: Art-Matters in the Present* (University Park, Pa., 1993), 73–92.

4. Wolf Tegethoff, *Mies van der Rohe: The Villas and Country Houses* (New York, 1985), 76. This study is sometimes overwrought but includes much of interest and many good plates. See now also Tegethoff's "From Obscurity to Maturity: Mies van der Rohe's Breakthrough to Modernism," in the fine collection edited by Franz Schulze, *Mies van der Rohe: Critical Essays* (New York, 1989), 28–94, esp. 83–4.

5. Immanuel Kant, *Observations on the Feeling of the Beautiful and Sublime* (1764), trans. John T. Goldthwait (Berkeley, Calif., 1960), 71ff.

6. Philip Johnson, "Architecture in the Third Reich," reprinted from *Hound & Horn,* 7(October–December, 1933), 137–9, in his *Writings,* with ed. comments by Robert A. M. Stern (New York, 1979), 52–4.

7. Ludwig Mies van der Rohe, quoted in Kenneth Frampton, *Modern Architecture: A Critical History* (New York, 1980), 231, with fig. 226 (Reichsbank drawing).

8. Walter Curt Behrendt, "The Architect in These Times," *American Magazine of Art,* 28, no. 3 (March 1935), 141–7 and back cover. Behrendt's article is a stream of bourgeois-materialist double-talk laced with high-minded quotations from Hegel and Schinkel. Most telling are his musings on a letter in the last chapter of Dostoevsky's *A Raw Youth* (1875) in which he resolves that, were he a novelist, he would choose characters from the old nobility to have benefit of an " 'outward semblance of fine order and aesthetic beauty' " (the word "order" pops up six times on Behrendt's first short page alone): this is Behrendt's way of understanding – please remember that we are talking architecture! – retreat to the tried-and-true.

9. Fritz Tugendhat, statement, in Tegethoff, *Mies,* 98.

10. Richard Hennessy, "What's All This About Photography?" *Artforum* (May 1979), 24.

11. Jeffrey Potter, *To a Violent Grave: An Oral Biography of Jackson Pollock* (New York, 1985), 104, 108; thanks to Mike Bidlo for calling my attention to this book.

12. Peter Carter, *Mies van der Rohe at Work* (London, 1974), quoted in Frampton, *Modern Architecture,* 234.

13. Although I tend to see it as conflating, if not confusing, some 1950s and 1960s phenomena, Dan Graham's "Eisenhower and the Hippies," *o to 9,* (Winter 1968–9), reprinted in his *Articles,* ed. R. H. Fuchs (Eindhoven, 1978), 21–6, is interesting on Eisenhowerean blandness in relation to minimalism. Also, now that some are prepared to see the cold war as an art-historical period, with New York somehow having Stolen the Idea of Modern Art, a remark of Willy Rotzler, *Constructive Concepts: A History of Constructive Art from Cubism to the Present* (New York, 1977), 215, takes on interest in respect to Moholy (d. 1946) and Mies, the last Bauhaus

director, in Chicago: "The European, who thinks of himself as the supplier, the exporter, will ask when, where and how the Americans first took over the ideas of a non-figurative art that employs – whether intuitively or rationally – geometric ordering principles."

14. Mies van der Rohe, statement, from Carter in *Architectural Design* (March 1961), quoted in Frampton, *Modern Architecture*, 161. I see that one of those high school chums of mine has published a study of the medieval rootedness of modern thought: Gerald J. Galgan, *The Logic of Modernity* (New York, 1982).

15. Erwin Panofsky, *Gothic Architecture and Scholasticism* (New York, 1957), 35.

16. Ibid., 38.

17. Ibid., 51ff. Something from 1959 that also struck me in a Miesian way, once I encountered it in the 1960s, was Meyer Schapiro's "A Note on the Wall Strips of Saxon Churches," *Journal of the Society of Architectural Historians*, 17, no. 4 (Dec. 1959), 123–5, reprinted in his *Selected Papers*, vol. 3 *Late Antique, Early Christian and Mediaeval Art* (New York, 1979), 242–8, where the derivation of a *fachwerk*-like angular system of wall articulation from native wood construction is affirmed (Mies had worked for an architect specializing in wood early on).

18. Fredric Jameson, foreword to Jean-François Lyotard, *The Postmodern Condition: A Report on Knowledge* (Minneapolis, 1984), xvii.

19. Meyer Schapiro, "Looking Forward to Looking Backward," reprinted from *Partisan Review* (1938) in William Phillips and Philip Rahv, eds., *The Partisan Reader: Ten Years of Partisan Review 1934–1944: An Anthology* (New York, 1946), 310–23. Since even the reprint is not accessible, here are excerpts: "Although he regards architecture as a simple reflection of society, their relations are anything but clear in Mumford's account. He does not limit himself to architectural forms or uses depending directly on the social objects in question, but dogmatically derives the artistic value of buildings from their social origin. . . . [His] banal tautologies and prejudices presuppose an indifference to the qualities of post-medieval architecture incredible in Mumford: it must issue from his prophetic zeal, not from his sensibility. When he admires a building, he infers that it is connected with the "dominant social sources of order," or with some still healthy part in a diseased organism; if it is bad, then it lacks such a connection" (314).

"The charge of stylelessness in architecture has been repeated already for a hundred years, but it is becoming more and more evident how much the architecture of the twentieth century owes to these revivals and what originality some of them possessed. Their nature is hardly exhausted by their imitative aspect. The values of a geometrical simplicity are already clear in neo-classic architecture (Ledoux, Soane and Schinkel have an imposing modernity); and the Gothic revival undoubtedly affected the modern taste for elusive, incommensurable arrangements and the interest in technical sources of forms, whatever the misunderstandings of the neo-Gothic architects (echoed by Mumford!) about the constructive and functional character of Gothic buildings. Conversely, Mumford tends to accept the programmatic definitions of functionalism uncritically, on their face value. And in assimilating, as he does, modern architectural style to cubism, which is anything but organic and social in his sense, his social judgement of the style becomes even more mysterious and confusing. If republican Germany produced it and the Nazis have restricted its use, it should also be remembered that the Italians have in turn welcomed it as 'rational architecture' " (p. 315).

More politically: "Today, when Marxists, liberals, fascists, and Christians all condemn capitalism, Mumford's denunciation is not in itself crucial. It is especially consoling to those who find capitalism intolerable, but the overthrow of capitalism equally unpleasant. . . . " (323).

20. Aldo Rossi, "Introduction" to Adolf Loos, *Spoken into the Void: Collected Essays, 1897–1900,* trans. Jane O. Newman and John H. Smith (Cambridge, Mass., 1982), xi.

21. Loos, "Building Materials," *Spoken,* 63–5, here 63.

22. Ibid., 65.

23. Loos, "The Principle of Cladding," *Spoken,* 66–9, here 67.

24. Jean Baudrillard, *Simulations,* trans. Paul Foss, Paul Patton, and Philip Beitchman (New York, 1983), "The Stucco Angel," 83–92.

25. Loos, "Principle," 68.

26. Charles Jencks, *Modern Movements in Architecture* (Garden City, N.Y., 1973), 95–108.

27. Quoted, ibid., 96.

28. Ibid., 99.

29. Subtle distinction is of the essence in Mies's art. Juxtaposing corner details of four of his buildings, Edward F. Sekler observes "variations which have little structural or constructional justification but which are most telling tectonically"; "Structure, Construction, Tectonics," in Gyorgy Kepes, ed., *Structure in Art and in Science,* Vision and Value (New York, 1965), 89–95, here 94 with figs. 5–8 on 92–3.

30. Ibid., 105.

31. Ibid., caption to fig. 49 on p. 95.

32. Moreover, with Skidmore, Owings & Merrill's Central Heating and Refrigeration Plant at Kennedy Airport, New York, built in 1957 (a year before that firm was asked to take over subsequent construction at IIT), ideas of Mies's Boiler Plant and Chapel are in a sense fused, and the housing of heavy utility equipment there takes on an earnest litheness tantamount to Miesian homage. Not without reason is the airport heating plant semiofficially called "splendid and wonderful": American Intitute of Architects, New York Chapter, *A.I.A. Guide to New York City,* 3d ed., ed. Elliot Willensky and Norval White (New York, 1988), 791.

8. Post Tenebras Lux

1. James Stirling, "Ronchamp: Le Corbusier's Chapel and the Crises of Rationalism," *Architectural Review,* 119 (March 1956), 155–61.

2. Stanislaus von Moos, "The Visualized Machine Age; or, Mumford and the European Avant-Garde," in Thomas P. Hughes and Agatha C. Hughes, eds., *Lewis Mumford: Public Intellectual* (New York, 1990), 181–232, with notes on 403–24; esp. 223–5.

3. Giulio Carlo Argan, "La Chiesa di Ronchamp (Le Corbusier)" (1956), in his *Progetto e destino,* La Cultura, 102 (Milan, 1965), 236–43, here 238–9.

4. See Chapter 6, this volume.

5. Tim Benton, "The Sacred and the Search for Myths," in the Hayward Gallery catalogue *Le Corbusier: Architect of the Century* (London, 1987), introd., 238–45, and "Notre-Dame du Haut, Ronchamp," 247–9, here 249.

6. Ibid., 241.

7. Ibid., 242.

8. Peter Blake, *Le Corbusier: Architecture and Form* (excerpted from his *The Master Builders,* 1964) (Baltimore, Md., 1966), 137–8.

9. Charles Jencks, *Le Corbusier and the Tragic View of Architecture* (Cambridge, Mass. 1973), 152–3.

10. Argan, "Chiesa," 242.

11. A contemporary Protestant theologian of ecumenical inclination explains this: "In conjunction with the principle of *ex opere operato* [from the work performed], the principle of *non ponens obicem* [not posing a hindrance], traditional in Catholic theology of the sacraments, is a safeguard against a donatist or a pelagian view that sacramental efficacy depends upon the worthiness of the minister or the autonomous effort of the recipient"; Geoffrey Wainwright, *Doxology: The Worship of God in Worship, Doctrine and Life: A Systematic Theology* (New York, 1980), 403.

12. Benton, "The Sacred," 245 n. 4.

13. Thanks to David Murphy for a discussion.

14. See Madeleine Barthélemy-Madaule, *Lamarck the Mythical Precursor: A Study of the Relations Between Science and Ideology* (1979), trans. M. H. Shank (Cambridge, Mass., 1982), 7, 14, with refs. to *Hydrogéologie* (1802) and writings of 1805–9.

15. Mircea Eliade, *Images and Symbols: Studies in Religious Symbolism* (1952), trans. Philip Mairet (Kansas City, Mo., n.d.), 137 with refs.

16. Vincent Scully, *Modern Architecture: The Architecture of Democracy,* Great Ages of World Architecture (New York, 1961), with illus. of drawing by Le Corbusier of a goddess sanctuary on Malta, from *L'Esprit nouveau,* and refs.

17. Ibid., 127. In "Stabat Mater" (1977), a Christian meditation on Mary's maternity, Julia Kristeva writes of "the female sexual organ changed into an innocent shell, holder of sound"; trans. León S. Roudiez in *The Julia Kristeva Reader,* ed. Toril Moi (New York, 1986), 160–86, here 173.

18. James S. Ackerman, "Dürer's Crab," in *Ars Auro Prior: Studia Ioanni Białłostocki sexagenario dicata,* ed. Juliusz A. Chroc'icki et al. (Warsaw, 1981), 291–5, wherein a 1495 watercolor of crab in the Boymans-van Beuningen Museum, Rotterdam, shows Dürer's attempt not to indulge Gothicism but rather to absorb a contemporary Venetian naturalism having, however unexpectedly, Hellenistic sculptural antecedents. There is, too, a Paduan bronze box, some 6¾ inches long, dating from the late fifteenth or early sixteenth century, in the Samuel H. Kress Collection of the National Gallery of Art, Washington.

19. *The Crystal Chain Letters: Architectural Fantasies by Bruno Taut and His Circle,* ed. and trans. Iain Boyd Whyte (Cambridge, Mass., 1985), 89, 81; for my review of this volume, see Joseph Masheck, "Expressionist Fantasias: The Crystal Chain Letters" (1986), in my *Modernities: Art-Matters in the Present* (University Park, Pa., 1993). Manfredo Tafuri, *Theories and History of Architecture* (1968; 4th ed., 1976), trans. Giorgio Verrecchia (New York, 1980), 99–100 n. 21, finds much of this material distasteful (though he himself accepts the metaphor of building as "organism"): "One should distinguish . . . between experiences that are at the base of a new code of values and those that are nothing more than clever eversions or tightrope walks."

20. Illus., Christopher Thacker, *The History of Gardens* (Berkeley, Calif., 1979), fig. 145 on p. 219. Philip Steadman, *The Evolution of Designs: Biological Analogy in Architecture and the Applied Arts,* Cambridge Urban and Architectural Studies (Cambridge, 1979), 41, notes that Le Corbusier likened "traditional load-bearing wall construction of stone" to the "restricting" shells of crustaceans (tortoises and lobsters), versus modern architectural endoskeletal structure; ref. to Le Corbusier, "Le

plan de la maison moderne," in his *Précisions sur un état présent de l'architecture et de l'urbanisme,* Collection *Esprit Nouveau* (Paris, 1960), 24.

21. Danièle Pauly, "The Chapel of Ronchamp as an Example of Le Corbusier's Creative Process," trans. Stephen Sartarelli, in Fondation Le Corbusier, *Maison Jaoul and Other Buildings and Projects, 1951–52,* The Le Corbusier Archive, 20 (New York, 1983) xiii–xxii, here xiv; Benton, "The Sacred," p. 248, gives 1946.

22. A selection of his writings: M.-A. Couturier, *Sacred Art,* ed. Dominique de Menil and Pie Duployé (Austin, Texas, n.d.), which I have reviewed: Masheck, "Readings: Cosmic Taste," *Arts Magazine,* 65, no. 2 (October 1990), 27–8.

23. Pauly, "Chapel," xv, quoting from a "Création Ronchamp" file in the Fondation Le Corbusier.

24. Jacques de Voragine, *La légende dorée,* trans. Theodor de Wyzewa (Paris, 1923), 338–47.

25. Timothy Husband, in the Metropolitan Museum exhibition catalog *The Wild Man: Medieval Myth and Symbolism* (New York, 1980), 100.

26. Fondation Le Corbusier, *Palais des Nations and Other Buildings and Projects, 1946–48,* The Le Corbusier Archive, 18 (New York, 1983), pls. on 314, 315.

27. Ibid., pls. on 324, 329, 344, 347.

28. Ibid., pls. on 327.

29. Paul Claudel, "An Underground Church," in his *Ways and Crossways,* trans. John O'Connor (1933; repr. Port Washington, N.Y., 1968), 189–99, here 189–90; thanks to Andrew Attaway for bringing this to my attention.

30. Ibid., 191.

31. Ibid., 191–2.

32. Ibid., 193.

33. Ibid., 195–6.

34. Ibid., 197.

35. Ibid., 198–9.

36. Jean Charlot, "Thirty Years At It," repr. from *Liturgical Arts,* February 1953, in *An Artist on Art: Collected Essays of Jean Charlot* (Honolulu, 1972), vol. 1, 283–97. *Liturgical Arts* was co-edited by Father Couturier.

37. Joseph Rykwert, *On Adam's House in Paradise: The Idea of the Primitive Hut in Architectural History,* 2d ed. (Cambridge, Mass., 1981), reproducing Le Corbusier's two figures, one a plan and elevation, the other a bird's-eye view (14–15), identifies them as "Primitive Temple – The Jewish Tabernacle in the Desert." Stuart Cohen and Steven Hurtt, "The Pilgrimage Chapel at Ronchamp," *Oppositions,* nos. 19–20 (Winter–Spring 1980), 142–57, treat the "hut/temple" of *Vers une architecture* as if oblivious to any religious significance in the illustrations.

38. Louis Bouyer, *Rite and Man: Natural Sacredness and Christian Liturgy* (Notre Dame, Ind., 1963), 159, quoting 2 Sam. 7:6.

39. Ibid., 163, with ref. to Bouyer's "La Schekinah: Dieu avec nous," *Bible et vie chrétienne,* 20 (1957), 7ff.

40. André Parrot, *The Temple of Jerusalem* (2d. ed., 1955), trans. B. E. Hooke, Studies in Biblical Archaeology, 5 (New York, 1955), 40.

41. Ibid., 34.

42. Quoted, ibid., 51, from Ernest Renan, *Histoire du peuple d'Israël,* vol. 2 (1891), 142; for an unflattering portrait of Renan as superstar poseur, see Jules Lemaitre, "Ernest Renan," in his *Les contemporains: Etudes et portraits littéraires: Première série, 1884 et*

1885 (Paris, 1903?), 193–215. If there were any more reason for a young Protestant interested in architecture than for a Catholic to pursue such matters, it might be the Reformation tradition of playing down the temple-function of the sacrifice of the Mass in favor of the church as synagogic; see M. C. Culotta, "The Temple, the Synagogue and Hebrew Precedent," *Journal of the History of Ideas*, 31 (1970), 273–6.

43. Yrjö Hirn, *The Sacred Shrine: A Study in the Poetry and Art of the Catholic Church* (1909) (London, 1958), 328; cf. below, p. 288 n. 167.

44. William S. Rubin, *Modern Sacred Art and the Church of Assy* (New York, 1961), 119–20.

45. Pauly, *Ronchamp: Lecture d'une architecture* (Paris, 1980), 61–2.

46. Benton, "The Sacred," 249.

47. Pauly, *Ronchamp*, 83.

48. *Boullée's Treatise on Architecture,* ed. Helen Rosenau (London, 1953), 84.

49. Pauly, *Ronchamp*, 132–6. The Saharan mosque – Argan quickly criticized this as a colonialist derivation (during the Algerian war), but it might as well be considered sympathetic on the part of the newly French (1930) architect – has "deep splays" and niches in its exterior wall, and is also all-white.

50. James S. Ackerman, Letter of March 12, 1991.

51. Pauly, "Chapel," xv.

52. Pauly, *Ronchamp*, 83.

53. Sigfried Giedion, *Architecture and the Phenomena of Transition: The Three Space Conceptions in Architecture* (Cambridge, Mass., 1971), 164, with figs. 133 (exterior) on p. 166 and fig. 134 (interior) on p. 167.

54. On the Albigensian ancestry: e.g., Jencks, *Le Corbusier,* 17.

55. Richard Aldington, *Introduction to Mistral* (London, 1956), 111–12.

56. "Rome n'est plus: et si l'architecture / Quelque umbre encor de Rome fait revoir, / C'est comme un corps par magique sçavoir / Tiré de nuict hors de sa sepulture": Joachim du Bellay, "Les Antiquités de Rome," no. 5, ll. 5–8, in *Les Regrets; suivis des Antiquités de Rome,* ed. Pierre Grimal (Paris, 1958), 249.

57. *Letters of Roger Fry,* ed. Denys Sutton, 2 vols. (New York, 1972), vol. 2, 467, letter 464.

58. Cf. Philibert Delorme, *L'Architecture (Nouvelles Inventions pour bien bastir et à petits frais,* 1561) (1567; ed. Rouen, 1648; repr. Ridgewood, N.J., 1964), book 4, prologue through chap. 7, ff. 85v–128v, followed by chapters applicable to church vaulting. On Delorme in relation to Louis I. Kahn, see Chapter 9, this volume.

9. Kahn

1. By the exhibition "Louis I. Kahn: In the Realm of Architecture," organized by the Museum of Contemporary Art, Los Angeles, and traveling from Philadelphia to Paris, New York, Gunma (Japan), Los Angeles, Fort Worth and Columbus in 1991–4, and its accompanying book: David B. Brownlee and David G. De Long, *Louis I. Kahn: In the Realm of Architecture* (New York, 1991), hereafter cited as "*Kahn.*"

2. De Long, "The Mind Opens to Realizations," in *Kahn,* 50–77, esp. 59, 66, 70.

3. Rudolf Wittkower, *Architectural Principles in the Age of Humanism,* 3d ed. (London, 1962), 27.

4. Alfred Powell, "W. R. Lethaby (1857–1931): Biographical Note," in W. R. Lethaby, *Architecture, Nature and Magic* (London, 1956), 9–13, here 10.

5. Lethaby, *Architecture,* 81.

6. Ibid., 81–2, with fig. 28 on p. 82.

7. I recall my own fascination, in about 1961–2, with foursquare structures in eighteenth-century poetry and architecture.

8. Lewis Mumford, preface to Lethaby, *Form in Civilization: Collected Papers on Art and Labour,* 2d ed. (London, 1957), xiii.

9. Meyer Schapiro, conversation of November 25, 1991.

10. Joseph Masheck, "Kuspit's LeWitt: Has He Got Style?" *Art in America,* 64, no. 9 (November–December 1976), 107–10; Donald B. Kuspit's response, "Letters," January–February; reply, "Letters," March–April.

11. See, for example, Evelyn Fox Kellert and Christine R. Grontkowski, "The Mind's Eye," in Sandra Harding and Merill B. Hintikka, eds., *Discovering Reality: Feminist Perspectives on Epistemology, Metaphysics, Methodology and Philosophy of Science* (Dordrecht [Netherlands], 1983), 207–25 (thanks to my colleague Silvia Federici for a copy). Among the great modern architects, Le Corbusier inherited a French classical sense of "masses" in light; Mies van der Rohe indulged a certain mystique of light (see Massimo Cacciari, "Mies's Classics," *Res: Anthropology and Aesthetics,* no. 16 [Autumn 1988], 9–16, esp. 13), but not, I think, in Kahn's polemical way.

12. "To us the vast majority of Latin writers seem never to have conceived of their language as a means of self-expression, but have used it much as do sixth-form boys, making versions instead of expressing themselves.... Homer and Sophocles wrote because they had something to say, Virgil and Seneca because it seemed right to say something.... Roman philosophy reminds one of an exceptionally high-toned debate in the House of Commons." Clive Bell, *Civilization* (1928) in his *"Civilization" and "Old Friends"* (Chicago, 1973), 39–40.

13. That to his contemporary Raphael, around 1500, Bramante's architecture was practically Greek in its paradigmatic classical truth is apparent in the critically confident presiding of Bramante's "new" Roman Tempietto over Raphael's great tapestry composition *Saint Paul Preaching at Athens,* c. 1514–16 (London, Victoria and Albert Museum).

14. What I tend to see as historical mannerism in Kahn's work is part and parcel of its linguistic richness and "ambiguity." Both matters are also intertwined in respect to modernist architecture in Colin Rowe and Robert Slutzky, "Transparency: Literal and Phenomenal," *Perspecta: The Yale Architectural Journal* (1963), repr. in Rowe's *The Mathematics of the Ideal Villa and Other Essays* (Cambridge, Mass., 1976), 159–83, and "Transparency: Literal and Phenomenal; Part II," *Perspecta,* nos. 13–14 (1971), 287–301. At several points the present essay, written before reviewing their astute study, might readily adapt to Rowe and Slutzky's terms.

15. Questions of Renaissance Romanism and protomodernism arise almost side by side in Anthony Blunt's consideration of Delorme's chateau of Anet (1549–52), in *Art and Architecture in France, 1500 to 1700* (1953), 2d ed. (Baltimore, 1970). With the chapel, an "emphasis on the circle is in accord with the practice of Bramante, but Philibert's application of it is quite different from his. In the Tempietto Bramante chooses the simplest combination of the mathematically pure forms of circle, cylinder and sphere, whereas de l'Orme, with an almost naive enthusiasm, seeks a much more complex solution" (52); yet the entrance pavilion is "designed almost without the use of classical elements ... and ... thought of as a series of blocks of

masonry, playing against each other almost in the manner of functionalist architecture," so that the piece "is perhaps the most striking example of Philibert's ability to think in monumental terms while at the same time remaining free from any tendency to imitate models of the Italian High Renaissance" (53).

16. Philibert Delorme, *Architecture* (ed. Rouen, 1648; repr. Ridgewood, N.J., 1964), book 3, chap. 8, headed "L'artifice des traicts geometriques, servir quand on veux faire d'une maison, ou de deux mal commencées ou imparfaictes (soit vieils logis ou autrement), une belle & parfaicte maison, y accomodant tous les membres, & parties du vieil edifice avecques le neuf'; 65r–7r, with pls. on f. 66r (before) and f. 67r (after).

17. Cf. ibid., illus. on ff. 121r (view of wall with inset barbican), 274v (plan of a cellar kitchen with inset cylindrical ovens), the former, however, borrowed from Fra Giocondo's Venice, 1511, edition of Vitruvius (illus. as such in Vitruvius's *The Ten Books on Architecture,* trans. Morris Hicky Morgan [Cambridge, Mass., 1914; repr. New York, 1960], 23).

18. My appreciation of Delorme owes much to my studies under Dorothea Nyberg.

19. Giedion's materialist Romanism inevitably collides with the tradition of seeing the Gothic as anticlassically protofunctionalist. As early as the 1830s, the engineering-attuned William Whewell, in *History of the Inductive Sciences from the Earliest to the Present Time* (1837), 3d ed., 2 vols. (New York, 1859), had rejected Roman imperial architecture for not being "mechanically consistent"; "The decorative members must represent a structure which has in it a principle of support and stability. . . . But to be content with colonnades and pediments, which, though they imitated the forms of the Grecian ones, were destitute of their mechanical truth, belonged to the decline of art; and showed that men had lost the idea of force, and retained only that of shape" (vol. 1, 191). Such was the "perverse inventiveness" of Roman building (192). "Building became not only a mere art, but an art exercised by masters without any skill, and without feeling for real beauty" until the Gothic revived mechanical truth (247). I am grateful to Meyer Schapiro for a discussion and for lending me this text.

20. If there was homage here, it was gracious at a difficult moment for Corbusier. Around the time this building was begun, in 1951, Le Corbusier was in America, struggling to defend his role in the United Nations project; his also politically difficult Unité d'Habitation (1947–52) was under construction at Marseilles; and his perhaps all the more understandably mold-breaking, meditational Ronchamp Chapel project (1950–5), by which doctrinaire modernists felt betrayed, was also under way. See Charles Jencks, *Le Corbusier and the Tragic View of Architecture* (Cambridge, Mass., 1973), section "The Brutalist Language," esp. 137–53, on these projects; on Ronchamp, see this volume, Chap. 8.

21. Patricia Cummings Loud, "Yale University Art Gallery," in *Kahn,* 314–17, esp. 315. Fuller himself described Tyng as "Louis Kahn's geometrical strategist": De Long, "The Mind," 53.

22. Vincent Scully, "Introduction," in *Kahn,* 12–14, here 13–14.

23. "Among the city's finest works of architecture": Eliot Willensky and Norval White, eds., *A.I.A. Guide to New York City,* 3d ed. (New York, 1988), 254.

24. As to I.M. Pei's concrete Herbert F. Johnson Museum of Art, Cornell University, Ithaca, New York, 1969–73, related insofar as it looks to be missing three floors in one side: like other works by that bestower of frigid corporate-authoritarian luxury, including the east wing of the National Gallery, it makes a big architectural

deal out of forms first proposed in minimal sculpture, by Tony Smith in particular (see this volume, Chap. 10).

25. Already there arises a problem of deep significance to architecture under industrial conditions: the common necessity of fudging over material discrepancy in the use of standardized units. If you try simply making a square shed out of standard four-by-eight-foot panels, you will realize that at least two panels will have to be cut down from standard width, or else you will have to settle for a shed that is not exactly square, in which case, goodbye to ideal form. More theoretically: J. N. L. Durand's early institution of graph paper in academic instruction, c. 1800, induced an emptying of centralized planning of sacred-symbolic significance except for an air of absolutist control – now the arbitrary centrality of an imposed, this-worldly ego. Here, too, ironically, begins the modernist cult of the plan as governing all else, and if Durand's influence had done nothing more, it would have secured for graph paper's underlying organizing grid an "abstract" independence from the grid's instrumental role as a pictorializing device in Renaissance perspective study (on this last, see Joseph Mascheck, "Alberti's 'Window': Art-Historiographic Notes on an Anti-Modernist Misprision" [1989; 1991], in my *Modernities: Art-Matters in the Present* [University Park, Pa., 1993], 13–29).

26. Rowe, "Neo-'Classicism' and Modern Architecture, II" (1973), *Mathematics*, 139–58, esp. 152ff.

27. Rowe and Slutzky, "Transparency," part 2, esp. 296–97.

28. Martin Heidegger, "Building Dwelling Thinking," in his *Poetry, Language, Thought,* trans. Albert Hofstadter (New York, 1975), 143–61. One could certainly imagine Kahn saying, for example, "A boundary is not that at which something stops but, as the Greeks recognized, the boundary is that from which something *begins its presencing*. . . . Space is in essence that for which room has been made, that which is let into its bounds" (154; emphasis in original), not to speak of Heidegger's complex "fourfold" as a transcendental far beyond the reach of mundane functionalism.

29. Wilder Green, "Louis I. Kahn, Architect: Alfred Newton Richards Medical Research Building," *Museum of Modern Art Bulletin*, no. 28 (1961).

30. An important early relief sculpture was made by Robert Smithson while this work was nearing completion: *Enantiomorphic Chambers*, of 1964 (lost), which consisted of two open, irregular boxes of sheet metal with interior mirrors, hanging side by side as complex mutual inversions of each other's structure; see Joseph Mascheck, "Smithson's Earth: Notes and Retrievals," in the New York Cultural Center catalogue *Robert Smithson: Drawings* (New York, 1974, 19–29, repr. (without illus.) as "Smithson's Earth: Spontaneous Retrievals" in my *Historical Present: Essays of the 1970s* (Ann Arbor, Mich., 1984), 127–36, esp. 127.

31. The unplanted starkness of the terrace, in itself beautiful, owes something to consultation with Luis Barragan in 1966; see Daniel S. Friedman, "Salk Institute for Biological Studies," in *Kahn*, 330–9, esp. 334.

32. Donald Hoffmann, *Frank Lloyd Wright's Robie House: The Illustrated Story of an Architectural Masterpiece* (New York, 1984), 29, with illustration.

33. Englished by James O'Gorman as *Principles of Architectural History* (1968); see Jean Castex, *Frank Lloyd Wright: Le printemps de la Prairie House* (Liège, 1985), 143–4, with fig. 87 on p. 146.

34. Mascheck, "Robert Mangold: A Humanist Geometry," *Artforum*, 12 no.6 (March 1974), 39–43, with diagrams; repr. in Amy Baker Sandback, ed., *Looking Crit-*

ically: 21 Years of Artforum (Ann Arbor, Mich., 1984), and also as "Mangold's Humanist Geometry," in Masheck, *Historical Present,* 103–07 (without illus.). The device of a circle centered within a semicircular tympanum appears, among other places, in the interior of Giuliano da Sangallo's projected Saint Peter's; on the facade of Bramante's House of Raphael, this in turn studied in a drawing by Palladio; on the facade of the mannerist Palazzo Branconio dell'Aquila, Rome; and in the gable of Vignola's original facade design for the church of the Gesù (1570).

35. Masheck, "Neo-Neo," *Artforum,* 18, no. 1 (September 1979), 40–8, repr. (without illus.) in *Historical Present,* 231–48, esp. 236–7. Harry B. Gutman, "Zur Ikonologie der fresken Raffaels in der Stanza della Segnatura," *Zeitschrift für Kunstgeschichte,* 21 (1958), 27–39, suggests oppositely but relevantly that building is under demolition and represents the Synagogue (32). Hearsay has it that Wright's great work for the Oak Park Unitarians has obscured a privately more orthodox Christian theology in his family.

36. James S. Ackerman, *The Architecture of Michelangelo,* 2d ed. (Chicago, 1986), 246, 250; also 251: "The scenographic Porta Pia was more like a painting than a statue."

37. Ibid., 254, 258.

38. Carla Yanni, "Fine Arts Center, School and Performing Arts Theater," in *Kahn,* 346–51, here 350.

39. Robert Venturi, *Complexity and Contradiction in Architecture,* Museum of Modern Art Papers in Architecture, 1 (New York, 1966), 64, 65.

40. Aware that in general Kahn's architecture is not supposed to be picturesque, I will fall back on my equally unauthorized sense of compositional picturesqueness in then-contemporary abstract sculpture by Anthony Caro, which I likened to earlier British painting, sculpture and architecture in Masheck, "Reflections on Caro's Englishness," *Studio International,* 188, no. 969 (September 1974), 93–6, repr. (without illus.) as "The Englishness of Caro" in *Historical Present,* 97–102.

41. De Long, "Assembly," in *Kahn,* 78–93, here 80, with refs. to J. Kieffer, *Louis I. Kahn and the Rituals of Architecture* (privately pub., 1981), as cited in Joseph Burton, "Notes from Volume Zero: Louis Kahn and the Language of God," *Perspecta,* no. 20 (1983), 80–3.

42. See Chapter 10.

43. In Baroque architecture, inversions of forms or of form-complexes manifest a general plasticity.

44. Reyner Banham, *A Concrete Atlantis: U.S. Industrial Building and European Modern Architecture* (Cambridge, Mass., 1986), esp. 22–107, for my review of which, see Masheck, "Temples to the Dynamo" (1987), in *Modernities,* 51–6.

45. Ironically, the Olivetti firm itself – which in the early 1960s was identified with the victory of modernist "good design" thanks largely to its original "Lettera 22" typewriter, which even had its own distinctive chamfer-serifed type face (and there was inexhaustible popular appeal to the sample typewriters on pylons, out on the sidewalk in front of Olivetti's Fifth Avenue showroom, around the corner from the Museum of Modern Art) – was here associating with traditionally clunky Underwood. Before long the once-coveted curvaceous Italian machine would be made in Mexico.

46. Wittkower, *Architectural Principles,* 76 with n. 2, 77; also "Pseudo-Palladian Elements in English Neoclassicism" (1945), in his *Palladio and Palladianism,* ed. Margot Wittkower (New York, 1974), 154–74. That Kahn's tympana are suppressed may itself be a mannerist symptom. Heinrich Wölfflin, *Renaissance and Baroque,* trans.

Kathrin Simon (London, 1964), speaking *avant le lettre* of a mannerist "effect of yielding to oppressive weight," commented, "The serene semicircular arch was depressed into an ellipse, first of all in the second storey of the Palazzo Farnese," which Vasari had noticed (45, with 165 n. 2).

47. Wolfgang Lotz, "The Roman Legacy in Sansovino's Venetian Buildings" (1963), in his *Studies in Italian Renaissance Architecture* (Cambridge, Mass., 1977), 140-51, with figs. 81-94 on pp. 164-71.

48. J. C. Krafft and N. Ransonnette, *Plans, coupes et élévations des plus belles maisons et des hôtels à Paris* (Paris, 1801-2); illus. in Alexander Tzonis and Liane Lefaivre, *Classical Architecture: The Poetics of Order* (Cambridge, Mass., 1986), figs. 170, 171 on pp. 240-1.

49. Don Judd, "Art and Architecture" (1983), fragment of a lecture given at the Yale School of Art and Architecture, in his Westfälischer Kunstverein book *Architektur* (Münster, 1990), 177-8.

50. Limerick, in Ireland, for instance, a city lucky at least architecturally to have remained untouched by money, now sports a lawned luxury apartment complex on the Shannon, with classico-moderne amenities in walking distance. At this writing, nearby Sarsfield House, a large modernist office block apparently deemed obsolete but of real architectural interest, is almost as sadly abandoned as the adjacent (genuine) neo-Palladian Customs House, 1765-9, by Davis Ducart.

51. Banham, *Concrete Atlantis*, 108-79.

52. Aloïs Riegl, *Late Roman Art Industry* (1901), trans. Rolf Winkes, Archaeologica, 36 (Rome, 1985), 33-4; in the original, *Spätrömische Kunstindustrie,* 2d ed. (Vienna, 1927; repr. Darmstadt, 1964), 49-50.

53. Henry-Russell Hitchcock, *Architecture: Nineteenth and Twentieth Centuries,* 2d ed., Pelican History of Art (Harmondsworth, 1963), 407. In *Modern Architecture: Romanticism and Reintegration* (New York, 1929), 87, not mentioning New Delhi at all (too contemporaneous?), Hitchcock writes that in 1900 Lutyens "may almost be said to have built all unwittingly the finest house of the New Tradition," Deanery Gardens, at Sonning, whose craftsmanly virtues are extolled while its "perfect adaptation of the plan to contemporary life" is conceded. With Denise Scott Brown, Robert Venturi, who worked in Kahn's office, embraced Lutyens against the rejections of Alison Smithson ("The Responsibility of Lutyens," also Peter Smithson, "The Viceroy's House in Imperial Delhi," both in the *Journal of the Royal Institute of British Architects,* April 1969): see "Learning from Lutyens: Reply to Alison and Peter Smithson" (1969), in Venturi and Brown's *A View from the Campidoglio: Selected Essays, 1953-1984* (New York, 1984), 20-3. At the same moment, Rudolf Wittkower was encouraging the present writer to look into C. R. Cockerell (1788-1863), then still overlooked by "Georgianists" (no doubt too eccentrically classical) and arguably a kind of Lutyens of a century earlier.

54. De Long, "Assembly . . . [sic] A Place of Transcendence," in *Kahn,* 78-93, observes that Kahn likened his wife, Harriet Patterson, a landscape architect, to Gertrude Jeckyll as landscape-architectural associate of Lutyens (80-1).

55. Manfredo Tafuri, *Theories and History of Architecture* (1968; 4th ed., 1976), trans. Giorgio Verrecchia (New York, 1980), 55-7.

56. Ibid., 63.

57. Ibid., 92.

58. Ibid., 97.

59. Ibid., 111.

60. See ibid., 113, 135-6 n. 21.

61. "Many of the pure geometrical objects projected by . . . cultured American architecture as obscure symbols of an existential condition torn between protest against the psychological squashing of *urban consumerism* and the fascination of the changeable, of the urban surreal, of *Kitsch,* are, in fact, architectural translations of the symbolism of the new *pop* realism"; ibid., 130.

62. Illustrated conveniently in Robert Tavernor, *Palladio and Palladianism,* World of Art (London, Thames and Hudson, 1991), fig. 103 on p. 103.

63. John Summerson, "The Mischievous Analogy," in his *Heavenly Mansions and Other Essays on Architecture* (New York, 1963), 195–218, esp. 203–4.

10. Crystalline Form, Worringer, and the Minimalism of Tony Smith

1. I have been scrutinizing photographs of a bronze Silenus of the late sixth century B.C. and David Smith's *Albany III,* 1959, of painted steel, but countless other comparable examples would serve as well.

2. A pair of critical essays written in the 1950s can be mentioned for their timely, worthy struggle with the ambiguity of "old" classicism versus the classic-modernity of the early twentieth century: Colin Rowe, "Neo-'Classicism' and Modern Architecture, I" and "Neo-'Classicism' and Modern Architecture, II" (both 1973), in his *The Mathematics of the Ideal Villa and Other Essays* (Cambridge, Mass., 1976), 119–38 and 139–58, respectively. William Curtis, "Modern Transformations of Classicism," *Architectural Review,* 176, no.1050 (August 1984), 39–47, understandably preoccupied under pressure of postmodernism, does not itself penetrate to a deeper sense of precedent.

3. See Joseph Mascheck, "Neolithic-Modern" (1984) and "On Cycladic Ultramodernity" (1989), in his *Modernities: Art-Matters in the Present* (University Park, Pa., 1993), 39–43.

4. Wilhelm Worringer, *Form Problems of the Gothic,* authorized American ed. (unsigned trans. dedicated in 1918) (New York, 1920?), 65.

5. William Rubin, ed., in his Museum of Modern Art exhibition catalog *Pablo Picasso: A Retrospective* (New York, 1980), 89.

6. Ibid., 87.

7. Heinrich Wölfflin, "Italien und das deutsche Formgefühl," collected in his *Gedanken zur Kunstgeschichte; gedrucktes und ungedrucktes* (1940), 4th ed. (Basel, 1947), 119–26, here 120: "Wie schlicht und leicht fassbar die Flächen und Kuben."

8. Mascheck, "Raw Art: 'Primitive' Authenticity and German Expressionism," *Res: Anthropology and Aesthetics,* no. 4 (Autumn 1982), 92–117; *Modernities,* 145–80.

9. Mascheck, "A Critical Contribution to Art" (brief comment), *Art-Rite* (New York), no. 1 (April 15, 1973), 5.

10. Henry-Russell Hitchcock, *Architecture: Nineteenth and Twentieth Centuries,* 2d ed., Pelican History of Art (Harmondsworth, 1963), 341.

11. Fritz Burger, *Einführung in die Moderne Kunst* (Burger et al., *Die Kunst des 19. und 20. Jahrhunderts,* I), Handbuch der Kunstwissenschaft (Berlin-Neubabelsberg, 1917), 18–19, with illus.

12. In the Westfälisches Landesmuseum catalog *Tony Smith: Skulpturen und Zeichnungen / Sculptures and Drawings / 1961–1969* (Münster, 1988), illus. on 25; references to this catalog given hereafter as *Tony Smith.*

13. Albrecht Dürer, *The Human Figure: The Complete "Dresden Sketchbook,"* ed. Walter L. Strauss (New York, 1972), cat. 138 on p. 280 with fig. on p. 281.

14. James Joyce, *Ulysses,* The Modern Library (New York, 1961), 181.

15. José A. Argüelles, *Charles Henry and the Formation of a Psychophysical Aesthetic* (Chicago, 1972), 60n–61n. Even though minimal art is generally antispiritual in the extreme, one might also think of the passionlessness, or dispassion, of *apatheia,* in mystics.

16. Recall that the great Viennese philosopher Ludwig Wittgenstein's *Philosophical Investigations* (posthumous) opens with an extended quotation from Augustine.

17. Robert Goldwater, *Primitivism in Modern Art,* rev. ed. (New York, 1967), 28; thanks to Marjorie Welish for calling my attention to this.

18. Johann Wolfgang von Goethe, *Italian Journey (1786–1788),* trans. W. H. Auden and Elizabeth Mayer (New York, 1968), 364. In *Naturphilosophie* the regularity of crystal structure was not at odds with "organic" structure, if only because what Goethe and others sought in organic structure was precisely a lawful order. In the eighteenth century crystals grown in solution were actually exhibited as "stone plants"; Philip Steadman, *The Evolution of Designs: Biological Analogy in Architecture and the Applied Arts,* Cambridge Architectural and Urban Studies (Cambridge, 1979), 26–7, quoting P. C. Ritterbush, *The Art of Organic Forms* (Washington, D.C., 1924), 14. A diary entry of Goethe's shows him thinking of "architecture . . . [as] being like mineralogy, botany and zoology" (quoted loc. cit. without citation; ellipsis Steadman's). A definitive text in the larger matter is Friedrich Wilhelm von Schelling's pantheistic *Ideen zu einer Philosophie der Natur* (1797).

19. Friedrich August Kekulé von Stradonitz, untitled address to the German Chemical Society, *Berichte der Deutschen Chemischen Gesellschaft* (Berlin), 23 (1890), 1302–11, here 1304, 1307.

20. Aloïs Riegl, *Late Roman Art Industry,* trans. and ed. Rolf Winkes, (series) Archaeologica, 36 (Rome, 1985), 194; in the original: *Stätrömische Kunstindustrie,* 2d ed. (Vienna, 1927; repr. Darmstadt, 1964), 343.

21. Ibid., English, 208.

22. Friedrich Nietzsche, *The Birth of Tragedy and The Case of Wagner,* trans. Walter Kaufmann (New York, 1967), 24.

23. Ibid., 39 (emphasis added).

24. Ibid., 41 (emphasis added to "stone by stone").

25. Ibid., 47.

26. Ibid., 67.

27. Worringer, *Abstraction and Empathy: A Contribution to the Psychology of Style,* 3d ed., trans. Michael Bullock (Cleveland, Ohio, 1967), 55; in the original: *Abstraktion und Einfühlung: ein Beitrag zur Stilpsychologie,* 4th ed. (Munich, 1916), 72.

28. Compare *Nymph and Satyr,* a bronze by Théodore Géricault, with a type of Paleolithic bone carving of wild beasts.

29. Worringer, *Abstraction,* English, 112–13.

30. *Viollet-le-Duc: Le dictionnaire d'architecture: Relevés et observations,* ed. Philippe Boudon and Philippe Deshayes (Brussels, 1979), 271–5, with fig. 5 on p. 275.

31. John Ruskin, *The Seven Lamps of Architecture* (New York, 1961), 104–5.

32. Ruskin, *The Stones of Venice,* ed. J. G. Links (New York, 1960; repr., New York, n.d.), 106.

33. Arthur Schopenhauer, *The World as Will and Representation,* trans. E. F. J. Payne, 2 vols. (Indian Hills, Colo., 1958), vol. 1, 258–9.

34. Ibid., 132.

35. Ibid., 155.

36. Ibid., vol. 2, 194–5 (emphasis in original).

271

37. Ibid., 296 (emphases in original).

38. Ibid., 416–19.

39. Georg Wilhelm Friedrich Hegel, *Aesthetics: Lectures on Fine Art,* trans. T. M. Knox, 2 vols. (Oxford, 1975), vol. 1, 130.

40. Ibid., 136.

41. Ibid., vol. 2, 653.

42. Ibid., 654; in the original, Hegel, *Vorlesungen über die Aesthetik (Werke,* 14), ed. Eva Moldenhauer and Karl Markus Michel (Frankfurt am/Main, 1970), vol. 2, 295 ("abstrakt und verständig" [intelligible]).

43. Johann Christoph Friedrich von Schiller, *"On Naive and Sentimental Poetry" and "On the Sublime": Two Essays,* trans. and ed. Julius A. Elias (New York, 1966), 105.

44. Ibid., 106; in the original: "Uber naive und sentimentalische Dichtung," in *Schillers Sämtliche Werke,* 14 vols. (Berlin, n.d.), vol. 14, 118–98, here 135.

45. Ibid., English, 142.

46. Ibid., English, 158; German, 174.

47. Ibid., English, 103 (emphasis in original). One might want to excavate still deeper, under Schiller's paired categories, to the different but not irrelevant opposition proposed in Oliver Goldsmith's "Essay on the Theatre; or, A Comparison Between Sentimental and Laughing Comedy" (1773).

48. Nietzsche, *Birth,* 43.

49. Schiller, *Naive and Sentimental Poetry,* English, 98; German, 129.

50. Immanuel Kant, *Critique of Judgement,* trans. J. H. Bernard, The Hafner Library of Classics (New York, 1951), 212.

51. Worringer, *Abstraction and Empathy,* 4; in the German ed., 4.

52. Joseph Masheck, "Kuspit's LeWitt: Has He Got Style?" *Art in America,* 64, no. 9 (November–December 1976), 107–10, with illus. on 109 (reprint in LeWitt anthology by Editrice Inonia, Rome, forthcoming); Donald Kuspit's response, January–February; reply, March–April.

53. Emil Kaufmann, *Architecture in the Age of Reason: Baroque and Post-Baroque in England, Italy and France* (Cambridge, Mass., 1955; repr. New York, 1968), esp. 225 n. 213, criticizing Rudolf Wittkower, "Principles of Palladio's Architecture," *Journal of the Warburg Institute,* 7 (1944), 102–22; 8 (1945), 68–106, esp. vol. 8, 98; this followed by Wittkower, "English Literature on Architecture" (1966), in his *Palladio and Palladianism,* ed. Margot Wittkower (New York, 1974), 94–112, esp. 104 (not mentioning Kaufmann). Morris's proportional cube plate is now also illustrated in Joseph Rykwert, *The First Moderns: The Architects of the Eighteenth Century* (Cambridge, Mass., 1980), on 191.

54. Kaufmann, *Architecture,* 225 n. 213, with ref. to Robert Morris, *Lectures on Architecture* (London, 1734–6), Lecture 9, 147.

55. Rykwert, *First Moderns,* 193.

56. Ibid., 191.

57. Walter Benjamin, "Louis-Philippe or the Interior," in his "Paris: The Capital of the Nineteenth Century" (finished 1935), trans. Quintin Hoare, in his *Charles Baudelaire: A Lyric Poet in the Era of High Capitalism,* ed. and trans. Harry Zohn (London, 1973), 167–9.

58. Benedetto Gravagnuolo, *Adolf Loos: Theory and Works,* trans. C. H. Evans (New York, 1982), 50.

59. On which see Ian Boyd Whyte, ed. and trans., *The Crystal Chain Letters: Architectural Fantasies by Bruno Taut and His Circle* (Cambridge, Mass., 1985); review by

Masheck, "Expressionist Fantasias: The Crystal Chain Letters" (1986), in his *Modernities,* 45–9.

60. Robert Rosenblum, *Transformations in Late Eighteenth-Century Art* (Princeton, N.J., 1970), 150–1, with pl. 181.

61. Kaufmann, *Architecture,* fig. 14 after p. 118.

62. In Angela Westwater and Carl Andre's Kunsthalle Bern catalog *Carl Andre: Sculpture, 1958–1974* (Bern, 1975), cat. no. 1966–1 (and following), *Equivalent I,* 1966 (destroyed; remade, 1969), on 21 with fig. on 18.

63. According to Wittkower, the authority of a generation on such matters, Morris was well versed in harmonic proportion theory, in the most orthodox line of Palladio; "English Literature," 94–112, here 104.

64. See the interesting study by Mary McLeod, " 'Architecture or Revolution': Taylorism, Technocracy and Social Change," *Art Journal,* 43 (1983), 132–47.

65. Gravagnuolo, *Adolf Loos,* 170, with illus.

66. Reyner Banham, *A Concrete Atlantis: U.S. Industrial Building and European Modern Architecture, 1900–1925* (Cambridge, Mass., 1986), 195, 197, 201; review by Masheck, "Temples to the Dynamo: The 'Daylight' Factory and the Grain Elevator" (1987), in his *Modernities.* Neil H. Donahue has shown that after Worringer's own *Abstraction and Empathy* (1908) had stimulated Walter Gropius's enthusiasm for American industrial buildings, Worringer himself reacted in fright in the later Weimar period, identifying, in *Agyptische Kunst* (1927), the ancient Egyptian and modern American cultures as similarly demasculinized and soulless, spiritually shallow and materialistic: "From Worringer to Baudrillard and Back: Ancient Americans and (Post)Modern Culture in Weimar Germany," *Deutsche Vierteljahrsschrift,* 66 (1992).

67. Worringer, *Form Problems,* title page.

68. Ibid., pl. 13, opp. p. 88.

69. Banham, *Concrete Atlantis,* 202.

70. Ibid., 258 n. 19.

71. Illus., *Tony Smith,* pl. on 38.

72. Geoffrey Scott, *The Architecture of Humanism: A Study in the History of Taste,* 2d ed. (London, 1924), 243, 244.

73. I rely here and below on Joan H. Pachner, "Tony Smith: Architecture into Sculpture," in *Tony Smith,* 48–71 (German and English on facing pages), here 62 (English) n. 7.

74. Ibid., 62 n. 2.

75. Ibid., 50, with fig. 2.

76. Ibid., with fig. 3 and fig. 7 on p. 52. On the vicissitudes of the church design, Steven Naifeh and Gregory White Smith, *Jackson Pollock: An American Saga* (New York, 1989), 657, 681, 761–2; also E. A. Carmean, "The Church Project: Pollock's Passion Themes," *Art in America,* 70 (Summer 1982), 110–22, the latter disputed furiously, seemingly as daring to entail religion at all, in Rosalind E. Krauss, "Reading Jackson Pollock, Abstractly" (1982), in her *The Originality of the Avant-Garde and Other Modernist Myths* (Cambridge, Mass., 1985), 221–42.

77. Pachner, "Tony Smith" 52 (English), with figs. 4, 5 on p. 51.

78. Pei's 1968 Everson Museum, at Syracuse, N.Y., and his Herbert F. Johnson Museum of Art for Cornell University, at Ithaca, of 1969–73, both carry over the hefty cantilevered blockiness of a Smith sculpture like *Keys to Given!,* of which the model dates from 1965 (illus. *Tony Smith,* pls. on 10, 11). As to Pei's later "East Wing" (disjunct from the old building) at the National Gallery, Washington,

for which the 1962 *Tower of the Winds* is a likely prototype: it is almost embarrassing to see Smith's *Wandering Rocks*, 1967, placed beside it.

79. Jaroslav Vokoun, "Czech Cubism," *Architectural Review*, 139 (March 1966), 229–33, offering, significantly, certain Bohemian Gothic anticipations; there are also Maria Benesova, "Architettura cubista in Boemia," *Casabella*, no. 314 (May 1967), 62–7, and Milos Pistorius, "Kubistická Architektura v Praze," *Staleta Praha*, 4 (1969), 135–54 (English summary, "Cubist Prague," 219–20). The wedgelike serifs of the 1966 title typeface resemble serifs, said to be influenced by Roman engraved inscriptions, in Celtic manuscript illumination.

80. Rosemary Haag Bletter, "The Interpretation of the Glass Dream: Expressionist Architecture and the History of the Crystal Metaphor," *Journal of the Society of Architectural Historians*, 40 (1981), 20–43, here 20, with figs. 3 on p. 21 (1919) and 4 on p. 22 (1920).

81. Jacob Boehme, "On the Supersensual Life . . . ; a Conversation of a Teacher and Student" (1622), the "sixth treatise" of *The Way to Christ*, trans. Peter Erb, The Classics of Western Spirituality (New York, 1978), 186–7.

82. Worringer, *Abstraction*, 127.

11. Form Behind Concept

1. Carl Andre, "Note on Bernhard and Hilla Becher," *Artforum*, 11, no. 4 (December 1972), 59–61.

2. For other remarks by Andre on photography, see his and Hollis Frampton's interesting *12 Dialogues, 1962–1963: Photographs by Hollis Frampton*, ed. Benjamin H. D. Buchloh (Halifax, 1981).

3. Roger Fry, "Some Questions in Aesthetics," in his *Transformations: Critical and Speculative Essays on Art* (New York, 1926), 1–43, here 37.

4. *Wanderings and Pencillings Amongst Ruins of the Olden Time: A Series of Seventy-Three Etchings by George Cuitt, Esq., with Descriptive Letterpress* (1848), rev. ed. (London, 1855), 36.

5. *Joseph Pennell's Pictures of the Wonder of Work: Reproductions of a Series of Drawings, Etchings, Lithographs Made by Him Around the World, 1881–1915, with Impressions and Notes by the Artist* (Philadelphia, 1916), notes accompanying pl. 25, as quoted in Joseph Masheck, "The Panama Canal and Other Works of Work" (1971), in my *Historical Present: Essays of the 1970s* (Ann Arbor, Mich. 1984), 117–25, here 125 n. 14. On such enthusiasms among European modernists, see Reyner Banham, *A Concrete Atlantis: U.S. Industrial Building and European Modern Architecture, 1900–1925* (Cambridge, Mass., 1986), reviewed by Masheck, "Temples to The Dynamo: The 'Daylight' Factory and the Grain Elevator" (1987), in my *Modernities: Art-Matters in the Present* (University Park, Pa., 1993), 51–6.

6. H. I. Brock, "A Span That Symbolizes the Steel Age," *New York Times Magazine*, September 6, 1931, 4, 5, 21, here 4. While it was uncertain whether the towers would stay unsheathed beyond the Depression, "The notion has got considerably diffused that what has already been achieved in carrying out the monumental design in steel provides an eyeful that could hardly be bettered by trying to make the steel towers look like stone piers – even stone piers designed by the architect of the Woolworth Building." For the "skeletons" of the bridge "have now a fascination for many, a fashion which is not less essentially sentimental because it attaches to a material usually conceived as starkly utilitarian." And, "New York will become familiar with . . . a steel bridge with steel towers expressing their structure in the

manner dear to the school that arrogates to itself the name of 'functionalist' " (4–5). Days later, the *Times* endorsed leaving the engineering structure exposed, in that it made "a special appeal to the present generation"; for, "Many New Yorkers who have watched these naked steel skeletons rise like giants against the skyline have been fascinated rather than repelled by their majestic contours." No one knows if "public favor [should] ultimately turn against this bit of self-expression in iron and steel," but the bridge, which "another generation might call uncouth . . . gaunt as it stands . . . speak[s] worlds for the esthetic sense of engineer and advisers": "A Bridge of Naked Steel," *New York Times,* September 9, 1931, 26, col. 4.

7. Illus. in the National Collection of Fine Arts catalog *Charles Sheeler* (Washington, 1968), fig. 106 (color) on p. 58, fig. on p. 73, respectively.

8. Donald Judd, "Twentieth-Century Engineering" (1964), in his *Architektur* (1989), 2d ed. (Münster: Westfälischer Kunstverein, 1990), 173–5, here 173. Later Judd would write, "Consideration of the function is enjoyable. It's not in the way of being creative – it's against 'creative,' a present delusion and one in the past as well." Faujas de Saint-Fond is quoted as saying of factories in 1797: "L'architecture est une peste pour ces sortes d'establissements!"; "Art and Architecture" (1987), ibid., 194–9, here 197.

9. Ibid., 174–5.

10. Masheck, "Robert Grosvenor's Fractured Beams," *Artforum,* 12, no. 9 (May 1974), 36–39: "Even to notice the striking similarity between *Topanga* and the . . . Solar Observatory . . . is to compare it with an extremely sculptural object, in fact, more a telescope than a building" (36); also illus. in relation to another minimal sculpture (Robert Murray's *Track,* 1966) in Masheck, "Formalism, Minimalism and Recent Developments," in Martin Friedman, ed., *Walker Art Center: Painting and Sculpture from the Collection* (Minneapolis, 1990), 72–85, fig. on 78.

11. Judd, "Engineering," 175.

12. See Bernd and Hilla Becher, *Framework Houses of the Siegen Industrial Region* (Munich, 1977).

13. Dan Graham, "Photographs," in Gregory Battcock, ed., *Minimalism: A Critical Anthology* (New York, 1968), 175–80; these images are from a wrongly edited photoessay, "Homes for America" (1966), now reconstructed in the Van Abbemuseum publication *Dan Graham: Articles* (Eindhoven, 1978), 5–10. In the same catalog Benjamin H. D. Buchloh, "Moments of History in the Work of Dan Graham," 73–7, here 73, rightly points out how mistaken could be even the "minimalist's perspective" of another artist (Dan Flavin), who in 1966 likened the same photographs to "the consistently clear and plain deviceless reportage of Henri Cartier-Bresson," applied "not to people, as he did, but to their 'feats' of banal vernacular architecture and landscape." Thus even to a sympathetic artist, "photographical information/documentation obviously could not even be conceived as possibly being 'art' (unless 'photographical' art)." The issue at the moment is somewhat different: whether the structures appearing in such images might not also be quasi-artistic, even when presented (revealed?) in light of (photoconceptual) art.

14. On Kelly: see Diane Waldman, *Ellsworth Kelly: Drawings, Collages, Prints* (Greenwich, Conn., n.d.), esp. figs. 1–22 (photographs by the artist) on pp. 30–3; Masheck, "Ellsworth Kelly at the Modern," *Artforum,* 12, no. 3 (November 1973), 54–7; Phyllis Tuchman, "Ellsworth Kelly's Photographs," *Art in America,* 62, no. 1 (January–February 1974), 55–61. On Mangold: Masheck, "A Humanist Geometry," *Artforum,* 12, no. 7 (March 1974), 36–9, reprinted in Amy Baker Sandback,

ed., *Looking Critically: 21 Years of Artforum* (Ann Arbor, Mich., 1984), and as "Mangold's Humanist Geometry" in my *Historical Present: Essays of the 1970s* (Ann Arbor, Mich., 1984), 103–7 (without illus.).

15. Wend Fischer, essay in Die Neue Sammlung (Staatliches Musem für angewandte Kunst) catalog *Industriebauten, 1830–1930: Ein fotografische Dokumentation von Bernd und Hilla Becher* (Munich, 1967), unpaginated.

16. J. M. Richards, *The Functional Tradition in Early Industrial Buildings*, photographs by Eric de Maré (London, 1958), 51.

12. Classical Sass

1. See Nikolaus Pevsner with Suzanne Lang, "The Doric Revival" (1948), in his *Studies in Art, Architecture and Design*, 2 vols. (London, 1968), vd. 1: *From Mannerism to Romanticism*, 196–211, with figs. 8, 10 on p. 199.

2. On affirmative recourse to classicism in contemporary art, see Joseph Mascheck, "Neo-Neo," repr. from *Artforum*, 18, no. 1 (September 1979), 40–8, in his *Historical Present: Essays of the 1970s* (Ann Arbor, Mich., 1984), 231–48 (without illus.).

3. John Miller, *Contamination* (New York, 1982), 5.

4. François René de Chateaubriand, *Itinéraire de Paris à Jerusalem*, ed. Georges Faugeron (Paris, 1964), 135.

5. See Victor Wolfgang von Hagen, *F. Catherwood: Architect-Explorer of Two Worlds* (Barre, Mass., 1968).

6. Gustave Flaubert, *Flaubert in Egypt: A Sensibility on Tour*, ed. and trans. Francis Steegmuller (Chicago, 1977), 159–60 (emphasis in original).

7. Henri Focillon, *The Life of Forms in Art*, rev. ed., trans. Charles Beecher Hogan and George Kubler, Documents of Modern Art (New York, 1948), 35.

8. Edmund Burke, *A Philosophical Enquiry into the Origin of Our Ideas of the Sublime and Beautiful*, ed. James T. Boulton (London 1958, repr. 1967), 80–1, continuing, "And this is not the only instance wherein the opposite extremes operate equally in favour of the sublime, which in all things abhors mediocrity."

9. Ibid., 81.

10. Karl Marx, *Grundrisse: Foundations of the Critique of Political Economy*, trans. Martin Nicolaus (New York, 1973), 110–11.

11. Theo van Doesburg, *Classique, Baroque, Moderne* (Antwerp, 1921), 12. The text is dated December 1918; the publication date appears in the colophon.

12. Benjamin H. D. Buchloh, "Figures of Authority, Ciphers of Regression: Notes on the Return of Representation in European Painting" (1981), in Brian Wallis and Marcia Tucker, eds., *Art after Modernism: Rethinking Representation* (New York, 1984), 106–35 (including important "Postscript" on the Reagan*zeit*); without pretending to bend his approach to mine, it can be said that Buchloh's stimulating historical study retains contextual relevance to the dilemma of contemporary painting in a postmodern(ist) context antithetical to modernist, if not all, painting.

13. Pevsner, "The Counter-Reformation and Mannerism" (1925), trans. David Britt, in his *Studies*, vol. 1, 10–33, esp. "Introduction" dated 1968, 11–12, on the historiography.

14. Ibid., 15.

15. Heinrich Wölfflin, *Renaissance and Baroque* (1888), trans. Kathrin Simon (London, 1964), 45.

16. John Shearman, *Mannerism* (Harmondsworth, 1967), 157.

17. Henri Zerner, "Observations on the Use of the Concept of Mannerism," in Frank-lin W. Robinson and Stephen G. Nichols, Jr., eds., *The Meaning of Mannerism* (Hanover, N.H., 1972), 105–21, esp. 115. If artistic significance, however, were principally art-historical, would it not become limited to what art history can find to say about itself before a given object? On the "end of art" as art's having now already fulfilled a certain historical destiny – that of representation – see the writings of Arthur C. Danto, including *The Transfiguration of the Commonplace* (Cambridge, Mass., 1981) and *The Philosophical Disenfranchisement of Art* (New York, 1986).

18. Smith's book itself is characterized as "portray[ing] Post-Modernism less as Mod-ernism's antithesis than as a cultural analogue of contemporary political and social revolutions in the United States during the 1960s": Michael Hollander, "Attitudes to Modern Architecture in Post-Modern Criticism," *Yale Review*, 69 (1980), 411–26, here 415.

19. Edith Wharton and Ogden Codman, Jr., *The Decoration of Houses*, 2d ed. (New York, 1902; repr., 1978).

20. William B. and Elizabeth Clay Blanford, *Beauport Impressions: An Introduction to Its Collections* (Boston, 1965), 45–6; Ms. Lorna Condon, Curator of Archives of the Society for the Preservation of New England Antiquities, who kindly checked this reference, has also mentioned Nancy Curtis, Richard C. Nylander et al., *Beauport: The Sleeper-McCann House* (Boston, 1990).

21. Henry-Russell Hitchcock, 1966 foreword to Hitchcock and Philip Johnson, *International Style* (New York, 1966), ix.

22. See the special issue of *Architectural Record*, 78, no. 6 (December 1935), 355–458, reprinted as a book, with same pagination: *The Restoration of Colonial Williamsburg in Virginia* (New York, 1935).

23. William Graves Perry, "Notes on the Architecture," *Restoration*, 363–81, here 363.

24. Ibid., 370.

25. An indication of the quasi-official diffusion of the cult of Williamsburg is the reprinting, for the United States Armed Forces Institute, as Education Manual MB550, of Ray Faulkner, Edwin Ziegfeld, and Gerald Hill's textbook *Art Today* (1941), 2d ed. (New York, 1949), in which photographs of rebuilt Williamsburg buildings as well as sixteen pages of text on the Williamsburg "community" serve to associate this model of eighteenth-century British Colonial taste with the sur-prisingly similar (!) "good taste" of markedly middle-class modern architecture and design.

26. Not Piers Court, Gloucestershire, as I reported in the original version of the present essay.

27. Frances Donaldson, *Evelyn Waugh: Portrait of a Country Neighbor* (London, 1967).

28. Illus., Peter Arnell and Ted Bickford, eds., *Robert A. M. Stern, 1965–1980: Toward a Modern Architecture After Modernism* (New York, 1981), 8, 58–65.

29. See this volume, Chap. 13.

30. Charles Jencks, *The Language of Post-Modern Architecture*, rev. ed. (New York, 1977), 72, caption to fig. 118. If this implies handling semantics like so much software, one might want to recall that from the 1950s, after the death of its founder, the Institute of General Semantics of Alfred Korzybski (*Science and Sanity: An Introduction to Non-Aristotelian Systems and General Semantics,* 1933) became known for promulgating a (capitalistically exploitable), proto-McLuhanesque sense of ad-vertising copy as tantamount to poetry in its potential for semantic analysis.

31. James Wines, in *Express* magazine, Fall 1982.

32. Miriam Gusevich, "Purity and Transgression: Reflections on the Architectural Avantgarde's Rejection of Kitsch," *Discourse: Journal for Theoretical Studies in Media and Culture,* 10, no. 1 (Autumn–Winter 1987–8), 90–115, here 109.

33. Barbaralee Diamondstein, conversation with Robert A. M. Stern, as repr. in *Interior Design: The New Freedom in Historic Preservation,* September–October 1982.

34. See Joseph Masheck, "Living Modern: James Stirling's Sackler Museum" (1986), in my *Modernities: Art-Matters in the Present* (University Park, Pa., 1993), 57–62.

35. Leopold Eidlitz, "The Architect of Fashion," *Architectural Record,* April–June 1894.

36. Manfredo Tafuri, *Theories and History of Architecture* (1968; 4th ed., 1976), trans. Giorgio Verrecchia (New York, 1980), 126 with 138 n. 41; see also Lawrence Alloway, "The Development of British Pop," in Lucy R. Lippard, ed., *Pop Art* (London, 1966), 26–68, esp. 29.

37. Ibid., 213.

38. Israel Silvestre, *Marche des marechaux de camp et des cinq quadrilles depuis la grande place derrière l'hostel de Vendosme jusqu'à l'entrée de l'amphithéatre* (Paris, 1664), fold-out engraving, 7¼ inches high by 14 feet, 4½ inches long.

39. Peter Plagens, "Los Angeles: The Ecology of Evil" (1972), in *Moonlight Blues: An Artist's Art Criticism* (Ann Arbor, Mich., 1986), 203–25, here 225.

40. See this volume, Chap. 10.

41. Plagens, "Architecture: Passion and Praxis" (1981), *Moonlight Blues,* 239–44.

42. Fredric Jameson, "Reification and Utopia in Mass Culture," *Social Text,* no. 1 (Winter 1979), 130–48, here 131–2.

43. Albert Camus, "Summer in Algiers," in his *The Myth of Sisyphus and Other Essays,* trans. Justin O'Brien (New York, 1959), 104–13; here, 109, 111.

13. Tired Tropes

1. Charles-Edouard Jeanneret (called Le Corbusier), *Towards a New Architecture,* trans. Frederick Etchells (1927), 2d ed. (London, 1946; repr. 1965), 23. Cf.: "By the use of inert materials and *starting from* conditions more or less utilitarian, you have established certain relationships which have aroused my emotions. This is architecture" (187; emphasis in original). Within a few years the architect and author shows concern over the vulgarization of *Vers une architecture's* "machine à habiter" ideal (on which see this volume, Chap. 6), wondering in "Température," an introductory essay for a new edition of the book dated January 1, 1928, about the sense of a "house-as-tool (*maison-outil*)": "Sanitary installations" may be taken seriously, but "the *sentiment* that dwells (*habite*) in our hearts" is by no means yet "expressed," has not "manifested itself." Against literalist misunderstanding he now dilates on the metaphorical character of his 1923 figure: "We have since provoked indignation afresh when we maintained that this machine might be a *palace.* And by palace we wanted to signify that each organ (*organe*) of the house, by virtue of its disposition in the ensemble, could enter into such moving rapports as to disclose the grandeur and nobility of an *intention.* And this intention was what we meant by *architecture.* To those now absorbed in the problem of the 'machine à habiter' who declare 'architecture is serving (*l'architecture, c'est servir*),' we have replied, 'architecture is moving (*l'architecture, c'est émouvoir*).' And with disdain we have been charged with being a 'poet.' " Charles-Edouard Jeanneret (called Le Corbusier), *Vers une architecture,* rev. ed. (Paris, 1928, repr. 1958), x–xi.

2. Ibid., 31, 202, 164, respectively.

3. Ibid., 75, and illus. of Blondel's 1671 Porte Saint-Denis, Paris – an engraving of

which appears proudly as a frontispiece to Blondel's own *Cours d'architecture enseigné dans l'Académie royale* (Paris, 1675) – on 63. It is Blondel's recourse to a determining compositional "unit of three" that Le Corbusier finds relevant to his own façades. It was rather maverick to say so: not that (re)claiming the academic past is necessarily maverick; but the protomodern Etienne-Louis Boullée had identified Blondel as the author of the Porte Saint-Denis in insulting François Blondel's "feeble" (Ancients') argument against (the Moderns') Claude Perrault; *Boullée's Treatise on Architecture,* ed. Helen Rosenau (London, 1953), 28.

4. Blondel, *Cours,* vol. 2, 137.

5. Anthony Blunt, *Art and Architecture in France, 1500 to 1700,* The Pelican History of Art, 2d ed. (Harmondsworth, 1970), 279 n. 58.

6. Blondel, *Cours,* vol. 1, 1, immediately continuing: "L'on appelle un bon bâtiment, celuy qui est solide, commode, sain & agreable" (One terms good a building that is solid, commodious, sound and agreeable) – a restatement of Vitruvius's traditional triad of *utilitas-firmitas-venustas,* but with the conspicuously proto-Corbusian addition of *sain,* "sound" in the sense of "healthy," or "hale."

7. *Boullée's Treatise,* 27.

8. Ibid., 27.

9. Ibid., 28; the claim is repeated on p. 33.

10. Ibid., 80.

11. Claude Nicolas Ledoux, *L'architecture considérée sous le rapport de l'art, des moeurs et de la législation* (Paris, 1804; repr. Nördlingen, 1981), 83.

12. Ibid., 96.

13. Ibid., 97.

14. Nikolaus Pevsner, *Outline of European Architecture* (New York, 1948), xix.

15. But not necessarily auteuristic "author"-ity, since the anonymity of much Gothic architecture has been romanticized. The Gothic work of Lincoln Cathedral (c. 1192) is attributed to a French architect, Geoffrey de Noiers (or Noyers).

16. Marcus Vitruvius Pollio, *The Ten Books on Architecture,* trans. Morris Hicky Morgan (Cambridge, Mass., 1914; repr. New York, 1960), 16.

17. *The Babylonian Talmud: Seder Mo'ed,* trans. and ed. I. Epstein (London, 1938), 8, continuing – "[and it can, therefore, be regarded as a "house": ed.], otherwise, they do not dwell therein." Thanks to David Shapiro, himself stimulated by Michal Govrin, for suggesting that I consider the Talmud.

18. I. e., "to serve as a dwelling for which purpose a house is built" (ed.); ibid., 9, with nn. 10–12.

19. Thus, for different but comparable juridical purpose, only "a house which is intended to stand," not a hovel "intended to be demolished" (3b); ibid., 11.

20. Antoine Arnauld and Gottfried Wilhelm Leibniz, *The Leibniz-Arnauld Correspondence,* ed. and trans. H. T. Mason (Manchester, 1967), Letter 26, Leibniz to Arnauld, Hanover, October 9, 1687, p. 144.

21. Le Corbusier, *New Architecture,* 11, "The Plan proceeds from within to without; the exterior is the result of an interior" (repeated, 164); also 44, "The plan is the generator" (repeated, 45); and "a plan proceeds *from within to without,* for a house or palace is an organism comparable to a living being" (166; emphasis in original); further, within "Architecture II: The Illusion of Plans," the section headed "A Plan Prodeeds from Within to Without" (167–70).

22. Rudolf Wittkower, "English Literature on Architecture" (1965), in his *Palladio and Palladianism,* ed. Margot Wittkower (New York, 1974), 94–112, esp. 108–9.

23. Giovanni Battised Piranesi, *Parere su l'architettura,* with *Osservazioni di Giovanni*

Battista Piranesi sopra la lettere de Monsieur Mariette (Rome, 1765), quoted in Manfredo Tafuri, *The Sphere and the Labyrinth: Avant-Gardes and Architecture from Piranesi to the 1970s* (1980), trans. Pellegrino d'Acierno and Robert Connolly (Cambridge, Mass., 1987), 45.

24. *Boullée's Treatise,* 27; cf. Joseph Rykwert, *On Adam's House in Paradise: The Idea of the Primitive Hut in Architectural History,* 2d ed. (Cambridge, Mass., 1981), esp. 70.

25. Ledoux, *L'architecture,* 15–16.

26. Ibid., 18.

27. Jean Nicole Durand, *Précis des leçons d'architecture données à l'Ecole polytechnique,* 2 vols. (Paris, 1802–5), vol. 1, "Introduction," 1–24 (esp. 1, 12, 14, 23); vol. 2, "Discours préliminaire" to Part 3, 1–20 (here, 1); thanks to Barbara Lekatsas for help with the last passage. On the wild boy: Jean-Marc-Gaspard Itard, "First Developments of the Young Savage of Aveyron" (1801), and "A Report to His Excellency the Minister of the Interior" (1806), together trans. as *The Wild Boy of Aveyron* by George and Muriel Humphrey, Century Psychology Series (New York, 1962), 8, 12, 24, 66, in the "Developments"; his lodging as a prison: 88, 95, in the "Report"; Roger Shattuck, *The Forbidden Experiment: The Wild Boy of Aveyron* (London, 1981) relates Itard's to other accounts.

28. Ledoux, *L'architecture,* 121–2. Cf. Leon Battista Alberti, *De Re aedificatoria,* 9.1 on an advisable restraint in building one's house, a point taken up in Donald Kieth Hedrick, "The Ideology of Ornament: Alberti and the Erotics of Renaissance Urban Design," *Word and Image,* 3 (1987), 111–37, esp. 132 (thanks to Jeremy Gilbert-Rolfe for a copy).

29. L. F. J. de Bausset, *Mémoires anecdotiques sur l'intérieur du palais de Napoléon,* 3d ed., 5 vols. (Paris, 1829), vol. 4, 237. A *charbonnier* is also a simple "coal-burner." May the key remark also allude to the expression "Charbonnier est maître chez soi" (A man's home is his castle)?

30. George Wilhelm Friedrich Hegel, *Aesthetics: Lectures on Fine Art,* trans. and ed. T. M. Knox, 2 vols. (Oxford, 1974), vol. 2, 653; in the original, *Vorlesungen über die Asthetik,* ed. Eva Moldenhauer and Kark Markus Michel, 3 vols. (*Werke,* 13–15) (Frankfurt am Main, 1970), vol. 2, 294.

31. "Whoever realizes that the purpose of art is to guide man even onwards and upwards, making him more God-like, senses that the fusion of art with functional ends is a profanation in the highest degree. Man does not allow the artist free play because he is not in sufficient awe of him and the crafts cannot unfold freely while loaded down by the heavy burden of idealised demands. . . . If we find a mound in the forest, six foot long and three foot wide, formed into a pyramid shape by a shovel, we become serious and something within us says, 'Someone lies buried here.' This is architecture." Adolf Loos, "Architecture" (written 1910; various eds. to 1931), trans. in Tim and Charlotte Benton, *Architecture and Design, 1890–1939: An International Anthology of Original Articles,* Whitney Library of Design (New York, 1975), 41–5, here 45; thanks to Joan Ockman for this reference.

32. Does it matter that in choosing Lincoln, Pevsner was not celebrating a Gothic tour de force of engineering but rather a transitional church begun in the Romanesque style in 1070 and later ornamentally Gothicized? Lincoln belongs fundamentally to a ground-hugging, hefty-walled category that, "merely embellished with decorative Gothic details," did not depend on flying buttresses: on the contrary, " 'scholastic' structuring of many parts, the logical buildup of a complex scaffolding of architectural members, is rejected for solid mural construction with cubic forms

added one to the other." Its Gothicization after an earthquake and fire, from 1192, included glaring, nonstructurally determined "crazy vaults" of "pure decorative fancy" in the choir. James Snyder, *Medieval Art: Painting, Sculpture, Architecture: 4th–14th Century* (Englewood Cliffs, N.J., 1989), 404–5, with fig. 518 on p. 404. On the "crazy vaults," see Pevsner and John Harvey, *Lincolnshire,* The Buildings of England (Harmondsworth, 1964), 93–4, admiring the way this system "invalidates . . . bay division."

33. Hegel, *Aesthetics,* vol. 2, 684–5; in the original, *Vorlesungen,* vol. 2, 330–1.

34. Arthur Schopenhauer, *The World as Will and Representation,* trans. E. F. J. Payne, 2 vols. (Indian Hills, Colo., 1958), vol. 1, 214; further: "Architecture is bound to suffer great restrictions through the demands of necessity and utility" (217).

35. Hugh Miller, *First Impressions of England and Its People* (London, 1847), 294.

36. Ibid., 293.

37. John Ruskin, *The Seven Lamps of Architecture* (New York, 1961), 15.

38. Ibid., emphasis added.

39. Ruskin, *Lectures on Architecture and Painting Delivered in Edinburgh in November 1853* (New York, 1854), lecture 1, 43.

40. William Whewell, *History of the Inductive Sciences from the Earliest to the Present Time* (1837), 3d ed., 2 vols. (New York: Appleton, 1859), vol. 1, 542–3, with 543 n. 5. referring to Rees's *Cyclopaedia,* q.v. "Oblique Arches," as attributing the form to an engineer named Chapman and noting the first such built in 1787 at Naas, County Kildare, Ireland. Thanks to Meyer Schapiro for introducing me to Whewell.

41. Ruskin, *Seven Lamps,* 117.

42. Eugène Viollet-le-Duc, *How to Build a House,* trans. Benjamin Bucknall (London, 1874), 144–5, as excerpted in *The Architectural Theory of Viollet-le-Duc: Readings and Commentary,* ed. M. F. Hearn (Cambridge, Mass., 1990), 193; thanks to Paul Zukofsky for a reference to this volume.

43. Conrad Fiedler, *On Judging Works of Visual Art,* trans. Henry Schaeffer-Simmern and Fulmer Mood (Berkeley, Calif., 1949), 17–18; in the original, Konrad Fiedler, "Uber die Beurteilung von Werken der bildenden Kunst," in his *Schriften zur Kunst* (1913–14), ed. Gottfried Boehm, Theorie und Geschichte der Literatur und der schönen Künste, 16 (Munich, 1971), 2 vols., vol 1, 1–79, here 20–1.

44. Gilbert Scott, *Lectures on the Rise and Development of Mediaeval Architecture Delivered at the Royal Academy,* 2 vols. (London, 1879), vol. 1, 46; emphasis in original.

45. Bruno Bettelheim, *Freud and Man's Soul* (New York, 1983).

46. John Russell, "The Morgan Honors a Renaissance Man," *New York Times,* September 30, 1984, Sect. H, p. 31: "As for Great Coxwell Barn, his friend the architect wrote the ideal caption for Frederick Evans's photograph when he said that 'Its magnitude, nice precision of building and dainty parts of pure architecture, all done in handsome freestone, make it as beautiful as a cathedral, but with no ostentation of building whatsoever.'" Thanks to Hope Mayo, of the Pierpont Morgan Library, for verifying the quotation. On Webb, see Robert Macleod, *Style and Society: Architectural Ideology in Britain, 1835–1914* (London, 1971).

47. Coventry Patmore, "Ideal and Material Greatness in Architecture," in his *Principle in Art* (London, 1898; repr. Farnborough, Hants., 1969), 210–17, esp. 211–13.

48. Michael Baxandall, *Patterns of Intention: On the Historical Explanation of Pictures* (New Haven, Conn., 1985), 24–5, quoting Thomas Mackay, *The Life of Sir John Fowler, Engineer* (London, 1900), 314–15. Any modernist must protest the title of this book: the Forth Bridge is not a picture; art is not painting, and painting is not "pictures" – a reactionary term that smells of the sales room. Baxandall discusses

the bridge interestingly, but, unlike the other works reproduced, he gives no author or even date for it. To Eric de Maré, *Photography,* 3d ed. (Harmondsworth, 1962), 187, such "architectural raw material . . . may, or may not, have aesthetic value as architecture"; also, illus. on 62 (top): "The central tower of the Forth Bridge snapped in a drizzle by the author." Neither writer mentions the stunning use to which the same bridge is put in Hitchcock's film *The Thirty-nine Steps* (1935).

49. Quoted in William Knight, *The Philosophy of the Beautiful; Being Outlines of the History of Aesthetics,* 2 vols. (London, 1903, 1904), vol. 2, 193 with n. 1.

50. Philip Steadman, *The Evolution of Designs: Biological Analogy in Architecture and the Applied Arts,* Cambridge Architectural and Urban Studies (Cambridge, 1979), 48, quoting Montgomery Schuyler, "Modern Architecture" (1894), in his *American Architecture and Other Writings* (abridged ed.), ed. William H. Jordy and Ralph Coe (New York, 1964), 77–8.

51. Ibid., 48n.

52. See ibid., 13–15, with illus.

53. A more recent commentator "has pointed to the mild structural deceit in the design of the bridge, in the way in which the outer span of each end cantilever has to be tied down to large quantities of ballast concealed in the piers of the approach, in order to prevent the cantilever tipping when loaded."; 14n, with ref. to R. J. Mainstone, *Developments in Structural Form* (London, 1975), 248. Nevertheless, nobody ever said that "mild structural deceit" was incompatible with art.

54. M. Malézieux, *Travaux publiques des Etats-Unis d'Amérique en 1870: Rapport de mission . . . publié par ordre de M. le Ministre des Travaux Publiques* (Paris, 1873), text vol., 100–15, here 100; see also plate vol., pls. 18–20.

55. Le Corbusier's dual personification of the Brooklyn and George Washington Bridges, in *When the Cathedrals Were White* (1938–9), suggests a second chance for modernity: "Brooklyn Bridge, which is old . . . is strong and rugged as a gladiator, while George Washington Bridge, built yesterday, smiles like a young athlete. In this [first] case the two large Gothic towers of stone are very handsome because they are *American* and not 'Beaux-Arts.' They are full of native sap and they are not graceful, but strong. . . . I come back to *the immense* and like a barbarian I enjoy it, or better, as a man animated by a constructive spirit, active but wearied by the depressing atmosphere of cowardice and abdication in Paris, crushed, often dishonored, treated as a madman and Utopian . . . here I find *reality.*" Le Corbusier, *When the Cathedrals Were White,* trans. Francis E. Hyslop, Jr. (1947; repr. New York, 1964), 77–8 (emphases and last ellipsis in original).

56. Alan Trachtenberg, *The Brooklyn Bridge: Fact and Symbol* (New York, 1965; repr. 1979), 79–81. Thanks to my student Barbara Solomon for making a point of this.

57. Schuyler, "The Brooklyn Bridge as a Monument" (1883), in his *American Architecture,* vol. 2, 331–44, here 344.

58. Schuyler, "Art in Modern Bridges" (1900), ibid., 351–71, here 358–9; Schuyler anticipates a futurist term with the comment that in the Brooklyn Bridge "the lines of force constitute the structure" ("Brooklyn Bridge," 343).

59. Schuyler, "New York Bridges" (1905), excerpted, ibid., 372–3.

60. Quoted, Lloyd Goodrich, *Thomas Eakins: His Life and Work* (New York, 1933), 21.

61. Henry Adams, *The Education of Henry Adams* (New York, 1931), 379–90, here 379.

62. Léonce Bénédite et al., *Exposition universelle de 1900: Les beaux-arts et les arts décoratifs,* Gazette des Beaux-Arts (Paris, 1900), 405.

63. Sadakichi Hartmann, "A Plea for the Picturesqueness of New York," repr. from

Camera Notes, no. 4 (1900), in his *The Valiant Knights of Daguerre: Selected Critical Essays on Photography and Profiles of Photographic Pioneers,* ed. Harry W. Lawton and George Knox with Wistaria Hartmann Linton (Berkeley, Calif., 1978), 56–63, here 56.

64. Hartmann, "A Photographic Enquête," *Camera Notes,* no. 5 (1901–2), 233–8, here 236. Brush's further comment, "Today is essentially a time when mean things are done so finely that future ages may refer to it as a period when the minor arts attracted the genius and energy diverted, by modesty or timidity, from heroic enterprises," might be comprehensible in respect to then–"artistic" photography, but hardly to the Brooklyn or Williamsburg Bridges (the Manhattan Bridge was built only in 1911).

65. Adams, *Education,* 380.

66. "A child of Benvenuto Cellini, smothered in an American cradle," ibid., 387.

67. Ibid., 388.

68. W. H. Auden, "The Virgin and the Dynamo," in his *The Dyer's Hand and Other Essays* (New York, 1968), 61–71, here 63; R. P. Blackmur, "The Virgin and the Dynamo," *Magazine of Art,* 45 (April 1952), 147–53, treats a poem written by Adams after seeing the exposition but before Adams composed the *Education,* a "Prayer to the Virgin of Chartres" that includes a "Prayer to the Dynamo."

69. Harry Francis Mallgrave, introd. to his ed. and trans. of Otto Wagner, *Modern Architecture: A Guidebook for His Students to this Field of Art* (Santa Monica, Calif., 1988), 45. Thanks to Wayne Dynes for calling my attention to this.

70. Gert Schiff, ed., *German Essays on Art History,* The German Library (New York, 1988), introd., Schlosser based his distinction on the work of Karl Vossler. See Julius von Schlosser, *L'Arte del Medioevo* (1923), trans. Carlo Sgorlon (Turin, 1961), 68–72, with introd. essay by Otto Kurz, "Julius von Schlosser: personalità, metodo, lavoro," ix–xxviii, esp. xxvi–xxvii.

71. Julius von Schlosser, "On the History of Art Historiography: The Gothic" (1910), trans. Peter Wortsman, in Schiff, *German Essays,* 206–33, here 212–13.

72. Roger Fry, as quoted in Virginia Woolf, *Roger Fry: A Biography* (New York, 1940), 185.

73. Fry, "A Possible Domestic Architecture" (1918), in his *Vision and Design* (London 1929; repr. New York, 1956), 272–8, here 272.

74. Fry, "Art and Life" (1917), *Vision,* 1–15, here 5. Fry focuses his accusation on the pilgrimage church of Paray-le-Monial, an experience of which once moved the present author as few buildings have.

75. James Joyce, *Ulysses,* The Modern Library (New York, 1961), 621, 635, 636, 653, 658, 660, respectively. If this seems trivial, consider the social stigma of "shanty Irish" (versus, say, "lace-curtain Irish"). After incidental mention of another in Great Brunswick (now Pearse) Street (77), this principal "cabman's shelter" in the novel is Skin-the-Goat Fitzharris's at Butt Bridge (also 136, 675, 729), in what is known as the "Eumaeus" episode. "These coffeehouse shelters were relatively small eight-sided buildings approximately ten feet by fifteen feet": Don Gifford and Robert J. Seidman, *Ulysses Annotated: Notes for James Joyce's "Ulysses"* (Berkeley, Calif., 1988), 534.

76. David Jones, *In Parenthesis* (London 1937; repr. 1969), 79 and note on p. 207.

77. Jones, *Epoch and Artist: Selected Writings* (New York, 1959), as already noticed in Robert Venturi, *Complexity and Contradiction in Architecture* (New York, 1966), 21.

78. Ian Boyd White, ed. and trans., *The Crystal Chain Letters: Architectural Fantasies by Bruno Taut and His Circle* (Cambridge, Mass., 1985), 101; for my review of this

book, see "Expressionist Fantasias: The Crystal Chain Letters" (1986), in *Modernities: Art-Matters in the Present* (University Park, Pa., 1993), 45–9.

79. Ibid., 163.

80. Henry-Russell Hitchcock and Philip Johnson, *The International Style* (1932), 2d ed. (New York, 1966), which includes Hitchcock, "The International Style Twenty Years Later" (1951), 237–55; here, 35.

81. Ibid., 36. Benjamin, in the *Passagen-Werk* (Arcades Project), seconded Giedion's enthusiasm for the "marvelous aspects" of nineteenth-century industrial structures, contrasting "the 'ornamental style' of . . . architects (which he connects with 'boredom') to Giedion's 'excellent examples' of bridge scaffolding"; Susan Buck-Morss, *The Dialectics of Seeing: Walter Benjamin and the Arcades Project* (Cambridge, Mass., 1991), 126–27, with refs. to Siegfried Giedion, *Bauen im Frankreich*, 2d ed. (Leipzig, 1928), as cited in Walter Benjamin, *Gesammelte Schriften*, 5, *Das Passagen-Werk*, ed. Rolf Tiedemann (Frankfurt, 1982), 218, and to 1016 in the latter.

82. Ibid., 80.

83. Ibid., 91.

84. Pevsner, *Pioneers of Modern Design from William Morris to Walter Gropius* (orig. *Pioneers of the Modern Movement*, London, 1936), 2d rev. ed (Harmondsworth, 1975), 133. Pevsner says that this occurs "at the very start" of the *Seven Lamps*, but he must mean the idea; the rat hole and other motifs I do not find there. At any rate, it cannot be the presumedly rote articulation alone of the hypothetical bicycle shed that matters – as where a blackbird is observed to have started fourteen different nests under adjacent rafters of a certain 150-meter-long bicycle shed, "muddled by the topographic similarity" (Karl von Frisch, with Otto von Frisch, *Animal Architecture*, trans. Lisbeth Gombrich [New York, 1974], 245–6, with fig. 91 [diagram] and pl. 100 [view of shed] on p. 246) – for the same nesting bird might have been as muddled by the endlessly long blind arcade of the Lincoln facade.

85. Pevsner, *Outline*, xix.

86. In a term paper written for my course "Form in the Art-Work," a former Harvard student of mine, Anne Ballard, wisely wondered where, by Pevsner's terms, a Quaker meetinghouse would stand.

87. Roman Ingarden, "The Architectural Work" (1946), in his *Ontology of the Work of Art: The Musical Work; the Picture; the Architectural Work; the Film*, trans. Raymond Meyer with John T. Goldthwait (Athens, Ohio, 1989), 253–313, here 255–6. See also Chap. 6, this volume, on Jan Mukařovský's essay, "On the Problem of Functions in Architecture" (1937–8).

88. Ibid., 259.

89. Ibid., 263.

90. Significantly, a city may have only a "pro-cathedral" (cf. Chap. 1, this volume), a provisional episcopal seat, until a more legally (or architecturally) suitable building is available.

91. Perhaps to make a symbolic point, as in connection with the "humiliation" theology of the Incarnation. A special case: at Portiuncula (Italy), where the little cell in which Saint Francis died is architecturally enshrined within a formidable (other) building, the grander architecture could never outrank the humble building within. Thanks to Andrew Attaway for a discussion.

92. Even the Archbishop of Paris cannot render a building a cathedral by magical fiat, because such acts are inevitably contextual. As every Catholic schoolchild used to know, the frivolous priest *cannot* by pronouncement of the words of consecration transubstantiate the contents of a bakery; and even the sacramental "I dos" of a

wedding must be exchanged in the company of a priest or other ceremonial witness. Marcel Duchamp himself had to change the world into art one piece at a time, and his "readymades" only make sense, or enough nonsense to register, in respect to (other) art; see Joseph Masheck, "Readymades: Art Accompli" (1975), chap. 7 in his *Modernities*.

93. Ingarden, "Architectural Work," 259, continuing, "Although this heap serves as its real basis (its bearer) and forms the point of departure of the act of consecration."

94. Ibid., 261.

95. Ibid., 262.

96. Ibid., 262–4.

97. Ibid., 271. Mies van der Rohe is known to have reembodied some of the same architectural designs in different buildings.

98. Ibid., 272.

99. Dewey does not exactly resort to self-evidence when he says, "*By common consent, the Parthenon is a great work of art*": John Dewey, *Art as Experience* (New York, 1934), 4 (emphasis added).

100. Igarden, "Architectural Work," 311 n. 5.

101. Ibid., 278.

102. Ibid., 289.

103. More subtly: without violating unity, "those moments of the work in which the mental individuality of its creator is perhaps expressed can fit into . . . [its] unity and confer upon it a peculiar stamp; they then only elevate the aesthetic value of the work. But they can also merely unconnectedly parallel each other, and either be completely without significance for the work or else counteract its structure and undermine the value it might otherwise have or even destroy it"; ibid., 290.

104. Ibid., 293.

105. Ibid., 294–5.

106. Ibid., 298.

107. Ingarden notes that, despite "neopositivists," the elemental "logemes" of language and literature are *not* of the real world; 300 and 312 n. 18.

108. I draw here above all on Dewey, *Art as Experience*.

109. At least one of the forms of *bauen* ("to build") recurring in Wittgenstein's posthumous *Philosophical Investigations,* these ordinarily rendered in terms of abstract "structure," has a peculiar architectural and metaphoric concreteness: in the phrase "des Wesen der Sprache – ihre Funktion, ihren Bau," in para. 92 of Part 1 ("complete by 1945"), given as "essence of language – its function, its structure" in Ludwig Wittgenstein, *Philosophische Untersuchungen / Philosophical Investigations,* trans. G. E. M. Anscombe (New York, 1953, repr. 1964), 43 (German), 43e (English), "ihre Funktion, ihren Bau," may remind one more literally, as "its function, its *building*," of Wittgenstein's direct architectural experience; on which see Bernhard Leitner, *Die Architektur von Ludwig Wittgenstein: eine Dokumentation / The Architecture of Ludwig Wittgenstein: A Documentation* (New York, 1976).

110. Ludwig Wittgenstein, *Culture and Value / Vermischte Bemerkungen,* ed. Georg Henrik von Wright and Heikki Nyman, trans. Peter Winch, 2d ed. (Oxford, 1980), 42 and 42e.

111. Ibid., 69, 69e.

112. Pevsner, *Outline,* 1.

113. Moholy-Nagy must have been translating from the original text published by Wasmuth as a preface to Wright's *Ausgeführte Bauten und Entwürfe* (Berlin, 1910);

the entire essay appears in English in Edgar Kaufmann and Ben Raeburn, *Frank Lloyd Wright: Writings and Buildings* (New York, 1960), 84–106, with the passage in question on 85.

114. Alexander Tzonis and Liane Lefaivre, *Classical Architecture: The Poetics of Order* (Cambridge, Mass., 1986), 276.

115. Quotations from Philip Johnson's Museum of Modern Art catalog *Mies van der Rohe* (New York, 1947), 140, without source; antiformalist statements of the 1920s, with sources, 183–8. According to Arthur Drexler, *Ludwig Mies van der Rohe,* The Masters of World Architecture (New York, 1960), 32, "Mies' most original buildings are one-story structures, and the greatest of these consist of one room. In this sense Mies has designed nothing but temples, which is to say that he has revealed the irrational mainspring of our technological culture."

116. Ludwig Mies van der Rohe, quoted in Kenneth Frampton, *Modern Architecture: A Critical History* (New York, 1980), 161, from Peter Carter in *Architectural Design,* March 1961.

117. Pevsner, *Outline,* 215.

118. Maxwell Fry, *Fine Building* (London, 1944, repr. 1945), 7; note the embedded formalist term "significant form."

119. Ibid., 18, 25.

120. "If I admire the great works of engineering that brought the railways into London and built the docks of its port, I must turn to deplore the fate of countless Irish workmen brought over to labour on these works and left to fend for themselves in the festering slums"; ibid., 33.

121. Ibid., 33, with pls. 5, 6 opp. p. 34; continuing, "Where do the 'Civils' stand to-day and what have they to say of their part in the rebuilding of the towns?" (The copy at hand, a reprint of 1945, carries on the copyright page the notice "For use of H.M. Forces; Not for resale.")

122. Bruce Allsopp, *The Study of Architectural History* (New York, 1970), 116.

123. Lucien Kroll, *An Architecture of Complexity* (originally *Composants,* 1983), trans. Peter Blundell Jones (Cambridge, Mass., 1987), 86.

124. Ibid., 11.

125. Witold Rybczynski, *The Most Beautiful House in the World* (New York, 1989), 3.

126. Ibid., 11, noting Horace Walpole's quip on Inigo Jones's Saint Paul's, Covent Garden, as "the handsomest barn in England," and James Playfair's modeling of an actual barn on the same church (11n). Well-read as he is, Rybczynski makes no mention of the importance of barns to Walter Horn's development of Joseph Strzygowski's (1924) thesis of the origins of the medieval bay system in North European wooden architecture, with barn evidence as early as the Iron Age: "On the Origins of the Medieval Bay System," *Journal of the Society of Architectural Historians,* 17 (1958), repr. in Harold Spencer, ed., *Readings in Art History,* 2 vols., vol. 1: *Ancient Egypt Through the Middle Ages,* 2d ed. (New York, 1976), 187–220.

127. One wonders just when Western culture began to perform the tedious sadomasochistic reversal, hardly a change of heart, of taking its own wisdom as folly while honoring everything else as revelation. Rybczynski reflects on his having been "a child of Polish parents in postwar Britain . . . a schoolboy with an English accent . . . and an unpronounceable name in a small town in Canada, and . . . an *anglais* in French-speaking Québec." It should be obvious enough not to be impertinent to say of one so positively European that less exotic spiritual resorts have been known to mollify such an unsettled condition in the wastes of North America.

128. Ibid., 74–7.

129. Ibid., 49.

130. Ibid., 100. In 1949 Hans Straub, *A History of Civil Engineering* (trans. E. Rockwell [Cambridge, Mass., 1964], 185) proclaimed a "modest locomotive shed or water tower" preferable to Jugendstil architectural pretension.

131. Ibid., 103.

132. Ibid., 111.

133. Ibid., 112.

134. Ibid., 136–7.

135. Ibid., 171–2, 180–1.

136. Ibid., 148.

137. It doesn't take imagination for a critic of *Le Monde* to ask the Centre Pompidou, "Is this a museum – this garage, this gasworks, this petroleum refinery?"; quoted ibid., 152, from *Architectural Design*, 47, no. 2 (1977). Rybczynski dilates: "It was not that Parisians disliked oil refineries but that the extravagant industrial imagery of the building suggested a glorification of the technical world that seemed to many of them to be at odds with the creative arts and with museums" (153).

138. Ibid., 186–9.

139. Ibid., 189.

140. To John Lobell I owed my awareness of this at the time.

141. Significantly attending to mannerist modes of composition was Colin Rowe's "Mannerism and Modern Architecture" (1950), in his *The Mathematics of the Ideal Villa and Other Essays* (Cambridge, Mass., 1976), 29–57.

142. John Shute, *The First and Chief Groundes of Architecture* (London, 1563; repr. London, n.d.), f. Ai (verso); orthography modernized and emphasis added.

143. Ibid., f. Aii (recto).

144. A certain Hanseatic gentility was still enjoyed in the Romantic period by none other than Engels, who, working at the age of 18 in an office in Bremen, delighted in studying and even drawing the mercantile architecture there: a letter of October 9, 1838, to his sister Marie, describes the merchants' houses with storehouses in the attic as "built in a very remarkable way," with a short end to the street and a large hall inside "just like a church"; *Letters of the Young Engels, 1838–1845* (Moscow, 1976), Letter 4 (trans. Jack Cohen), 41, with illus.

145. Robert C. Wheeler, "Frank Lloyd Wright Filling Station, 1958," *Journal of the Society of Architectural Historians*, 19 (1960), 174–5.

146. The latter, illus., David Spaeth, *Mies van der Rohe* (New York, 1985), figs. 185 on p. 154, 186 on p. 155.

147. Wilfrid Sheed, *Frank and Maisie: A Memoir with Parents* (New York, 1985), 208.

148. On "Colonial Williamsburg," Virginia, see this volume, Chap. 12.

149. Venturi, *Complexity*, 59.

150. Nancy Marmer, "Pop Art in California," in Lucy R. Lippard, et. al., *Pop Art* (London, 1966), 139–61, here 151.

151. Peter Plagens, *Sunshine Muse: Contemporary Art on the West Coast* (New York, 1974), 142.

152. Ledoux, *L'architecture*, 83–4.

153. A name and logotype that would date with the advent of a newly consolidated Exxon in the time of Nixon (and Vietnam military-industrial activity), in seeming obliviousness to the notoriety of the classic Standard Oil antitrust case.

154. Hitchcock and Johnson, *International Style*, 76.

155. Venturi, "A Buildingboard Involving Movies, Relics, and Space" (1968), in Ven-

turi and Denise Scott Brown, *A View from the Campidoglio: Selected Essays, 1953–1984,* ed. Peter Arnell, Ted Bickford, and Catherine Bergart (New York, 1984), 14–18, here 15–16.

156. Ibid., 15.

157. Cf.: "The Iconoclasts had failed to distinguish 'between the sacred and the profane,' calling the image of the Lord and his saints 'like unto the statues of diabolic idols' "; Aidan Nichols, "The Horos of Nicea II: A Theological Reappropriation," *Annuarium Historiae Conciliorum,* 20 (1988), 171–81, here 173, quoting (with Greek) the prologue to the "minutes" of the Second Nicene Council (AD 787).

158. Venturi, "A Definition of Architecture as Shelter with Decoration on It, and Another Plea for a Symbolism of the Ordinary in Architecture" (1978), in Venturi and Brown, *View from the Campidoglio,* 62–7, here 64, 67 (emphasis in original).

159. Karl Ernst Osthaus, *Henry Van de Velde: Leben und Schaffen des Künstlers* (Hagen, 1920; repr. Berlin, 1984), 133, with illus. on 135–9. Osthaus already writes poetically of docking zeppelins, with exciting engine noise, evoking Greek galleys full of naked youths (134).

160. Venturi, "Definition," 65.

161. Ibid., 63.

162. James Abbott McNeill Whistler, *The Gentle Art of Making Enemies* (London, 1892; repr. New York, 1967), 144.

163. Venturi, "Definition," 63. If one did not yet think of McDonald's in conjunction with the disappearing South American rain forest, one did already think of Las Vegas in terms of organized crime.

164. Ibid., 65–6.

165. Ibid.

166. Illus. of the plan, published in 1804, in Peter Collins, *Changing Ideals in Modern Architecture, 1750–1950* (London, 1965), pl. iv.

167. Earlier examples can be found, if retroactively. T. Leplus's Church of the Magdalene at Lille, 1675–1713, seems rather womblike in plan: Louis Hautecoeur, *Histoire de l'architecture classique en France,* vol. 2 (Paris, 1948), fig. 556 on p. 727.

168. Houston, University of St. Thomas, *Visionary Architects: Boullée, Ledoux, Lequeu* (Houston, Texas, 1967), cat. 118 on p. 196 with illus. of this undated watercolor in the Bibliothèque nationale; in the caption, "High up [inside the "cow"] is a hayloft lighted and ventilated by the eyes of the animal," etc. In Philippe Duboy's engagingly surreal *Le Queu: An Architectural Enigma,* trans. Francis Scarfe and Brad Divitt (London, 1986), which tropes Jean-Jacques Le Queu (1756–1825) into the twentieth-century company of Marcel Duchamp, the design for the *Cow Byre Facing South on the Cool Meadow,* with enormous blanket over the "animal" and an urn atop its head, appears as pl. 239 (bottom); that for the *Tomb of Isocrates, Athenian Orator,* dated 1789, a sheep with a mermaid riding on it, as pl. 335; on the architect's modern reputation, see esp. 63–76.

169. Ibid., 9.

170. Collins, *Changing Ideals,* 122–3.

171. Charles Jencks, *The Language of Post-Modern Architecture,* rev. ed. (New York, 1977), 45.

172. Ibid., caption to fig. 65 on p. 45.

173. Petros Martinidis, "Semiotics of Architectural Theories: Toward an Epistemology

of Architecture," *Semiotica*, 59 (1986), 371–86. In general, Martinidis tends, I think, to hand too much architectural meaning over to verbal culture, while the *artistic* illiteracy of yuppie classicism testifies that there are those whose sense of formal significance, like their political behavior, merely follows suit from a caricatural look of puritanical wealth that is style *qua* lifestyle. It is unfortunate that semiotic writings on architecture by Jan Mukařovský, of the Prague Linguistic Circle between the World Wars, were made available in English only in 1977, including the lecture "On the Problem of Functions in Architecture" (1937–8), in *Structure, Sign and Function: Selected Essays by Jan Mukařovský*, ed. and trans. John Burbank and Peter Steiner, Russian and East European Studies, 14 (New Haven, 1978), 236–50.

174. Museum of Modern Art, *What is Modern Architecture?*, Introductory Series to the Modern Arts, 1, 2 ed. (New York, 1946), 6. The exhibition was prepared by John McAndrew and Elizabeth Mack.
175. Ibid., 17. As farcically bogus, the indulgent "pomo" speculation of Baudrillard on stucco (which extends a traditional antipathy toward the Italian baroque) encourages a frustrated, puritanical, pseudo-modernist sense of material integrity in surfacing: Jean Baudrillard, *Simulations*, trans. Paul Foss, Paul Patton and Philip Beitchman (New York, 1983), "The Stucco Angel," 83–92. Adolf Loos's rigorous "principle of cladding," which prohibited only redundant imitation, allowed that "stucco can take any ornament with just one exception – rough brickwork"; "The Principle of Cladding" (1898), in Loos's *Spoken Into the Void: Collected Essays, 1897–1910*, trans. Jane Ockman Newman and John H. Smith, Oppositions Books (Cambridge, Mass., 1982), 66–9, here 68. Even in the most rigorous 1920s International Style architecture a coating of stucco was more than tolerated in order to effect "a continuous even covering" of the surface; indeed, by the orthodox theory of the time, "A material like stucco but elastic and with a wide color range, which could be laid over various bases, would be ideal" (Hitchcock and Johnson, *International Style*, 50). This view is not unrelated to later formalist critique on monochrome in sculpture. Today it is better argued that the stimulation of Raphael and others in the sixteenth century to make stucco, or gesso, architectural decorations of their own, by the contemporary discovery of Roman gesso decoration, exemplifies a lively congruence of historical art and connoisseurship with artistic practice; Alan Colquhoun, "Postmodernism and Structuralism: A Retrospective Glance" (1988), in his *Modernity and the Classical Tradition: Architectural Essays, 1980–1987* (Cambridge, Mass., 1989), 243–55, here 253.
176. Klaus Herdeg, *The Decorated Diagram: Harvard Architecture and the Failure of the Bauhaus Legacy* (Cambridge, Mass., 1983), 8.
177. Michael Hollander, "Attitudes to Modern Architecture in Post-Modern Criticism," *The Yale Review*, 69 (1980), 411–26, here 422–3; emphasis added.
178. Nelson Goodman, "How Buildings Mean," from Goodman and Catherine Z. Elgin, *Reconceptions in Philosophy and Other Arts and Sciences* (Cambridge, 1988), in George Dickie, Richard Sclafani and Ronald Roblin, eds., *Aesthetics: A Critical Anthology*, 2d ed. (New York, 1989), 544–55, here 545, 552, 550, 551, respectively.
179. Richard Rogers, *Architecture: A Modern View*, Walter Neurath Memorial Lecture (London, 1990), 20–2.
180. There is abroad the notion that this beautiful structure enjoys a historical priority by virtue of the postmodern, hypothetical look of permanent nonfinality in its exposed workings. But there is an instance of this from the previous generation

in Harrison and Abromowitz's United Nations Headquarters (1948–50), where the interior of the Economic and Social Council Chamber, designed by Sven Markelius, has a partial ceiling floating under exposed ducts and such – symbolizing, or so it used always to be told by the U.N. guides, the provisional work of this council. Le Corbusier's 1930 Swiss Pavilion at the Cité Universitaire, Paris, is also said to have sported exposed ventilation ducts.

181. Rogers, *Architecture*, 26.
182. Hitchcock and Johnson, *International Style*, 38.
183. Rogers, *Architecture*, 58 (caption), 59 (caption).
184. Robert Venturi, Denise Scott Brown and Steven Izenour, *Learning from Las Vegas: The Forgotten Symbolism of Architectural Form*, rev. ed. (Cambridge, Mass., 1977), 105–6.
185. Carol Lutfy, "Isozaki's Architecture Bridges East and West" (interview), *Journal of Art*, 4, no. 7 (September 1991), 17.
186. Wilhelm Worringer, *Form Problems of the Gothic*, anon. trans., authorized American ed. (New York, 1920?), 88, with pl. opposite.
187. Milton W. Brown, *American Painting from the Armory Show to the Depression* (Princeton, N.J., 1955; repr., 1970), 113.
188. *Joseph Pennell's Pictures of the Panama Canal: Reproductions of a Series of Lithographs Made by Him on the Isthmus of Panama, January–March 1912, Together with Impressions and Notes by the Artist* (Philadelphia, 1912), 14, as quoted in Joseph Masheck, "The Panama Canal and Other Works of Work" (1971), in my *Historical Present: Essays of the 1970s* (Ann Arbor, Mich., 1984), 117–25, here 123. Smithson, for his part considering that at a "Dam Foundation Site" in Texas, being projected by him in 1966–7 as consultant to Tippetts-Abbott-McCarthy-Stratton (engineers and architects), once the mammoth slab of the dam was functioning, the visual grandeur of its last days before completion would disappear: hence, "If viewed as a 'discrete stage' it becomes an abstract work of art that vanishes as it develops"; Robert Smithson, "Towards the Development of an Air Terminal Site" (1967), in *The Writings of Robert Smithson: Essays with Interpretations*, ed. Nancy Holt (New York, 1979), 40–7, here 43 (caption).
189. Frank Gehry, "No, I'm an Architect" (interview with Peter Arnell), in Arnell and Ted Bickford, eds., *Frank Gehry: Buildings and Projects* (New York, 1985), xiii–xviii, esp. xiii–xiv.
190. *Joseph Pennell's Pictures of the Wonder of Work: Reproductions of a Series of Drawings, Etchings, Lithographs Made by Him Around the World, 1881–1915, with Impressions and Notes by the Artist* (Philadelphia, 1916), notes accompanying pl. 25, as quoted in Masheck, "Panama Canal," 117–25, here 125 n. 14.
191. Pierre Hepp, "Le Salon d'Automne," *Gazette des Beaux-Arts*, 3d period, 40 (1908), 381–401, pl. opp. 398.
192. Manfredo Tafuri, "The New Babylon: The 'Yellow Giants' and the Myth of Americanism," in his *The Sphere and the Labyrinth: Avant-Gardes and Architecture from Piranesi to the 1970s*, trans. Pellegrino d'Acierno and Robert Connolly (Cambridge, Mass., 1987), 171–95.
193. George Gordon Coulton, "The Peasants' Search for Salvation," excerpted from his *The Medieval Scene* (1959) in Bernard S. Bachrach, ed., *The Medieval Church: Success or Failure?* (New York, 1972), 97–102, here 99.
194. James Joyce, *Finnegans Wake* (New York, 1939; repr. 1957), 4.

Index

Italic numbers indicate pages on which illustrations appear.